"I know where to go to learn what I don't know."

library

» show library menu

ebook

American Democracy Now
Harrison, 2e

jump to pg go   book contents   search ebook go

CHAPTER 14. The Judiciary

reading   images   exercises

my notebook

Chapter 14 Sections

ASSIGNED
Page 517

Judges as Policy Makers

Courts make law—common law—by deciding cases and establishing legal principles that bind future litigants and judges. The lawmaking function of courts ensures that judges have a powerful role as public policy makers.[37] This is particularly true of judges who serve in appellate courts such as the state supreme courts, the federal circuit courts of appeals, and the U.S. Supreme Court.

Because of their policy-making role, judges participate in a larger political discourse that goes far beyond the concerns of individual litigants. As we consider in this section, judges are not free to act completely independently of the other branches of the government, but they *are* able to weigh in on some of the country's most important issues. Supreme

The integrated eBook takes students to the place in the text where the material they don't know is explained.

"I get an individual learning plan."

connect

LESS MANAGING.
MORE TEACHING.
GREATER LEARNING.

ENGAGE STUDENTS WITH POWERFUL

Connect includes many features that will help students learn faster, study more efficiently and retain more knowledge.

WATCH INTRO VIDEO
VIEW FULL PRODUCT TOUR
GET STARTED

Introduction 101

Create assignments and assessments from the library or anything you find on the Web.

SELECT ANY OF THE 6 SUBJECT AREAS (e.g. BUSINESS AND ECONOMICS, CAREER)

| BUSINESS AND ECONOMICS | CAREER | HUMANITIES AND SOCIAL SCIENCES | BIOLOGICAL SCIENCES AND NUTRITION | PHYSICAL AND EARTH SCIENCES | ENGINEERING |

FIND YOUR SALES REP · GET STARTED · REQUEST A LIVE PRODUCT TOUR

The rich reporting tools give students and instructors detailed views of how well a student is performing during the semester.

LearnSmart generates an individualized learning plan so students study most what they understand least.

AMERICAN DEMOCRACY NOW

BRIGID CALLAHAN HARRISON

Montclair State University

JEAN WAHL HARRIS

University of Scranton

WITH

MICHELLE D. DEARDORFF
Jackson State University

SECOND EDITION

Mc
Graw
Hill

Connect
Learn
Succeed™

Boston   Burr Ridge, IL   Dubuque, IA   Madison, WI   New York   San Francisco   St. Louis
Bangkok   Bogotá   Caracas   Kuala Lumpur   Lisbon   London   Madrid   Mexico City
Milan   Montreal   New Delhi   Santiago   Seoul   Singapore   Sydney   Taipei   Toronto

The McGraw·Hill Companies

Connect
Learn
Succeed™

Published by McGraw-Hill, an imprint of The McGraw-Hill Companies, Inc., 1221 Avenue of the Americas, New York, NY 10020. Copyright © 2011 and 2009 by The McGraw-Hill Companies. All rights reserved. No part of this publication may be reproduced or distributed in any form or by any means, or stored in a database or retrieval system, without the prior written consent of The McGraw-Hill Companies, Inc., including, but not limited to, in any network or other electronic storage or transmission, or broadcast for distance learning. This book is printed on acid-free paper.

1 2 3 4 5 6 7 8 9 0 DOW/DOW 9 8 7 6 5 4 3 2 1 0

ISBN: 978-0-07-337907-4
MHID: 0-07-337907-7

Vice President, Editorial: *Michael Ryan*
Director, Editorial: *Beth Mejia*
Sponsoring Editor: *Mark Georgiev*
Marketing Manager: *Patrick Brown*
Director of Development: *Dawn Groundwater*
Developmental Editor: *Judith Kromm*
Editorial Coordinator: *Amy Flauaus*
Text Permissions Editor: *Marcy Lunetta*
Production Editor: *Leslie Racanelli*
Manuscript Editor: *Carole Crouse*
Illustrator: *Ayelet Arbel*
Designers: *Cassandra Chu & Linda Beaupré*
Photo Research Coordinator: *Alexandra Ambrose*
Photo Researcher: *David Tietz*
Buyer: *Louis Swaim*
Media Project Managers: *Shannon Gattens & Jami Woy*
Composition: *10/12 ITC Legacy Serif Book by Thompson Type*
Printing: *45# Libery Dull by R.R. Donnelley & Sons*
Cover: Flag © Stockbyte/Getty Images; iPhone © Kacper Kida/Alamy

Credits: The credits section for this book begins on page 625 and is considered an extension of the copyright page.

Library of Congress Cataloging-in-Publication Data

American Democracy Now / Brigid Callahan Harrison ... [et al.].
    p. cm.
  Includes bibliographical references and index.
  ISBN-13: 978-0-07-337907-4
  MHID: 0-07-337907-7
  1. United States—Politics and government—Textbooks.   2. Political participation—
United States—Textbooks.   I. Harrison, Brigid, C.

2010940519

The Internet addresses listed in the text were accurate at the time of publication. The inclusion of a Web site does not indicate an endorsement by the authors or McGraw-Hill, and McGraw-Hill does not guarantee the accuracy of the information presented at these sites.

www.mhhe.com

BRIEF CONTENTS

CONTENTS

Part I: Foundations of American Democracy

3 FEDERALISM 80

Part II: Fundamental Principles

4 CIVIL LIBERTIES 110

5 CIVIL RIGHTS 146

Part III: Linkages Between the People and Government

9 ELECTIONS, CAMPAIGNS, AND VOTING 272

10 THE MEDIA 306

Part IV: Institutions of Government

11 CONGRESS 334

14 THE JUDICIARY 430

Part V: Public Policy

15 ECONOMIC POLICY 462

PERFORMANCE

means students actively and critically engage in discussing their government—a course in which students' opinions are well formed and evidence based.

Introducing Performance-Based Learning for *American Democracy Now*

Imagine that YOU . . .

- could recreate the one-on-one experience of working through difficult concepts in office hours with every one of your students
- could see at a glance how well each of your students or sections was performing in each segment of your course
- could spend more time in class teaching what you want to teach

Imagine *American Democracy Now!*

American Democracy Now does what no other learning program does. It directly complements the way instructors teach by directly reinforcing core learning objectives for the course. *American Democracy Now* benefits instructors by allowing them easily to see all student activity and progress, identifying challenging learning objectives, and evaluating each student's degree of mastery. Equipped with this information, instructors can tailor lectures, assignments, and exams for each class and each student.

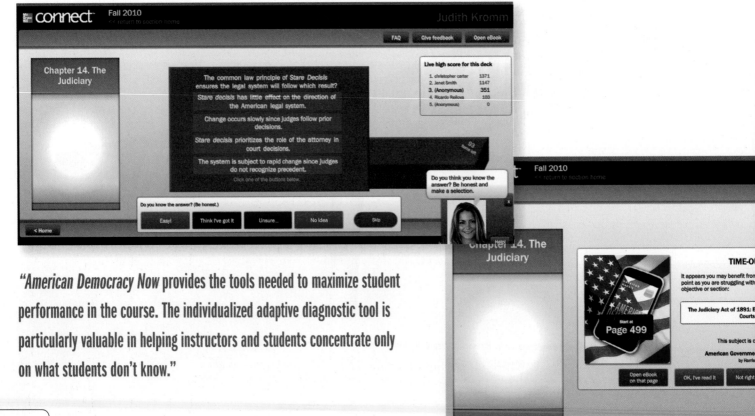

"*American Democracy Now* provides the tools needed to maximize student performance in the course. The individualized adaptive diagnostic tool is particularly valuable in helping instructors and students concentrate only on what students don't know."

Imagine that YOUR STUDENTS . . .

- **are actively and critically engaged in discussing their government**
- **have opinions that are well formed and evidence based**
- **come to class prepared and perform better on quizzes and exams**

Imagine *American Democracy Now!*

American Democracy Now is a first: a truly integrated learning program for American government that provides individualized instruction through an adaptive diagnostic coupled with pedagogical tools that are anchored in research on critical thinking. By showing students what they know, *American Democracy Now* focuses students on specific learning objectives they need to master in order to achieve better performance in the course. Better performance leads to greater student engagement and ultimately to a classroom in which true critical thinking can be achieved and applied. *American Democracy Now*'s individualized, adaptive learning program guides students away from merely expressing opinion to forming a point of view based in critical thinking, analysis, and evidence.

"I know that I know"

Individualized adaptive learning and outcomes based activities

"I am confident"

Engage in the content and participate in the course

Think critically about the issues in American government

"I know how to ask questions. I analyze issues. I apply what I learn."

In this way, *American Democracy Now*'s individualized, adaptive learning program is both a studying environment and a teaching environment—researched and designed to help students interact more with material, perform better during the course, and become more active, engaged citizens in the world.

Thinking Critically About American Government

At the heart of *American Democracy Now* is a rich set of instructional tools that move students along the path to critical thinking.

CHAPTER

12

The Presidency

367

THEN

Presidential power grew over the centuries to "imperial" proportions and then ebbed in the late twentieth century in the wake of scandals.

NOW

The power of modern presidents varies, and is affected by congressional actions and public opinion.

NEXt

Will future presidents continue down the path of an imperial presidency?

What checks will constrain future presidents' exercise of power?

ill the relationship between people change

A *Then, Now, Next* framework encourages students to understand historical contexts and precedents, so they can weigh them against current political events and actions, begin to formulate an informed judgment about politics, and consider how the past and present might shape the future.

THEN◄ NOW◄ NEXt◄

How the Media Have Shaped Entertainment and the Information Highways

THEN (1960s)	NOW (2011)
Television programming matured and revolutionized how the media entertained and provided information.	The Internet matures and revolutionizes how we are entertained and how we get information.
Television accentuated a new set of candidate qualities—including being telegenic—that had not mattered much in earlier political campaigns.	The Internet accentuates a new set of candidate qualities—including being tech savvy and Net organized—that were unheard of a generation ago.
Communication between the media and voters was one-way: people got information but could not "talk back."	Information flow is two-way, thanks to talk radio and the Internet—including blogs, YouTube, and social-networking sites.

WHAT'S NEXt?

> What new media technologies will shape campaigns and political participation in the future?

> For individuals seeking information about policy issues and political campaigns, what might be the negative consequences of the abundance of information flowing through the electronic media?

> How will technology change political participation in the future?

ANALYZING THE SOURCES

CONFIDENCE IN THE MEDIA

The Gallup Organization has asked the following question in surveys since 1972: "In general, how much trust and confidence do you have in the mass media—such as newspapers, T.V., and radio—when it comes to reporting the news fully, accurately, and fairly: a great deal, a fair amount, not very much, or none at all?"

SOURCE: The Gallup Poll, Media Use and Evaluation, www.galluppoll.com/poll/1663/Media-Use-Evaluation.aspx

The line graph illustrates survey respondents' views on that question, showing data at various times between May 1972 and September 2009. You can see that able changes have occurred in people's assessment of news organizations in th

Evaluating the Evidence

① Describe trends during the 1970s in people's confidence in the media, citing specific data from the graph.

② Describe trends since 2001 in people's confidence in the media, citing specific data.

③ What do the latest surveys indicate about respondents' opinions on the issue of confidence in the media?

④ What do the data say about the overall trends with regard to people's confidence in the media?
...ctors could have contributed
...people's assess-

> "Analyzing the Sources" guides students in thinking through original resources in American politics.

> "Thinking Critically About Democracy" gives students a comprehensive appreciation of the many sides of a political issue and an opportunity to formulate well-reasoned opinions.

THINKING CRITICALLY ABOUT DEMOCRACY

SHOULD CONGRESS REGULATE THE INTERNET INFRASTRUCTURE?

The Issue: The technological revolution has brought ongoing, exponential growth in Internet traffic. As rising numbers of people turn to the Internet for more and more uses—from viewing videos online to sending pictures to Grandma, and from buying gifts and personal items to calling friends and relatives—the volume of information that the broadband infrastructure of the Internet must transmit is becoming overwhelming. The owners of that infrastructure—corporate giants such as AT&T, Verizon, and Comcast—seek legislation that would allow them to charge companies that produce high volumes of traffic. In effect, this legislation would set up a two-tiered system of broadband access in which one tier is an "express lane" with tolls, and the other an older, slower lane with free access. One problem is that many of today's services require the faster access to make them effective.

Yes: Congress should regulate the Internet infrastructure. We need a two-tiered system of broadband access. The telecommunications titans in command of the Internet infrastructure argue that to keep up with the increasing demand for broadband space, they will have to expand and improve the system continually. Corporate advocates of a two-tiered system of broadband access are also interested in providing premium-quality broadband service to their own clientele. Thus, for example, Verizon wants to ensure that its Internet subscribers (rather than the subscribers of its competitors) have high-quality access to the broadband infrastructure technology that Verizon owns so that its subscribers do not get caught in an Internet traffic jam.

with soaring demand. In addition, the security of the system is crucial to continued business activity and corporate financial growth, as well as to national economic health. Broadband availability is a national security issue because if law enforcers, airports, hospitals, nuclear power plants, and first responders do not have adequate or immediate access to the information they need to perform their jobs, human lives are at risk. Because of these critical financial and security implications, a tax or user fee could be instituted that would pay for Internet infrastructure improvements.

What do you think?

① Do you believe that Congress should reject proposals to create a for-fee fast lane for Internet traffic? If so, why? Or do you think the marketplace should determine which services get faster access to broadband lines? If so, why would the latter be preferable?

② What impact would the creation of a two-tiered Internet structure have on Internet business development? On national security?

③ Should the federal government help to defray the costs of improvements to the Internet infrastructure? Why, or why not?

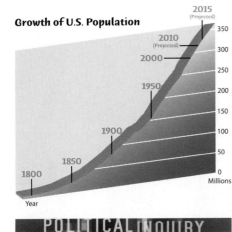

Growth of U.S. Population

POLITICAL INQUIRY

FIGURE 1.2 ■ From 1790 to 1900, the population of the United States increased gradually, and it did not reach 100 million until the second decade of the twentieth century. What factors caused the steep rise during the twentieth century? How will these forces continue to affect the size of the U.S. population during this century?

SOURCE: U.S. Census, www.census.gov/population/www/documentation/twps0056.html, and www.census.gov/compendia/stabab/cats/population/estimates_and_projections _by_age_sex_raceethnicity.html.

> Students continue to build skills through additional tools, such as "Political Inquiry," which prompts them to analyze data and images presented in the program.

Teaching and Studying *American Democracy Now*

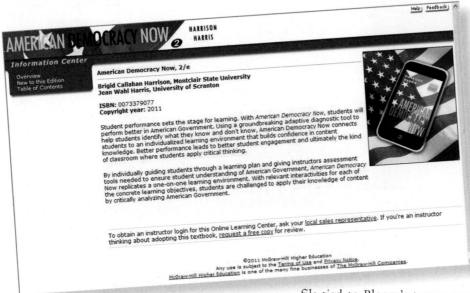

American Democracy Now, 2/e

Brigid Callahan Harrison, Montclair State University
Jean Wahl Harris, University of Scranton

ISBN: 0073379077
Copyright year: 2011

Student performance sets the stage for learning. With *American Democracy Now*, students will perform better in American Government. Using a groundbreaking adaptive diagnostic tool to help students identify what they know and don't know, *American Democracy Now* connects students to an individualized learning environment that builds confidence in content knowledge. Better performance leads to better student engagement and ultimately the kind of classroom where students apply critical thinking.

By individually guiding students through a learning plan and giving instructors assessment tools needed to ensure student understanding of American Government, *American Democracy Now* replicates a one-on-one learning environment. With relevant interactivities for each of the concrete learning objectives, students are challenged to apply their knowledge of content by critically analyzing American Government.

To obtain an instructor login for this Online Learning Center, ask your local sales representative. If you're an instructor thinking about adopting this textbook, request a free copy for review.

American Democracy Now is supported by a set of integrated supplements for instructors teaching and students studying American Government. Together with the core materials, these supplements are readily available on the instructor side of the Online Learning Center for *American Democracy Now*.

ONLINE LEARNING CENTER

The password-protected instructor side of the Online Learning Center (**www.mhhe.com/harrisonadn2e**) contains the Instructor's Manual that goes beyond lecture topics and outlines by tying all text features to individual and group projects in and out of class and a full test item file tied to Bloom's taxonomy, as well as PowerPoint slides, Classroom Performance System (CPS) Questions, and an Image Gallery. See more information about specific assets below. Ask your local McGraw-Hill representative for password information.

- The **Instructor's Manual** includes chapter summaries, chapter outlines, lecture outlines with integrated PowerPoints, and abundant class activities.

- The **Test Bank** includes more than 1000 multiple-choice and short-answer questions to accompany the chapters in *American Democracy Now,* along with questions to be used in class (with PowerPoints) and student self check questions.

CREATE   Craft your teaching resources to match the way you teach! With McGraw-Hill Create, **www.mcgrawhillcreate.com,** you can easily rearrange chapters, combine material from other content sources, and quickly upload content you have written like your course syllabus or teaching notes. Find the content you need in Create by searching through thousands of leading McGraw-Hill textbooks. Arrange your book to fit your teaching style. Create even allows you to personalize your book's appearance by selecting the cover and adding your name, school, and course information. Order a Create book and you'll receive a complimentary print review copy in 3–5 business days or a complimentary electronic review copy (eComp) via email in about one hour. Go to www.mcgrawhillcreate.com today and register. Experience how McGraw-Hill Create empowers you to teach your students *your* way.

COURSESMART E-TEXTBOOK This text is available as an e-Textbook at **www .CourseSmart.com.** At CourseSmart your students can take advantage of significant savings off the cost of a print textbook, reduce their impact on the environment, and gain access to powerful web tools for learning. CourseSmart e-Textbooks can be viewed online or downloaded to a computer. The e-Textbooks allow students to do full text searches, add highlighting and notes, and share notes with classmates. CourseSmart has the largest selection of e-Textbooks available anywhere. Visit www.CourseSmart.com to learn more and to try a sample chapter.

Do More

BLACKBOARD McGraw-Hill Higher Education and Blackboard have teamed up. What does this mean for you?

1. **Your life, simplified.** Now you and your students can access McGraw-Hill's Connect™ and Create™ right from within your Blackboard course—all with one single sign-on. Say goodbye to the days of logging in to multiple applications.

2. **Deep integration of content and tools.** Not only do you get single sign-on with Connect™ and Create™, you also get deep integration of McGraw-Hill content and content engines right in Blackboard. Whether you're choosing a book for your course or building Connect™ assignments, all the tools you need are right where you want them—inside of Blackboard.

3. **Seamless gradebooks.** Are you tired of keeping multiple gradebooks and manually synchronizing grades into Blackboard? We thought so. When a student completes an integrated Connect™ assignment, the grade for that assignment automatically (and instantly) feeds your Blackboard grade center.

4. **A solution for everyone.** Whether your institution is already using Blackboard or you just want to try Blackboard on your own, we have a solution for you. McGraw-Hill and Blackboard can now offer you easy access to industry leading technology and content, whether your campus hosts it, or we do. Be sure to ask your local McGraw-Hill representative for details.

Staying Current

CHAPTER BY CHAPTER CHANGES IN *AMERICAN DEMOCRACY NOW*, SECOND EDITION

This second edition includes important new material in a streamlined format. Each chapter has also been updated to reflect recent events and trends. Key content changes, chapter by chapter, include the following:

CHAPTER 1 PEOPLE, POLITICS, AND PARTICIPATION
- Updated coverage of the changing demographics and ideological shifts in American politics
- Revised coverage of the role of technology in politics

CHAPTER 2 THE CONSTITUTION
- Reorganized for better flow and to increase understanding of how the Constitution addressed the concerns of the framers, state rights advocates, and citizens
- Revised, more comprehansive coverage of the first state constitutions and their influence on the U.S. Constitution's separation of powers and Bill of Rights
- Additional coverage of the deficiencies of the Articles of Confederation and the call for a Constitutional convention
- Added a critical presentation of the innovative constitutional ratification process

CHAPTER 3 FEDERALISM
- Updated data in tables and figures throughout the chapter
- Added tables and figures on the number of local governments in each state and the number of recognized Indian tribes in each state

- Added information on the federal Race to the Top grant program
- Added information on the 2009 American Recovery and Reinvestment Act (ARRA)
- Added coverage on the debate over the minimum drinking age in the new Thinking Critically About Democracy feature
- The section on Today's Federalism has been revised to capture the difference between the federal system of government presented by Madison in *Federalist* No. 45 and the reality of today's federalism–intergovernmental relations

CHAPTER 4 CIVIL LIBERTIES
- Emphasis on the theoretical framework of the tension between liberty and societal order integrated throughout the chapter
- Added coverage of new Supreme Court decisions related to civil liberties
- Updated coverage of the Obama Administration's approach to ethnic profiling and the infringement of personal liberties in the War on Terror
- Integration of new sources that reflect current events (e.g., updating footnotes to the Obama Administration)
- New emphasis on social networking media, including Twitter
- New charts addressing changes in the death penalty and marriage rights by the states

CHAPTER 5 CIVIL RIGHTS
- Tests used by the courts to determine legal and illegal discrimination moved to the beginning of the chapter, establishing a framework for understanding the evolution of civil rights
- Updated information on voter registration and minority representation in elected offices
- Added information on the Indian Gaming Regulatory Act
- Added discussion of the 2008 ADA amendments

CHAPTER 6 POLITICAL SOCIALIZATION AND PUBLIC OPINION
- Updated with the most recent data available concerning U.S. public opinion, including confidence in institution trends and policy priorities

CHAPTER 7 INTEREST GROUPS
- New coverage of the regulatory environment that structures interest group behavior

CHAPTER 8 POLITICAL PARTIES
- New discussion of the Tea Party movement, the struggle in the national Republican party, and an Obama-led Democratic party
- New discussion of the post-2010 party environment, including the use of technology by the political parties

CHAPTER 9 ELECTIONS, CAMPAIGNS, AND VOTING
- New discussion of California's Proposition 8
- New discussion of how technology has revolutionized the art of political campaigning
- Added discussion of the *Citizen United* decision, including its impact on the PACs
- Increased discussion of voter turnout within states

CHAPTER 10 THE MEDIA
- Increased discussion of the responsibility of consumers of the media
- Increased discussion of verifiability, particularly concerning the role of citizen journalists in politics
- Expanded coverage of the changing face of the media, especially new media outlets

CHAPTER 11 CONGRESS
- Preliminary discussion of the impact of the 2010 census on reapportionment and redistricting
- Added coverage of the 2010 congressional election
- Increased discussion of congressional policymaking, including earmarks and health care legislation

CHAPTER 12 THE PRESIDENCY
- Increased comparisons of Bush administration policies and Obama administration policies—including stimulus spending
- Integrated the latest research regarding presidential communication
- Added coverage of the Obama administration personnel
- New discussion of Obama presidential approval ratings

CHAPTER 13 THE BUREAUCRACY
- Updated data on demographics of bureaucrats and added data on the type of work bureaucrats do
- Updated data on the number of federal bureaucrats in each department and each department's budget.

CHAPTER 14 THE JUDICIARY
- New coverage of the Roberts court, including the appointments of Sotomayor and Kagan
- Added coverage of new policy decisions

CHAPTER 15 ECONOMIC POLICY
- Integrated discussion of the Bush and Obama administrations' use of fiscal policy to bolster faltering financial institutions and address the great recession
- New Analyzing the Sources box critiquing the GDP and the unemployment rate as measures of economic health
- Increased coverage of the Federal Reserve System
- Added coverage of the debate over new financial and banking regulations
- Updated coverage of the status of U.S. economy, the global economy, and the American dream

CHAPTER 16 DOMESTIC POLICY
- Coverage of the April 2010 Masey mine disaster in West Virginia and the BP oil rig disaster in the discussion of threats posed by energy production
- Discussion of the Obama administration's work on climate change legislation, the House of Representatives American Clean Energy and Security Act, and the Senate Energy and Natural Resources Committee's Clean Energy and Leadership Act
- New discussion of the sustainability of OASI
- New discussion of the March 2010 federal health care law, the Patient Protection and Affordable Care Act, and the debate over requiring people to purchase health care
- Revised section on homeland security policy to focus on the dilemmas legislators confront in homeland security policy deliberations
- New coverage of the controversial Arizona immigration law

CHAPTER 17 FOREIGN POLICY AND NATIONAL SECURITY
- New coverage of the Obama doctrine in foreign policy
- Increased coverage of the war in Afghanistan
- Re-evaluation of the motivations driving U.S. foreign policy

CHAPTER 18 STATE AND LOCAL GOVERNMENT
- Updated information on recent ballot measures and recall efforts
- New discussion of the battle for statehood for Washington, D.C.
- Enhanced discussion of the federal government's role as fiscal equalizer, with a focus on the impact of the American Recovery and Reinvestment Act (ARRA) on state budgets
- Updated data on minority representation and female representation in state legislatures

ACKNOWLEDGMENTS

We owe a debt of thanks to all of the people who contributed their thoughts and suggestions to the development of *American Democracy Now*.

Manuscript Reviewers

Stephen Anthony, *Georgia State University*
Stephen Baker, *Jacksonville University*
Michael Baranowski, *Northern Kentucky University*
Kyle Barbieri, *Georgia Perimeter College*
Wendell Broadwell, *Georgia Perimeter College*
Vida Davoudi, *Lone Star College–Kingwood*
Jacqueline DeMerritt, *University of North Texas*
Kevin Dockerty, *Kalamazoo Valley Community College*
Cecil Dorsey, *San Jacinto College*
Matthew Eshabaugh-Soha, *University of North Texas*
Glen Findley, *Odessa College*
John Forshee, *San Jacinto College*
Myrtle Freeman, *Tarrant County College–South*
Dana Glencross, *Oklahoma City Community College*
James Michael Greig, *University of North Texas*
Alexander Hogan, *Lone Star College–CyFair*
Richard Kiefer, *Waubonsee Community College*
Melinda Kovacs, *Sam Houston State University*
Nancy Kral, *Lone Star College–Tomball*
Fred Lokken, *Truckee Meadows*
Vinette Meikle-Harris, *Houston Community College–Central*
Fran Moran, *New Jersey City University*
Joseph Moskowitz, *New Jersey City University*
Yamini Munipalli, *Florida State College*
Kathleen Murnan, *Ozarks Technical Community College*
Martha Musgrove, *Tarrant County College–South*
Glynn Newman, *Eastfield College*
Cecil Larry Pool, *El Centro College*
Sean Reed, *Wharton County Junior College*
Shauna Reilly, *Northern Kentucky University*
Elizabeth Rexford, *Wharton County Junior College*
Shyam Sriram, *Georgia Perimeter College*
Adam Stone, *Georgia Perimeter College*
Steve Tran, *Houston Community College*
Dennis Toombs, *San Jacinto College–North*
David Uranga, *Pasadena City College*
Ron Vardy, *University of Houston*
Sarah Velasquez, *Fresno Community College*

American Government Symposia

Since 2006, McGraw-Hill has conducted several symposia in American Government for instructors from across the country. These events offered a forum for instructors to exchange ideas and experiences with colleagues they might not have met otherwise. They also provided an opportunity for editors from McGraw-Hill to gather information about the needs and challenges of instructors of American Government. The feedback we have received has been invaluable and has contributed—directly and indirectly—to the development of *American Democracy Now*. We would like to thank the participants for their insights.

Melvin Aaron, *Los Angeles City College*
Yan Bai, *Grand Rapids Community College*
Robert Ballinger, *South Texas College*
Nancy Bednar, *Antelope Valley College*
Jeffrey Birdsong, *Northeastern Oklahoma A&M College*
Amy Brandon, *San Jacinto College-North*
Jane Bryant, *John A. Logan College*
Dan R. Brown, *Southwestern Oklahoma State University*
Monique Bruner, *Rose State College*
Anita Chadha, *University of Houston–Downtown*
John Clark, *Western Michigan University–Kalamazoo*
Kathleen Collihan, *American River College*
Steven Collins, *Oklahoma State University–Oklahoma City*
John Davis, *Howard University*
Kevin Davis, *North Cedntral Texas College*
Paul Davis, *Truckee Meadows Community College*
Vida Davoudi, *Lone Star College – Kingwood*
Robert De Luna, *Saint Philips College*
Jeff DeWitt, *Kennesaw State University*
Kevin Dockerty, *Kalamazoo Valley Community College*
Cecil Dorsey, *San Jacinto College – South*
Hien Do, *San Jose State University*
Jay Dow, *University of Missouri–Columbia*
Manar Elkhaldi, *University of Central Florida*
Karry Evans, *Austin Community College*
Pearl Ford, *University of Arkansas–Fayetteville*
John Forshee, *San Jacinto College–Central*
Ben Riesner Fraser, *San Jacinto College*
Daniel Fuerstman, *Dutchess Community College*
Jarvis T. Gamble, *Owens Community College*
Marilyn Gaar, *Johnson County Community College*

Michael Gattis, *Gulf Coast community College*
William Gillespie, *Kennesaw State University*
Dana K. Glencross, *Oklahoma City Community College*
Larry Gonzalez, *Houston Community College–Southwest*
Nirmal Goswami, *Texas A&M University–Kingsville*
Daniel Gutierrez, *El Paso Community College*
Richard Gutierrez, *University of Texas, El Paso*
Michelle Kukoleca Hammes, *St. Cloud State University*
Cathy Hanks, *University of Nevada, Las Vegas*
Wanda Hill, *Tarrant County Community College*
Joseph Hinchliffe, *University of Illinois at Urbana–Champaign*
John Hitt, *North Lake College*
Mark Jendrysik, *University of North Dakota*
Brenda Jones, *Houston Community College–Central*
Franklin Jones, *Texas Southern University*
Lynn Jones, *Collin County Community College*
James Joseph, *Fresno City College*
Jason Kassel, *Valdosta State University*
Manoucher Khosrowshahi, *Tyler Junior College*
Rich Kiefer, *Waubonsee Community College*
Robert J. King, *Georgia Perimeter College*
Melinda Kovacs, *Sam Houston State University*
Chien-Pin Li, *Kennesaw State University*
Fred Lokken, *Truckee Meadows Community College*
John Mercurio, *San Diego State University*
Janna Merrick, *University of South Florida*
Joe Meyer, *Los Angeles City College*
Eric Miller, *Blinn College*
Kent Miller, *Weatherford College*
Charles Moore, *Georgia State University*
Eduardo Munoz, *El Camino College*
Kay Murnan, *Ozarks Technical Community College*
Carolyn Myers, *Southwestern Illinois College*
Blaine Nelson, *El Paso Community College*
Theresa Nevarez, *El Paso Community College*
James A. Norris, *Texas A & M International University*
Kent Park, *U.S. Military Academy at West Point*
Eric Rader, *Henry Ford Community College*
Elizabeth Rexford, *Wharton County Junior College*
Tara Ross, *Keiser University*
Carlos Rovelo, *Tarrant Community College–South*
Ryan Rynbrandt, *Collin County Community College*
Ray Sandoval, *Richland College*
Craig Scarpelli, *California State University–Chico*
Louis Schubert, *City College of San Francisco*
Edward Senu-Oke, *Joliet Junior College*
Mark Shomaker, *Blinn College*
Thomas Simpson, *Missouri Southern University*
Henry Sirgo, *McNeese State University*
Amy Smith, *North Lake College*
Daniel Smith, *Northwest Missouri State University*
John Speer, *Houston Community College–Southwest*
Jim Startin, *University of Texas at San Antonio*
Sharon Sykora, *Slippery Rock University*
Tressa Tabares, *American River College*
Beatrice Talpos, *Wayne County Community College*
Alec Thomson, *Schoolcraft College*
Judy Tobler, *Northwest Arkansas Community College*

Steve Tran, *Houston Community College*
Beth Traxler, *Greenville Technical College*
William Turk, *University of Texas - Pan American*
Ron Vardy, *University of Houston*
Sarah Velasquez, *Fresno City College*
Ron VonBehren, *Valencia Community College – Osceola*
Albert C. Waite, *Central Texas College*
Van Allen Wigginton, *San Jacinto College–Central*
Charlotte Williams, *Pasadena City College*
Ike Wilson, *U.S. Military Academy*
Paul Wilson, *San Antonio College*
John Wood, *Rose State College*
Robert Wood, *University of North Dakota*
Larry Wright, *Florida A & M University*
Ann Wyman, *Missouri Southern State University*
Kathryn Yates, *Richland College*

Personal Acknowledgments

We must thank our team at McGraw-Hill: Steve Debow, president of the Humanities, Social Science, and Languages group; James Headley, national sales manager; Mike Ryan, vice president and editor in-chief; and Lisa Pinto, executive director of development have supported this project with amazing talent and resources. Beth Mejia, editorial director for political science, has been a strong advocate for this project, and a dear friend. With kind and thoughtful leadership and sharp intellect, Mark Georgiev, sponsoring editor, took us by the hand and gently led us to where we needed to be. We benefited from steady guidance and wisdom from Dawn Groundwater, director of development. Senior developmental editor Judith Kromm has been a pleasure to work with. Naomi Friedman and Marjorie Anderson provided valuable development support. Marketing manager Patrick Brown's energy and enthusiasm have meant a great deal to us. Leslie Racanelli, our production editor, and her team showed patience, innovation, and flexibility. We would particularly like to thank Cassandra Chu and Linda Beaupré, our designers; Ayelet Arbel, our illustrator; and David Tietz, our photo researcher. Amy Flauaus provided invaluable support with good humor in her role as Editorial Coordinator. We are extraordinarily grateful to all of you.

We would also like to thank the contributors to our first edition: Susan Tolchin at George Mason University, Suzanne U. Samuels at Ramapo College, Elizabeth Bennion at Indiana University, Carol Whitney, and Naomi Friedman.

For their patience, understanding, and support, the authors also wish to thank: Caroline, Alexandra, and John Harrison, Paul Meilak, Rosemary Fitzgerald, Patricia Jillard, Kathleen Cain, John Callahan, Teresa Biebel, Thomas Callahan, Michael Harris, Jim and Audrey Wahl and the Wahl "girls"—Eileen Choynowski, Laura McAlpine, Audrey Messina, and Jaimee Conner.

John and Rosemary Callahan and Jim and Audrey Wahl first began the conversation of democracy with us and we thank them and all of the students and colleagues, friends and family members, who continue that conversation now.

BRIGID CALLAHAN HARRISON

JEAN WAHL HARRIS

A letter from the AUTHORS

Welcome to the second edition of *American Democracy Now!* In creating the first edition of this text, we sought to merge our years of experience as classroom instructors and our desire to captivate students with the compelling story of their democracy into a student-centered text. In this second edition, we are delighted to refine those goals with an integrated learning program for American government that will maximize student performance.

One of the most exciting facets of the second edition is the ability to create individualized study plans. Using an adaptive diagnostic tool combined with research-based teaching tools, students are guided in their critical thinking about American government. These tools value student performance by showing what they know, and then creating individualized learning objectives that will facilitate their success in completing the course. The result is higher student achievement, greater interest, more critical thinking, and a classroom environment that sizzles with the excitement of success, learning, mastery, and engagement.

The key to student success is the ability to think critically about American government and politics. *American Democracy Now,* 2e, teaches students the essential elements, institutions, and dynamics of American government. As they gain an understanding of the fundamental character of our political process, they also learn to ask the questions that make their understanding of American government meaningful to them. They learn how the fundamental principles of American democracy inform their understanding of the politics and policies of today, so that they can think about the policies they would like to see take shape tomorrow. In short, they learn to inquire: how does then and now shape what's going to happen next? This then, now, next approach to critical thinking serves as the basis for student participation.

American Democracy Now, 2e, takes a broader view of participation than the textbooks we have used in the past. To us, participation encompasses a variety of activities from the modest, creative, local or even personal actions students can take to the larger career choices they can make. And today, technology plays an enormous role in shaping political participation—particularly the participation of young people. By recognizing the legitimacy of new forms of political participation, we are giving students the tools to define what participation means to them and make active choices about where, when, and how to participate. And choosing how to participate makes American government matter.

As the students in our American Government classroom become ever more diverse, the challenge is not to appeal directly to their personal backgrounds; the challenge is to hone their critical thinking skills, foster and harness their energy, and create tools that facilitate their success in the American government course. We know we have succeeded when students apply their knowledge and sharpened skills to consider the outcomes they—as students, citizens, and participants—would like to see.

Facilitating their success means joining students where they are. The second edition of *American Democracy Now* further integrates technology into our students' study of politics, so that their engagement with content is seamless. Facebook, YouTube, and Twitter are not only powerful social networking tools, but also powerful political and educational tools. New technologies help politicians to communicate with citizens, citizens to communicate with each other, and you to communicate with your students. We invite you to, and we wish you and your students success.

BRIGID CALLAHAN HARRISON

JEAN WAHL HARRIS

Brigid Callahan Harrison

Brigid Harrison specializes in the civic engagement and political participation of Americans, especially the Millennial Generation, the U.S. Congress, and the Presidency. Brigid has taught American government for over fifteen years. She takes particular pride in creating in the classroom a learning experience that shapes students' lifelong understanding of American politics, sharpens their critical thinking about American government, and encourages their participation in civic life. She enjoys supervising student internships in political campaigns and government and is a frequent commentator in print and electronic media on national and New Jersey politics. She currently serves as president of the National Women's Caucus for Political Science. She received her B.A. from The Richard Stockton College, her M.A. from Rutgers, The State University of New Jersey, and her Ph.D. from Temple University. Harrison lives in Galloway, NJ and has three children: Caroline (16), Alexandra (10), and John (7). Born and raised in New Jersey, Harrison is a fan of Bruce Springsteen and professor of political science and law at Montclair State University.

Jean Wahl Harris

Jean Harris's research interests include political socialization and engagement, federalism, and the evolution and institutionalization of the first ladyship and the vice presidency. She regularly teaches introductory courses in local, state, and national government and upper level courses in public administration and public policy. In the classroom, Jean seeks to cultivate students' participation in the political conversation so vital to American civic life and to convey the profound opportunities that the American political system affords an active, critical, and informed citizenry. She earned her B.A., M.A., and Ph.D. from the State University of New York at Binghamton. In 1994 the University of Scranton named her its CASE (Council for Advancement and Support of Education) professor of the year. She was an American Council on Education (ACE) Fellow during the 2007–2008 academic year. She currently serves as chairperson for the Political Science Department at the University of Scranton. Jean lives in Nicholson, Pennsylvania with her husband Michael. She enjoys reading on her deck overlooking the Endless Mountains of Northeast Pennsylvania.

People, Politics, and Participation

THEN

Cynicism, distrust, and apathy characterized Americans' relationship with their government for the past generation.

NOW

New information technologies, new political leadership, generational politics, and a diversifying population give cause for optimism as the nation responds to the challenges of a new millennium.

NEXT

Will the present generation break the cycle of cynicism that has pervaded the politics of the recent past?

Will new information technologies facilitate and energize political participation?

Will the face of American politics change as the nation's population grows and shifts?

The United States was founded

by individuals who believed in the power of democracy to respond to the will of citizens. Historically, citizen activists have come from all walks of life, but they have shared one common attribute: the belief that, in the ongoing conversation of democracy, their government listens to *people like them*. This idea is vital if individuals are to have an impact on their government; people who don't believe they can have any influence rarely try. From the Pilgrims' flight from religious persecution, to the War for Independence, to the Civil War, to the Great Depression, to World War II, and to the great movements for social justice—civil rights, women's liberation, and more—the story of the United States is the story of people who are involved with their government, who know what they want their government to do, and who have confidence in their ability to influence its policies.[1] *American Democracy Now* tells the story of how today's citizen activists are participating in the conversation of democracy—in the politics, governance, and civic life of their communities and their nation during a time of technological revolution and unprecedented global change. This story is the next chapter in America's larger story.

The history of democracy in the United States is rife with examples of ordinary people who have made and are making a difference.[2] Throughout this book, we describe the impact that individuals and groups have had, and continue to have, in creating and changing the country's institutions of government. We also explore how individuals have influenced the ways in which our governments—national, state, and local—create policy.[3] These stories are important not only in and of themselves but also as motivators for all of us who want to live in a democracy that responds to all its citizens.

A fundamental principle underlying this book is that your beliefs and your voice—and ultimately how you use those beliefs and that voice—matter. Whatever your beliefs, it is important that you come to them thoughtfully, by employing introspection and critical thinking. Similarly, however you choose to participate, it is crucial that you take part in the civic life of your community. This book seeks both to inform and to inspire your participation. A sentiment voiced by American anthropologist Margaret Mead expresses a powerful truth: "Never doubt that a small group of thoughtful, committed citizens can change the world. Indeed, it's the only thing that ever has."

y shd u stdy am dem now? Or, Why Should You Study American Democracy Now?

Politics as practiced today is not your parents' brand of politics. **Politics**—the process of deciding who benefits in society and who does not—is a much different process today than it was even a decade ago. Advances in technology have altered the political landscape in many ways, including how voters and candidates communicate with each other, how governments provide information to individuals, how people get their news about events, and how governments administer laws. The political landscape has also changed because of world events. In particular, the terrorist attacks of September 11, 2001, and the wars in Afghanistan and Iraq

---

This chapter provides a framework for your study of American government in this textbook.

FIRST, we delve into the basic question, *why should you study American democracy now?*

SECOND, we explore *what government does.*

THIRD, we explain how political scientists categorize the various *types of government.*

FOURTH, we consider the *origins of American democracy,* including the ideas of natural law, a social contract, and representative democracy.

FIFTH, we examine *political culture and American values,* which centrally include liberty; equality; consent of the governed; capitalism; and the importance of the individual, the family, and the community.

SIXTH, we focus on *the changing face of American democracy* as the population grows and diversifies.

SEVENTH, we look at *ideology as a prism* through which American politics can be viewed.

politics
the process of deciding who benefits in society and who does not

have markedly changed many aspects of American life. Americans have become immune to the latest reports of suicide bombings in Iraq, Afghanistan, and elsewhere, and they have become all too familiar with reports of local soldiers killed in war. These shifts in how Americans interact with government and in what issues concern them represent distinct changes that make the study of politics today interesting, exciting, and important.

How Technology Has Changed Politics

It would be difficult to overstate the impact of the technological revolution on politics as it is practiced today. In electoral politics, faster computers and the Internet have revolutionized a process that, until the advent of the personal computer and the Internet, was not very different in 1990 from the way it was carried out in 1890. Today, many voters get much of their information from Internet-based news sites and Weblogs. Campaigns rely on e-mail; instant and text messaging; Web sites; and social-networking pages on MySpace, Facebook, BlackPlanet, Cyloop, and similar sites to communicate with and organize supporters. State governments rely on computers to conduct elections.

But the impact of technology is not limited to elections. Would you like to help your grandfather apply for his Social Security benefits? You no longer need to go to the local Social Security office or even mail an application; instead, you can help him apply online, and his check can be deposited into his bank account electronically. Do you want to communicate your views to your representatives in Congress? You do not need to call or send a letter by snail mail—their e-mail addresses are available online. Do you want to find out which government agencies are hiring recent college graduates? Go to usajobs.gov. Do you need to ship a package using the U.S. Postal Service? The postal service Web site provides guidelines.

Because of these unprecedented shifts in the ways politics happens and government is administered, Americans today face both new opportunities and new challenges. How might we use technology to ensure that elections are conducted fairly? How might the abundance and reach of media technology be directed toward informing and enriching us rather than overwhelming us or perpetuating the citizen cynicism of recent years? What privacy rights can we be sure of in the present digital age? Whatever your age, as a student, you are a member of one of the most tech-savvy groups in the country, and your input, expertise, and participation are vital to sorting out the opportunities and obstacles of this next stage of American democracy.

The Political Context Now

September 11, 2001, and the subsequent wars in Afghanistan and Iraq have had a marked effect on the U.S. political environment. These events have been a catalyst for changes in the attitudes of many Americans, including young Americans, about their government and their role in it.

Since the early 1970s—a decade blemished by the intense unpopularity of the Vietnam War and by scandals that ushered in the resignation of President Richard Nixon in 1974—Americans' attitudes about government have been dismal.[4] Numerous surveys, including an ongoing Gallup poll that has tracked Americans' opinions, have demonstrated low levels of trust in government and of confidence in government's ability to solve problems.[5] Young people's views have mirrored those of the nation as a whole. In 2000, one study of undergraduate college students, for example, showed that nearly two-thirds (64 percent) did not trust the federal government to do the right thing most of the time, an attitude that reflected the views of the larger population.[6] Distrust; lack of **efficacy,** which is a person's belief that he or she has the ability to achieve something desirable and that the government genuinely listens to individuals; and apathy among young people were reflected in the voter turnout for the 2000 presidential election, when only 36 percent of eligible college-age voters went to the polls.

The events of September 11, 2001, jolted American politics and the nation, and the altered political context provoked changes in popular views—notably, young people's opinions. "The attacks of 9/11 . . . changed the way the Millennial Generation thinks about

efficacy
citizens' belief that they have the ability to achieve something desirable and that the government listens to people like them

Technology and Political Participation

THEN (1970s)	NOW (2011)
47 percent of 18- to 20-year-olds voted in the 1976 presidential election.	About 53 percent of 18- to 20-year-olds voted in the 2008 presidential election, though that figure dropped in the 2010 congressional midterm elections.
People got their national news from one half-hour-long nightly news broadcast.	People get their news from an array of sources, including twenty-four-hour news networks and Internet news services available on demand via computers and cell phones.
Many people participated in civic life primarily through demonstrations, protests, and voting.	People still participate through demonstrations and protests but Tea Party activists rely on electronic communications to spread the word about demonstrations and protests. Other forms of political participation, including volunteerism, social networking, and targeted purchasing, characterize civic participation now.

WHAT'S NEXT?

> How might advancing media technologies further transform the ways that people "consume" their news?

> Will the upswing of voter participation by 18- to 20-year-olds continue?

> What new forms of civic participation will emerge?

> Will the highly competitive 2008 presidential race motivate a new wave of voters to remain active participants in the electoral process?

politics. Overnight, their attitudes were more like [those of] the Greatest Generation [the generation of Americans who lived through the Great Depression and World War II]," observed John Della Volpe, a pollster who helped Harvard University students construct a national poll of young people's views.[7]

As patriotic spirits soared, suddenly 60 percent of college students trusted government to do the right thing. Ninety-two percent considered themselves patriotic. Some 77 percent thought that politics was relevant to their lives.[8] In the immediate aftermath of the September 11, 2001 attacks, then-President George W. Bush and Congress enjoyed record-high approval ratings. Roughly 80 percent of young people and nearly that same percentage of all Americans supported U.S. military actions in Afghanistan. Beyond opinions, actions changed as well:

- More than 70 percent of college students gave blood, donated money, or volunteered in relief efforts.
- Nearly 70 percent volunteered in their communities (up from 60 percent in 2000).
- Eighty-six percent believed their generation was ready to lead the United States into the future.[9]

Then the political context changed again, over months and then years, as wars in Afghanistan and Iraq wore on, as casualties mounted, and as military spending skyrocketed. Trust in government, particularly of the president, plummeted. The changes after September 11, 2001 continued to affect how Americans, particularly young Americans, participate in politics.

An important trend is visible in one of the most easily measured contexts: voter turnout. Figure 1.1 shows the jump in participation by young voters in the 2004 presidential election. (In contrast, for voters aged 66–74, participation actually *de*creased in 2004.) Among voters aged 18–21, the largest increases in turnout occurred among 19-year-olds, whose turnout rivaled that of voters in their 30s. Americans are debating the importance of this upswing in turnout over the long haul. (See "Thinking Critically About Democracy" on page 8.) In 2008, that trend continued, with estimates indicating that voters aged 18–20 increased by 2.2 million, surpassing the young voter turnout since 18-year-olds voted for the first time in 1972.

As these statistics demonstrate, lingering media characterizations of a cynical young electorate are off the mark. Evidence indicates that many young people are enthusiastic participants in civic and political life.[10] Witness the strong political support that Barack Obama's presidential campaign garnered from young people, some of whom packed their bags and traveled with the Obama team during the primary season that led to the Democratic convention in August 2008 (see "Analyzing the Sources") on page 9. Others are taking part in ways that have not traditionally been thought of, and measured as, participation. These include, for example, Internet activism and using one's power as a consumer to send political messages. For many students, that foundation of political participation, volunteerism, or community action has already provided them with a rationale for increasing their knowledge of, and participation in, their communities.

Individuals who engage in politics and civic life experience many benefits. Engaged citizens are knowledgeable about public issues; actively communicate with policy makers and others; press government officials to carry out the people's will; advocate for their own self-interest and the interests of others; and hold public officials accountable for their decisions and actions. You will find that advocating for your own interests or working with others in similar situations will sometimes (perhaps to your surprise) lead to desired outcomes. This is efficacy in action. And you will discover that with experience you will become more effective at advocacy—the more you do, the better you get. Furthermore, you will derive social and psychological benefits from being civically engaged.

In addition, and importantly, local communities, states, and the nation benefit from an engaged populace. Governments are more effective when people voice their views. As we explore throughout this book, American democracy provides citizens and others more opportunities to influence governmental action than at any other time in history. If you have the knowledge and tools, you should be able to make the most of these opportunities.

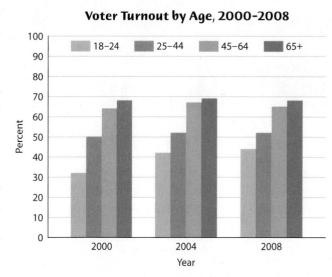

Voter Turnout by Age, 2000-2008

FIGURE 1.1 ■ **VOTER TURNOUT IN PRESIDENTIAL ELECTIONS (2000–2008) BY VOTER AGE How has the turnout rate changed over time for voters aged 18–24? For other age groups?**

SOURCE: www.census.gov/hhes/www/socdemo/voting/publications/historical/index.html.

POLITICAL INQUIRY

Civic Engagement: Acting on Your Views

One vitally important goal of this book is to encourage you to engage in a respectful, continuing conversation about your views and to make the connection between having ideas and opinions and acting on them. Political scientist Michael Delli Carpini has defined **civic engagement** as

> individual and collective actions designed to identify and address issues of public concern. Civic engagement can take many forms, from individual voluntarism to organizational involvement to electoral participation. It can include efforts to directly address an issue, work with others in a community to solve a problem or interact with the institutions of representative democracy.[11]

The possibilities for citizen involvement are so broad and numerous that the idea of civic engagement encompasses a range of activities. Civic engagement might include everything from tutoring an underprivileged child to volunteering at a conservative think tank. In this book, we focus in particular on civic engagement that takes the form of **political engagement**—that is, citizen actions that are intended to solve public problems through political means. As you will find as you read the book, a wide variety of political actions are possible, from boycotting and *buycotting* (buying goods produced by companies whose policies you agree with) to running for office.

We hope that this book not only empowers you by teaching you about the institutions, policies, and processes of the government but also inspires you to become civically and politically engaged. You can take part in your democracy by organizing a fund-raising event, joining a volunteer group,

civic engagement
individual and collective actions designed to identify and address issues of public concern

political engagement
citizen actions that are intended to solve public problems through political means

> One way in which individuals articulate their political views is through the products they choose to purchase. By purchasing "fair trade" coffee, consumers use their purchasing power to express their political viewpoints. Have you ever boycotted or buycotted a manufacturer based on your political view?

DOES THE YOUTH VOTE MATTER?

The Issue: During the 2008 presidential election, much emphasis was placed on the importance of the youth vote. Many pollsters and pundits, noting the strong support among younger voters for candidate Barack Obama, asserted that the youth vote had the potential to determine the outcome of that year's presidential race.

To that end, we saw a plethora of individuals from politicians to rappers to clothing designers urging young people to come out and vote. The national political parties took notice too: because Americans aged 18–29, drawn exclusively from the vast millennial generation, constitute a larger cohort than similar age brackets, the parties sought to tap the potential of this potential sleeping giant in the 2008 election.

Yes: The youth vote did matter in 2008, and it will continue to play an important role in future elections. The 2008 presidential election saw near-historic participation by young Americans: about 44 percent of those aged 18–24 voted. And although that is not a turnout rate comparable to that of older segments of the population (whose turnout rate ranged from 52 to 68 percent, depending upon age), it was the highest turnout for younger Americans in nearly forty years, when turnout was bolstered in the first presidential election in which 18–20 year-olds could vote. But the significance of the higher turnout rate was magnified by the large proportion of young Americans who voted for Barack Obama. Fully 66 percent of those aged 18–29 voted for Obama. This breakdown was the first sign of a new era of generational politics, and those who came of age politically in the era of Obama will be loyal to the Democratic party for years to come.

No: The turnout of young Americans, though increasing historically, will not be the determining factor in federal elections. The low participation rate by young Americans in 2010 indicates that the Obama phenomenon was a flash-in-the-pan occurrence, and that Democrats cannot count young Americans among their loyal party supporters. As a candidate, Barack Obama relied upon a message and an electronic medium that was attractive to young Americans, but those tactics are difficult to replicate in the complicated process of governing, and the 2010 turnout among young people is indicative of a disenchantment with both President Obama in particular and politics in general by those young voters.

Other approaches: Younger voters were attracted to Obama's brand of politics, and they will remain loyal to him in 2012. But as the 2010 turnout indicated, that support does not translate into support for other Democratic candidates. Nonetheless, today's younger voters—millennial voters—will become the determining constituency in federal elections in years to come, both because of the size of their generation and because of the unique set of political viewpoints they bring to the political table as a result of being socialized in a post–September 11 world.

What do you think?

① How did the impact of the youth vote in 2010 compare with that of 2008?

② What issues motivate young voters to vote? What kinds of candidates motivate younger voters?

③ Do the positions of millennial voters differ from those of older voters?

---

volunteering for a campaign, calling or writing to an elected official, or even participating in a protest march, to name just a few of the many options available to you. Consider which potential volunteer activities pique your interest. Think about what might best suit your schedule, lifestyle, and personal and professional goals. By taking part, you will ensure that your voice is heard, and you will derive the satisfaction of knowing that your community and the nation benefit from your actions as well.

What Government Does

government
the institution that creates and implements policies and laws that guide the conduct of the nation and its citizens

citizens
members of the polity who, through birth or naturalization, enjoy the rights, privileges, and responsibilities attached to membership in a given nation

In this section, we look at the nature of government and the functions a government performs. **Government** is an institution that creates and implements the policy and laws that guide the conduct of a nation and its citizens. **Citizens** are those members of a political community—town, city, state, or country—who, through birth or naturalization, enjoy the rights, privileges, and responsibilities attached to membership in a given nation. **Natural-**

The figure below shows the results of a Gallup poll that measures party identification by age. Notice that there are significant differences between people of various ages when it comes to their party identification.

Democrats currently enjoy a party identification advantage over Republicans among Americans at every age between 18 and 85. The Democrats' greatest advantages come from those in their 20s and from baby boomers in their late 40s and 50s. Republicans, on the other hand, come closest to parity with Democrats among Generation Xers in their late 30s and early 40s and among seniors in their late 60s.

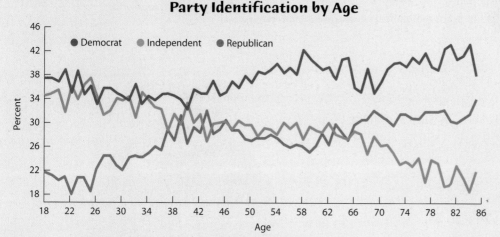

Party Identification by Age

● Democrat ● Independent ● Republican

SOURCE: www.gallup.com/poll/118285/Democrats-Best-Among-Generation-Baby-Boomers.aspx.

Evaluating the Evidence

① Describe the party breakdown of the millennial generation. Which party are members of that generation most likely to identify with? The least likely to identify with? Why do you think this is the case?

② Among which generation are there likely to be nearly equal proportions of Democrats and Republicans?

③ Which voters are least likely to be Independents? Why do you think this might be the case?

ization is the process of becoming a citizen by means other than birth, as in the case of immigrants. Although governments vary widely in how well they perform, most national governments share some common functions.

To get a clear sense of the business of government, consider the following key functions performed by government in the United States and many other national governments:

■ **To protect their sovereign territory and their citizenry and to provide national defense.** Governments protect their *sovereign territory* (that is, the territory over which they have the ultimate governing authority) and their citizens at home and abroad. Usually they carry out this responsibility by maintaining one or more types of armed services, but governments also provide for the national defense through counter-terrorism efforts.

In the United States, the armed services include the Army, Navy, Marines, Air Force, and Coast Guard. In 2008, the U.S. Department of Defense budget was approximately $480 billion. This excludes about $235 billion in emergency appropriations for military operations in Afghanistan and Iraq, plus about $38 billion in funding for the Department of Homeland Security.

Governments also preserve order domestically. In the United States, domestic order is preserved through the National Guard and federal, state, and local law enforcement agencies.

naturalization

the process of becoming a citizen by means other than birth, as in the case of immigrants

GLOBAL CONTEXT

CHALLENGES FOR THE GOVERNMENT OF AFGHANISTAN

When Barack Obama was elected president of the United States in November 2008, many Americans applauded, others were disappointed, but acceptance of the election results as a free and fair expression of the will of the American people was near universal. Contrast that with the Afghani elections held in August 2009. In the aftermath of those elections, both international and domestic critics charged that the elections were corrupt, thereby tainting the reelection of Afghan president Hamid Karzai, and calling into question the legitimacy of the Afghani government. In fact, when the Gallup polling organiza-

tion surveyed 1,000 Afghanis in June 2009, it found that eight in ten Afghans had asserted that corruption was widespread.

Because of the pervasive perception of corruption, the government's ability to perform other functions, including preserving order and stability and establishing a legitimate legal system, also suffers. Nonetheless, many Afghanis view the current situation as an improvement over earlier times.

SOURCE: Gallup World Poll, http://74.125.155.132/search?sourceid=navclient &ie=UTF-8&rlz=1T4DKUS_enUS304US304&q=cache:http%3A%2F%2F www.gallup.com%2Fpoll%2Fworld.aspx.

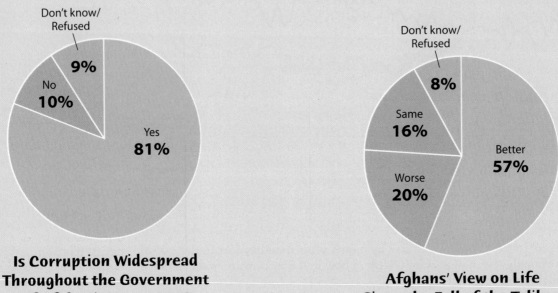

Is Corruption Widespread Throughout the Government of Afghanistan, or Not?

Don't know/Refused **9%**
No **10%**
Yes **81%**

Afghans' View on Life Since the Fall of the Taliban

Don't know/Refused **8%**
Same **16%**
Worse **20%**
Better **57%**

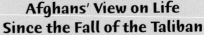

■ **To preserve order and stability.** Governments also preserve order by providing emergency services and security in the wake of disasters. For example, after Hurricane Katrina struck the Gulf Coast and the city of New Orleans in August 2005, the National Guard was sent in to provide security in the midst of an increasingly dangerous situation (though in the eyes of many critics, including local and state elected officials, the action came too late to preserve order). Governments also maintain stability by providing a political structure that has **legitimacy:** a quality conferred on government by citizens who believe that its exercise of power is right and proper.[12] (See "Global Context.")

■ **To establish and maintain a legal system.** Governments create legal structures by enacting and enforcing laws that restrict or ban certain behaviors. In the United States, the foundation of this legal structure is the federal Constitution.[13] Govern-

legitimacy
a quality conferred on government by citizens who believe that its exercise of power is right and proper

ments also provide the means to implement laws through the actions of local police and other state and national law enforcement agencies. By means of the court system, governments administer justice and impose penalties.

- **To provide services.** Governments distribute a wide variety of services to their citizens. In the United States, government agencies provide services ranging from inspecting the meat we consume to ensuring the safety of our workplaces. Federal, state, and local governments provide roads, bridges, transportation, education, and health services. They facilitate communication, commerce, air travel, and entertainment.

    Many of the services governments provide are called **public goods** because their benefits, by their nature, cannot be limited to specific groups or individuals. For example, everyone enjoys national defense, equal access to clean air and clean water, airport security, highways, and other similar services. Because the value and the benefits of these goods are extended to everyone, government makes them available through revenue collected by taxes. Not all goods that government provides are public goods, however; some goods, such as access to government-provided health care, are available only to the poor or to older Americans.

- **To raise and spend money.** All the services that governments provide, from national protection and defense to health care, cost money.[14] Governments at all levels spend money collected through taxes. Depending on personal income, between 25 and 35 cents of every dollar earned by those working in the United States and earning above a certain level goes toward federal, state, and local income taxes. Governments also tax *commodities* (commercially exchanged goods and services) in various ways—through sales taxes, property taxes, sin taxes, and luxury taxes.

- **To socialize new generations.** Governments play a role in *socialization,* the process by which individuals develop their political values and opinions. Governments perform this function, for example, by providing funding for schools, by introducing young people to the various "faces" of government (perhaps through a police officer's visiting a school or a mayor's bestowing an honor on a student), and by facilitating participation in civic life through institutions such as libraries, museums, and public parks. In these ways, governments transmit cultural norms and values such as patriotism and build commitment to fundamental values such as those we explore later in this chapter. For a detailed discussion of political socialization, see Chapter 6.

public goods
goods whose benefits cannot be limited and that are available to all

> Children are socialized to the dominant political culture from a very early age. When children emulate firefighters, for example, they begin the process of learning about the functions governments perform.

Types of Government

When social scientists categorize the different systems of government operating in the world today, two factors influence their classifications. The first factor is *who participates in governing or in selecting those who govern.* These participants vary as follows, depending on whether the government is a monarchy, an oligarchy, or a democracy:

monarchy
government in which a member of a royal family, usually a king or a queen, has absolute authority over a territory and its government

oligarchy
government in which an elite few hold power

democracy
government in which supreme power of governance lies in the hands of its citizens

■ In a **monarchy,** a member of a royal family, usually a king or a queen, has absolute authority over a territory and its government. Monarchies typically are inherited—they pass down from generation to generation. Most modern monarchies, such as those in Great Britain and Spain, are *constitutional monarchies,* in which the monarch plays a ceremonial role but has little actual say in governance, which is carried out by elected leaders. In contrast, in traditional monarchies, such as the Kingdom of Saudi Arabia, the monarch is both the ceremonial and the governmental head of state.

■ In an **oligarchy,** an elite few hold power. Some oligarchies are *dictatorships,* in which a small group, such as a political party or a military junta, supports a dictator. North Korea and Myanmar (formerly Burma) are present-day examples of oligarchies.

■ In a **democracy,** the supreme power of governance lies in the hands of citizens. The United States and most other modern democracies are *republics,* sometimes called *representative democracies,* in which citizens elect leaders to represent their views. We discuss the republican form of government in Chapter 2.

Social scientists also consider *how governments function* and *how they are structured* when classifying governments:

totalitarianism
system of government in which the government essentially controls every aspect of people's lives

authoritarianism
system of government in which the government holds strong powers but is checked by some forces

constitutionalism
government that is structured by law, and in which the power of government is limited

limited government
government that is restricted in what it can do so that the rights of the people are protected

■ Governments that rule according to the principles of **totalitarianism** essentially control every aspect of their citizens' lives. In these tyrannical governments, citizens enjoy neither rights nor freedoms, and the state is the tool of the dictator. Totalitarian regimes tend to center on a particular ideology, religion, or personality. North Korea is a contemporary example of a totalitarian regime, as was Afghanistan under the Islamic fundamentalist regime of the Taliban.

■ When a government rules by the principles of **authoritarianism,** it holds strong powers, but they are checked by other forces within the society. China and Cuba are examples of authoritarian states because their leaders are restrained in their exercise of power by political parties, constitutions, and the military. Individuals living under an authoritarian regime may enjoy some rights, but often those rights are not protected by the government.

■ **Constitutionalism,** a form of government structured by law, provides for **limited government**—a government that is restricted in what it can do so that the rights of the people are protected. Constitutional governments can be democracies or monarchies. In the United States, the federal Constitution created the governmental structure, and this system of government reflects both the historical experiences and the norms and values of the founders.

The Constitution's framers (authors) structured American government as a *constitutional democracy.* In this type of government, a constitution creates a representative democracy in which the rights of the people are protected. We can trace the roots of this modern constitutional democracy back to ancient times.

The Origins of American Democracy

The ancient Greeks first developed the concept of a democracy. The Greeks used the term *demokratia* (literally, "people power") to describe some of the 1,500 *poleis* ("city-states"; also the root of *politics*) on the Black and Mediterranean seas. These city-states were not democracies in the modern sense of the term, but the way they were governed provided the philosophical origins of American democracy. For example, citizens decided public issues using majority rule in many of the city-states. However, in contrast to modern democracies, the Greek city-states did not count women as citizens. The Greeks also did not count slaves as citizens. American democracy also traces some of its roots to the Judeo-Christian tradition and the English common law, particularly the ideas that thrived during the Protestant Reformation.[15]

Democracy's Origins in Popular Protest: The Influence of the Reformation and the Enlightenment

We can trace the seeds of the idea of modern democracy almost as far back as the concept of monarchy—back to several centuries ago, when the kings and emperors who ruled in Europe claimed that they reigned by divine sanction, or God's will. The monarchs' claims reflected the political theory of the **divine right of kings,** articulated by Jacques-Benigne Bossuet (1627–1704), who argued that monarchies, as a manifestation of God's will, could rule absolutely without regard to the will or well-being of their subjects. Challenging the right of a monarch to govern or questioning one of his or her decisions thus represented a challenge to the will of God.

At odds with the theory of the divine right of kings was the idea that people could challenge the crown and the church—institutions that seemed all-powerful. This idea took hold during the Protestant Reformation, a movement to reform the Catholic Church. In October 1517, Martin Luther, a German monk who would later found the Lutheran Church, posted his *95 Theses,* criticizing the harmful practices of the Catholic Church, to the door of the church at Wittenberg Castle. The Reformation continued throughout the sixteenth century, during which time reform-minded Protestants (whose name is derived from *protest*) challenged basic tenets of Catholicism and sought to *purify* the church.

In England, some extreme Protestants, known as Puritans, thought that the Reformation had not gone far enough in reforming the church. Puritans asserted their right to communicate directly with God through prayer rather than through an intermediary such as a priest. This idea that an individual could speak directly with God lent support to the notion that the people could govern themselves. Faced with persecution in England, congregations of Puritans, known to us today as the Pilgrims, fled to America, where they established self-governing colonies, a radical notion at the time. Before the Pilgrims reached shore in 1620, they drew up the Mayflower Compact, an example of a **social contract**—an agreement between people and their leaders, whereby the people give up some liberties so that their other liberties will be protected. In the Mayflower Compact, the Pilgrims agreed to be governed by the structure of government they formed, thereby establishing consent of the governed.

In the late seventeenth century came the early beginnings of the Enlightenment, a philosophical movement that stressed the importance of individuality, reason, and scientific endeavor. Enlightenment scientists such as Sir Isaac Newton (1642–1727) drastically changed how people thought about the universe and the world around them, including government. Newton's work in physics, astronomy, math, and mechanics demonstrated the power of science and repudiated prevalent ideas based on magic and superstition. Newton's ideas about **natural law,** the assertion that the laws that govern human behavior are derived from the nature of humans themselves and can be universally applied, laid the foundation for the ideas of the political philosophers of the Enlightenment.

divine right of kings
the assertion that monarchies, as a manifestation of God's will, could rule absolutely without regard to the will or well-being of their subjects

social contract
an agreement between people and their leaders in which the people agree to give up some liberties so that their other liberties are protected

natural law
the assertion that standards that govern human behavior are derived from the nature of humans themselves and can be universally applied

> In his scientific work, Sir Isaac Newton demonstrated the power of science to explain phenomena in the natural world and discredited prevalent ideas based on magic and superstition. Newton's ideas laid the foundation for the political philosophers of the Enlightenment.

The Modern Political Philosophy of Hobbes and Locke

The difficulty of individual survival under the rule of an absolute monarch is portrayed in British philosopher Thomas Hobbes' book *Leviathan* (1651). Hobbes (1588–1679), who

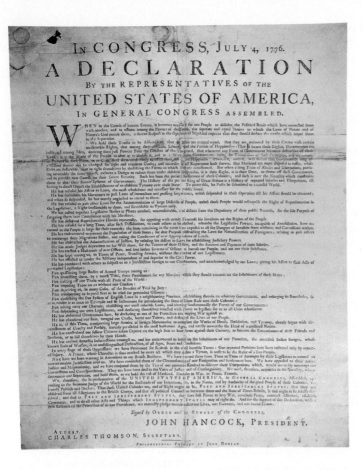

believed in the righteousness of absolute monarchies, argued that the strong naturally prey upon the weak and that through a social contract, individuals who relinquish their rights can enjoy the protection offered by a sovereign. Without such a social contract and without an absolute monarch, Hobbes asserted, anarchy prevails, describing this state as one lived in "continuall feare, and danger of violent death; And the life of man, solitary, poore, nasty, brutish, and short."[16]

John Locke (1632–1704) took Hobbes's reasoning concerning a social contract one step further. In the first of his *Two Treatises on Civil Government* (1689), Locke systematically rejected the notion that the rationale for the divine right of kings is based on scripture. By providing a theoretical basis for discarding the idea of a monarch's divine right to rule, Locke paved the way for more radical notions about the rights of individuals and the role of government. In the second *Treatise,* Locke argued that individuals possess certain unalienable (or natural) rights, which he identified as the rights to life, liberty, and property, ideas that would prove pivotal in shaping Thomas Jefferson's articulation of the role of government and the rights of individuals found in the Declaration of Independence. Locke, and later Jefferson, stressed that these rights are inherent in people as individuals; that is, government can neither bestow them nor take them away. When people enter into a social contract, Locke said, they do so with the understanding that the government will protect their natural rights. At the same time, according to Locke, they agree to accept the government's authority; but if the government fails to protect the inherent rights of individuals, the people have the right to rebel.

The French philosopher Jean-Jacques Rousseau (1712–1778) took Locke's notion further, stating that governments formed by social contract rely on **popular sovereignty,** the theory that government is created by the people and depends on the people for the authority to rule. **Social contract theory,** which assumes that individuals possess free will and that every individual possesses the God-given right of self-determination and the ability to consent to be governed, would eventually form the theoretical framework of the Declaration of Independence.

The Creation of the United States as an Experiment in Representative Democracy

The American colonists who eventually rebelled against Great Britain and who became the citizens of the first thirteen states were shaped by their experiences of living under European monarchies. Many rejected the ideas of absolute rule and the divine right of kings, which had been central to rationalizing the monarchs' authority. The logic behind the rejection of the divine right of kings—the idea that monarchs were not chosen by God—was that people could govern themselves.

In New England, where many colonists settled after fleeing England to escape religious persecution, a form of **direct democracy,** a structure of government in which citizens discuss and decide policy through majority rule, emerged in *town meetings* (which still take place today). In every colony, the colonists themselves decided who was eligible to participate in government, and so in some localities, women and people of color who owned property participated in government well before they were granted formal voting rights under amendments to the federal Constitution.

Beyond the forms of direct democracy prevalent in the New England colonies, nearly all the American colonies had councils structured according to the principle of representative democracy, sometimes called **indirect democracy,** in which citizens elect representatives

popular sovereignty
the theory that government is created by the people and depends on the people for the authority to rule

social contract theory
the idea that individuals possess free will, and every individual is equally endowed with the God-given right of self-determination and the ability to consent to be governed

direct democracy
a structure of government in which citizens discuss and decide policy through majority rule

indirect democracy
sometimes called a *representative democracy,* a system in which citizens elect representatives who decide policies on behalf of their constituents

who decide policies on their behalf. These representative democracies foreshadow important political values that founders such as Thomas Jefferson and James Madison would incorporate into key founding documents, including the Declaration of Independence and the Constitution.

Political Culture and American Values

On September 11, 2002, the first anniversary of the terrorist attacks on the United States, the *New York Times* ran an editorial, "America Enduring," that described how the United States and its residents had weathered the difficult year after 9/11. "America isn't bound together by emotion. It's bound together by things that transcend emotion, by principles and laws, by ideals of freedom and justice that need constant articulation."[17] These ideals are part of American **political culture**—the people's collective beliefs and attitudes about government and the political process. These ideals include liberty, equality, capitalism, consent of the governed, and the importance of the individual (as well as family and community).

Liberty

The most essential quality of American democracy, **liberty** is both freedom from government interference in our lives and freedom to pursue happiness. Many of the colonies that eventually became the United States were founded by people who were interested in one notion of liberty: religious freedom. Those who fought in the War for Independence were intent on obtaining economic and political freedom. The framers of the Constitution added

political culture
the people's collective beliefs and attitudes about government and political processes

liberty
the most essential quality of American democracy; it is both the freedom from governmental interference in citizens' lives and the freedom to pursue happiness

> Thomas Jefferson's ideas about the role of government shaped the United States for generations to come. In 1999, descendants of Thomas Jefferson, including those he fathered with his slave, Sally Hemings, posed for a group photo at his plantation, Monticello, in Charlottesville, Virginia.

to the structure of the U.S. government many other liberties,[18] including freedom of speech, freedom of the press, and freedom of association.[19]

There is evidence all around us of ongoing tensions between people attempting to assert their individual liberty on the one hand and the government's efforts to exert control on the other. For example, issues of religious freedom are in play in school districts where some parents object to the teaching of the theory of evolution because the theory contradicts their religious beliefs. The struggle for privacy rights—and how those rights are defined—continues unabated as the government's counterterrorism efforts result in officials' seeking greater access to our communications.

Throughout history and to the present day, liberties have often conflicted with efforts by the government to ensure a secure and stable society by exerting restraints on liberties. When government officials infringe on personal liberties, they often do so in the name of security, arguing that such measures are necessary to protect the rights of other individuals, institutions (including the government itself), or society as a whole. As we consider in Chapter 4, these efforts include, for example, infringing on the right to free speech by regulating or outlawing hate speech or speech that compels others to violence. Governments may also impinge on privacy rights; think of the various security measures that you are subject to before boarding an airplane.

> Many Americans began to change their views about their country on September 11, 2001, when terror attacks killed more than 2,700 people with the destruction of the World Trade Center, the crash at the Pentagon, and United Airlines Flight 93 in Shanksville, Pennsylvania. Here, a woman and child look over the flowers in the reflecting pool at Ground Zero during a memorial ceremony on September 11, 2009 in New York City. Nearly a decade later these views are still evolving.

The meaning of liberty—how we define our freedoms—is constantly evolving. In light of September 11 and the digital revolution, difficult questions have arisen about how much liberty Americans should have and how far the government should go in curtailing liberties to provide security. Should law enforcement officers be allowed to listen in on an individual's phone conversations if that person is suspected of a crime? Or should they be required to get a warrant first? What if that person is suspected of plotting a terrorist attack—should the officer be required to obtain a warrant first in that situation? What if one of the suspected plotters is not a U.S. citizen?

Equality

The Declaration of Independence states that "all men are created equal . . ." But the founders' notions of equality were vastly different from those that prevail today. Their ideas of equality evolved from the emphasis the ancient Greeks placed on equality of opportunity. The Greeks envisioned a merit-based system in which educated freemen could participate in democratic government rather than inheriting their positions as a birthright. The Judeo-Christian religions also emphasize the idea of equality. All three major world religions—Christianity, Judaism, and Islam—stress that all people are equal in the eyes of God. These notions of equality informed both Jefferson's assertion about equality in the Declaration of Independence and, later, the framers' structuring of the U.S. government in the Constitution.[20]

The idea of equality evolved during the nineteenth and twentieth centuries. In the early American republic, all women, as well as all men of color, were denied fundamental rights, including the right to vote. Through long, painful struggles—including the abolition movement to free the slaves; the suffrage movement to gain women the right to vote; various immigrants' rights movements; and later the civil rights, Native American rights, and women's rights movements of the 1960s and 1970s (see Chapter 5)—members of these disenfranchised groups won the rights previously denied to them.

Several groups are still engaged in the struggle for legal equality today, notably gay and lesbian rights organizations and groups that advocate for fathers', children's, and immigrants' rights. And historic questions about the nature of equality have very modern implications: Are certain forms of inequality, such as preventing gay couples from enjoying the rights of married heterosexual couples, acceptable in American society? Are the advantages of U.S. democracy reserved only for citizens, or should immigrants living legally in the United States also enjoy these advantages?

Beyond these questions of legal equality, today many arguments over equality focus on issues of economic equality, a concept about which there is substantial disagreement. Some in the United States believe that the government should do more to eliminate disparities in wealth—by taxing wealthy people more heavily than others, for example, or by providing more subsidies and services to the poor. Others disagree, however, and argue that although people should have equal opportunities for economic achievement, their attainment of that success should depend on factors such as education and hard work, and that success should be determined in the marketplace rather than through government intervention.

Capitalism

Although the founders valued the notion of equality, capitalism was equally important to them. **Capitalism** is an economic system in which the means of producing wealth are privately owned and operated to produce profits. In a pure capitalist economy, the marketplace determines the regulation of production, the distribution of goods and services, wages, and prices. In this type of economy, for example, businesses pay employees the wage that they are willing to work for, without the government's setting a minimum wage by law. Although capitalism is an important value in American democracy, the U.S. government imposes certain regulations on the economy: it mandates a minimum wage, regulates and inspects goods and services, and imposes tariffs on imports and taxes on domestically produced goods that have an impact on pricing.

One key component of capitalism is **property**—anything that can be owned. There are various kinds of property: businesses, homes, farms, the material items we use every day, and even ideas are considered property. Property holds such a prominent position in American culture that it is considered a natural right, and the Constitution protects some aspects of property ownership.

capitalism
an economic system in which the means of producing wealth are privately owned and operated to produce profits

property
anything that can be owned

Consent of the Governed

The idea that, in a democracy, the government's power derives from the consent of the people is called the **consent of the governed.** As we have seen, this concept, a focal point of the rebellious American colonists and eloquently expressed in Jefferson's Declaration of Independence, is based on John Locke's idea of a social contract. Implicit in Locke's social contract is the principle that the people agree to the government's authority, and if the government no longer has the consent of the governed, the people have the right to revolt.

The concept of consent of the governed also implies **majority rule**—the principle that, in a democracy, only policies with 50 percent plus one vote are enacted, and only candidates who attain 50 percent plus one vote are elected. In the United States and other democracies, often the candidate with a plurality (the most votes, but not necessarily a majority) wins. Governments based on majority rule include the idea that the majority has the right of self-governance and typically also protect the rights of people in the minority. A particular question about this ideal of governing by the consent of the governed has important implications for the United States in the early twenty-first century: Can a democracy remain stable and legitimate if less than a majority of its citizens participate in elections?

consent of the governed
the idea that, in a democracy, the government's power derives from the consent of the people

majority rule
the idea that, in a democracy, only policies with 50 percent plus one vote are enacted, and only candidates that win 50 percent plus one vote are elected

Individual, Family, and Community

Emphasis on the individual is a preeminent feature of American democratic thought. In the Constitution, rights are bestowed on, and exercised by, the individual. The importance of the individual—an independent, hearty entity exercising self-determination—has powerfully shaped the development of the United States, both geographically and politically.

Family and community have also played central roles in the U.S. political culture, both historically and in the present day. A child first learns political behavior from his or her family, and in this way the family serves to perpetuate the political culture. And from the earliest colonial settlements to today's blogosphere, communities have channeled individuals' political participation. Indeed, the intimate relationship between individualism and community life is reflected in the First Amendment of the Constitution, which ensures individuals' freedom of assembly—one component of which is their right to form or join any type of organization, political party, or club without penalty.

The Changing Face of American Democracy

Figure 1.2 shows how the U.S. population has grown since the first census in 1790. At that point, there were fewer than 4 million Americans. By 2000, the U.S. population had reached 281 million, and it will soar well over 300 million by the next census, in 2010.

Immigrants have always been part of the country's population growth, and over the centuries they have made innumerable contributions to American life and culture.[21] Immigrants from lands all around the world have faced the kinds of struggles that today's undocumented immigrants encounter. Chinese Americans, for example, were instrumental in pioneering the West and completing the construction of the transcontinental railroad in the mid-nineteenth century, but the Chinese Exclusion Act of 1881 prevented them from becoming U.S. citizens. Faced with the kinds of persecution that today would be considered hate crimes, Chinese Americans used civil disobedience to fight against the so-called Dog Tag Laws that required them to carry registration cards. In one incident, in 1885, they fought back against unruly mobs that drove them out of the town of Eureka, California, by suing the city for reparations and compensation.[22]

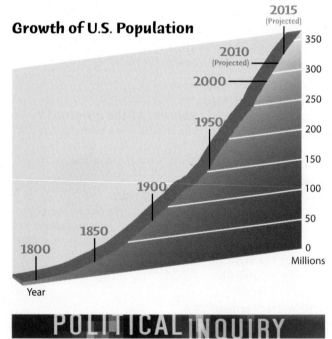

Growth of U.S. Population

A Population That Is Growing— and on the Move

Between 1960 and 2000, the population of the United States increased by more than 50 percent. As the population increases, measures of who the American people are and what percentage of each demographic group makes up the population have significant implications for the policies, priorities, values, and preferred forms of civic and political participation of the people. All the factors contributing to U.S. population growth—including immigration, the birth rate, falling infant mortality rates, and longer life spans—influence both politics and policy as the ongoing debate about immigration reform shows. Generational differences in preferred methods of participation are yet another, as is the national conversation about the future of Social Security.

Accompanying the increase in population over the years has been a shift in the places where people live. For example, between 1990 and 2000, 684 of the nation's 3,142 counties, most of them in the Midwest and Plains states, reported a loss in population. But 80 counties, primarily in the West and the South, had population growth of more than 50 percent. In five counties, two in Georgia and three in Colorado, the population jumped by more than 100 percent.

An Aging Population

As the U.S. population increases and favors new places of residence, it is also aging. Figure 1.3 shows the distribution of the population by age and by sex as a series of three pyramids for three different years. The 2000 pyramid shows the "muffin top" of the baby boom-

FIGURE 1.2 ■ From 1790 to 1900, the population of the United States increased gradually, and it did not reach 100 million until the second decade of the twentieth century. What factors caused the steep rise during the twentieth century? How will these forces continue to affect the size of the U.S. population during this century?

SOURCE: U.S. Census, www.census.gov/population/www/documentation/twps0056.html, and www.census.gov/compendia/stabab/cats/population/estimates_and_projections _by_age_sex_raceethnicity.html.

ers, who were 36 to 55 years old in that year. A quarter-century later, the echo boom of the millennials, who will be between the ages of 30 and 55 in 2025, is clearly visible. The pyramid evens out and thickens by 2050, showing the effects of increased population growth and the impact of extended longevity, with a large number of people (women in particular) expected to live to the age of 85 and older.

Some areas of the United States are well-known meccas for older Americans. For example, the reputation of Florida and the Southwest as the premier retirement destinations in the United States is highlighted in Figure 1.4 on page 20, which shows that older Americans are concentrated in those areas, as well as in a broad north–south band that runs down the United States' midsection. Older people are concentrated in the Midwest and Plains states because of the high levels of emigration from these areas by younger Americans, who are leaving their parents behind to look for opportunity elsewhere.

A Changing Complexion: Race and Ethnicity in the United States Today

The population of the United States is becoming not only older but also more racially and ethnically diverse. Figure 1.5 on page 20 shows the racial and ethnic composition of the U.S. population in 2010. Notice that Hispanics* now make up a greater proportion of the U.S. population than do blacks. As Figure 1.5 also shows, this trend has been continuous over the past several decades. Figure 1.5 also indicates that the percentage of Asian Americans has more than doubled in recent decades, from just over 2 percent of the U.S. population in 1980 to over 4 percent today. The Native American population has increased marginally but still constitutes less than 1 percent of the whole population. Figure 1.5 also shows the proportion of people reporting that they belonged to two or more racial groups, a category that was not an option on the census questionnaire until 2000.

As Figures 1.6 (on page 21) and 1.7 (on page 22) show, minority populations tend to be concentrated in different areas of the United States. Figure 1.6 shows the concentration of non-Hispanic African Americans. At 12 percent of the population, African Americans are the largest racial minority in the United States. (Hispanics are an ethnic minority.) As the map illustrates, the African American population tends to be centered in urban areas and in the South, where, in some counties, African Americans constitute a majority of the population.

Hispanics, on the other hand, tend to cluster in Texas and California along the border between the United States and Mexico and in the urban centers of New Mexico, as shown in Figure 1.7 (on page 22). Concentrations of Hispanic populations are also found in Florida and the Northeast. Hispanics are the fastest-growing ethnic group in the United States, with a projected 16 percent of the U.S. population identifying themselves as Hispanic in 2010, an increase of nearly 10 percent since 1980. Among people of Hispanic ethnicity, Mexicans make up the largest number (about 7 percent of the total U.S. population), followed by Puerto Ricans (1 percent in 2000) and Cubans (0.4 percent).

* A note about terminology: When discussing data for various races and ethnicities for the purpose of making comparisons, we use the terms *black* and *Hispanic,* because these labels are typically used in measuring demographics by the Bureau of the Census and other organizations that collect this type of data. In more descriptive writing that is not comparative, we use the terms *African American* and *Latino* and *Latina,* which are the preferred terms at this time. Although the terms *Latino* and *Latina* exclude Americans who came from Spain (or whose ancestors did), these people compose a very small proportion of this population in the United States.

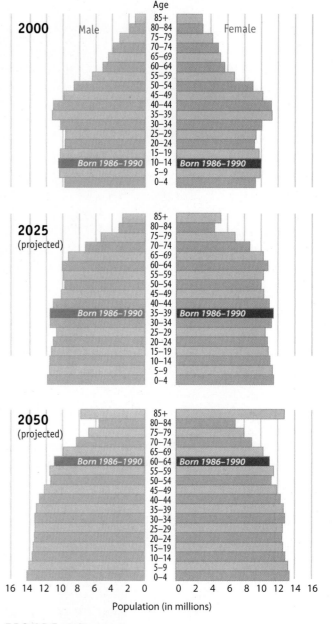

FIGURE 1.3

The Aging U.S. Population, 2000–2050

SOURCE: U.S. Census Bureau, National Population Projections, www.census.gov/population/www/projections/natchart.html.

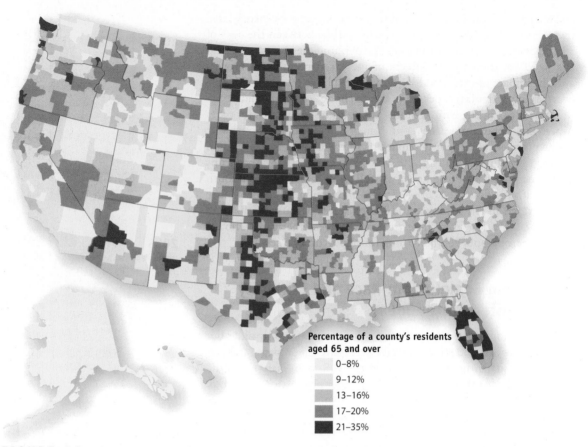

Percentage of a county's residents aged 65 and over

- 0–8%
- 9–12%
- 13–16%
- 17–20%
- 21–35%

FIGURE 1.4

Where the Older Americans Are

SOURCE: www.CensusScope.org, Social Science Data Analysis Network, University of Michigan, www.ssdan.net.

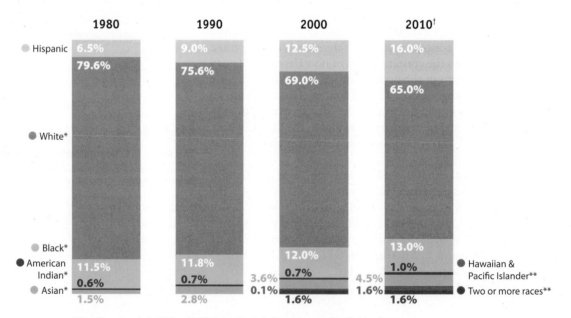

	1980	1990	2000	2010†
Hispanic	6.5%	9.0%	12.5%	16.0%
White*	79.6%	75.6%	69.0%	65.0%
Black*	11.5%	11.8%	12.0%	13.0%
American Indian*	0.6%	0.7%	0.7%	1.0%
Asian*	1.5%	2.8%	3.6% / 0.1%	4.5% / 1.6%
			1.6%	1.6%

- Hawaiian & Pacific Islander**
- Two or more races**

*Non-Hispanic only; in 1980 and 1990 "Asians" included Hawaiians and Pacific Islanders

**Option available for the first time in 2000 census

†Projected

FIGURE 1.5

Population by Race Since 1980

SOURCE: www.CensusScope.org, Social Science Data Analysis Network, University of Michigan, www.ssdan.net, and www.census.gov/compendia/statab/cats/population/estimates_and_projections_by_age_sex_raceethnicity.html.

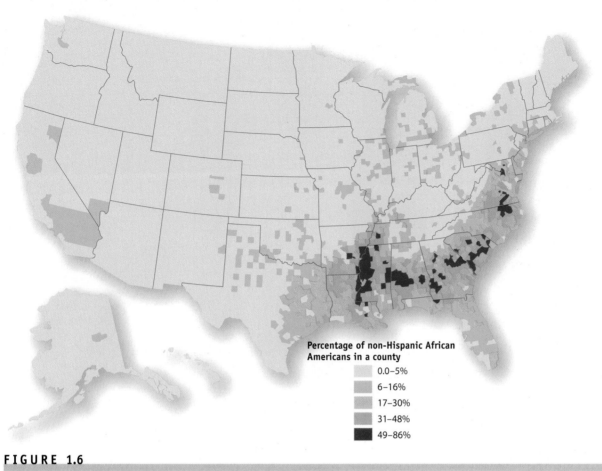

Percentage of non-Hispanic African Americans in a county

0.0–5%
6–16%
17–30%
31–48%
49–86%

FIGURE 1.6

Where African Americans Live

SOURCE: www.CensusScope.org, Social Science Data Analysis Network, University of Michigan, www.ssdan.net.

Changing Households: American Families Today

The types of families that are counted by the U.S. census are also becoming more diverse. The *nuclear family,* consisting of a stay-at-home mother, a breadwinning father, and their children, was at one time the stereotypical "ideal family" in the United States. Many—though hardly all—American families were able to achieve that cultural ideal during the prosperous 1950s and early 1960s. But since the women's liberation movement of the 1970s, in which women sought equal rights with men, the American family has changed drastically. As Figure 1.8 on page 23 shows, these changes continued between 1990 and 2000, with the percentage of married couples declining from 55 percent to 52 percent. Explanations for this decline include the trend for people to marry at an older age and the fact that as the population ages, rising numbers of individuals are left widowed. The percentage of female householders without spouses (both with and without children) remained constant between 1990 and 2000 after experiencing a significant increase from 1970 through 1990. The proportion of male householders without spouses increased slightly, and men without a spouse are more likely to be raising children than they were in 1980. Finally, the proportion of the population living in nonfamily households, both those living alone and those living with others, rose slightly.

Why the Changing Population Matters for Politics and Government

Each of the changes to the U.S. population described here has implications for American democracy. As the nature of the electorate shifts, a majority of the nation's people may have different priorities, and various policies may become more and less important. For example,

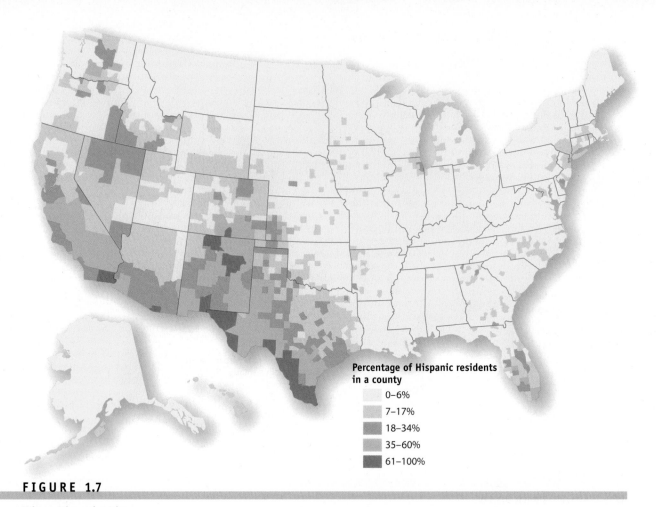

FIGURE 1.7

Where Hispanics Live

SOURCE: www.CensusScope.org, Social Science Data Analysis Network, University of Michigan, www.ssdan.net.

Percentage of Hispanic residents in a county

- 0–6%
- 7–17%
- 18–34%
- 35–60%
- 61–100%

swift population growth means that demand for the services government provides—from schools, to highways, to health care—will continue to increase. The aging population will inevitably increase the burden on the nation's Social Security and government-supported health care system, which will be forced to support the needs of that rising population.

Changes in the population's racial and ethnic composition also matter, as does the concentration of racial minorities in specific geographic areas. The racial and ethnic makeup of the population (along with other influences) can significantly affect the nation's political culture and people's political attitudes. It has implications, too, for who will govern, as more and more representatives of the country's various racial and ethnic groups become candidates for political office and as *all* political candidates must reach out to increasingly diverse groups of voters—or possibly pay the price at the ballot box for failing to do so.

Ideology: A Prism for Viewing American Democracy

Besides focusing on the demographic characteristics of the U.S. population, another way of analyzing political events and trends is by looking at them through the prism of ideology. **Political ideology** is an integrated system of ideas or beliefs about political values in general and the role of government in particular. Political ideology provides a framework for thinking about politics, about policy issues, and about the role of government in people's everyday lives. In the United States, one key component of various ideologies is the extent to which adherents believe that the government should have a role in people's everyday

political ideology
integrated system of ideas or beliefs about political values in general and the role of government in particular

U.S. Household Trends

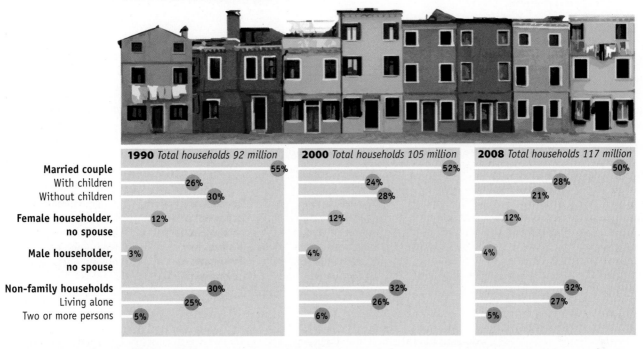

	1990 *Total households 92 million*	**2000** *Total households 105 million*	**2008** *Total households 117 million*
Married couple	55%	52%	50%
With children	26%	24%	28%
Without children	30%	28%	21%
Female householder, no spouse	12%	12%	12%
Male householder, no spouse	3%	4%	4%
Non-family households	30%	32%	32%
Living alone	25%	26%	27%
Two or more persons	5%	6%	5%

POLITICAL INQUIRY

FIGURE 1.8 ■ **What factors might explain the increase in male householders without spouses between 1990 and 2000? What factors might explain the increase in nonfamily households? What impact, if any, might these trends have on policy in the future?**

SOURCE: www.CensusScope.org/us/chart_house.html, Social Science Data Analysis Network, University of Michigan, www.ssdan.net, and www.census.gov/population/www/socdemo/hh-fam/cps2008.html.

lives, in particular, the extent to which the government should promote economic equality in society.

For all of the twentieth century, the ideologies of liberalism and conservatism dominated U.S. politics. Although liberalism and conservatism have remained powerful ideologies in the early years of the twenty-first century, neoconservatism has also become increasingly important. Table 1.1 on page 24 summarizes the key ideologies we consider in this section.

Liberalism

Modern **liberalism** in the United States is associated with the ideas of liberty and political equality; its advocates favor change in the social, political, and economic realms to better protect the well-being of individuals and to produce equality within society. They emphasize the importance of civil liberties, including freedom of speech, assembly, and the press, as outlined in the Bill of Rights. Modern liberals also advocate the separation of church and state, often opposing measures that bring religion into the public realm, such as prayer in the public schools. In addition, they support political equality, advocating contemporary movements that promote the political rights of gay and lesbian couples and voting rights for the disenfranchised.

The historical roots of modern liberalism reach back to the ideals of classical liberalism: freedom of thought and the free exchange of ideas, limited governmental authority, the consent of the governed, the rule of law in society, the importance of an unfettered market economy, individual initiative as a determinant of success, and access to free public education. These also were the founding ideals that shaped American democracy as articulated in the Declaration of Independence and the Constitution.

liberalism
an ideology that advocates change in the social, political, and economic realms to better protect the well-being of individuals and to produce equality within society

The Traditional Ideological Spectrum

TABLE 1.1

	Socialism	Liberalism	Middle of Road (Moderate)	Conservatism	Libertarianism
Goal of government	Equality	Equality of opportunity, protection of fundamental liberties	Nondiscrimination in opportunity, protection of some economic freedoms, security, stability	Traditional values, order, stability, economic freedom	Absolute economic and social freedom
Role of government	Strong government control of economy	Government action to promote opportunity	Government action to balance the wants of workers and businesses; government fosters stability	Government action to protect and bolster capitalist system, few limitations on fundamental rights	No governmental regulation of economy, no limitations on fundamental rights

Modern liberalism, which emerged in the early twentieth century, diverged from its classical roots in a number of ways. Most important, modern liberals expect the government to play a more active role in ensuring political equality and economic opportunity. Whereas classical liberals emphasized the virtues of a free market economy, modern liberals, particularly after the Great Depression that began in 1929, advocated government involvement in economic affairs. Today, we see this expectation in action when liberals call for affirmative action; increases in social welfare programs such as Social Security, Medicare, and Medicaid; and government regulation of business and workplace conditions.

Conservatism

conservatism
an ideology that emphasizes preserving tradition and relying on community and family as mechanisms of continuity in society

Advocates of **conservatism** recognize the importance of preserving tradition—of maintaining the status quo, or keeping things the way they are. Conservatives emphasize community and family as mechanisms of continuity in society. Ironically, some conservative ideals are consistent with the views of classical liberalism. In particular, the emphasis on individual initiative, the rule of law, limited governmental authority, and an unfettered market economy are key components of both classical liberalism and contemporary conservatism.

Traditionally, one of the key differences between modern liberals and conservatives has been their view of the role of government. In fact, one of the best ways of determining your own ideology is to ask yourself the question, To what extent should the government be involved in people's everyday lives? Modern liberals believe that the government should play a role in ensuring the public's well-being, whether through the regulation of industry or the economy, through antidiscrimination laws, or by providing an economic "safety net" for the neediest members of society. By contrast, conservatives believe that government should play a more limited role in people's everyday lives. They think that government should have a smaller role in regulating business and industry and that market forces, rather than the government, should largely determine economic policy. Conservatives believe that families, faith-based groups, and private charities should be more responsible for protecting the neediest and the government less so. When governments must act, conservatives prefer decentralized action by state governments rather than a nationwide federal policy. Conservatives also believe in the importance of individual initiative as a key determinant of success. Conservative ideas are the fundamental basis of policies such as the Welfare Reform Act of 1996, which placed the development and administration of welfare (Temporary Aid to Needy Families, or TANF) in the hands of the states rather than the federal government.

> Protests and demonstrations are tactics that have been used by people across the ideological spectrum. Often, those who rely on protests are outside the mainstream power structure. What groups do you think will be most likely to use protest as a key method in the next several years?

Other Ideologies on a Traditional Spectrum: Socialism and Libertarianism

Although liberals and conservatives dominate the U.S. political landscape, other ideologies reflect the views of some Americans. In general, those ideologies tend to be more extreme than liberalism or conservatism. Advocates of certain of these ideologies call for *more* governmental intervention than modern liberalism does, and supporters of other views favor even *less* governmental interference than conservatism does.

For example, **socialism**—an ideology that stresses economic equality, theoretically achieved by having the government or workers own the means of production (businesses and industry)—lies to the left of liberalism on the political spectrum.[23] Although socialists play a very limited role in modern American politics, this was not always the case.[24] In the early part of the twentieth century, socialists had a good deal of electoral success. Two members of Congress (Representative Meyer London of New York and Representative Victor Berger of Wisconsin), more than seventy mayors of cities of various sizes, and numerous state legislators (including five in the New York General Assembly and many municipal council members throughout the country) were socialists. In 1912, Socialist Party presidential candidate Eugene Debs garnered 6 percent of the presidential vote—six times what Green Party candidate Ralph Nader netted in 2004.

According to **libertarianism,** on the other hand, government should take a "hands-off" approach in most matters. This ideology can be found to the right of conservatism on a traditional ideological spectrum. Libertarians believe that the less government intervention, the better. They chafe at attempts by the government to foster economic equality or to promote a social agenda, whether that agenda is the equality espoused by liberals or the traditional values espoused by conservatives. Libertarians strongly support the rights of property owners and a *laissez-faire* (French for "let it be") capitalist economy.

socialism
an ideology that advocates economic equality, theoretically achieved by having the government or workers own the means of production (businesses and industry)

libertarianism
an ideology whose advocates believe that government should take a "hands-off" approach in most matters

Neoconservatism

The term *neoconservatism,* which emerged in the early 1970s, describes the "new conservatives," or "neo-cons"; the prefix *neo* indicates that many of the prominent thinkers who developed this ideology were new to conservatism. Many people who espouse neoconservative ideology were previously socialists or liberal Democrats who then turned to a more traditional perspective.

Neoconservatives differ from traditional conservatives in several ways. Whereas traditional conservatives tend to advocate an isolationist foreign policy and reliance on traditional foreign policy tactics such as diplomacy, neoconservatives are often characterized as "hawks" because they tend to advocate military over diplomatic solutions. Often, too, neoconservatives press for unilateral (one-sided) military action rather than the collective effort of a multinational military coalition. And unlike traditional conservatives, who emphasize a limited role for government, particularly in social policy, neoconservatives are less concerned with restraining government activity than they are with taking an aggressive foreign policy stand. During the Cold War, neoconservatives were defined by their militaristic opposition to communism. Today they are defined by their fierce advocacy of U.S. superiority and their stance against predominantly Arab states that are alleged to support or harbor terrorists or pose a threat to the state of Israel.

The ideology of neoconservatism was a powerful force during the George W. Bush administration (2000–2008). Indeed, the U.S. war in Iraq is often cited as an example of the power of neoconservatives in that era

neoconservatism

an ideology that advocates military over diplomatic solutions in foreign policy and is less concerned with restraining government activity in domestic politics than traditional conservatives

A Three-Dimensional Political Compass

The rise of neoconservatism demonstrates the limitations of a one-dimensional ideological continuum. For example, although an individual may believe that government should play a strong role in regulating the economy, he or she may also believe that the government should allow citizens a high degree of personal freedom of speech or religion. Even the traditional ideologies do not always fit easily into a single continuum that measures the extent to which the government should play a role in citizens' lives. Liberals supposedly advocate a larger role for the government. But while this may be the case in matters related to economic equality, liberals generally take a more laissez-faire approach when it comes to personal liberties, advocating strongly for privacy and free speech. And although conservatives support less governmental intervention in the economy, they sometimes advocate government action to promote traditional values, such as constitutional amendments to ban flag burning and abortion and laws that mandate prayer in public schools.

Scholars have developed various *multidimensional scales* that attempt to represent peoples' ideologies more accurately.[25] Many of these scales measure people's opinions on the proper role of government in the economy on one axis and their beliefs about personal freedom on a second axis. As shown in Figure 1.9, these scales demonstrate that traditional liberals (upper left quadrant) and traditional conservatives (lower right quadrant) believe in social liberty and economic equality, and economic liberty and social order, respectively. But the scale also acknowledges that some people prioritize economic equality and social order, whereas others embrace economic liberty and social order. One Web site, *The Political Compass* (www.politicalcompass.org), allows visitors to plot their ideology on the site's multidimensional scale.

Multi-Dimensional Ideological Scale

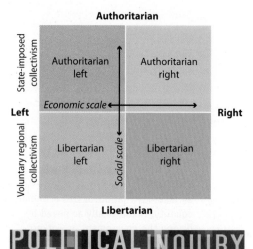

POLITICAL INQUIRY

FIGURE 1.9 ■ Where would you place yourself on this scale? How has your socialization formed your ideology? Can you imagine future circumstances that might cause your views to change?

SOURCE: http://politicalcompass.org/analysis2.

Now is an exciting time to study American democracy. And the fast-paced changes in American society today make participation in government and civic life more vitally important than ever. The effects of participating in the continuing conversation of American democracy through both words and actions are unequivocally positive—for you, for others, and for the government—and can have large ripple effects.

Will the present generation break the cycle of cynicism that has pervaded the politics of the recent past? Today, it is clear that generational changes, particularly the distinctive political opinions of the millennial generation, underscore why it is essential for members of that generation to voice their views. Millennials are participating in the civic life of their communities and the nation through unprecedented—and efficacious—new forms of political participation and community activism. Technology will continue to play a significant role in how they and the population at large communicate and participate in politics and how government creates and administers policy. Exciting changes have come to pass in the political realm, and there is no end to them in sight.

Demographic changes in American society—particularly the aging and growing diversity of the U.S. population—are giving rise to new public policy demands and creating new challenges. Challenges mean opportunities for those who are ready for them, and citizens who respond to those challenges will have an impact on the future of the nation.

Summary

1. y shd u stdy am dem now? Or, Why Should You Study American Democracy Now?

American democracy is at a crossroads with respect to the impact of technology, war, and the continuing terrorist threat on politics. The young Americans of today differ from earlier generations in notable ways, and their fresh opinions and means of organizing and communicating with one another make them a significant political force.

2. What Government Does

Governments perform a variety of essential functions. They provide for the national defense, preserve order and stability, establish and maintain a legal system, distribute services, raise and spend money, and socialize new generations of citizens.

3. Types of Government

In categorizing governmental systems, political scientists evaluate two factors. One factor is who participates in governing or in selecting those who govern. In a monarchy, a king or a queen has absolute authority over a territory and its government (though most of today's monarchies are constitutional), whereas in an oligarchy, an elite few hold power. In a democracy, the people hold and exercise supreme power. Scholars also categorize governmental systems according to how governments function and are structured. Totalitarian governments effectively control every aspect of their citizens' lives. Authoritarian governments have strong powers but are checked by other forces within the society. In democracies, the people have a say in their governance either by voting directly or, as in the United States, by electing representatives to carry out their will.

4. The Origins of American Democracy

American democracy was shaped by individuals who believed in the right of citizens to have a voice in their government. Through principles developed by Enlightenment philosophers such as Thomas Hobbes, John Locke, and Jean-Jacques Rousseau, the key tenets of American democracy emerged, including the idea of a social contract creating a representative democracy.

5. Political Culture and American Values

Political culture refers to the people's collective beliefs and attitudes about the government and the political process. Though aspects of political culture change over time, certain fundamental values have remained constant in American democracy. These include liberty, which is both freedom *from* government interference in daily life and freedom *to* pursue happiness; and equality, the meaning of which has fluctuated significantly over the course of U.S. history. Capitalism—an economic system in which the means of producing wealth are privately owned and operated to produce profits—is also a core value of American political culture, as is consent of the governed, with its key components of popular sovereignty and majority rule. Finally, the American political system values the importance of the individual, the family, and the community.

6. The Changing Face of American Democracy

The population of the United States is growing, aging, and becoming increasingly diverse. Hispanics now make up the country's largest ethnic minority. U.S. families have undergone fundamental structural alterations, as the number of nonfamily households and of households headed by single people has increased in recent times. These changes have already had an impact on communities, and their effect on government policies will intensify. The demographic shifts may create demand for changes in current policies, or they may indicate that the nature of the electorate has shifted and that different priorities are favored by a majority of the people.

7. Ideology: A Prism for Viewing American Democracy

Liberals emphasize civil liberties, separation of church and state, and political equality. Conservatives prefer small government, individual initiative, and an unfettered market economy. Socialists advocate government intervention in the economy to promote economic equality, whereas libertarians argue that government should take a "hands-off" approach to most matters. Neoconservatism, with its emphasis on military rather than diplomatic solutions in foreign policy, and with its comparatively small concern for restraining government activity, has become a growing force in politics and government. Some social scientists prefer to use a three-dimensional framework rather than a two-dimensional continuum for understanding and analyzing political ideology. Regardless of their ideology, citizens can and should act upon their views through civic and political engagement.

Key Terms

authoritarianism 12	indirect democracy 14	political culture 15
capitalism 17	legitimacy 10	political engagement 7
citizens 8	liberalism 23	political ideology 22
civic engagement 7	libertarianism 25	politics 4
consent of the governed 17	liberty 15	popular sovereignty 14
conservatism 24	limited government 12	property 17
constitutionalism 12	majority rule 17	public goods 11
democracy 12	monarchy 12	social contract 13
direct democracy 14	natural law 13	social contract theory 14
divine right of kings 13	naturalization 9	socialism 25
efficacy 5	neoconservatism 26	totalitarianism 12
government 8	oligarchy 12	

For Review

1. In what ways has technology changed how politics happens and how government works? What impact did September 11, 2001 and the subsequent war on terror have on how Americans thought—and think—about their government?

2. Explain the functions that governments perform.

3. Describe how social scientists categorize governments.

4. How did the ideas of the Enlightenment shape people's views on the proper role of government?

5. Explain the fundamental values of American democracy.

6. Describe the general trends with regard to population change in the United States.

7. Contrast liberals' and conservatives' views on government. How do the views of neo-conservatives differ from these other perspectives?

For Critical Thinking and Discussion

1. In what ways do you use technology in your daily life? Do you use technology to get information about politics or to access government services? How? If not, what information and services may be obtained using technological tools?

2. Do you believe there are differences between your political views and those held by members of other generations? Explain. Have the wars in Afghanistan and Iraq changed how you view government? Describe.

3. Why do governments perform the functions they do? Can you think of any private entities that provide public goods?

4. Think of the advantages and disadvantages of direct versus indirect democracies. Do you participate in any form of direct decision making? If so, how well, or poorly, does it work?

5. Examine the demographic maps of the United States in this chapter, and describe what they reveal about the population in your home state.

PRACTICE QUIZ

MULTIPLE CHOICE: Choose the lettered item that answers the question correctly.

1. The institution that creates and implements policies and laws that guide the conduct of the nation and its citizens is called
   - **a.** a democracy.
   - **b.** efficacy.
   - **c.** government.
   - **d.** citizenry.

2. Public goods include
   - **a.** clean air.
   - **b.** clean water.
   - **c.** highways.
   - **d.** all of the above.

3. The economic system in which the means of producing wealth are privately owned and operated to produce profits is
   - **a.** capitalism.
   - **b.** monetarism.
   - **c.** socialism.
   - **d.** communism.

4. Emphasizing the importance of conserving tradition and of relying on community and family as mechanisms of continuity in society is known as
   - **a.** communism.
   - **b.** conservatism.
   - **c.** liberalism.
   - **d.** libertarianism.

5. Citizens' belief that they have the ability to achieve something desirable and that the government listens to them is called
   - **a.** popular sovereignty.
   - **b.** democracy.
   - **c.** civic engagement.
   - **d.** efficacy.

6. A system in which citizens elect representatives who decide policies on behalf of their constituents is referred to as
   - **a.** an indirect democracy.
   - **b.** a representative democracy.
   - **c.** consent of the governed.
   - **d.** both (a) and (b).

7. A belief by the people that a government's exercise of power is right and proper is
   - **a.** authoritarianism.
   - **b.** democracy.
   - **c.** popular sovereignty.
   - **d.** legitimacy.

8. The principle that the standards that govern human behavior are derived from the nature of humans themselves and can be universally applied is called
   - **a.** the social contract.
   - **b.** neoconservatism.
   - **c.** natural law.
   - **d.** representative democracy.

9. An agreement between the people and their leaders in which the people agree to give up some liberties so that other liberties are protected is called
   - **a.** a Mayflower compact.
   - **b.** a social contract.
   - **c.** republicanism.
   - **d.** natural law.

10. A form of government that essentially controls every aspect of people's lives is
    - **a.** socialism.
    - **b.** neoconservatism.
    - **c.** liberalism.
    - **d.** totalitarianism.

FILL IN THE BLANKS.

11. _____ is individual and collective actions designed to identify and address issues of public concern.

12. _____ is the institution that creates and implements policy and laws that guide the conduct of the nation and its citizens.

13. _____ is the idea that in a democracy, only policies with 50 percent plus one vote are enacted.

14. _____ are services governments provide that are available to everyone, such as clean air, clean water, airport security, and highways.

15. A form of government that is structured by law, and in which the power of government is limited, is called _____ .

Answers: 1. c; 2. d; 3. a; 4. b; 5. d; 6. d; 7. d; 8. c; 9. b; 10. d; 11. Civic engagement; 12. Government; 13. Majority rule; 14. Public goods; 15. constitutionalism.

Internet Resources

American Democracy Now
Web site www.mhhe.com/harrison2e Consult the book's Web site for study guides, interactive activities, simulations, and current hot-links for additional information on American politics and political and civic engagement in the United States.

Circle: the Center for Information & Research on Civic Learning & Engagement
www.civicyouth.org Circle is the premier clearinghouse for research and analysis on civic engagement.

American Association of Colleges and Universities
www.aacu.org/resources/civicengagement/index.cfm The AACU's Web site offers a clearinghouse of Internet resources on civic engagement.

American Political Science Association
www.apsanet.org/section_245.cfm The professional association for political scientists offers many resources on research about civic engagement, education, and participation.

The Statistical Abstract of the United States
www.census.gov/compendia/statab This is "the authoritative and comprehensive summary of statistics on the social, political, and economic organization of the United States." It provides a plethora of data about the population of the United States.

The 2010 Census
http://2010.census.gov/2010census/ The U.S. Census Bureau's 2010 census Web site is a clearinghouse for information about the census, including information on why the census is important, data, and how you can get involved in the census.

Internet Activism

The Census Bureau
http://2010.census.gov/2010census/index.php The U.S. Census is one of the most important sources of demographic information. Go to the Web site and use the interactive tools to learn how census data affects funding levels for institutions such as hospitals and schools, and how the data collected even shape congressional representation.

Recommended Readings

Levine, Peter. *The Future of Democracy: Developing the Next Generation of American Citizens.* Medford, MA: Tufts University Press (UPNE), 2007. An examination of how today's youth are participating in poli-tics differently from previous generations and of how they lack the skills necessary to facilitate some forms of civic participation. The author proposes educational, political, and institutional changes to correct this problem.

Putnam, Robert D. *Bowling Alone: The Collapse and Revival of American Community.* New York: Touchstone, 2000. A classic volume demon-strating the decline in traditional forms of civic participation.

Verba, Sidney, Kay Lehman Schlozman, and Henry E. Brady. *Voice and Equality: Civic Voluntarism in American Politics.* Cambridge, MA: Harvard University Press, 1995. An analysis of how people come to be activists in their communities, what issues they raise when they participate, and how activists from various demographic groups differ.

Winograd, Morley, and Michael D. Hais. *Millennial Makeover: MySpace, YouTube, and the Future of American Politics.* New Brunswick, NJ: Rutgers University Press, 2008. A study of the impact of millen-nials' use of changing technology on political life.

Zukin, Cliff, Scott Keeter, Molly Andolina, Krista Jenkins, and Michael X. Delli Carpini. *A New Engagement? Political Participation, Civic Life and the Changing American Citizen.* Oxford: Oxford University Press, 2006. A study of participation and political viewpoints across generations.

Movies of Interest

The Messenger (2009)
This film, starring Ben Foster and Woody Harrelson, depicts one side of the ravages of war through the experiences of Army's Casu-alty Notification service officers. Through their experiences, viewers explore the values of the families of fallen soldiers, as well as those of society at large.

V for Vendetta (2005)
Actor Natalie Portman becomes a revolutionary in this thriller, which depicts an uprising against an authoritarian government.

Blind Shaft (2003)
This Chinese thriller explores the interaction between free market incentives and aspects of political culture, including traditional communal values and human decency, in the context of an increas-ingly globalized economy.

Blue Collar (1978)
This classic film tracing the experience of three autoworkers in the late 1970s explores racial and economic strife in the United States.

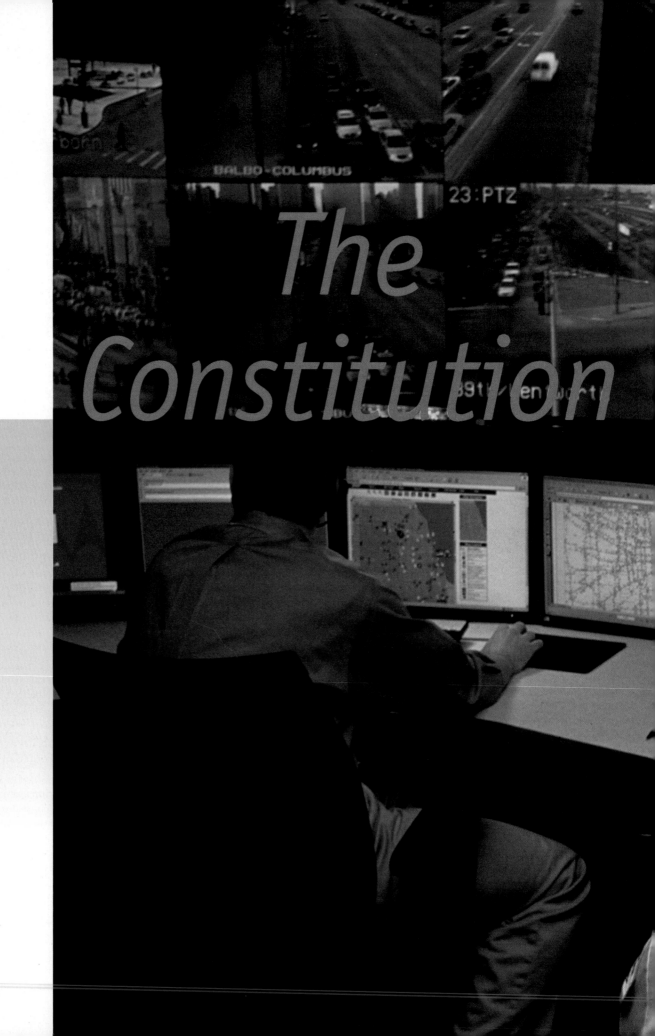

The Constitution

THEN

The Constitution's framers distributed government power between the federal and the state governments, and divided power and created checks and balances among the three branches of the national government to ensure a representative democracy that protected individual liberties.

NOW

The courts continue to probe and interpret the Constitution's meaning, and members of Congress introduce proposed constitutional amendments annually.

NEXT

How will the courts resolve the continuing tensions between individual liberties and majority rule?

Will Congress call for a second constitutional convention?

Will the Constitution's third century witness a greater volume of ratified constitutional amendments as the people's efforts to ensure "a more perfect union" intensify?

We trace various constitutional conflicts throughout this textbook. So that you can understand these conflicts, this chapter concentrates on the roots of the U.S. Constitution and the basic governing principles, structures, and procedures it establishes.

FIRST, we probe the question, *what is a constitution?* by considering the three main components of constitutional documents: descriptions of mission, foundational structures, and essential operating procedures.

SECOND, we explore the political, economic, and social factors that were the catalysts for *the creation of the United States of America.*

THIRD, we survey the *crafting of the Constitution* and the processes of *compromise, ratification, and quick amendment.*

FOURTH, we focus on *the Constitution as a living, evolving document*—a vitality that derives from the alteration (formal amendment) of its written words and from the Supreme Court's (re)interpretation of its existing language to create new meaning.

People in the United States of

America have lived under two constitutions since the American colonies declared their independence from Great Britain in 1776. The Articles of Confederation (1781–1789)—the first U.S. constitution—and the Constitution of the United States (1789–present)—the second and current constitution—established very different government bodies and operating procedures to achieve the same vision of government. The framers of both constitutions were striving to achieve the vision presented in the Declaration of Independence.

The Declaration of Independence (Appendix A) claims that the "laws of nature and of nature's God" give people the rights of life, liberty, and the pursuit of happiness. In addition, the Declaration argues that people have a natural right to create governments in order to protect their life, liberty, and pursuit of happiness. Moreover, when a government infringes on its citizens' natural rights, the Declaration maintains that the people have not only a right but also an obligation to separate from the offending government and establish a new government.

In their efforts to create a new government that would protect their natural rights better than did the government of Great Britain, the newly independent colonists sought a democratic system of government. By ratifying the Articles of Confederation, the founding generation of Americans established a friendly alliance (a confederation) among the existing state governments that composed the United States of America. Within a few years, citizens were criticizing this system of government for its inability to protect life, liberty, and the pursuit of happiness. Less than a decade after the Articles went into effect, the "people of the United States, in order to form a more perfect union," replaced it with the Constitution of the United States. The Constitution established an innovative system of government, which, its framers argued, would better protect the people's natural rights and would create and maintain a healthy economy and a strong nation.

This chapter explores the colonists' experiences under British rule and their subsequent efforts to create the structures and operating procedures of a democratic government that protects the people's life, liberty, and pursuit of happiness. In the process of replacing the problematic confederation with a more perfect union, the architects of the Constitution resolved major conflicts over principles and structures of government through compromise and agreement on frequently ambiguous language. Today, the debates over the vision of the Declaration and the meaning of constitutional language that began even before the states ratified the Constitution continue (see "Thinking Critically About Democracy").

What Is a Constitution?

constitution
the fundamental principles of a government and the basic structures and procedures by which the government operates to fulfill those principles; may be written or unwritten

A **constitution** presents the fundamental principles of a government and establishes the basic structures and procedures by which the government operates to fulfill those principles. Constitutions may be written or unwritten. An *unwritten constitution,* such as the constitution of Great Britain, is a collection of written laws approved by a legislative body and unwritten common laws established by judges, based on custom, culture, habit, and previ-

SHOULD CONGRESS CALL FOR A SECOND CONSTITUTIONAL CONVENTION?

The Issue: Today, many citizens believe that parts of the Constitution are not working. Major national economic problems, including huge deficits and debt, excessive influence of special interest groups, a presidential election decided by the U.S. Supreme Court, and questions about the balance between civil rights and liberties and national security have led citizens and several political scientists to call for a second constitutional convention. Should Congress call for a second constitutional convention?

Yes: The framers expected that the conversation of democracy would be ongoing, as would be attempts to perfect the union. To accommodate those expectations, they authorized two distinct factions (or interests) to propose constitutional amendments. Congress can propose constitutional amendments. Recognizing that the interests of the states may differ from those of Congress, the framers also gave the states authority to propose amendments by means of a constitutional convention. Unfortunately, the states must apply to Congress for a constitutional convention. Although applications for a constitutional convention have been submitted to Congress by all fifty state legislatures, Congress has never called for a constitutional convention. Article V of the Constitution states that Congress "shall call a convention for proposing amendments" to the Constitution "on the application of the legislatures of two thirds of the several states." Congress must call a convention, or else it is violating the Constitution.

No: Article V does not specify how Congress determines when two-thirds of the states have applied for a constitutional convention, nor does it detail how the convention would operate. In 1788, Virginia, New York, and North Carolina submitted applications for a constitutional convention. Should Congress count those applications as three of the thirty-four required today (two-thirds of the fifty states) to call a convention? No! Congress and the states already addressed concerns of 1788 with the states' ratification of the Bill of Rights in 1791. Moreover, the lack of specificity in the Constitution means that a convention could be free to consider and propose any amendments, including a whole new constitution, which is what happened at the last constitutional convention. Given the overwhelming success of the current Constitution, no one wants that.

Other approaches: Before calling a convention, Congress could propose legislation to fill in the gaps left by Article V's lack of details. That could ease fears that a runaway convention would propose a new constitution. Those fears could also be allayed by reminding the public that any proposal produced by a convention would need the approval of three-quarters of the states. Such a supermajority vote would prevent ratification of radical changes for which there is not a national consensus.

What do you think?

1. Who should decide if the 750 applications for a convention submitted previously by the fifty states are valid? Explain your answer.

2. Should the states review their previous applications and then report to Congress whether or not they are valid? How do you think Congress would react to that?

3. Do you think the states have grounds to sue Congress for violation of Article V? Explain.

4. Should citizens with specific proposals to amend the Constitution work through their members of Congress to get them proposed? How successful do you think they would be? Justify your answer.

---

ous judicial decisions. A *written constitution,* such as the Constitution of the United States, is one specific document supplemented by judicial interpretations that clarify its meaning.

If you read a government's written constitution, or even your school's student government constitution, you will find a statement of the government's mission, descriptions of its foundational structures, which are the core government bodies that will do what is necessary to accomplish the mission, and details of its essential operating procedures. Typically, constitutions begin with a description of the mission, the long-term goals of the government as envisioned by its founders. For example, the first sentence in the Constitution of the United States, known as the Preamble, states:

> *We the People of the United States, in Order to form a more perfect Union, establish Justice, insure domestic Tranquility, provide for the common defence, promote the general Welfare, and secure the Blessings of Liberty to ourselves and our Posterity, do ordain and establish this Constitution for the United States of America.*

The U.S. Constitution describes three foundational government bodies—the legislative, executive, and judicial branches—and articulates the responsibilities of each body as well as the relationships among those bodies. The Constitution also details essential operating procedures, including those used to select national government officials, to make laws, and to amend the Constitution, as well as the process by which the Constitution was to be ratified.

In addition to finding the mission statement, descriptions of foundational structures, and details of essential operating procedures in a constitution, you will typically find some vague and ambiguous language. For example, reread the Constitution's Preamble. What do you think "promote the general welfare" means? Does it mean that the government is responsible for ensuring that all people living in the nation have decent health care so that people do not pass their illnesses to others? Does it mean that the government needs to ensure that all people have sufficient and nutritious food and safe housing? Do you know what liberties the government must secure for you and your children and grandchildren? Does it include the freedom to marry whomever you want? Does it include the freedom to decide whether to buy health insurance?

Debates over the meaning of constitutional language were taking place in living rooms, in bars, in legislative chambers, in executive offices, in courtrooms, and on the streets even before the states ratified the Constitution. Ultimately, the United States Supreme Court has the final word on the meaning of constitutional language. You will learn as you read the chapters in this book that members of the Supreme Court do not always agree on what constitutional language means. Moreover, throughout U.S. history, as the members of the Supreme Court changed and the nation's economy, technology, and culture evolved, societal understanding of constitutional language changed, as has citizen and judicial interpretation.

To comprehend today's debates about constitutional language, we need to first develop an understanding of what the framers of the Constitution and the citizens who debated it were hoping to achieve. What was their vision of a more perfect union?

The Creation of the United States of America

Unlike British subjects living in England in the period before the War for Independence (1775–1783), the colonists, who also regarded themselves as British subjects, were largely shut out of participating in the political processes. As the eighteenth century unfolded, that exclusion increasingly rankled the American colonists, especially as parliamentary legislation put more and more restrictions on their freedoms and their pursuit of economic well-being. Eventually, the colonists' private and public conversations about the British government's damaging treatment of them coalesced around the principles of government by the people (popular sovereignty) and for the people (government established to protect the people's liberties).

Colonization and Governance of America

In the 1600s, waves of Europeans made the dangerous sea voyage to America to start new lives. Some people with connections to the king of England were rewarded with large grants of land and the authority to govern. Many more voyagers came as *indentured servants,* who would work for a number of years for a master who paid for their passage. Others came to create communities with people of the same religion so that they could practice their faith without government interference. Countless others—Africans who were brought to the colonies as slaves—came against their will. In short, a diversity of people and a mix of economic classes migrated to the colonies, joining the Native American peoples who already inhabited North America.

By the early eighteenth century, a two-tier system of governing the American colonies had evolved, with governance split between the colonies and Britain. The colonists elected local officials to assemblies that had the authority to rule on day-to-day matters (including criminal law and civil law) and to set and collect taxes. Back in England, Parliament, with no representatives from the colonies, enacted laws with which the colonists had to comply.

Governors appointed by the king oversaw the enforcement of British law in the colonies. Initially, those laws focused on international trade—the regulation of colonial imports and exports. But that focus soon shifted.

British Policy Incites a Rebellion

Between 1756 and 1763, Britain and France were engaged in the Seven Years' War, a military conflict that involved all the major European powers of the era. At the same time they were fighting on European soil, British and French forces (and France's Native American allies) were battling in North America, in a conflict known as the French and Indian War. To help pay the towering costs of waging the Seven Years' War and the French and Indian War, and postwar costs of maintaining peace in America as westward-moving colonists encroached on Indian lands, the British Parliament turned to the colonies for increased revenues. The first new tariff imposed after the end of the war was the Sugar Act (1764). In addition to increasing the taxes on such imported goods as molasses, coffee, and textiles, the Sugar Act directed that all the taxes thus collected be sent directly to Britain instead of to the colonial assemblies, as had been the practice until then.[1] Almost immediately, the colonists condemned the law, saying that because they had no representatives in Parliament, they had no obligation to pay taxes imposed by that body. Their anger intensified in 1765 when Parliament passed the Stamp Act, which taxed the paper used for all legal documents, bills of sale, deeds, advertisements, newspapers, and even playing cards.[2] The Stamp Act introduced a new level of British involvement (some thought interference) in the day-to-day matters of the colonies.

The colonists responded to the Sugar and Stamp acts by boycotting imported goods from Great Britain. Women, including groups of upper-class women known as Daughters of Liberty, substituted homegrown or homespun goods for the banned items. Although the boycotts were largely peaceful, other acts of resistance were not. The Sons of Liberty, founded by Boston brewer Samuel Adams in 1765, opposed the Stamp Act by intimidating British stamp commissioners and sometimes engaging in acts of violence.

Parliament followed the Sugar and Stamp acts with passage of the Quartering Act in 1765. The Quartering Act directed each colonial assembly to provide supplies to meet the basic needs of the British soldiers stationed within its colony. Parliament expanded this law in 1766 to require the assemblies to ensure housing for the soldiers.[3] Throughout the colonies, violent reactions to the quartering law erupted.[4]

Although Parliament repealed the hated Stamp Act in 1766, it paired that repeal with passage of the Declaratory Act. This new law gave Parliament the blanket power to assert control over colonies "in any way whatsoever."[5] This development was a clear indication that the two-tier system of colonial government, in which the colonies exerted some local governing authority, was dissolving. The next year, the colonists understood how momentous this law was, when Parliament used the Declaratory Act as the basis for a new series of laws that would culminate in war. Significant among these laws was the Townshend Duties Act of 1767, which not only expanded the list of imported goods that would be taxed but also stated that Parliament had unilateral power to impose taxes as a way of raising revenue and that the colonists had no right to object.[6] With this new law, the colonists dramatically stepped up their civic resistance.

Specifically, activist Samuel Adams circulated a letter arguing against British taxation of the colonists without their representation in Parliament, and calling for repeal of the Townshend Act. In 1768, the Massachusetts colonial legislature petitioned King George III to repeal the Act. In 1770, Parliament repealed the Townshend duties, except for the duty on tea. At the same time, Parliament reaffirmed its right to tax the colonists.

A "MASSACRE" AND A TEA PARTY By 1770, more than 4,000 British soldiers were quartered in the homes of the 16,000 civilians living in Boston. To make matters worse, the British soldiers quartered in the city sought additional work as rope makers and in other crafts, competing with the colonists for those jobs.[7] On March 5, 1770, an angry mob of nearly 1,800 struggling colonists clashed with the British soldiers, who shot into the crowd, leaving five dead and six wounded.

Almost immediately, Samuel Adams—an expert at "spinning" a news story—condemned the event as "the Boston Massacre." Partnering with Adams to shape public opinion were silversmith Paul Revere and wealthy shipping merchant John Hancock. The communications of the two men stressed that the colonists respected the rule of law but emphasized that the British king, George III, cared more about preserving his own power than about his subjects' well-being. Therefore, Revere and Hancock asserted, there could be no assurance that he would respect the colonists' rights and liberties. This problem, they argued, could be rectified only by ending the American colonists' relationship with Britain.

In 1772, Adams created the Massachusetts Committee of Correspondence, a group dedicated to encouraging and maintaining the free flow of information and the spread of calls for rebellion among the Massachusetts colonists. Radicals in other colonies followed his lead.[8] Revere published pamphlets aimed at keeping the colonists together in their battle with the Crown, talking boldly about "our rights," "our liberties," and "our union."[9] These communication networks served as a kind of colonial-era Internet, facilitating the sharing of news among the colonists. But in this case, the swift transmission of information occurred by way of riders on horseback and printers at their presses rather than by the keystrokes of citizens typing on computers and cell phones—today's vital communication network for rallying people behind a cause and mobilizing political activism.

Adding fuel to the fire, in 1773 Parliament passed the Tea Act, which gave the East India Tea Company a monopoly on tea imported into the colonies. By questioning the Act's legitimacy, the Sons of Liberty successfully swayed public opinion and became the catalyst for an event that would become known as the Boston Tea Party. In November 1773, the first post–Tea Act shipment of tea arrived in Boston Harbor on three East India ships. Under cover of darkness on the night of December 16, 1773, fifty colonists, dressed as Mohawk Indians, boarded the three ships, broke open hundreds of crates, and dumped thousands of pounds of tea into the harbor.[10] The Boston Tea Party had a cataclysmic effect, not only on the relationship between Britain and the colonies, but also on relationships among the colonists themselves.

> The Tea Party movement emerged in 2009 evoking images and themes of the pre-Revolutionary era, specifically the Boston Tea Party's (1773) anti-tax and government-by-the-people messages. Tea Party protesters demand fewer and lower taxes and cuts in government spending, greater protection of individual liberties, and less government regulation of the economy.

Parliament responded with the Coercive Acts (Intolerable Acts), which closed the port of Boston and kept it closed until the colonists paid for the lost tea. In addition, the new laws imposed martial law, shut down the colonial assembly, and banned virtually all town meetings, thus curtailing legal opportunities for political engagement.[11] At the same time, the Crown stepped up enforcement of the Quartering Act.

THE CONTINENTAL CONGRESS'S DEMANDS FOR POLITICAL RIGHTS

Sympathy for Massachusetts's plight, along with rising concerns about how the Crown was generally abusing its powers, reinforced the colonists' growing sense of community and their shared consciousness of the need for collective action. The Massachusetts and Virginia colonial assemblies requested a meeting of delegates from all the colonies to develop a joint statement of concern that would be sent to the king. In September 1774, every colony but Georgia sent delegates to what became known as the First Continental Congress.

The Congress (the assembled delegates) adopted and sent to the king the Declaration of Rights and Grievances. This declaration listed numerous rights to which the delegates argued the colonists were entitled. Some of the rights included in the list were life, liberty, and property; participation in colonial legislatures; participation in Parliament's policy-making processes when the policies affected them; peaceable assembly; consideration of their grievances and petitions to the king; and protection from the king's standing armies.[12] The Congress also adopted the Articles of Association, which put forth a plan of association for the colonies, detailed the colonies' agreement to boycott (no longer import or consume) goods from Great Britain, and the creation of county, city, and town committees to monitor this boycott.[13] Finally, the Congress scheduled a second meeting—the Second Continental Congress—to discuss the king's response to their declaration of rights and list of grievances.

When the king refused to respond to the Congress's declaration, private and public discussions about pursuing independence from Great Britain increased. On April 19, 1775, before the Second Continental Congress met, shots rang out at Lexington and Concord, Massachusetts, as British troops moved inland to seize the colonists' store of guns and ammunition. On May 10, 1775, the Second Continental Congress convened. The assembled delegates empowered the Congress to function as an independent government and to prepare for war with Britain, appointing George Washington to command the to-be-created Continental Army.

The Common Sense of Declaring Independence

In July 1775, the Second Continental Congress made one last effort to avert a full-blown war. The Congress petitioned King George III to end hostile actions against the colonists. The king refused and sent even more troops to the colonies to put down the rebellion. Yet even as the Congress prepared for war, many colonists remained unsure about cutting their ties with Britain. A pamphlet written by Thomas Paine, a recently arrived radical from Britain, and published in January 1776 transformed many such wavering colonists into patriots. Paine's *Common Sense* argued that war with Great Britain was not only necessary but also unavoidable. Without war, the colonies and their people would continue to suffer "injuries" and disadvantages. Only through independence would Americans attain civil and religious liberty.[14]

In May 1776, Richard Henry Lee, Virginia delegate to the Congress, asserted "that these united Colonies are, and of right ought to be free and independent States, [and] that they are absolved from all allegiance to the British crown."[15] This "declaration of independence," which congressional delegates from other colonies subsequently echoed, led the Congress to approve a resolution empowering a committee of five to write down, in formal language, a collective declaration of independence. The committee selected Virginia delegate Thomas Jefferson, a wealthy plantation owner, to draft the declaration.

Unanimously endorsed by the Second Continental Congress on July 4, 1776, Jefferson's Declaration of Independence drew upon the work of John Locke and Jean-Jacques Rousseau, as Table 2.1 on page 40 highlights. Recall from Chapter 1 that Thomas Hobbes (1588–1679) argued that people enter into social contracts that create governments, giving up some of their liberties to protect their life and property. Locke built on this social contract theory, arguing that people, all of whom are born free and equal, agree to create government to protect their **natural rights** (also called **unalienable rights**), which are rights possessed by all humans as a gift from nature, or God, including the rights to life, liberty, and the pursuit of happiness. Rousseau took Locke's theory further, stating that people create governments, and therefore governments get their authority from the people.

Jefferson's Declaration was a radical statement. Its two central principles—that all men are equal and have rights that are unalienable (that is, fundamental and existing before governments are established) and that all government must be based on the consent of the governed—may seem obvious from the vantage point of the twenty-first century. But in 1776, the idea that the people had a right not only to choose their government but also to abolish it made the Declaration of Independence unlike anything before it.

After establishing those two central principles, the Declaration spelled out a list of grievances against King George in an attempt to convince the colonists and the European powers that the break with England was necessary

natural rights
(also called *unalienable rights*), the rights possessed by all humans as a gift from nature, or God, including the rights to life, liberty, and the pursuit of happiness

> Jefferson's Declaration of Independence, drawing on the work of philosophers John Locke and Jean-Jacques Rousseau, delivered the radical message that people have a right not only to choose their government but also to abolish it when it no longer serves them.

TABLE 2.1

John Locke's Theories: *Two Treatises of Government* (1690)	Thomas Jefferson's Application of Locke and Rousseau: Declaration of Independence (1776)
All people are born free and equal.	All men are created equal.
All people are born into a "state of nature" and choose to enter into government for protection against being harmed.	All men are endowed with certain unalienable rights, among which are life, liberty, and the pursuit of happiness.
Every person has the right to "life, liberty and property," and government may not interfere with this right.	To secure these rights, men create governments, which derive their powers from the consent of the governed.
Jean-Jacques Rousseau's Theories: ***The Social Contract* (1762)**	King George III failed to respect the unalienable rights of the American colonists and instead created an "absolute tyranny" over them.
All power ultimately resides in the people.	If government is destructive of people's rights, the people can alter or abolish it and create a new government.
People enter into a "social contract" with the government to ensure protection of their lives, liberties, and property.	
If government abuses its powers and interferes with the people's exercise of their civil liberties, then the people have both the right and the duty to create a new government.	

POLITICAL INQUIRY

What ideas did Jefferson take from Locke and Rousseau with respect to human rights and liberties? How would you summarize the views of the three men on the purposes of government and the source of government power?

and justified. The Declaration won the hearts and minds of people in the colonies and abroad. Until this point, the patriots were united in their hatred toward Britain but lacked a rallying point. The Declaration provided that rallying point by promising a new government that would be based on the consent of the people, with liberty and equality as its central goals.

In 1777, as a brutal war over colonial independence raged between England and the colonies, the Second Continental Congress turned to the pressing task of establishing a new, *national* government by drafting a constitution, the Articles of Confederation. By that year, too, each colony had adopted a constitution, establishing new *state* governments. In these ways, the colonies had become thirteen states with independent, functioning governments. It was to those governments that the Second Continental Congress sent the Articles of Confederation for ratification in 1777.

The State Constitutions

In May 1776, the Continental Congress encouraged the legislative assembly of each colony to write a state constitution establishing its independence from Great Britain. By the end of 1776, eight states had enacted state constitutions. New York, Georgia, and Vermont followed suit in 1777. After four years of intense deliberation, Massachusetts adopted a state constitution in 1780. Connecticut and Rhode Island continued to operate under their royal charters until they enacted new constitutions in 1818 and 1843, respectively.[16] In Massachusetts, citizen voters ratified the state constitution; in all other states, elected representatives ratified the state constitutions. The new state constitutions were revolutionary for two primary reasons. First, they were each a single, written document that specified the principles, structures, and operating procedures of the government established by the consent of the people. Second, they were adopted at a specific moment in time, unlike constitutions before them, which were accumulations of disparate laws written over time or created by judges through the years, based on customs and traditions.[17]

The framers of the first state constitutions attempted to implement the principles of popular sovereignty and natural rights presented in the Declaration of Independence. Each state constitution established a **republic,** better known today as representative democracy. Moreover, most state constitutions explicitly asserted that the people held the power—government was by consent of the people. Whereas the Articles of Confederation would create one national governing body, state governments included three governing bodies—the legislative, executive, and judicial branches. **Bicameral legislatures,** which are legislatures comprising two parts, called *chambers,* were the norm in the states. State legislators, who were directly elected by voters in most states, were delegated more governing powers than members of the other two branches, who were not typically elected by voters. The prevailing view of people of the time was that the legislature offered the best prospects for representative government.

The mission of all the state governments was to ensure natural rights. Two weeks before adopting its state constitution, Virginia representatives approved a Declaration of Rights. In addition to affirming that all government's power derives from the people, this declaration endorsed rights such as trial by jury and religious freedom. Other state constitutions included protections for liberties including free speech and press, protection from excessive fines and bail, the right of the accused to be informed of the charges against them, and protection from unreasonable search and seizure. Authors of the first state constitutions wrote into them limits to prevent state governments from infringing on individuals' life, liberties, and pursuit of happiness, infringements the colonists experienced under British rule. Hence, the inclusion of a written list of citizens' liberties, a **bill of rights,** limited government by ensuring that both the people and the government knew what freedoms the government could not violate.

The states of the new American republic used their new constitutions to guide them in handling their day-to-day domestic matters. Meanwhile, members of the Second Continental Congress turned their attention to creating a national government that would allow the states to engage collectively in international affairs.

republic
a government that derives its authority from the people and in which citizens elect government officials to represent them in the processes by which laws are made; a representative democracy

bicameral legislature
legislature comprising two parts, called chambers

bill of rights
a written list of citizens' liberties within a constitution that establishes a limited government by ensuring that both the people and the government know what freedoms the government cannot violate

confederation
a union of independent states in which each state retains its sovereignty, rights, and power, which is not by their agreement expressly delegated to a central governing body

unicameral legislature
a legislative body with a single chamber

The Articles of Confederation (1781–1789)

Because of the colonists' bitter experience under the British Crown, the people and their delegates to the Second Continental Congress distrusted a strong, distant central government; they preferred limited local government, which they established in their state constitutions. The delegates nevertheless recognized the need for a unified authority to engage in international trade, foreign affairs, and defense. For a model of government, they needed to look no further than a league formed by several Indian tribes of the northeastern United States and eastern Canada.

The Iroquois League was an alliance of five tribes. Under the league, the tribes pursued their own self-interest independently of one another, and the only condition was that they maintain peace with one another. A Grand Council presided over the league, and its fifty representatives, who were chosen by the tribes, had very limited authority. This council served as a unified front and was charged simply with keeping intertribal peace—and later, with negotiating with the Europeans.[18]

The Iroquois League's influence is evident in the first four articles in the Articles of Confederation, which was submitted to the states for ratification in 1777 and which the required number of states (thirteen) ratified by 1781. The Articles of Confederation established a **confederation:** a union of independent states in which each state retains its sovereignty, rights, and power, which is not by their agreement expressly delegated to a central governing body. Through the Articles of Confederation, the states created an alliance for mutual well-being in the international realm yet continued to pursue their own self-interest independently.

STRUCTURE AND AUTHORITY OF THE CONFEDERATION Structurally, the Articles created only one governing body, a Congress. The Congress was a **unicameral legislature,** meaning that it had only one chamber. Every state had from two to seven delegates in Congress, but only one vote. Each state determined how its delegates would be

> This flag represents the original five nations of the Iroquois Confederacy: Seneca, Cayuga, Onondaga, Mohawk, and Oneida. The needles of the white pine, in the middle, grow in clusters of five. The influence of the Iroquois Confederacy is evident in the first four articles of the first constitution of the United States, the Articles of Confederation.

selected. However, the Articles specified one-year terms and a term limit of no more than three out of every six years. Approving policies and ratifying treaties required nine affirmative votes. The Articles did not create a judicial branch, an executive branch, or a chief executive officer. Congressional delegates would select one of their members to serve as president, to preside over the meetings of Congress. State courts would resolve legal conflicts, unless the dispute was between states, in which case Congress would resolve it. State governments would implement and pay for congressionally approved policies. Finally, and important to remember, amending the Articles of Confederation required unanimous agreement among all thirteen states.

The Congress had very limited authority. Although it could approve policies relevant to foreign affairs, defense, and the coining of money, it was not authorized to raise revenue through taxation. Only state governments could levy and collect taxes. Therefore, to pay the national government's bills, Congress had to request money from each state.

WEAKNESSES OF THE CONFEDERATION   The Articles of Confederation emphasized the sovereignty of individual, independent states at the expense of a powerful national government and national identity. Citizens' allegiance was to their states; there was no mass national conscience. Under the Articles of Confederation, the states retained ultimate authority in matters of commerce. As a result, other nations were not willing to negotiate trade policies with national officials. In addition, each state taxed all goods coming into the state from foreign nations and from other states. Moreover, the states issued their own money and required the use of that currency for all business within the state. The cumulative effect of these state policies hampered interstate and international commerce, putting the nation's economic health in jeopardy.[19] Many politicians and the elite viewed the uprisings that resulted from these economic problems as examples of the dangers of democracy.

In Massachusetts, economic pressures reached a head in 1786 when small farmers, many of whom had fought in the War for Independence, could not pay their legal debts and faced bankruptcy and the loss of their land. Farmer and war veteran Daniel Shays led an uprising, today known as Shays's Rebellion, of those debt-burdened farmers. The rebels first broke into county courthouses and burned all records of their debts, then proceeded to the federal arsenal. Massachusetts asked Congress for assistance in putting down the rebellion. Congress appealed to each state for money to fulfill that request, but only Virginia complied. Eventually, through private donations, Massachusetts raised enough money to hire a militia to end the rebellion, but the weaknesses of the national confederacy and the need for a stronger central government were becoming apparent.

Five states sent delegates to Annapolis, Maryland, in 1786, to "remedy defects of the Federal Government," as the government created by the Articles of Confederation was known at that time. The states charged their delegates with considering the trade and commerce problems of the United States. However, in the report of their proceedings, the delegates noted that the "embarrassments which characterize the present State of our national affairs, foreign and domestic" suggested that trade and commerce were not the only problems of the federal government. Therefore, the delegates called for a future convention, to be attended by representatives from all thirteen states, to devise amendments to the Articles of Confederation that would fix its weaknesses and to submit its proposals to "the United States in Congress assembled."[20]

Crafting the Constitution: Compromise, Ratification, and Quick Amendment

The convention called to address the defects of the Articles of Confederation was held in Philadelphia from May 25 through September 17, 1787. All states except Rhode Island sent delegates. The delegates to this Constitutional Convention were among the most elite Americans. Some 80 percent had served as members of the Continental Congress, and most were lawyers, businessmen, or plantation owners. Many were engaged in highly lucrative international trade, and all were wealthy. These elites contrasted sharply with the masses, who included the country's hard-pressed farmers, struggling local merchants, and those engaged in trade. In fact, historian Charles Beard contended in 1913 that the Constitution's framers succeeded in forging a government that protected their elite status.[21]

Early in the convention, the delegates agreed on the need for a stronger national government than the Articles had created, but there was conflict over how best to structure a representative democracy that would protect liberties, with property rights a priority for the delegates. There was also conflict over the issue of slavery. In working through those conflicts to create compromises they could support, the delegates were pragmatic. They had to balance their preference for a strong central government with the citizens' distrust of a strong central government. Ultimately, the delegates framed a new constitution, establishing new foundational government structures and operating procedures to achieve the principles laid out in the Declaration of Independence. Thereafter, proponents of the Constitution would win its ratification only after acknowledging the need to amend it quickly by adding a bill of rights to limit the power of the national government it created.

Consensus

The framers had to send their final proposal to Congress for action. Remember that the Congress, as structured by the Articles of Confederation—the constitution in effect at the time of the convention—was made up of representatives of the state governments. The framers recognized that these representatives were not likely to ratify a document that created a strong central government at the expense of the existing state governments. Therefore, the framers had to balance a strong central government, national sovereignty, and existing state sovereignty. That balance would hinge on delegating governing powers to the national government in the policy areas that were problematic under the Articles—interstate and international trade, foreign affairs, and defense—and leaving the remaining domestic matters with the states.

DUAL SOVEREIGNTY   The framers created an innovative system of government with **dual sovereignty**—a system of government in which ultimate governing authority is divided between two levels of government—a central government and regional governments—with each level having ultimate authority over different policy matters. Today, we call this a *federal system* of government. Article I of the Constitution lists the matters over which the national legislature (Congress) has lawmaking authority, such as regulating interstate and foreign commerce, coining money, raising and funding an army, and declaring war. Article I also prohibits state governments from engaging in several specific activities, such as negotiating treaties. (Chapter 3 focuses on dual sovereignty and the constitutional distribution of power between the national and the state governments.)

dual sovereignty
a system of government in which ultimate governing authority is divided between two levels of government, a central government and regional governments, with each level having ultimate authority over different policy matters

NATIONAL SUPREMACY   Being pragmatic, the framers anticipated that this system of dual sovereignty would cause tension between the national government and the state governments. Therefore, they included in Article VI of the Constitution a **supremacy clause,** which states that the Constitution and the treaties and laws created by the national government in compliance with the Constitution are the supreme law of the land.

The framers did not include a list or even a vague outline of the matters over which the states had sovereignty. Citizens apprehensive of a strong central government would argue that this vacuum of information on state sovereignty was a major fault in the Constitution, because it would allow the national government to infringe on state sovereignty. The lack of a list of individual liberties to limit the power of the national government was also a major concern for citizens afraid of a strong central government.

supremacy clause
a clause in Article VI of the Constitution that states that the Constitution and the treaties and laws created by the national government in compliance with the Constitution are the supreme law of the land

SEPARATION OF POWERS WITH INTEGRATED CHECKS AND BALANCES
Another area where there was convergence of opinion among the framers was that of the foundational structures of the new government they were creating. Borrowing from the states and from *The Spirit of the Laws* (1748), by French political thinker Baron de Montesquieu

(1689–1755), the framers separated the primary governing functions among three branches of government—referred to as the **separation of powers**—so that no one group of government officials controlled all the governing functions. Under the terms of the separation of powers, each branch of the government has specific powers and responsibilities that allow it to operate independently of the other branches: the legislative branch has authority to formulate policy; the executive branch has authority to implement policy; the judicial branch has authority to resolve conflicts over the law.

As suggested by Montesquieu's work, once the framers separated the primary functions, they established various mechanisms by which each branch can monitor and limit the functions of the other branches to ensure that no branch acts to the detriment of citizens' natural rights. These mechanisms collectively form a system of **checks and balances.** If one branch tries to move beyond its own sphere or to behave tyrannically, this arrangement ensures that the other branches can take action to stop it. Figure 2.1 shows how specific checks and balances contribute to the separation of powers.

The delegates spent most of the first two months of debate arguing about the national legislature and focused primarily on the question of state representation in Congress. They devoted less than a month to the other issues before them, including the structure of the executive and judicial branches; the relationship between the federal and the state governments; the process for amending the new plan of government, should the need arise to do so; the procedures for the Constitution's ratification; and a series of compromises over the slave trade.[22]

Conflict and Compromise over Representative Democracy

Among the delegates' top points of contention was representation in the national government. There was disagreement about two elements of representation. First, how should the government officials in each of the three branches of this newly formed republican national government be selected? Second, how would the states be represented in the national government?

THE CONNECTICUT COMPROMISE Virginian James Madison arrived at the convention with a plan in hand for restructuring the national government. The **Virginia Plan,** drafted by Madison and proposed by the Virginia delegation, called for a radically revamped government, consisting of three branches: a bicameral legislature (Congress), an executive elected by the legislature, and a separate national judiciary. State representation in Congress would be proportional, based on state population. The people would elect members to the lower house, and members of the lower house would elect the members of the upper house.

The states with smaller populations quickly and aggressively responded to Madison's Virginia Plan with a proposal of their own. Their concerns about the Virginia Plan were obvious. Because the Virginia Plan called for proportional representation in Congress based on state population, the small states stood to lose significant power. (Remember that under the Articles of Confederation, each state, no matter what its population and no matter how many representatives it had in the Congress, had one vote.) On behalf of the less populous states, William Paterson of New Jersey presented a series of resolutions known as the **New Jersey Plan.** Unlike the Virginia Plan, this was not a radical proposal—it essentially reworked the Articles of Confederation. Under the New Jersey Plan, a unicameral national legislature would remain the centerpiece of the government, and all states would have an equal voice (equal representation) in this government. The New Jersey Plan also called for Congress to elect several people to form an executive office, and the executive office had the authority to appoint members to a Supreme Court.

The disagreement and negotiation over the Virginia and New Jersey plans resulted in several compromises, most notably the **Connecticut Compromise** (also known as the *Great Compromise*). This compromise created today's bicameral Congress, with state representation in the House of Representatives based on state population and equal state representation in the Senate (two senators per state).

THE CONSTITUTION'S CHECKS ON REPRESENTATIVE DEMOCRACY At the heart of representative democracy is the participation of citizens in electing their government officials. Yet the framers built a number of checks into the Constitution that

Separation of Powers with Checks and Balances

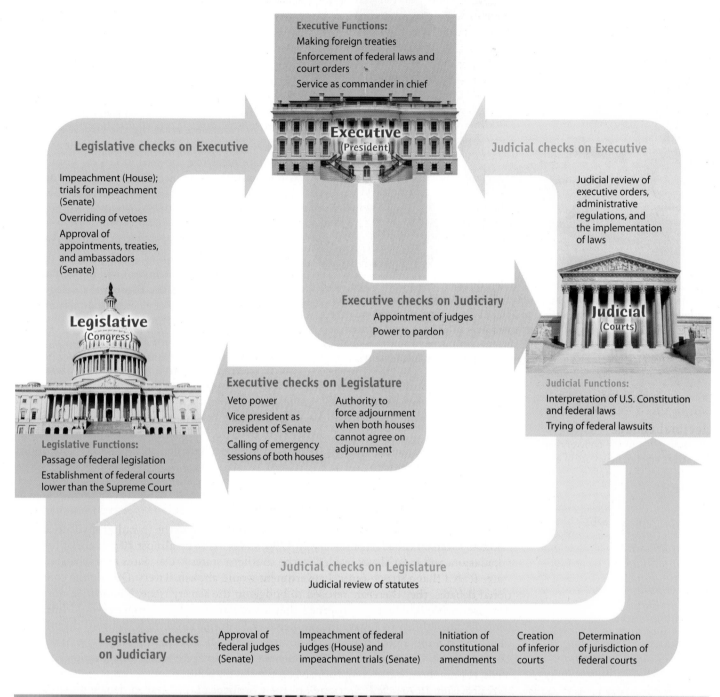

Executive Functions:

Making foreign treaties

Enforcement of federal laws and court orders

Service as commander in chief

Executive (President)

Legislative checks on Executive

Impeachment (House); trials for impeachment (Senate)

Overriding of vetoes

Approval of appointments, treaties, and ambassadors (Senate)

Judicial checks on Executive

Judicial review of executive orders, administrative regulations, and the implementation of laws

Executive checks on Judiciary

Appointment of judges

Power to pardon

Legislative (Congress)

Judicial (Courts)

Executive checks on Legislature

Veto power

Vice president as president of Senate

Calling of emergency sessions of both houses

Authority to force adjournment when both houses cannot agree on adjournment

Judicial Functions:

Interpretation of U.S. Constitution and federal laws

Trying of federal lawsuits

Legislative Functions:

Passage of federal legislation

Establishment of federal courts lower than the Supreme Court

Judicial checks on Legislature

Judicial review of statutes

Legislative checks on Judiciary	Approval of federal judges (Senate)	Impeachment of federal judges (House) and impeachment trials (Senate)	Initiation of constitutional amendments	Creation of inferior courts	Determination of jurisdiction of federal courts

POLITICAL INQUIRY

FIGURE 2.1 ■ Why did the Constitution's framers separate powers among the three branches of the national government? What specific powers does each branch have? What is the purpose of the Constitution's checks and balances? For each branch of the government—legislative, executive, judicial—name a specific check that it can exert on each of the other two.

significantly *limited* representative democracy, and in doing so they effectively took most of the governing institutions out of the hands of the people. Although the Constitution allowed citizens to elect members of the House directly, it specified the election of senators by the state legislatures. This protocol remained in effect until 1913, when the ratification of the Seventeenth Amendment to the Constitution gave voters the power to elect the members of the Senate.

> Charnisha Thomas signs in to vote in New Orleans during Louisiana's 2008 presidential primary. Before the Constitution was formally amended, it did not guarantee any citizen the right to vote. Rather, state governments determined voting rights. Today the Constitution guarantees the right to vote to citizens who are at least 18 years old (Twenty-Sixth Amendment), regardless of their race (Fifteenth Amendment) or sex (Nineteenth Amendment).

The process that the framers devised for the election of the president and the vice president prevented citizens from directly selecting the nation's chief executive and the second-in-command. The Constitution delegates to states the authority to appoint individuals (*electors*), using a process determined by the state legislature, to elect the president and the vice president. Before ratification of the Twelfth Amendment (1804), these electors would cast two votes for president. The candidate receiving the largest majority of electors' votes would become president and the candidate receiving the second largest number of votes would become vice president. Since ratification of the Twelfth Amendment, each elector casts one vote for president and one vote for vice president. Today, in nearly every state, your presidential vote, combined with the votes of other citizens from your state, determines which political party's slate of representatives (*electors*) will participate on behalf of your state in the **Electoral College,** the name given to the body of electors that actually selects the president and the vice president.

In addition to limiting the number of officials directly elected by citizens, the framers effectively limited voting rights to a minority of citizens. Existing state constitutions had established that only property-owning white men could vote. The one exception was New Jersey, where property-owning white women could also vote until 1807, when the state constitution was amended to deny women the right to the vote. The framers left to the states the authority to determine eligibility to vote. Hence, women and many men, including Native Americans and slaves, were denied the right to vote under the new Constitution.

Electoral College
the name given to the body of representatives elected by voters in each state to elect the president and the vice president

Conflict and Compromise Over Slavery

Delegates to the Constitutional Convention also disagreed on the "peculiar institution" (as Thomas Jefferson called it) of slavery. In 1790, slaves made up almost 20 percent of the U.S. population, and most slaves resided in the southern states.[23] Delegates from the southern states feared that a strong central government would abolish slavery. During the constitutional debates, they therefore refused to budge on the slavery issue. Meanwhile, northern delegates, who were widely concerned that a weak national government would limit the United States' ability to engage in commerce and international trade, believed that the nation needed a more powerful central government than had existed under the Articles of Confederation. Ultimately, to get the southern states to agree to a stronger central government, the northern states compromised on the slavery issue.

A provision in Article I, Section 9, of the Constitution postponed debate on the legality of slavery—and consequently kept it legal—by prohibiting Congress from addressing the importation of new slaves into the United States until January 1, 1808. Moreover, Article IV, which deals with interstate relations, established the states' obligation to deliver all fugitive slaves back to their owners. This measure aimed to ensure that people in non-slaveholding states would continue to respect the property rights of slaveholders—including the right to own slaves, who were legally property, not people with natural rights.

Although the slaves were legally property, Article I, Section 2, established a formula for "counting" slaves for purposes of representation in the House of Representatives, apportionment of electors for the Electoral College, and the allocation of tax burdens among the states. This **Three-Fifths Compromise** counted each slave as three-fifths of a free man. The southern states benefited by this compromise: they gained greater representa-

Three-Fifths Compromise
the negotiated agreement by the delegates to the Constitutional Convention to count each slave as three-fifths of a free man for the purpose of representation and taxes

tion in the House and in the Electoral College than they would have if only nonslaves were counted. The benefit to the northern states was that if the national government imposed a direct tax on the states based on their populations, southern states would pay more than they would if only nonslaves were counted (The national government has never imposed such a direct tax on the states.)

James Madison, while deploring slavery, argued that the delegates' "compromise" over slavery was "in the spirit of accommodation which governed the Convention." He insisted that without the compromise, the Constitution would never have been signed.

So in the delegates' debates and deliberations, they resolved some disagreements, such as the large state–small state conflict over congressional representation. They put on hold other differences, such as their divisions over slavery. In the end, the document that the framers sent to the states for ratification described a government structure that aimed to fulfill the principles of the Declaration of Independence, for a select group of people. Foremost among those principles was the idea that it is up to the people to found a government that protects their natural rights to life, liberty, and the pursuit of happiness. To ensure those rights, which were initially meant only for white, property-owning men, the framers devised two key arrangements: the separation of powers with an integrated system of checks and balances, and a federal system in which the national and state governments had distinct, ultimate authorities.

The Changing Face of Popular Representation

	CONSTITUTIONAL CONVENTION (1787)	111TH CONGRESS (2009–2010)	CURRENT U.S. POPULATION*
Women	0%	17%**	51%
African Americans	0%	8%†	12%
Asian Americans	0%	2%	4%
Hispanics	0%	6%	15%
Native Americans	0%	0%	1%

*U.S. Census Bureau, 2006 American Community Survey.
**www.cawp.rutgers.edu/Facts2.html.
†www.ethnicmajority.com/congress.htm.

WHAT'S NEXT?

> What is different about the composition of the delegates to the Constitutional Convention and the composition of the 111th Congress? What explains the differences?

> Why do you think the demographic representation among lawmakers in the 111th Congress does not mirror the composition of the U.S. population at large more closely?

> Do you think future Congresses will be more "representative" of the nation's population? Explain.

Congress Sends the Constitution to the States for Ratification

On September 17, 1787, thirty-nine convention delegates signed the Constitution. Following the Articles of Confederation, the delegates delivered their proposed constitution to the standing Congress. However, fearful that the document would not garner the approval of all thirteen state legislatures as mandated by the Articles' amendment process, the framers suggested an innovative ratification process.

The framers requested that Congress send the proposed constitution to the states and that the state legislatures each establish a special, popularly elected convention to review and ratify the Constitution. One argument made to support this suggested ratification process, which violated the Articles of Confederation, was that ratification by popularly elected conventions would validate the Constitution as the supreme law of the land, legitimized by the consent of the people. Congress acquiesced to the framers' request, and sent the proposed constitution to the states for ratification votes in special conventions.

The proposed constitution sent to the states was a product of conflict, deliberation, discernment, compromise, and pragmatism. In seven articles, the framers established a new national government with structures modeled after the state governments—distributing the basic governing functions among three branches and giving each branch a means to check the others—and a radical new system of government, a federal system, with dual sovereignty. Before exploring the states' debate and ratification of the Constitution, we review the blueprint of government embodied in the constitution sent to the states. To explore the entire Constitution, as amended since 1791, turn to the annotated Constitution that follows this chapter on pages 61–79.

ARTICLE I: THE LEGISLATIVE BRANCH Article I of the Constitution delegates lawmaking authority to Congress, describes the structure of the legislative branch, and outlines the legislative process. Article I specifies that the legislature is bicameral, comprising the House of Representatives and the Senate. Each state is represented in the House based on its population. In contrast, state representation in the Senate is equal, with each state having two senators.

According to Article I, a proposed piece of legislation—a *bill*—requires simple majority votes (50 percent plus one vote) in both the House and the Senate to become a law. This requirement means that the House and the Senate can check each other in the legislative process, because even if one chamber garners a majority vote, the other chamber can kill the bill if its majority does not support it. Because all pieces of legislation supported by the majority of the House and the majority of the Senate go to the president for approval or rejection, the president has a check on the legislative authority of Congress.

ARTICLE II: THE EXECUTIVE BRANCH Article II of the Constitution describes the authority of the president. This article gives the president authority to ensure that the laws are faithfully executed, to appoint people to assist in administering the laws, to negotiate treaties, and to command the military. In addition to those executive functions, Article II allows the president several checks on the power of the other two branches of government.

As already noted, the president checks the legislative authority of Congress. All pieces of legislation approved by the House and the Senate are forwarded to the president's desk. The president has ten days to act on a bill, or it will automatically become law. Within those ten days, the president can either sign the bill into law or send it back to Congress—**veto** it—with his objections noted. Because Congress has primary responsibility for legislative functions, it can set aside the president's veto—that is, override the veto—with two-thirds of House members and two-thirds of the senators voting to approve the vetoed bill.

With respect to the legislature's checks on the executive, the Constitution gives the Senate a check on presidential authority to negotiate treaties by specifying that the Senate can approve or reject any negotiated treaties. The Senate also checks the executive power through its constitutional authority of **advice and consent,** which is the power to approve or reject the president's appointments. The Senate's advice and consent authority extends to the president's judicial nominees as well. Although the president nominates the individuals who will serve as judges in the federal judicial branch—ultimately, the people who will interpret the Constitution—the Senate must approve those candidates.

ARTICLE III: THE JUDICIAL BRANCH Article III describes the judicial branch. More specifically, Article III establishes the U.S. Supreme Court, and it delegates to Congress the authority to establish other, inferior (lower) courts. The Supreme Court and the other federal courts established by Congress have the authority to resolve lawsuits arising under the Constitution, federal laws, and international treaties. In 1803, in the case of ***Marbury v. Madison,*** the Supreme Court interpreted Article III to mean that the Court has the authority to determine whether an action taken by any government official or governing body violates the Constitution; this is the power of **judicial review.**

ARTICLE IV: STATE-TO-STATE RELATIONS The Constitution does not include a list of state powers, rights, or responsibilities as it does for the national government. However, in Article IV, the Constitution does describe how the states must respect the rights and

veto
the president's rejection of a bill, which is sent back to Congress with the president's objections noted

advice and consent
the Senate's authority to approve or reject the president's appointments

Marbury v. Madison
the 1803 Supreme Court case that established the power of judicial review, which allows courts to determine that an action taken by any government official or governing body violates the Constitution

judicial review
court authority to determine that an action taken by any government official or governing body violates the Constitution; established by the Supreme Court in the 1803 *Marbury v. Madison* case

liberties of the citizens of all states as well as the legal proceedings and decisions of the other states. Article IV also establishes the means by which Congress can add new states to the union at the same time it prohibits Congress from changing state borders without consent of the affected states. This amendment also obligates the national government to ensure that all states are representative democracies and to protect the states from domestic violence.

ARTICLE V: THE AMENDMENT PROCESS

The framers recognized that the Constitution was a compromise born of their attempts to resolve existing problems, and therefore future generations would want to, and need to, revise the document in light of their own experiences and circumstances. Therefore, the framers provided processes to amend the Constitution.

The Constitution's framers wanted to ensure that widespread deliberation among the American people would precede any and all changes in the written Constitution. Thus, they made it no easy matter to amend the U.S. Constitution—that is, to change its written language. Amendment is a two-step process, entailing, first, the proposal of the amendment and, second, the ratification of the proposed amendment. Article V describes two different procedures for *proposing* an amendment (see Figure 2.2). The first method requires a two-thirds majority vote in both the House and the Senate, after which the congressionally approved proposal is sent to the states for ratification. The second method (which has never been used) requires a special constitutional convention. If two-thirds of the state legislatures petition Congress to consider an amendment, such a convention, where state delegates vote on the possible amendment, takes place; an approved proposal then goes to the states for ratification.

Article V also outlines two avenues by which the second step, ratifying a proposed amendment, may occur. An amendment is ratified by a vote of approval in either three-quarters of the state legislatures or three-quarters of the special state conventions. Citizens have no vote in the process by which the U.S. Constitution is amended, nor did they have a vote in the original Constitution's ratification. In contrast, forty-nine of the fifty states in the United States do mandate that their citizens approve amendments to their state constitutions as well as new state constitutions. Many countries also mandate citizen approval of constitutional amendments.

ARTICLE VI: SUPREMACY OF THE CONSTITUTION

Article VI proclaims that the new national government will be legally responsible for all debts incurred by the Congress of the United States established by the Articles of Confederation. In addition, the article states that the Constitution, and laws and treaties made in compliance with it by the national government, are the supreme law of the land. Moreover, all national and state government officials must uphold the Constitution of the United States.

ARTICLE VII: THE CONSTITUTIONAL RATIFICATION PROCESS

According to Article VII of the Constitution, ratification of the Constitution required the affirmative vote of special conventions in nine of the thirteen original states. After the delegates signed the Constitution, the standing Congress forwarded it to the states, directing them to hold ratification conventions. See "Global Context" on page 50 for a description of the recent constitutional development and ratification process in Iraq.

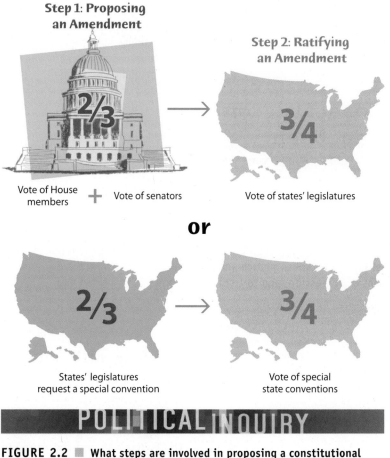

Amending the Constitution

Step 1: Proposing an Amendment

2/3

Vote of House members + Vote of senators

Step 2: Ratifying an Amendment

3/4

Vote of states' legislatures

or

2/3

States' legislatures request a special convention

3/4

Vote of special state conventions

POLITICAL INQUIRY

FIGURE 2.2 ■ What steps are involved in proposing a constitutional amendment? In what two ways can an amendment be ratified? Who has the authority to ratify amendments to the Constitution? Why is the designation of this authority important to the balance of power between the national and state governments? Explain.

THE IRAQI CONSTITUTION OF 2005

On March 20, 2003, multinational forces led by the United States and the United Kingdom invaded Iraq to search for nuclear weapons allegedly created and maintained in violation of United Nations (UN) resolutions prohibiting them. Within one month of the invasion, the United States established the Coalition Provisional Authority (CPA), which the UN and the international community recognized as the legitimate government in Iraq as it transitioned from rule under Saddam Hussein to a democratic government.

Will the Iraqi Constitution of 2005 stay in force for as long as the U.S. Constitution has been in force?

The CPA appointed an Iraqi Governing Council, which drafted a temporary constitution mandating the creation of a constitution to be approved or rejected by the Iraqi people. After considerable negotiation and compromise, and the promise of quick consideration of amendments to the constitution once ratification occurred, the Iraqi people voted to approve the proposed constitution on October 15, 2005.

The Preamble of the Iraqi Constitution of 2005 presents the mission of the newly created government. "We the people of Iraq . . . who are looking with confidence to the future through a republican, federal, democratic, pluralistic system, have resolved with the determination of our men, women, the elderly and youth, to respect the rules of law, to establish justice and equality, to cast aside the politics of aggression, and to tend to the concerns of women and their rights, and to the elderly and their concerns, and to children and their affairs, and to spread a culture of diversity and defusing terrorism."

The document goes on to describe fundamental principles of the Republic of Iraq, among them the concept of popular sovereignty, with government by consent of the people. It further enumerates civil and political rights and liberties of Iraqis, including equality before the law for all Iraqis, the right to personal privacy, and prohibitions against inhumane treatment.

The foundational government bodies established by the Iraqi Constitution include a central (federal) government with the executive, legislative, and judicial powers distributed among three branches. Iraqis elect the members of one of the two chambers of the legislative branch, and these elected members will then elect the president of the republic. The fourth section of the Iraqi Constitution enumerates the powers of the federal government, and the fifth section enumerates the powers of the regional governments. The regional governments are delegated the authority to adopt constitutions that define the structure of regional government bodies. The final section of the Iraqi Constitution presents provisions for the transition to this new system of government, including the requirement that the constitution will go into force after the approval of the majority of the people voting in a general referendum.

> An Iraqi woman takes advantage of her constitutional right to vote in a parliamentary election in March 2010.

The Federalist–Anti-Federalist Debate

Two days after thirty-nine delegates signed the Constitution, it was published in a special issue of a newspaper called the *Pennsylvania Packet*. Almost immediately, opponents of the proposed Constitution began to write letters, issue pamphlets, and make stirring speeches urging the state legislatures to reject the document. The debate developed as one between the Federalists and the Anti-Federalists. The **Federalists** supported the Constitution as presented by the convention delegates. The **Anti-Federalists** opposed the Constitution on the grounds that it gave the national government too much power—power that would erode states' authority and endanger individual freedoms.

The weak national government created by the Articles of Confederation was a federal government, as Americans understood the term before the ratification battle. Indeed, the critics of the Articles who called for the constitutional convention called for remedying the "defects of the *federal government.*" However, those supporting ratification of the Constitution called themselves federalists in an effort to persuade citizens that the states retained considerable powers under the Constitution.

It was in the Pennsylvania debate between the Federalists and the Anti-Federalists that the call first clearly emerged for the inclusion of a bill of rights that would limit the powers of the federal government. Geared toward addressing the main Anti-Federalist complaints about the Constitution, the proposal for a bill of rights became the dominant point of contention in the ratification campaign. In the end, the success or failure of the ratification process would hinge on it.

THE FEDERALIST PAPERS: IN SUPPORT OF A STRONG NATIONAL GOVERNMENT

The Federalists made their most famous arguments in a series of essays known as *The Federalist Papers,* which appeared in newspapers across the new nation. The authors, James Madison, Alexander Hamilton, and John Jay, knew that achieving ratification depended on convincing the public and state legislators that the Constitution would empower the new nation to succeed. They also understood that many of the Anti-Federalists' concerns centered on how much power the national government would have under the Constitution and how that authority would affect the states and individual freedoms. Consequently, they approached the ratification debate strategically, penning eloquently reasoned essays (in the form of letters) to consider those specific issues.

Addressing fears of lost state power, Hamilton argues in *Federalist* No. 9 that "a FIRM Union will be of the utmost moment to the peace and liberty of the States, as a barrier against domestic faction and insurrection."[24] Similarly, in *Federalist* No. 51, Madison explains how the Constitution's provision of both a separation of powers and a system of checks and balances would prevent the national government from usurping the powers of the states and also ensure that no one branch of the federal government would dominate the other two.[25]

With regard to protecting individual rights, in *Federalist* No. 10, Madison reassuringly details how the republican government created by the Constitution would ensure that

Federalists

individuals who supported the new Constitution as presented by the Constitutional Convention in 1787

Anti-Federalists

individuals who opposed ratification of the Constitution because they were deeply suspicious of the powers it gave to the national government and of the impact those powers would have on states' authority and individual freedoms

The Federalist Papers

a series of essays, written by James Madison, Alexander Hamilton, and John Jay, that argued for the ratification of the Constitution

> James Madison, Alexander Hamilton, and John Jay wrote *The Federalist Papers,* a series of newspaper articles that justified and argued for the governing structures and procedures established in the U.S. Constitution. Because Madison and Hamilton had attended the Constitutional Convention, they had an insider's view of the arguments for and against the Constitution.

> Mercy Otis Warren was one of the rare, respected, politically engaged women of the eighteenth century. Her significant influence extended to the citizenry and to the authors of the Constitution and the Bill of Rights, with many of whom she discussed and debated governance and politics. Her political writings include the *Anti-Federalist Papers* and her extraordinary *History of the Rise, Progress, and Termination of the American Revolution* (1805).

many views would be heard and that a majority of the population would not be permitted to trample the rights of the numerical minority.[26] And writing in *Federalist* No. 84, Hamilton argues that because "the people surrender nothing, and as they retain every thing" by way of the Constitution, there was no danger that the new government would usurp individual rights and liberties.[27]

THE ANTI-FEDERALIST RESPONSE: IN OPPOSITION TO A STRONG NATIONAL GOVERNMENT

On the other side of the debate, Anti-Federalists penned countless letters, speeches, and essays warning of the dangers of the new government and urging Americans to reject it. Anti-Federalists agonized that the Constitution ceded much too much power to the national government, at the expense of both the states and the people. Without a bill of rights, they reasoned, there was no way of truly limiting the actions the new government might take to achieve its goals.

Articulating Anti-Federalist views, Thomas Jefferson insisted that the inclusion of a bill of rights in the Constitution was essential. Federalist Alexander Hamilton countered that listing those rights might endanger the very kind of individual freedoms and rights they sought to safeguard. It was possible, Hamilton reasoned, that the list would be incomplete and that at some future time people might legitimately argue that because a given right was not specifically enumerated, it did not exist. (Was Hamilton correct? Consider the debate today about abortion.) Jefferson's response was that "half a loaf is better than no bread" and that "if we cannot secure all our rights, let us secure what we can."[28]

Along with Jefferson, Mercy Otis Warren was among the most influential Anti-Federalists. Through her political writings and personal relationships with many of the leading politicians of her time, Warren affected the public debate over declaring independence from Great Britain and ratifying the Articles of Confederation and the Constitution. Under the pen name "A Columbian Patriot," Warren wrote a pamphlet that presented a comprehensive argument against the proposed Constitution. The circulation of her pamphlet was larger than that of Hamilton, Madison, and Jay's *Federalist Papers.* Political scientist James McGregor Burns cited the "Columbian Patriot"—that is, Warren—as the spokesperson for the Anti-Federalist position.[29]

In the end, Jefferson's and Warren's views and the larger civic discourse about states' rights and individuals' liberties placed significant pressure on the Federalists to reconsider their opposition to a bill of rights. With the proviso that a bill of rights would be the first order of business for the new Congress, Massachusetts, Maryland, South Carolina, and New Hampshire—the last four states of the nine needed for ratification—ratified the Constitution in 1788. Ultimately, all original thirteen states ratified the Constitution.

The Bill of Rights (1791): Establishing Civil Liberties

In the opening days of the first session of the newly constituted Congress in March 1789, Virginia congressman James Madison introduced a bill of rights. Comprising twelve amendments, this proposed addition to the Constitution powerfully reflected the public concerns voiced during the ratification debates by enumerating limits on the government's right to infringe on the natural rights of life, liberty, and the pursuit of happiness, and by preserving the states' authority. Congress passed all twelve amendments and sent them to the states for approval. By 1791, the required number of states had quickly ratified ten of the twelve amendments, which we refer to today as the **Bill of Rights.**

The first eight amendments in the Bill of Rights establish the government's legal obligation to protect several specific liberties to which the Declaration of Independence re-

Bill of Rights
the first ten amendments to the Constitution, which were ratified in 1791, constituting an enumeration of the individual liberties with which the government is forbidden to interfere

ferred when it stated that men were "endowed by their creator with certain unalienable rights." These natural rights became government-protected liberties, *civil liberties,* through the ratification process. The Ninth Amendment indicates that the list of liberties in the first eight amendments is not exhaustive and therefore "shall not be construed to deny or disparage others retained by the people." (Chapter 4 discusses in depth the civil liberties established in the Bill of Rights.) The tenth and last amendment in the Bill of Rights, preserves the states' rights. The Tenth Amendment states that the powers not delegated to the national government by the Constitution "nor prohibited by it to the states, are reserved to the states respectively, or to the people."

The Constitution as a Living, Evolving Document

The authors of the Constitution were pragmatic men who were willing to compromise to resolve the problems confronting the new nation and to get a new constitution ratified.[30] To garner the votes needed to move the document from first draft through ratification, the framers had to negotiate and compromise over constitutional language. As a result of this give-and-take, the Constitution is replete with vague and ambiguous phrases, which the framers expected judges to interpret later. Alexander Hamilton wrote, "A constitution is in fact, and must be, regarded by judges as a fundamental law. It therefore belongs to them to ascertain its meaning as well as the meaning of any particular act proceeding from the legislative body. ... The courts must declare the sense of the law...."[31] As Supreme Court justice Charles Evans Hughes (1862–1948) more recently observed, "The Constitution is what the Judges say it is."[32]

Judges—and principally the justices sitting on the U.S. Supreme Court, which has the final authority to rule on what the Constitution means—have reinterpreted constitutional clauses many times. The Constitution has been formally amended, meaning the states have approved changes to the words in the document, only twenty-seven times, however. The reason for the relatively low number of constitutional amendments is that the framers established a difficult amendment process, requiring supermajority votes in Congress and among the states. They did so to ensure that nationwide public discourse would take place before the Constitution, the supreme law of the land, could be formally changed.

The alteration of this document—through both the formal passage of amendments and the less formal, but no less important, judicial reinterpretation of key clauses—derives from a continuing conversation among citizens about the core beliefs and principles of the framers and the generations that have followed them, including Americans today. In this concluding section, we consider the amendments that have been approved to date as the American people have undertaken efforts to perfect the union established by the Constitution, and we look at the process by which these amendments became a reality.

Formal Amendment of the Constitution

Every term, members of Congress introduce between one hundred and two hundred proposals for new constitutional amendments. That amounts to more than ten thousand proposals since 1789! Members of Congress who oppose a ruling by the U.S. Supreme Court or a law that engenders a great deal of public debate may propose an amendment to supersede the Court ruling or the law. Often, members of Congress introduce amendments knowing that they will never be ratified but wanting to appease their core constituencies by at least instigating public discourse about how our government should function and what rights and freedoms individuals possess.

Only a tiny fraction of the thousands of proposed amendments have cleared Congress—in fact, only thirty-three have achieved the two-thirds vote necessary in Congress—and, as noted, the states have ratified only twenty-seven. The amendments that the states have ratified fit into one of three categories: they have (1) extended civil liberties and civil rights (equal protection of laws for citizens), (2) altered the selection or operation of the branches of the national government, or (3) dealt with important policy issues. Table 2.2 (on page 54) summarizes the eleventh through the twenty-seventh constitutional amendments and organizes them by category.

The Eleventh Through Twenty-Seventh Amendments to the Federal Constitution

TABLE 2.2

Amendments That Protect Civil Liberties and Civil Rights

Thirteenth	1865	Banned slavery
Fourteenth	1868	Established that all people have the right to equal protection and due process before the law, and that all citizens are guaranteed the same privileges and immunities
Fifteenth	1870	Guaranteed that the right to vote could not be abridged on the basis of race or color
Nineteenth	1920	Guaranteed that the right to vote could not be abridged on the basis of sex
Twenty-third	1961	Defined how the District of Columbia would be represented in the Electoral College
Twenty-fourth	1964	Outlawed the use of a poll tax, which prevented poor people from exercising their right to vote
Twenty-sixth	1971	Lowered the voting age to 18 years

Amendments That Relate to the Selection of Government Officials or the Operation of the Branches of Government

Eleventh	1795	Limited federal court jurisdiction by barring citizens of one state from suing another state in federal court
Twelfth	1804	Required the electors in the Electoral College to vote twice: once for president and once for vice president
Seventeenth	1913	Mandated the direct election of senators by citizens
Twentieth	1933	Set a date for the convening of Congress and the inauguration of the president
Twenty-second	1951	Limited to two the number of terms the president can serve
Twenty-fifth	1967	Established the procedure for presidential succession in the event of the disability or death of the president; established the procedure for vice-presidential replacement when the position becomes vacant before the end of the term
Twenty-seventh	1992	Required that there be an intervening election between the time when Congress votes itself a raise and when that raise can be implemented

Amendments That Address Specific Public Policies

Sixteenth	1913	Empowered Congress to establish an income tax
Eighteenth	1919	Banned the manufacture, sale, and transportation of liquor
Twenty-first	1933	Repealed the ban on the manufacture, sale, and transportation of liquor

Interpretation by the U.S. Supreme Court

Beyond the addition of formal amendments, the Constitution has changed over time through reinterpretation by the courts. This reinterpretation began with the U.S. Supreme Court's landmark *Marbury v. Madison* decision in 1803, in which the Court established the important power of judicial review—the authority of the courts to rule on whether acts of government officials and governing bodies violate the Constitution. Although the U.S. Su-

ANALYZING THE SOURCES

CONSTITUTIONAL PRINCIPLES IN RECENT SECOND AMENDMENT CASES

Consider the following chronology related to the Second Amendment and its legal protections. Has the court made the meaning of the Second Amendment clear and unambiguous?

1791   **Second Amendment** states that "a well regulated Militia, being necessary to the security of a free State, the right of the people to keep and bear Arms, shall not be infringed."

1976   **Washington, D.C., law** is passed banning all handguns in homes unless they were registered before 1976. The law's intent is to decrease gun violence.

2007   **Majority opinion of the U.S. Court of Appeals for D.C. Circuit,** *Parker v. District of Columbia,* finds the 1976 Washington, D.C., ban unconstitutional and explains, "We . . . take it as an expression of the drafters' view that the people possessed a natural right to keep and bear arms, and that the preservation of the militia was the right's most salient political benefit—and thus the most appropriate to express in a political document."*

2008   **Majority opinion of the U.S. Supreme Court in** *District of Columbia and Adrian M. Felty v. Dick Anthony Heller* declares, "There seems to us no doubt, on the basis of both text and history, that the Second Amendment conferred an individual right to keep and bear arms." The decision goes on to say, "Like most rights, the Second Amendment right is not unlimited. It is not a right to keep and carry any weapon whatsoever in any manner whatsoever and for whatever purpose."**

*Parker v. District of Columbia, 478 F. 3d 370 (D.C. Circuit 2007).
**District of Columbia and Adrian M. Fenty v. Dick Anthony Heller, 544 U.S.

Evaluating the Evidence

① What do you think was the intent of the authors of the Second Amendment? Did they intend to protect a natural, individual right to bear arms? Did they mean to ensure that resources (that is, people with the right to bear arms) for protecting domestic tranquility and national defense would be readily available? Did they seek to ensure both?

② What do you imagine the majority of Americans think the Second Amendment means? Why? Where might you get data to support your prediction?

③ Do you agree with the majority opinion in the *Parker* case or the majority opinion in the *D.C. v. Heller* case? Explain.

④ What impact on public safety will the divergent interpretations of the Second Amendment have?

---

preme Court's interpretation is final, if the Supreme Court does not review constitutional interpretations made by lower federal courts, then the interpretations of those lower courts are the final word.

How do judges decide what the Constitution means? To interpret its words, they may look at how courts have ruled in past cases on the phrasing in question or what the custom or usage of the words has generally been. They may try to ascertain what the authors of the Constitution meant. Alternatively, the judges may consider the policy implications of differing interpretations, gauging them against the mission presented in the Constitution's Preamble. In any given case, the deciding court must determine which of those points of reference it will use and how it will apply them to interpret the constitutional principles under consideration. For a taste of how the courts determine the meaning of the Constitution, see "Analyzing the Sources."

The power of judicial review has allowed the courts to continue to breathe life into the Constitution to keep up with societal norms and technological change. For example, in 1896 the Supreme Court decreed that the Fourteenth Amendment allowed laws requiring the segregation of white and black citizens.[33] Then in 1954, in the case of *Brown v. The Board of Education of Topeka, Kansas,*[34] the Supreme Court declared such segregation to be an unconstitutional violation of the Fourteenth Amendment.

> In 2004, the U.S. Supreme Court ruled that U.S. federal courts had jurisdiction to decide lawsuits filed by foreigners detained at the U.S. naval base in Guantanamo Bay, Cuba (Gitmo). President George W. Bush and Congress responded to that ruling by enacting a law removing those lawsuits from federal court jurisdiction. In 2006, the Supreme Court found that law unconstitutional because of procedural errors in its enactment. Then Congress passed another law, following correct procedures, to remove the detainees' lawsuits from federal court jurisdiction. In 2008, the Supreme Court ruled that the Gitmo detainees had a constitutionally guaranteed right to have their lawsuits resolved in the federal courts. Today, federal courts hear lawsuits filed by Gitmo detainees.

Technology also drives constitutional reinterpretation. The framers naturally never conceived of the existence of computers and telecommunications. Yet by reviewing and freshly interpreting the Fourth Amendment, which prohibits unreasonable searches and seizures by government officials, the courts have uncovered the principles behind this amendment that apply to our technologically advanced society. Consequently, this provision, whose original intent was to limit governments' physical searches of one's property and person, can be used today to determine, for example, whether governmental surveillance of computer databases is permissible.

Sometimes, the Supreme Court's opinions ignite a debate or intensify a debate already under way. Court decisions that are viewed as a "win" for one side and a "loss" for the other often generate fierce responses in the other branches or levels of the government. For example, the executive branch might decide not to implement a Court decision. Or the legislative branch might write a new law that challenges a Court decision. Unless a lawsuit allows the Court to rule the new law unconstitutional, the new law takes effect.

Although controversial Court decisions often capture significant media attention, in most cases, the Court's rulings are in step with public opinion. Analysts note that the Court does not often lead public opinion—in fact, it more often follows it.[35] And even if the justices wanted to take some very controversial and unpopular action, the system of checks and balances forces them to consider how the other branches would react. Recall that the Court has the power to interpret the law; it does not have the power to implement or to enforce the law and must be concerned about how the other branches might retaliate against it for highly unpopular decisions. Therefore, for the most part, changes to the Constitution, both formal and informal, are incremental and further the will of the people because they are the product of widespread public discourse—an ongoing conversation of democracy.

The governing principles proclaimed in the Declaration of Independence successfully unified American colonists to fight the War for Independence. Government created by the consent of the people with the mission of protecting the people's natural rights of life, liberty, and the pursuit of happiness has proven difficult. The tensions between individual liberties and popular sovereignty first witnessed under the Articles of Confederation have continued under the Constitution of the United States. These tensions loom large, especially during times when national security is threatened and economic health is poor. Under such circumstances, the courts often play a role in interpreting the language of the Constitution. How will the courts resolve the continuing tensions between individual liberties and popular sovereignty?

Today, many Americans believe that parts of the Constitution are not working. Some argue that the government is not serving the people well; that the government is infringing on individual liberties and the pursuit of happiness. Others focus on the foundational structures and operating procedures established by the Constitution, claiming that the government is not properly implementing them. Many argue that the more perfect union envisioned by the founders is not being fulfilled. To address these contemporary governing defects, some have proposed constitutional amendments. Others are calling for a constitutional convention.

As Americans continue to work for a more perfect union, will Congress respond to state applications for a constitutional convention by calling for a second constitutional convention? Will the Constitution's third century witness a greater volume of ratified constitutional amendments as the people's efforts to ensure a more perfect union intensify?

Summary

1. What Is a Constitution?
A constitution presents the fundamental principles of a government and establishes the basic structures and procedures by which the government operates to fulfill those principles. Constitutions may be written or unwritten.

2. The Creation of the United States of America
By the mid-eighteenth century, the American colonists were protesting the effect of British rule on their lives and livelihoods. Pamphlets, newspaper articles, public discourse, and eloquent revolutionaries persuaded the colonists that it was common sense, as well as their obligation, to declare their independence from Britain and to create a new government. Yet the weak national government established by the country's first constitution, the Articles of Confederation, did not serve the people well.

3. Crafting the Constitution: Compromise, Ratification, and Quick Amendment
In response to severe economic problems and tensions among the states, and to growing desires for a more perfect union of the states, representatives from the states met in Philadelphia in 1787 to amend the Articles of Confederation. Debate and deliberation led to compromise and a new constitution, supported by the Federalists and opposed by the Anti-Federalists. The addition of the Bill of Rights two years after the states ratified the Constitution addressed the primary concerns about individual liberties and states' authority that the Anti-Federalists had raised during the debates over ratification of the Constitution of the United States.

4. The Constitution as a Living, Evolving Document

The Constitution of the United States has been formally amended a mere twenty-seven times over its 220-plus years of life. This rare occurrence of formal change to the Constitution's written words belies the reality of its perpetual revision through the process of judicial review and interpretation. The U.S. Supreme Court ultimately decides what the written words in the Constitution mean, and through that authority, the Court clarifies and modifies (hence, revises) the Constitution yearly.

Key Terms

advice and consent 48

Anti-Federalists 51

bicameral legislature 41

bill of rights 41

Bill of Rights 52

checks and balances 44

confederation 41

Connecticut Compromise
(Great Compromise) 44

constitution 34

dual sovereignty 43

Electoral College 46

The Federalist Papers 51

Federalists 51

judicial review 48

Marbury v. Madison 48

natural rights (unalienable
rights) 39

New Jersey Plan 44

republic 41

separation of powers 44

supremacy clause 43

Three-Fifths Compromise 46

unicameral legislature 41

veto 48

Virginia Plan 44

For Review

1. Describe the three main components of a written constitution.

2. How did the events leading up to the War for Independence shape the core principles of the U.S. Constitution?

3. How did conflict and compromise influence the drafting and ratification of the Constitution? What specific issues caused conflict and required compromise for their resolution? On what matters was there early consensus among the framers?

4. What are the formal and informal mechanisms for changing the Constitution?

For Critical Thinking and Discussion

1. What was the relationship between the state constitutions, many of which were created immediately after the signing of the Declaration of Independence, and the U.S. Constitution, which was written more than a decade later?

2. Think about important debates in American society today. Describe one that you think is linked in some way to the compromises upon which the Constitution is based.

3. Imagine that you are living during the Revolutionary era and writing an article for a newspaper in England. You are trying to explain why the colonists have destroyed thousands of pounds of British tea at the Boston Tea Party. How might you, as an English citizen living in England, characterize the colonists' motives? How might you, as an English citizen living in the colonies, characterize the colonists' motives?

4. What do you think would have happened had the Anti-Federalists, rather than the Federalists, prevailed in the ratification process of the Constitution? What kind of government would they have shaped? How would that government have dealt with the difficult issues facing the new republic—slavery, concerns about mob rule, and continuing hostility in the international community?

MULTIPLE CHOICE: Choose the lettered item that answers the question correctly.

1. According to the Declaration of Independence, the natural, unalienable rights include all the following except
   a. liberty.
   b. life.
   c. property.
   d. the pursuit of happiness.

2. The existence of three branches of government, each responsible for a different primary governing function, is the implementation of the foundational organizational structure called
   a. judicial review.
   b. the federal system.
   c. representative democracy.
   d. separation of powers.

3. *Marbury v. Madison* (1803) is a landmark case because it
   a. clarified the Electoral College system.
   b. clarified congressional legislative authority.
   c. clarified the courts' judicial review authority.
   d. clarified presidential appointment authority.

4. Ratification of an amendment to the U.S. Constitution requires
   a. approval of the majority of citizens voting in a referendum.
   b. approval of three-quarters of the members of Congress.
   c. approval of three-quarters of either the House or the Senate.
   d. approval of three-quarters of the state legislatures or special conventions.

5. All of the following were authors of *The Federalist Papers* except
   a. John Jay.
   b. Thomas Jefferson.
   c. Alexander Hamilton.
   d. James Madison.

6. The document (or set of documents), grounded in social contract theory and stating that citizens have an obligation to replace their government if it is not serving them and protecting their unalienable rights, is
   a. the Articles of Confederation.
   b. the Constitution of the United States of America.
   c. the Declaration of Independence.
   d. *The Federalist Papers*.

7. At the Constitutional Convention, the delegates devoted the bulk of their time to resolving the issue of

   a. procedures for electing the president and the vice president.
   b. representation in the national legislature.
   c. the necessity for a bill of rights.
   d. slavery.

8. The ultimate authority to interpret the meaning of constitutional language, and hence to decide what is the supreme law of the land, comes from
   a. the majority of members of Congress.
   b. the majority of members of state legislatures.
   c. the majority of justices on the U.S. Supreme Court.
   d. the president of the United States.

9. The required nine states ratified the Constitution of the United States in
   a. 1776.
   b. 1781.
   c. 1788.
   d. 1791.

10. One check that the Senate has on both the executive branch and the judicial branch is its power of
    a. advice and consent.
    b. impeachment.
    c. ratification of treaties.
    d. veto override.

FILL IN THE BLANKS.

11. Currently there are _____ amendments to the U.S. Constitution, and the last amendment was added in the year _____ .

12. The United States' first constitution was the _____ .

13. _____ wrote a pamphlet that summarized the Anti-Federalist position in the debate leading to ratification of the Constitution.

14. The Virginia delegate to the Second Continental Congress who wrote the Declaration of Independence was _____ .

15. Many of the Anti-Federalist criticisms of the Constitution were addressed in 1791 with the ratification of the _____ .

Answers: 1. c; 2. d; 3. c; 4. d; 5. b; 6. c; 7. b; 8. c; 9. c; 10. a; 11. 27 and 1992; 12. Articles of Confederation; 13. Mercy Otis Warren (the Columbian Patriot); 14. Thomas Jefferson; 15. Bill of Rights

RESOURCES FOR RESEARCH AND ACTION

Internet Resources

FindLaw
www.findlaw.com This site offers links to news regarding current cases before the U.S. Supreme Court as well as access to decisions of all federal and state appellate courts.

Library of Congress Memory Project
www.loc.gov/rr/program/bib/ourdocs/PrimDocsHome.htm
This comprehensive Web site, created by the Library of Congress as part of its Memory Project, includes a wealth of information about the early American republic, including primary documents such as *The Federalist Papers*.

The U.S. Constitution Online
www.USConstitution.net This interesting site helps to place the U.S. Constitution in a contemporary context. Its current events section discusses how the pending issues are affected by constitutional principles.

Internet Activism

YouTube
www.youtube.com/watch?v=TtGOyznDDEM&feature=related
Take a short test, developed by the Friends of the Article V Convention, to assess how much you know about the U.S. Constitution.

Twitter
http://twitter.com/aclu The American Civil Liberties Union (ACLU) is a nonprofit, nonpartisan, public interest organization devoted to protecting the basic civil liberties of everyone in America.

Facebook
www.facebook.com/pages/Philadelphia-PA/National-Constitution-Center/59543893235?ref=nfl The National Constitution Center is an interactive museum about the history of the Constitution.

Blog
http://blogs.archives.gov/aotus/ David Ferriero, the archivist for the National Archives, offers his take on transparency, collaboration, and participation at the National Archives. The National Archives preserves and makes accessible more than 9 billion valuable records of the Federal government, including the Declaration of Independence and the U.S. Constitution.

Recommended Readings

Breyer, Stephen. *Active Liberty: Interpreting Our Democratic Constitution.* New York: Random House, 2005. A short, readable book in which Supreme Court justice Stephen Breyer argues that constitutional interpretation must be guided by the foundational principle of government by the people and that the courts must ensure that they protect and facilitate citizens' participation in government.

Hamilton, Alexander, James Madison, and John Jay. *The Federalist Papers.* Cutchogue, NY: Buccaneer Books, 1992. A compilation of the eighty-five newspaper articles written by the authors to persuade the voters of New York to ratify the proposed Constitution of the United States, featuring a comprehensive introduction that puts the articles in context and outlines their principal themes—and hence, the underlying principles of the Constitution.

Roberts, Cokie. *Founding Mothers: The Women Who Raised Our Nation.* New York: Perennial Press, 2004. An examination of the Revolution and its aftermath, focusing on how women contributed to the war effort and to wider discussions about how the new government should be structured and what goals it should advance.

Sabato, Larry. *A More Perfect Constitution: 23 Proposals to Revitalize Our Constitution and Make America a Fairer Country.* New York: Walker Publishing, 2007. An exploration by political scientist Larry Sabato into why a constitutional convention is needed. The book includes proposals for twenty-three amendments—many of which citizens support, according to a poll commissioned by the author—that Sabato argues will perfect the Constitution. His real goal in writing the book was to kindle a national conversation on what he perceives as the deficiencies in U.S. representative democracy.

Movies of Interest

National Treasure (2004)
Starring Nicholas Cage, this adventure-packed film traces a hunt for treasure that a family's oral history says the nation's founding fathers buried. Clues are found hidden in the country's early currency and even on the back of the Declaration of Independence. The hunt exposes the viewer to the workings of the National Archives and its Preservation Room and features images of the founding fathers not typically reproduced in textbooks.

Return to the Land of Wonder (2004)
This documentary follows Adnan Pachachi's return to Iraq in 2003, after thirty-seven years in exile, to head a committee charged with drafting a new constitution and bill of rights. The movie focuses on the torturous process of trying to resolve conflicts created by the demands of the United States and the expectations of Iraqis, as well as the realities of everyday life in Iraq in 2003.

An Empire of Reason (1998)
A thought-provoking answer to an intriguing "what if ?" question: What if the ratification debates were held using the media tools of the twenty-first century, specifically television?

Amistad (1997)
This film depicts the mutiny and subsequent trial of Africans aboard the ship *Amistad* in 1839–1840. Viewers get a glimpse of the intense civic discourse over slavery in the period leading up to the Civil War.

Preamble

We the People of the United States, in Order to form a more perfect Union, establish Justice, insure domestic Tranquility, provide for the common defence, promote the general Welfare, and secure the Blessings of Liberty to ourselves and our Posterity, do ordain and establish this Constitution for the United States of America.

ARTICLE I. (Legislative Branch)

Section 1. (Bicameral Legislative Branch)

All legislative Powers herein granted shall be vested in a Congress of the United States, which shall consist of a Senate and House of Representatives.

Section 2. (The House of Representatives)

Clause 1: The House of Representatives shall be composed of Members chosen every second Year by the People of the several States, and the Electors in each State shall have the Qualifications requisite for Electors of the most numerous Branch of the State Legislature.

Clause 2: No Person shall be a Representative who shall not have attained to the age of twenty five Years, and been seven Years a Citizen of the United States, and who shall not, when elected, be an Inhabitant of that State in which he shall be chosen.

Clause 3: Representatives and direct Taxes shall be apportioned among the several States which may be included within this Union, according to their respective Numbers, which shall be determined by adding to the whole Number of free Persons, including those bound to Service for a Term of Years, and excluding Indians not taxed, three fifths of all other Persons. The actual Enumeration shall be made within three Years after the first Meeting of the Congress of the United States, and within every subsequent Term of ten Years, in such Manner as they shall by Law direct. The Number of Representatives shall not exceed one for every thirty Thousand, but each State shall have at Least one Representative; and until such enumeration shall be made, the State of New Hampshire shall be entitled to chuse three, Massachusetts eight, Rhode-Island and Providence Plantations one, Connecticut five, New-York six, New Jersey four, Pennsylvania eight, Delaware one, Maryland six, Virginia ten, North Carolina five, South Carolina five, and Georgia three.

Clause 4: When vacancies happen in the Representation from any State, the Executive Authority thereof shall issue Writs of Election to fill such Vacancies.

> The Preamble states that "the People" are creating a new government, which is described in the Constitution. The Preamble also decrees that it is the mission of this new government to serve the people better than did the government established by the Articles of Confederation, which had been in effect since before the end of the War for Independence.

> Article I presents the organization, procedures, and authority of the lawmaking branch, the Congress, a bicameral (two-chamber) legislature comprising the House of Representatives and the Senate.

> House members are elected to serve a two-year term.

> The Constitution specifies only three qualifications to be elected to the House: you must be at least 25 years old; you must be a U.S. citizen for at least seven years (so a foreign-born, naturalized citizen can be a House member); and you must be a resident of the state you will represent. By tradition, House members live in the district that they represent.

> The number of seats in the House increased as the population of each state grew until 1911, when Congress set the number of House seats at 435. Congress distributes these seats among the fifty states according to each state's share of the total population, as determined by a census (official count of the country's inhabitants) conducted every ten years. Every state must have at least one seat in the House. The "three-fifths" clause decreed that when conducting the census the government would not count Native Americans and would count each slave as three-fifths of a person while counting every other inhabitant as one person. The Thirteenth Amendment (1865) abolished slavery, and the Fourteenth Amendment (1868) repealed the three-fifths clause. Today every inhabitant of the United States is counted as one person in the census, and House seats are redistributed every ten years based on the census to ensure that each House member is elected by (and therefore represents) approximately the same number of people.

> Governors have the authority to call for a special election to fill any of their states' House seats that become vacant.

> House members select their presiding officer, the Speaker of the House. The Speaker is in line to succeed the president if both the president and the vice president are unable to serve. The Constitution gives the House a check on officials of the executive and judicial branches through its power of impeachment: the power to accuse such officials formally of offenses such as treason, bribery, and abuse of power. If the officials are subsequently found guilty in a trial held by the Senate, they are removed from office.

Clause 5: The House of Representatives shall chuse their Speaker and other Officers; and shall have the sole Power of Impeachment.

POLITICAL INQUIRY: *Because members of the House of Representatives run for reelection every two years, they are perpetually raising money for, and worrying about, their next election campaign. Recently an amendment was introduced that would increase their term from two to four years. What would be the consequences of such a change? How would this change make members of the House more, or less, responsive to their constituents' concerns?*

Section 3. (The Senate)

Clause 1: The Senate of the United States shall be composed of two Senators from each State, chosen by the Legislature thereof, for six Years; and each Senator shall have one Vote.

> Initially, senators were selected by the members of their state's legislature, not by their state's voters. The Seventeenth Amendment (1913) changed this election process; today, senators are elected by the voters in their state. This amendment also authorized each state's governor to call for elections to fill vacancies as well as authorizing the state's legislature to determine how its state's vacant Senate seats would be temporarily filled until the election of a new senator.

> Every even-numbered year, congressional elections are held in which one-third of the Senate's 100 seats and all 435 House seats are up for election. Every state elects two senators, who serve six-year terms.

Clause 2: Immediately after they shall be assembled in Consequence of the first Election, they shall be divided as equally as may be into three Classes. The Seats of the Senators of the first Class shall be vacated at the Expiration of the second Year, of the second Class at the Expiration of the fourth Year, and of the third Class at the Expiration of the sixth Year, so that one third may be chosen every second Year; and if Vacancies happen by Resignation, or otherwise, during the Recess of the Legislature of any State, the Executive thereof may make temporary Appointments until the next Meeting of the Legislature, which shall then fill such Vacancies.

Clause 3: No Person shall be a Senator who shall not have attained to the Age of thirty Years, and been nine Years a Citizen of the United States, and who shall not, when elected, be an Inhabitant of that State for which he shall be chosen.

> Senators must be at least 30 years old, either natural-born citizens or immigrants who have been citizens for at least nine years, and—like members of the House—residents of the state they are elected to represent.

Clause 4: The Vice President of the United States shall be President of the Senate but shall have no Vote, unless they be equally divided.

> The vice president serves as the president of the Senate, with the authority to preside over meetings of the Senate and to vote when there is a tie.

> Although the first few vice presidents did preside over daily meetings of the Senate, the vice president rarely does so today.

Clause 5: The Senate shall chuse their other Officers, and also a President pro tempore, in the Absence of the Vice President, or when he shall exercise the Office of President of the United States.

Clause 6: The Senate shall have the sole Power to try all Impeachments. When sitting for that Purpose, they shall be on Oath or Affirmation. When the President of the United States is tried the Chief Justice shall preside: And no Person shall be convicted without the Concurrence of two thirds of the Members present.

> The Senate exercises a check on officials of the executive and judicial branches of the federal government by trying them once they have been impeached by the House of Representatives.

Clause 7: Judgment in Cases of Impeachment shall not extend further than to removal from Office, and disqualification to hold and enjoy any Office of honor, Trust or Profit under the United States: but the Party convicted shall nevertheless be liable and subject to Indictment, Trial, Judgment and Punishment, according to Law.

> If the Senate convicts an impeached official, he or she is removed from office and may be subject to prosecution in the criminal courts.

POLITICAL INQUIRY: *The framers of the Constitution, who did not expect members of Congress to serve more than one or two terms, would be shocked to learn that Senator Robert C. Byrd (D-West Virginia) was in his fifty-first year of service to the Senate when he died in 2010 at the age of 92. Concerned about such longevity in office, some have proposed a constitutional amendment that would limit the number of times a House member or a senator could win reelection to the same seat. How would term limits benefit citizens? What problems might term limits cause?*

Section 4. (Congressional Elections)

Clause 1: The Times, Places and Manner of holding Elections for Senators and Representatives, shall be prescribed in each State by the Legislature thereof; but the Congress may at any time by Law make or alter such Regulations, except as to the Places of chusing Senators.

> Though states have the authority to organize and conduct elections, today they rely heavily on local governments to assist them. Congress has passed numerous laws to ensure constitutionally guaranteed voting rights. The first such law was passed shortly after ratification of the Fifteenth Amendment to criminalize attempts to deny black men their newly won right to vote. Congress has also enacted laws to make voter registration easier. For example, a 1996 federal law requires states to allow citizens to register to vote through the mail.

POLITICAL INQUIRY: *Voter turnout (the percentage of eligible voters that vote on election day) has increased in Oregon since that state changed its laws to allow voters to vote by mail. What are some additional arguments that could be made in support of a national law allowing citizens to vote by mail? What are some arguments that could be made against such a national law?*

Clause 2: The Congress shall assemble at least once in every Year, and such Meeting shall be on the first Monday in December, unless they shall by Law appoint a different Day.

> Congress must meet at least once each year. Since ratification of the Twentieth Amendment (1933), the regular annual session of Congress begins on January 3 of each year; however, the Twentieth Amendment gives Congress the authority to change the date on which its session begins.

Section 5. (Powers and Responsibilities of the House)

Clause 1: Each House shall be the Judge of the Elections, Returns and Qualifications of its own Members, and a Majority of each shall constitute a Quorum to do Business; but a smaller Number may adjourn from day to day, and may be authorized to compel the Attendance of absent Members, in such Manner, and under such Penalties as each House may provide.

> Each chamber decides whether the election of each of its members is legitimate. A majority of the members of each chamber must be present to conduct business: at least 218 members for the House and 51 senators for the Senate.

Clause 2: Each House may determine the Rules of its Proceedings, punish its Members for disorderly Behaviour, and, with the Concurrence of two thirds, expel a Member.

> After each congressional election, both the House and the Senate determine how they will conduct their business, and each chamber selects from among its members a presiding officer. Moreover, the members of each chamber establish codes of behavior, which they use to judge and—if necessary—punish members' misconduct.

Clause 3: Each House shall keep a Journal of its Proceedings, and from time to time publish the same, excepting such Parts as may in their Judgment require Secrecy; and the Yeas and Nays of the Members of either House on any question shall, at the Desire of one fifth of those Present, be entered on the Journal.

> The House and the Senate must keep and publish records of their proceedings, including a record of all votes for and against proposals, except those that they decide require secrecy. However, if one-fifth of the members of a chamber demand that a vote be recorded, it must be recorded. Congress publishes a record of its debates called the *Congressional Record.*

Clause 4: Neither House, during the Session of Congress, shall, without the Consent of the other, adjourn for more than three days, nor to any other Place than that in which the two Houses shall be sitting.

> To close down business for more than three days during a session, or to conduct business at another location, each chamber needs to get approval from the other one. This ensures that one chamber cannot stop the legislative process by refusing to meet.

Section 6. (Rights of Congressional Members)

Clause 1: The Senators and Representatives shall receive a Compensation for their Services, to be ascertained by Law, and paid out of the Treasury of the United States. They shall in all Cases, except Treason, Felony and Breach of the Peace, be privileged from Arrest during their Attendance at the Session of their respective Houses, and in going to and returning from the same; and for any Speech or Debate in either House, they shall not be questioned in any other Place.

> Today, each member of Congress earns at least $174,000 per year, paid by taxes collected by the national government. Members of Congress are protected from civil lawsuits and criminal prosecution for the work they do as legislators. They are also protected from arrest while Congress is in session except for a charge of treason, of committing a felony, or of committing a breach of the peace.

Clause 2: No Senator or Representative shall, during the Time for which he was elected, be appointed to any civil Office under the Authority of the United States, which shall have been created, or the Emoluments whereof shall have been encreased during such time; and no Person holding any Office under the United States, shall be a Member of either House during his Continuance in Office.

> To ensure the separation of basic governing functions, no member of Congress can hold another federal position while serving in the House or Senate. Moreover, members of Congress cannot be appointed to a position in the executive or judicial branch that was created during their term of office.

Section 7. (The Legislative Process)

> This section details the legislative process.

Clause 1: All Bills for raising Revenue shall originate in the House of Representatives; but the Senate may propose or concur with amendments as on other Bills.

> Although all revenue-raising bills, such as tax bills, must originate in the House, the Senate reviews them and has the authority to make modifications; ultimately the House and the Senate must approve the identical bill for it to become law.

> After the House and the Senate approve, by a simple majority vote in each chamber, the identical bill, it is sent to the president for approval or rejection. The president has ten days in which to act, or the bill will automatically become law (unless Congress has adjourned, in which case the bill dies—a pocket veto). If the president signs the bill within ten days, it becomes law. If the president rejects—vetoes—the bill, he or she sends it back to the chamber of its origin with objections. Congress can then rewrite the vetoed bill and send the revised bill through the legislative process. Or Congress can attempt to override the veto by garnering a supermajority vote of approval (two-thirds majority) in each chamber.

> The president must approve or veto everything that Congress approves except its vote to adjourn or any resolutions that do not have the force of law.

Clause 2: Every Bill which shall have passed the House of Representatives and the Senate, shall, before it become a law, be presented to the President of the United States: If he approve he shall sign it, but if not he shall return it, with his Objections to that House in which it shall have originated, who shall enter the Objections at large on their Journal, and proceed to reconsider it. If after such Reconsideration two thirds of that House shall agree to pass the Bill, it shall be sent, together with the Objections, to the other House, by which it shall likewise be reconsidered, and if approved by two thirds of that House, it shall become a Law. But in all such Cases the Votes of both Houses shall be determined by Yeas and Nays, and the Names of the Persons voting for and against the Bill shall be entered on the Journal of each House respectively. If any Bill shall not be returned by the President within ten Days (Sundays excepted) after it shall have been presented to him, the Same shall be a Law, in like Manner as if he had signed it, unless the Congress by their Adjournment prevent its Return, in which Case it shall not be a Law.

Clause 3: Every Order, Resolution, or Vote to which the Concurrence of the Senate and House of Representatives may be necessary (except on a question of Adjournment) shall be presented to the President of the United States; and before the Same shall take Effect, shall be approved by him, or being disapproved by him, shall be repassed by two thirds of the Senate and House of Representatives, according to the Rules and Limitations prescribed in the Case of a Bill.

POLITICAL INQUIRY: *The presidential veto power is limited to an all-or-nothing decision. Presidents must either approve or veto entire bills; they cannot approve part of a bill and veto other parts of it. Many who worry about the national debt have called for a new type of presidential veto: a line-item veto. This type of veto would authorize the president to overrule parts of a bill that provide spending authority while approving other parts of the same bill. Would giving the president authority to exercise a line-item veto make it easier for the national government to enact a balanced annual budget (a budget in which the money spent in the budget year is equal to or less than the money raised in that year)? Why or why not? What arguments might members of Congress make against giving the president a line-item veto, hence giving up their final say on spending bills?*

Section 8. (The Lawmaking Authority of Congress)

Clause 1: The Congress shall have Power To lay and collect Taxes, Duties, Imposts and Excises, to pay the Debts and provide for the common Defence and general Welfare of the United States; but all Duties, Imposts and Excises shall be uniform throughout the United States;

Clause 2: To borrow Money on the credit of the United States;

> This section specifies the constitutionally established congressional powers. These powers are limited to those listed and any other powers that Congress believes are "necessary and proper" for Congress to fulfill its listed powers. Congress has used the "necessary and proper" clause (Clause 18) to justify laws that expand its listed powers. Laws that appear to go beyond the listed powers can be challenged in the courts, with the Supreme Court ultimately deciding their constitutionality.

> The power to raise money and to authorize spending it for common defense and the general welfare is one of the most essential powers of Congress. The Sixteenth Amendment (1913) authorizes a national income tax, which was not previously possible given the "uniformity" requirement in Clause 1.

> Today, after years of borrowing money to pay current bills, the national government has a debt of over $13 trillion.

POLITICAL INQUIRY: *Some economists, politicians, and citizens fear that the national debt harms the United States by limiting the amount of money available to invest in growing the economy. Moreover, citizens worry that their children and grandchildren, saddled with the obligation of paying back this debt, may face limited government services. Therefore, there have been repeated calls for a balanced budget amendment, which would force Congress to spend no more than the money it raises in each budget year. What arguments might the members of Congress, elected officials who want to be reelected, put forth against ratification of a balanced budget amendment? What national situations might require spending more money than is raised in a budget year?*

Clause 3: To regulate Commerce with foreign Nations, and among the several States, and with the Indian Tribes;

Clause 4: To establish an uniform Rule of Naturalization, and uniform Laws on the subject of Bankruptcies throughout the United States;

Clause 5: To coin Money, regulate the Value thereof, and of foreign Coin, and fix the Standard of Weights and Measures;

Clause 6: To provide for the Punishment of counterfeiting the Securities and current Coin of the United States;

Clause 7: To establish Post Offices and post Roads;

Clause 8: To promote the Progress of Science and useful Arts, by securing for limited Times to Authors and Inventors the exclusive Right to their respective Writings and Discoveries;

Clause 9: To constitute Tribunals inferior to the supreme Court;

Clause 10: To define and punish Piracies and Felonies committed on the high Seas, and Offences against the Law of Nations;

Clause 11: To declare War, grant Letters of Marque and Reprisal, and make Rules concerning Captures on Land and Water;

Clause 12: To raise and support Armies, but no Appropriation of Money to that Use shall be for a longer Term than two Years;

Clause 13: To provide and maintain a Navy;

Clause 14: To make Rules for the Government and Regulation of the land and naval Forces;

Clause 15: To provide for calling forth the Militia to execute the Laws of the Union, suppress Insurrections and repel Invasions;

Clause 16: To provide for organizing, arming, and disciplining, the Militia, and for governing such Part of them as may be employed in the Service of the United States, reserving to the States respectively, the Appointment of the Officers, and the Authority of training the Militia according to the discipline prescribed by Congress;

> With the Supreme Court's support, Congress has interpreted Clause 3 in a way that has allowed it to expand its involvement in the economy and the daily lives of U.S. citizens, using this clause to regulate business as well as to outlaw racial segregation. However, state governments have frequently challenged Congress's expansion of power by way of the commerce clause when they believe that Congress is infringing on their constitutional authority.

> Congress has the authority to establish the process by which foreigners become citizens (Clause 4). Recently, national legislation has made it more difficult for individuals to file for bankruptcy.

> The authority to make and regulate money as well as to standardize weights and measures is essential to the regulation of commerce (Clause 5).

> Congress exercised its authority under Clause 9 to create the federal court system other than the Supreme Court, which was established under Article III of the Constitution.

> Every nation in the world possesses the authority to establish its own laws regarding crimes outside its borders and violations of international law (Clause 10).

> Clauses 11 through 15 collectively delegate to Congress the authority to raise and support military troops, to enact rules to regulate the troops, to call the troops to action, and to declare war. However, the president as commander in chief (Article II) has the authority to wage war. Presidents have committed armed troops without a declaration of war, leading to disputes over congressional and presidential war powers. Clause 11 also provides Congress with the authority to hire an individual for the purpose of retaliating against another nation for some harm it has caused the United States—that is, to provide a *letter of Marque,* an outdated practice.

> Clauses 15 and 16 guarantee the states the right to maintain and train a militia (today's National Guard), but state control of the militia is subordinate to national control when the national government needs the support of these militias to ensure that laws are executed, to suppress domestic uprisings, and to repel invasion.

POLITICAL INQUIRY: *Several state governments, specifically states that have needed their National Guard troops to help with crises such as massive forest fires, have raised questions about the right of the national government to send National Guard troops to foreign lands such as Afghanistan. Imagine you are arguing in front of the Supreme Court on behalf of the states. What argument would you make to support the states' claim that the national government does not have the right to send National Guard troops to Afghanistan? Now imagine that you are arguing in front of the Court on behalf of the national government. What argument would you make to support the right of the national government to send National Guard troops anywhere in the world?*

Clause 17: To exercise exclusive Legislation in all Cases whatsoever, over such District (not exceeding ten Miles square) as may, by Cession of Particular States, and the Acceptance of Congress, become the Seat of the Government of the United States, and to exercise like Authority over all Places purchased by the Consent of the Legislature of the State in which the Same shall be, for the Erection of Forts, Magazines, Arsenals, dock-Yards and other needful Buildings;—And

> Congress has the authority to govern Washington D.C., which is the seat of the national government. Today, citizens living in Washington D.C. elect local government officials to govern the city with congressional oversight. The national government also governs federal lands throughout the states that are used for federal purposes, such as military installations.

POLITICAL INQUIRY: *Article IV of the Constitution delegates to Congress the authority to admit new states to the union. The citizens of Washington D.C. have petitioned Congress to become a state. What would be the benefits*

> Clause 18 grants Congress authority to make all laws it deems necessary and proper to fulfill its responsibilities under the Constitution, including those listed in Section 8. This clause also authorizes Congress to pass laws it deems necessary to ensure that the other two branches are able to fulfill their responsibilities. Congress has also used this clause to expand its powers.

> Article I, Section 9 limits Congress's lawmaking authority and mandates that Congress be accountable to the people in how it spends the public's money.

> Clause 1 barred Congress from passing laws to prohibit the slave trade until 1808 at the earliest. The Thirteenth Amendment (1865) made slavery illegal.

> Clauses 2 and 3 guarantee protections to those accused of crimes. Clause 2 establishes the right of imprisoned persons to challenge their imprisonment in court (through a *writ of habeas corpus*). It notes that Congress can deny the right to a writ of habeas corpus during times of a rebellion or invasion if public safety is at risk.

> Congress cannot pass laws that declare a person or a group of people guilty of an offense (Bills of Attainder). Only courts have the authority to determine guilt. Congress is also prohibited from passing a law that punishes a person tomorrow for an action he or she took that was legal today (ex post facto law).

> Clause 4 prohibits Congress from directly taxing individual people, such as imposing an income tax. The Sixteenth Amendment (1913) authorized congressional enactment of a direct income tax on individual people.

> Congress is prohibited from taxing goods that are exported from any state, either those sent to foreign lands or to other states (Clause 5).

> Congress cannot favor any state over another in its regulation of trade (Clause 6).

> The national government can spend money only as authorized by Congress through enacted laws (no more than authorized and only for the purpose authorized) and must present a public accounting of revenues and expenditures.

> Congress cannot grant individuals special rights, privileges, or a position in government based on their heredity (birth into a family designated as nobility), which is how kings, queens, and other officials were granted their positions in the British monarchy. In addition, federal officials cannot accept gifts from foreign nations except those Congress allows (which today are gifts of minimal value).

> Clause 1 specifically prohibits states from engaging in several activities that the Constitution delegates to the national government, including engaging in foreign affairs and creating currency. In addition, it extends several of the prohibitions on Congress to the states.

> Clause 2 prevents states from interfering in foreign trade without congressional approval.

> States cannot, without congressional approval, levy import taxes, sign agreements or treaties with foreign nations, or enter into compacts (agreements) with other states.

Clause 18: To make all Laws which shall be necessary and proper for carrying into Execution the foregoing Powers and all other Powers vested by this Constitution in the Government of the United States, or in any Department or Officer thereof.

Section 9. (Prohibitions on Congress)

Clause 1: The Migration or Importation of such Persons as any of the States now existing shall think proper to admit, shall not be prohibited by the Congress prior to the Year one thousand eight hundred and eight, but a Tax or duty may be imposed on such Importation, not exceeding ten dollars for each Person.

Clause 2: The Privilege of the Writ of Habeas Corpus shall not be suspended, unless when in Cases of Rebellion or Invasion the public Safety may require it.

Clause 3: No Bill of Attainder or ex post facto Law shall be passed.

Clause 4: No Capitation, or other direct, Tax shall be laid, unless in Proportion to the Census of Enumeration herein before directed to be taken.

Clause 5: No Tax or Duty shall be laid on Articles exported from any State.

Clause 6: No Preference shall be given by any Regulation of Commerce or Revenue to the Ports of one State over those of another: nor shall Vessels bound to, or from, one State, be obliged to enter, clear or pay Duties in another.

Clause 7: No Money shall be drawn from the Treasury, but in Consequence of Appropriations made by Law; and a regular Statement and Account of the Receipts and Expenditures of all public Money shall be published from time to time.

Clause 8: No Title of Nobility shall be granted by the United States: And no Person holding any Office of Profit or Trust under them, shall, without the Consent of the Congress, accept of any present, Emolument, Office, or Title, of any kind whatever, from any King, Prince or foreign State.

Section 10. (Prohibitions on the States)

Clause 1: No State shall enter into any Treaty, Alliance, or Confederation; grant Letters of Marque and Reprisal; coin Money; emit Bills of Credit; make any Thing but gold and silver Coin a Tender in Payment of Debts; pass any Bill of Attainder, ex post facto Law, or Law impairing the Obligation of Contracts, or grant any Title of Nobility.

Clause 2: No State shall, without the Consent of the Congress, lay any Imposts or Duties on Imports or Exports, except what may be absolutely necessary for executing its inspection Laws: and the net Produce of all Duties and Imposts, laid by any State on Imports or Exports, shall be for the Use of the Treasury of the United States; and all such Laws shall be subject to the Revision and Controul of the Congress.

Clause 3: No State shall, without the Consent of Congress, lay any Duty of Tonnage, keep Troops, or Ships of War in time of Peace, enter into any Agreement or Compact with another State, or with a foreign Power, or engage in War, unless actually invaded, or in such imminent Danger as will not admit of delay.

ARTICLE II. (Executive Branch)

Section 1. (Executive Powers of the President)

Clause 1: The executive Power shall be vested in a President of the United States of America. He shall hold his Office during the Term of four Years, and, together with the Vice President, chosen for the same Term, be elected, as follows:

Clause 2: Each State shall appoint, in such Manner as the Legislature thereof may direct, a Number of Electors, equal to the whole Number of Senators and Representatives to which the State may be entitled in the Congress: but no Senator or Representative, or Person holding an Office of Trust or Profit under the United States, shall be appointed an Elector.

Clause 3: The Electors shall meet in their respective States, and vote by Ballot for two Persons, of whom one at least shall not be an Inhabitant of the same State with themselves. And they shall make a List of all the Persons voted for, and of the Number of Votes for each; which List they shall sign and certify, and transmit sealed to the Seat of the Government of the United States, directed to the President of the Senate. The President of the Senate shall, in the Presence of the Senate and House of Representatives, open all the Certificates, and the Votes shall then be counted. The Person having the greatest Number of Votes shall be the President, if such Number be a Majority of the whole Number of Electors appointed; and if there be more than one who have such Majority, and have an equal Number of Votes, then the House of Representatives shall immediately chuse by Ballot one of them for President; and if no Person have a Majority, then from the five highest on the List the said House shall in like Manner chuse the President. But in chusing the President, the Votes shall be taken by States, the Representatives from each State having one Vote; a quorum for this Purpose shall consist of a Member or Members from two thirds of the States, and a Majority of all the States shall be necessary to a Choice. In every Case, after the Choice of the President, the Person having the greatest Number of Votes of the Electors shall be the Vice President. But if there should remain two or more who have equal Votes, the Senate shall chuse from them by Ballot the Vice President.

POLITICAL INQUIRY: *The Electoral College system is criticized for many reasons. Some argue that deciding the presidential election by any vote other than that of the citizens is undemocratic. Others complain that in 2000 the system allowed George W. Bush to become president, even though he had not won the popular vote. Many argue that the Electoral College system should be eliminated and replaced by direct popular election of the president and the vice president. What is (are) the benefit(s) of eliminating the Electoral College? What might be the potential harm to the nation of eliminating the Electoral College?*

Clause 4: The Congress may determine the Time of chusing the Electors, and the Day on which they shall give their Votes; which Day shall be the same throughout the United States.

Clause 5: No Person except a natural born Citizen, or a Citizen of the United States, at the time of the Adoption of this Constitution, shall be eligible to the Office of President; neither shall any person be eligible to that Office who shall not have attained to the Age of thirty five Years, and been fourteen Years a Resident within the United States.

> Article II outlines the authority of the president and the vice president and the process of their selection.

> The Constitution delegates to the president the authority to administer the executive branch of the national government. The term of office for the president and his vice president is four years. No term limit was specified; until President Franklin D. Roosevelt, there was a tradition of a two-term limit. President Roosevelt served four terms.

> The Electoral College system was established as a compromise between those who wanted citizens to elect the president directly and others who wanted Congress to elect the president. Each state government has the authority to determine how their state's electors will be selected.

> Electors, who are selected through processes established by the legislatures of each state, have the authority to select the president and the vice president. Citizens' votes determine who their state's electors will be. Electors are individuals selected by officials of the state's political parties to participate in the Electoral College if the party wins the presidential vote in the state. Before passage of the Twelfth Amendment (1804), each elector had two votes. The candidate receiving the majority of votes won the presidency, and the candidate with the second highest number of votes won the vice presidency. Today, when the electors meet as the Electoral College, each elector casts one vote for the presidency and one vote for the vice presidency. If no presidential candidate wins a majority of the electoral votes, the House selects the president. If no vice-presidential candidate wins a majority of the electoral votes, the Senate selects the vice president.

> Today, by law, national elections are held on the Tuesday following the first Monday in November, in even-numbered years. During presidential election years, the electors gather in their state capitals on the Monday after the second Wednesday in December to vote for the president and the vice president. When Congress convenes in January after the presidential election, its members count the electoral ballots and formally announce the newly elected president and vice president.

> The president (and the vice president) must be at least 35 years old and must have lived within the United States for at least fourteen years. Unlike the citizenship qualification for members of the House and Senate, the president and vice president must be natural-born citizens; they cannot be immigrants who have become citizens after arriving in the United States. Therefore, prominent public figures such as California governor Arnold Schwarzenegger, who was born in Austria, Madeleine Albright, secretary of state under President Clinton, who was born in what is now the Czech Republic, and Senator Mel Martinez (R-Florida), who was born in Cuba, could never be elected president.

> Clause 6 states that the powers and duties of the presidency are transferred to the vice president when the president is no longer able to fulfill them. It also states that Congress can pass legislation to indicate who shall act as president if both the president and the vice president are unable to fulfill the president's powers and duties. The "acting" president would serve until the disability is removed or a new president is elected. The Twenty-Fifth Amendment (1967) clarifies when the vice president acts as president temporarily—such as when the president undergoes surgery—and when the vice president actually becomes president.

Clause 6: In Case of the Removal of the President from Office, or of his Death, Resignation, or Inability to discharge the Powers and Duties of the said Office, the Same shall devolve on the Vice President, and the Congress may by Law provide for the Case of Removal, Death, Resignation or Inability, both of the President and Vice President, declaring what Officer shall then act as President, and such Officer shall act accordingly, until the Disability be removed, or a President shall be elected.

> Currently the president's salary is $400,000 per year plus numerous benefits including a nontaxable expense account.

Clause 7: The President shall, at stated Times, receive for his Services, a Compensation, which shall neither be encreased nor diminished during the Period for which he shall have been elected, and he shall not receive within that Period any other Emolument from the United States, or any of them.

Clause 8: Before he enter on the Execution of his Office, he shall take the following Oath or Affirmation:—"I do solemnly swear (or affirm) that I will faithfully execute the Office of President of the United States, and will to the best of my Ability, preserve, protect and defend the Constitution of the United States."

> Under the Constitution, the authority to ensure that laws are carried out is delegated to the president. The president and the vice president are elected to serve concurrent four-year terms. The call for a term limit followed President Franklin Roosevelt's election to a fourth term. The Twenty-Second Amendment (1951) established a two-term limit for presidents.

Section 2. (Powers of the President)

> The president is the commander of the military and of the National Guard (militia of the several states) when it is called to service by the president. When they are not called to service by the president, the state divisions of the National Guard are commanded by their governors. The president is authorized to establish the cabinet, the presidential advisory body comprising the top officials (secretaries) of each department of the executive branch. As the chief executive officer, the president can exercise a check on the judicial branch by decreasing or eliminating sentences and even pardoning (eliminating guilty verdicts of) federal prisoners.

Clause 1: The President shall be Commander in Chief of the Army and Navy of the United States, and of the Militia of the several States, when called into the actual Service of the United States; he may require the Opinion, in writing, of the principal Officer in each of the executive Departments, upon any Subject relating to the Duties of their respective Offices, and he shall have Power to Grant Reprieves and Pardons for Offences against the United States, except in Cases of Impeachment.

> The Constitution provides a check on the president's authority to negotiate treaties and appoint foreign ambassadors, top officials in the executive branch, and Supreme Court justices by requiring that treaties be ratified or appointments confirmed by the Senate. Congress can create additional executive branch positions and federal courts and can decree how these legislatively created positions will be filled.

Clause 2: He shall have Power, by and with the Advice and Consent of the Senate, to make Treaties, provided two thirds of the Senators present concur; and he shall nominate, and by and with the Advice and Consent of the Senate, shall appoint Ambassadors, other public Ministers and Consuls, Judges of the supreme Court, and all other Officers of the United States, whose Appointments are not herein otherwise provided for, and which shall be established by Law: but the Congress may by Law vest the Appointment of such inferior Officers, as they think proper, in the President alone, in the Courts of Law, or in the Heads of Departments.

Clause 3: The President shall have Power to fill up all Vacancies that may happen during the Recess of the Senate, by granting Commissions which shall expire at the End of their next Session.

> If vacancies occur when the Senate is not in session and is therefore not available to confirm presidential appointees, the president can fill the vacancies. The appointees serve through the end of the congressional session.

POLITICAL INQUIRY: *In recent years, Presidents Bush and Obama have both taken advantage of the constitutional loophole that allows presidents to appoint people without Senate confirmation to make controversial appointments. Should the Constitution be amended to limit further the time an appointee who has not been confirmed can serve by requiring the Senate to consider the appointment when it next reconvenes? Why or why not?*

Section 3. (Responsibilities of the President)

He shall from time to time give to the Congress Information on the State of the Union, and recommend to their Consideration such Measures as he shall judge necessary and expedient; he may, on extraordinary Occasions, convene both Houses, or either of them, and in Case of Disagreement between them, with Respect to the Time of Adjournment, he may adjourn them to such Time as he shall think proper; he shall receive Ambassadors and other public Ministers; he shall take Care that the Laws be faithfully executed, and shall Commission all the Officers of the United States.

> As chief executive officer of the nation, the president is required to ensure that laws are properly implemented by overseeing the executive-branch agencies to be sure they are doing the work of government as established in law. The president is also required from time to time to give an assessment of the status of the nation to Congress and to make recommendations for the good of the country. This has evolved into the annual televised State of the Union Address, which is followed within days by the presentation of the president's budget proposal to Congress. The president can also call special sessions of Congress.

Section 4. (Impeachment)

The President, Vice President and all Civil Officers of the United States, shall be removed from Office on Impeachment for and Conviction of, Treason, Bribery, or other high Crimes and Misdemeanors.

> Presidents, vice presidents, and other federal officials can be removed from office if the members of the House of Representatives formally accuse them of treason (giving assistance to the nation's enemies), bribery, or other vaguely defined abuses of power ("high Crimes and Misdemeanors") and two-thirds of the Senate find them guilty of these charges.

ARTICLE III. (Judicial Branch)

Section 1. (Federal Courts and Rights of Judges)

The judicial Power of the United States, shall be vested in one supreme Court, and in such inferior Courts as the Congress may from time to time ordain and establish. The Judges, both of the supreme and inferior Courts, shall hold their Offices during good Behaviour, and shall, at stated Times, receive for their Services, a Compensation, which shall not be diminished during their Continuance in Office.

> Article III presents the organization and authority of the U.S. Supreme Court and delegates to Congress the authority to create other courts as its members deem necessary.

> To ensure that judges make neutral and objective decisions, and are protected from political influences, federal judges serve until they retire, die, or are impeached by the House and convicted by the Senate. In addition, Congress cannot decrease a judge's pay.

POLITICAL INQUIRY: *Although age discrimination is illegal, the government has allowed a retirement age to be established for some positions. For example, there is a retirement age for airline pilots, and most states have established retirement ages for state judges. What would be the arguments for or against amending the Constitution to establish a retirement age for federal judges?*

Section 2. (Jurisdiction of Federal Courts)

Clause 1: The judicial Power shall extend to all Cases, in Law and Equity, arising under this Constitution, the Laws of the United States, and Treaties made, or which shall be made, under their Authority;—to all Cases affecting Ambassadors, other public ministers and Consuls;—to all Cases of admiralty and maritime Jurisdiction;—to Controversies to which the United States shall be a Party;—to Controversies between two or more States;—between a State and Citizens of another State;—between Citizens of different States;—between Citizens of the same

> Federal courts have the authority to hear all lawsuits pertaining to national laws, the Constitution of the United States, and treaties. They also have jurisdiction over cases involving citizens of different states and citizens of foreign nations. Note that the power of judicial review, that is, the power to declare acts of government officials or bodies unconstitutional, is not enumerated in the Constitution.

State claiming Lands under Grants of different States, and between a State, or the Citizens thereof, and foreign States, Citizens or Subjects.

POLITICAL INQUIRY: *Today there are nine Supreme Court justices, yet the Constitution does not set a specific number for Supreme Court justices. With the increasing number of cases appealed to the Supreme Court, what would be the arguments for or against increasing the number of Supreme Court justices?*

> The Supreme Court hears cases involving foreign diplomats and cases in which states are a party. Today, such cases are rare. For the most part, the Supreme Court hears cases on appeal from lower federal courts.

Clause 2: In all Cases affecting Ambassadors, other public Ministers and Consuls, and those in which a State shall be Party, the supreme Court shall have original Jurisdiction. In all the other Cases before mentioned, the supreme Court shall have appellate Jurisdiction, both as to Law and Fact, with such Exceptions, and under such Regulations as the Congress shall make.

> Defendants accused of federal crimes have the right to a jury trial in a federal court located in the state in which the crime was committed.

Clause 3: The Trial of all Crimes, except in Cases of Impeachment, shall be by Jury; and such Trial shall be held in the State where the said Crimes shall have been committed; but when not committed within any State, the Trial shall be at such Place or Places as the Congress may by Law have directed.

Section 3. (Treason)

> This clause defines treason as making war against the United States or helping its enemies. At least two witnesses to the crime are required for a conviction.

Clause 1: Treason against the United States, shall consist only in levying War against them, or in adhering to their Enemies, giving them Aid and Comfort. No Person shall be convicted of Treason unless on the Testimony of two Witnesses to the same overt Act, or on Confession in open Court.

> This clause prevents Congress from redefining treason. Those found guilty of treason can be punished, but their family members cannot be (no "Corruption of Blood").

Clause 2: The Congress shall have Power to declare the Punishment of Treason, but no Attainder of Treason shall work Corruption of Blood, or Forfeiture except during the Life of the Person attainted.

ARTICLE IV. (State-to-State Relations)

> Article IV establishes the obligations states have to each other and to the citizens of other states.

> States must respect one another's legal judgments and records, and a contract agreed to in one state is binding in the other states.

Section 1. (Full Faith and Credit of legal proceedings and decisions)

Full Faith and Credit shall be given in each State to the public Acts, Records, and judicial Proceedings of every other State. And the Congress may by general Laws prescribe the Manner in which such Acts, Records and Proceedings shall be proved, and the Effect thereof.

POLITICAL INQUIRY: *States have had the authority to legally define marriage since before the Constitution was ratified. Today, one of the many issues being debated is whether states with laws defining marriage as a contract between one man and one woman need to give full faith and credit to a same-sex marriage contract from a state where such marriages are legal, such as Massachusetts. Which level of government do you think has the right to define marriage? Explain your choice. Does the full faith and credit clause require states that deny marriage contracts to same-sex couples to recognize legal same-sex marriage contracts from other states? Can you identify a compelling public interest that you believe can only be achieved by the government denying marriage contracts to same-sex couples?*

Section 2. (Privileges and Immunities of Citizens)

> No matter what state they find themselves in, all U.S. citizens are entitled to the same privileges and rights as the citizens of that state.

Clause 1: The Citizens of each State shall be entitled to all Privileges and Immunities of Citizens in the several States.

> If requested by a governor of another state, a state is obligated to return an accused felon to the state from which he or she fled.

Clause 2: A Person charged in any State with Treason, Felony, or other Crime, who shall flee from Justice, and be found in another State, shall on Demand of the executive Authority of the State from which he fled, be delivered up, to be removed to the State having Jurisdiction of the Crime.

Clause 3: No Person held to Service or Labour in one State, under the Laws thereof, escaping into another, shall, in Consequence of any Law or Regulation therein, be discharged from such Service or Labour, but shall be delivered up on Claim of the Party to whom such Service or Labour may be due.

> The Thirteenth Amendment (1865) eliminated a state's obligation to return slaves fleeing from their enslavement in another state.

Section 3. (Admission of New States)

Clause 1: New States may be admitted by the Congress into this Union; but no new State shall be formed or erected within the Jurisdiction of any other State; nor any State be formed by the Junction of two or more States, or Parts of States, without the Consent of the Legislatures of the States concerned as well as of the Congress.

> Congress can admit new states to the union, but it cannot alter established state borders without the approval of the states that would be affected by the change.

Clause 2: The Congress shall have Power to dispose of and make all needful Rules and Regulations respecting the Territory or other Property belonging to the United States; and nothing in this Constitution shall be so construed as to Prejudice any Claims of the United States, or of any particular State.

> The federal government has authority to administer all federal lands, wherever they are located, including national parks and historic sites as well as military installations.

Section 4. (National Government Obligations to the States)

The United States shall guarantee to every State in this Union a Republican Form of Government, and shall protect each of them against Invasion; and on Application of the Legislature, or of the Executive (when the Legislature cannot be convened) against domestic Violence.

> The national government must ensure that every state has a representative democracy, protect each state from foreign invasion, and assist states in addressing mass breaches of domestic tranquility. Under this section, Congress has authorized the president to send in federal troops to protect public safety. During the civil rights movement, for example, federal troops ensured the safety of black students attending newly desegregated high schools and colleges.

ARTICLE V. (Formal Constitutional Amendment Process)

The Congress, whenever two thirds of both Houses shall deem it necessary, shall propose Amendments to this Constitution, or, on the Application of the Legislatures of two thirds of the several States, shall call a Convention for proposing Amendments, which, in either Case, shall be valid to all Intents and Purposes, as Part of this Constitution, when ratified by the Legislatures of three fourths of the several States, or by Conventions in three fourths thereof, as the one or the other Mode of Ratification may be proposed by the Congress; Provided that no Amendment which may be made prior to the Year One thousand eight hundred and eight shall in any Manner affect the first and fourth Clauses in the Ninth Section of the first Article; and that no State, without its Consent, shall be deprived of its equal Suffrage in the Senate.

> Article V details the process by which the Constitution can be amended.

> Amendments can be proposed either by Congress or by a special convention called at the request of the states. States have the authority to ratify amendments to the Constitution; three-fourths of the state legislatures must ratify an amendment for it to become part of the Constitution. Every year dozens of constitutional amendments are proposed in Congress, yet only twenty-seven have been ratified since 1789.

ARTICLE VI. (Supremacy of the Constitution)

Clause 1: All Debts contracted and Engagements entered into, before the Adoption of this Constitution, shall be as valid against the United States under this Constitution, as under the Confederation.

> Article VI decrees that the Constitution is the supreme law of the land.

> This provision states that the new federal government created by the Constitution was responsible for the financial obligations of the national government created by the Articles of Confederation.

Clause 2: This Constitution, and the Laws of the United States which shall be made in Pursuance thereof; and all Treaties made, or which shall be made, under the Authority of the United States, shall be the supreme Law of the Land; and the Judges in every State shall be bound thereby, any Thing in the Constitution or Laws of any state to the Contrary notwithstanding.

> The Constitution, and all laws made to fulfill its mission that are in compliance with it, is the supreme law of the land; no one is above the supreme law of the land.

Clause 3: The Senators and Representatives before mentioned, and the Members of the several State Legislatures, and all executive and judicial Officers, both of the United States and of the several States, shall be bound by Oath or Affirmation, to support this Constitution; but no religious Test shall ever be required as a Qualification to any Office or public Trust under the United States.

> All national and state officials must take an oath promising to uphold the Constitution. This article also prohibits the government from requiring officeholders to submit to a religious test or swear a religious oath, hence supporting a separation of government and religion.

> Article VII outlines the process by which the Constitution will be ratified.

> When the Constitutional Convention presented the proposed second constitution, the Constitution of the United States, to the states for ratification, the Articles of Confederation (the first constitution) were still in effect. The Articles required agreement from all thirteen states to amend it, which some argued meant that all thirteen states had to agree to replace the Articles of Confederation with the Constitution. Yet the proposed second constitution decreed that it would replace the Articles when nine states had ratified it. The first Congress met under the Constitution of the United States in 1789.

ARTICLE VII. (Constitutional Ratification Process)

Clause 1: The Ratification of the Conventions of nine States, shall be sufficient for the Establishment of this Constitution between the States so ratifying the same.

Clause 2: Done in Convention by the Unanimous Consent of the States present the Seventeenth Day of September in the Year of our Lord one thousand seven hundred and Eighty seven and of the Independence of the United States of America the Twelfth. In witness whereof We have hereunto subscribed our Names,

G. Washington—Presid't.
and deputy from Virginia

Delaware	George Read
	Gunning Bedford, Jr.
	John Dickinson
	Richard Bassett
	Jacob Broom
Maryland	James McHenry
	Daniel of St. Thomas Jenifer
	Daniel Carroll
Virginia	John Blair
	James Madison, Jr.
North Carolina	William Blount
	Richard Dobbs Spaight
	Hugh Williamson
South Carolina	John Rutledge
	Charles Cotesworth Pinckney
	Charles Pinckney
	Pierce Butler
Georgia	William Few
	Abraham Baldwin

New Hampshire	John Langdon
	Nicholas Gilman
Massachusetts	Nathaniel Gorham
	Rufus King
Connecticut	William Samuel Johnson
	Roger Sherman
New York	Alexander Hamilton
New Jersey	William Livingston
	David Brearley
	William Patterson
	Jonathan Dayton
Pennsylvania	Benjamin Franklin
	Thomas Mifflin
	Robert Morris
	George Clymer
	Thomas FitzSimons
	Jared Ingersoll
	James Wilson
	Gouverneur Morris

Amendments to the Constitution of the United States of America

THE BILL OF RIGHTS: AMENDMENTS I–X
(ratified in 1791)

Amendment I (1791)

Congress shall make no law respecting an establishment of religion, or prohibiting the free exercise thereof; or abridging the freedom of speech, or of the press; or the right of the people peaceably to assemble, and to petition the Government for a redress of grievances.

> Government cannot make laws that limit freedom of expression, which includes freedom of religion, speech, and the press, as well as the freedom to assemble and to petition the government to address grievances. None of these individual freedoms is absolute, however; courts balance the protection of individual freedoms (as provided for in this Constitution) with the protection of public safety, including national security.

POLITICAL INQUIRY: *Currently, freedom of speech protects symbolic speech such as the burning of the U.S. flag to make a statement of protest. What reasons are there to amend the Constitution to make burning the flag unconstitutional and hence a form of speech that is not protected by the Constitution? What reasons are there not to do so?*

Amendment II (1791)

A well regulated Militia, being necessary to the security of a free State, the right of the people to keep and bear Arms, shall not be infringed.

> Today, states and the federal government balance the right of the people to own guns with the need to protect the public.

POLITICAL INQUIRY: *Does the phrase "a well regulated Militia" limit the right to bear arms to those engaged in protecting public peace and safety? Why or why not?*

Amendment III (1791)

No Soldier shall, in time of peace be quartered in any house, without the consent of the Owner, nor in time of war, but in a manner to be prescribed by law.

> Military troops cannot take control of private homes during peacetime.

Amendment IV (1791)

The right of the people to be secure in their persons, houses, papers, and effects, against unreasonable searches and seizures, shall not be violated, and no Warrants shall issue, but upon probable cause, supported by Oath or affirmation, and particularly describing the place to be searched, and the persons or things to be seized.

> Government officials must obtain approval before they search or seize a person's property. The approval must come either from the person whose private property they are searching or seizing or from a judge who determines that the government is justified in taking this action to protect public safety and therefore signs a search warrant.

POLITICAL INQUIRY: *Since the terrorist attacks on September 11, 2001, the national government has tried to balance the right of people to be secure in their person and property with public safety and national security. What reasons have the president and members of Congress offered in defense of allowing intelligence agencies to bypass the requirement to get judicial permission to conduct searches or seizures of phone records of suspected terrorists? How valid are those reasons? In your opinion, can they be reconciled with constitutional protections?*

Amendment V (1791)

No person shall be held to answer for a capital, or otherwise infamous crime, unless on a presentment or indictment of a Grand Jury, except in cases arising in the land or naval forces, or in the Militia, when in actual service in time of War or public danger; nor shall any person be

> The Fifth Amendment provides much more than the familiar protection against self-incrimination that we hear people who are testifying before Congress and the courts claim by "taking the Fifth." For example, before the government can punish a person for a crime (take away a person's life, liberty, or pursuit of happiness), it must follow certain procedures specified in law; it must follow *due process of the law.* The federal government guarantees those accused of federal crimes a grand jury hearing in which the government presents its evidence to a selected group of citizens who determine whether there is sufficient evidence to go to trial. If a defendant is found not guilty of a specific criminal offense, he or she cannot be brought to trial again by the same government for the same offense. If the government determines it needs private property for a public use, the owner is compelled to sell the land, and the government must pay a fair price based on the market value of the property.

subject for the same offence to be twice put in jeopardy of life or limb; nor shall be compelled in any criminal case to be a witness against himself, nor be deprived of life, liberty, or property, without due process of law; nor shall private property be taken for public use, without just compensation.

Amendment VI (1791)

In all criminal prosecutions, the accused shall enjoy the right to a speedy and public trial, by an impartial jury of the State and district wherein the crime shall have been committed, which district shall have been previously ascertained by law, and to be informed of the nature and cause of the accusation; to be confronted with the witnesses against him; to have compulsory process for obtaining witnesses in his favor, and to have the Assistance of Counsel for his defence.

> The Sixth Amendment outlines additional procedures that the government must follow before taking away a person's life, liberty, or pursuit of happiness. People accused of crimes have the right to know what they are accused of doing, to hear from witnesses against them, and to defend themselves in a trial that is open to the public within a reasonable amount of time after the accusations are made. An indigent (very poor) person is guaranteed a government-provided lawyer in serious criminal cases. It is assumed all others can afford to hire a lawyer.

POLITICAL INQUIRY: *The resources needed to provide an adequate defense in a criminal case can be quite steep. For example, to ensure a fair trial, a lawyer may use government money to pay for expert witnesses. Argue for or against the need to limit such expenditures for indigent defendants accused of serious crimes.*

Amendment VII (1791)

In Suits at common law, where the value in controversy shall exceed twenty dollars, the right of trial by jury shall be preserved, and no fact tried by a jury, shall be otherwise re-examined in any Court of the United States, than according to the rules of the common law.

> Either party (the complainant or the person accused of causing harm or violating a contract) in a federal civil lawsuit involving more than $20 can demand a jury trial.

Amendment VIII (1791)

Excessive bail shall not be required, nor excessive fines imposed, nor cruel and unusual punishments inflicted.

> The Eighth Amendment protects those accused of crimes as well as those found guilty from overly punitive decisions. Bail, a payment to the government that can be required to avoid incarceration before and during trial, cannot be set at an excessively high amount, unless the judge determines that freedom for the accused would jeopardize public safety or that he or she might flee. The punishment imposed on those convicted of crimes is expected to "fit" the crime: it is to be reasonable given the severity of the crime. Punishment cannot be excessive or cruel.

POLITICAL INQUIRY: *When the Constitution was written, imprisonment was viewed as cruel and unusual punishment of the convicted. Today, there is debate over whether the death penalty (capital punishment) is cruel and unusual. Whatever your opinion is of the death penalty itself, consider some of the techniques used by the government to put people to death. Are they cruel and unusual? Make a case for or against the use of lethal injection, for example.*

Amendment IX (1791)

The enumeration in the Constitution, of certain rights, shall not be construed to deny or disparage others retained by the people.

Amendment X (1791)

The powers not delegated to the United States by the Constitution, nor prohibited by it to the States, are reserved to the States respectively, or to the people.

> The Ninth Amendment acknowledges that there are additional rights, not listed in the preceding eight amendments, that the government cannot deny to citizens. The Supreme Court has interpreted the First Amendment, Fifth Amendment, and the Ninth Amendment to collectively provide individuals with a right to privacy.

> The Tenth Amendment acknowledges that state governments retain all authority they had before ratification of the Constitution that has not been delegated to the national government by the Constitution. This amendment was demanded by the Anti-Federalists, who opposed ratification of this Constitution. The Anti-Federalists feared that the national government would infringe on people's freedoms and on the authority of the state governments. The vagueness of the rights retained by the states continues to cause tensions and disputes between the state governments and the national government.

> The courts have interpreted this amendment to mean that federal courts do not have the authority to hear lawsuits brought by citizens against their own state or against another state, or brought by foreigners against a state.

Amendment XI (1795)

The Judicial power of the United States shall not be construed to extend to any suit in law or equity, commenced or prosecuted against one of the United States by Citizens of another State, or by Citizens or Subjects of any Foreign State.

Amendment XII (1804)

The Electors shall meet in their respective states and vote by ballot for President and Vice-President, one of whom, at least, shall not be an inhabitant of the same state with themselves; they shall name in their ballots the person voted for as President, and in distinct ballots the person voted for as Vice-President, and they shall make distinct lists of all persons voted for as President, and of all persons voted for as Vice-President, and of the number of votes for each, which lists they shall sign and certify, and transmit sealed to the seat of the government of the United States, directed to the President of the Senate;—The President of the Senate shall, in the presence of the Senate and House of Representatives, open all the certificates and the votes shall then be counted;—The person having the greatest Number of votes for President, shall be the President, if such number be a majority of the whole number of Electors appointed; and if no person have such majority, then from the persons having the highest numbers not exceeding three on the list of those voted for as President, the House of Representatives shall choose immediately, by ballot, the President. But in choosing the President, the votes shall be taken by states, the representation from each state having one vote; a quorum for this purpose shall consist of a member or members from two-thirds of the states, and a majority of all the states shall be necessary to a choice. And if the House of Representatives shall not choose a President whenever the right of choice shall devolve upon them, before the fourth day of March next following, then the Vice-President shall act as President, as in the case of the death or other constitutional disability of the President—The person having the greatest number of votes as Vice-President, shall be the Vice-President, if such number be a majority of the whole number of Electors appointed, and if no person have a majority, then from the two highest numbers on the list, the Senate shall choose the Vice-President; a quorum for the purpose shall consist of two-thirds of the whole number of Senators, and a majority of the whole number shall be necessary to a choice. But no person constitutionally ineligible to the office of President shall be eligible to that of Vice-President of the United States.

Amendment XIII (1865)

Section 1. Neither slavery nor involuntary servitude, except as a punishment for crime whereof the party shall have been duly convicted, shall exist within the United States, or any place subject to their jurisdiction.

Section 2. Congress shall have power to enforce this article by appropriate legislation.

Amendment XIV (1868)

Section 1. All persons born or naturalized in the United States and subject to the jurisdiction thereof, are citizens of the United States and of the State wherein they reside. No State shall make or enforce any law which shall abridge the privileges or immunities of citizens of the United States; nor shall any State deprive any person of life, liberty, or property, without due process of law; nor deny to any person within its jurisdiction the equal protection of the laws.

POLITICAL INQUIRY: *Recently some citizens and politicians have claimed that illegal immigrants and their children, who are citizens if they were born in the United States, cost the nation's taxpayers a great deal of money in public services guaranteed to all citizens, including public education. Argue for or against amending the Constitution to deny citizenship to those born in the United States to parents who are in the country illegally.*

Section 2. Representatives shall be apportioned among the several States according to their respective numbers, counting the whole number of

> The presidential election in 1800 ended with a tie in Electoral College votes between Thomas Jefferson and Aaron Burr. Because the candidate with the most votes was to become president and the candidate with the second highest number of votes was to become vice president, the tie meant that the job of selecting the president was turned over to the House of Representatives. The House selected Jefferson. Calls to change the procedure were answered by the enactment of this amendment. Today, each elector has two votes; one for a presidential candidate and one for a vice-presidential candidate. The presidential candidate who wins the majority of electoral votes wins the presidency, and the same is true for the vice-presidential candidate. If no presidential candidate wins a majority of the votes, the House selects the president. If no vice-presidential candidate wins a majority of the votes, the Senate selects the vice president.

> This amendment abolished slavery.

> This amendment extends the rights of citizenship to all those born in the United States and those who have become citizens through naturalization. States are prohibited from denying U.S. citizens their rights and privileges and must provide all people with due process before taking away their life, liberty, or pursuit of happiness. States must also treat all people equally and fairly. The courts have also used this section of the Fourteenth Amendment to require that states ensure citizens their protections under the Bill of Rights.

> This section of the Fourteenth Amendment is the first use of the term "male" in the Constitution. This section requires that if a state denies men over the age of 21 the right to vote, its representation in the House will be diminished accordingly. The Fifteenth Amendment makes this section unnecessary.

> The intent of this section was to prevent government officials who supported the Confederacy during the Civil War from serving in government. In 1898 Congress voted to eliminate this prohibition.

> All male citizens meeting their state's minimum age requirement are guaranteed the right to vote.

> This amendment authorizes the national government to establish taxes on personal and corporate income.

> Since the ratification of the Seventeenth Amendment in 1913, senators are elected by the citizens in each state rather than by state legislatures. The amendment also allows each state legislature to establish the process by which vacancies in the Senate will be filled, either through special election or by gubernatorial appointment.

persons in each State, excluding Indians not taxed. But when the right to vote at any election for the choice of electors for President and Vice President of the United States, Representatives in Congress, the Executive and Judicial officers of a State, or the members of the Legislature thereof, is denied to any of the male inhabitants of such State, being twenty-one years of age, and citizens of the United States, or in any way abridged, except for participation in rebellion, or other crime, the basis of representation therein shall be reduced in the proportion which the number of such male citizens shall bear to the whole number of male citizens twenty-one years of age in such State.

Section 3. No person shall be a Senator or Representative in Congress, or elector of President and Vice President, or hold any office, civil or military, under the United States, or under any State, who, having previously taken an oath, as a member of Congress, or as an officer of the United States, or as a member of any State legislature, or as an executive or judicial officer of any State, to support the Constitution of the United States, shall have engaged in insurrection or rebellion against the same, or given aid or comfort to the enemies thereof. But Congress may by a vote of two-thirds of each House, remove such disability.

Section 4. The validity of the public debt of the United States, authorized by law, including debts incurred for payment of pensions and bounties for services in suppressing insurrection or rebellion, shall not be questioned. But neither the United States nor any State shall assume or pay any debt or obligation incurred in aid of insurrection or rebellion against the United States, or any claim for the loss or emancipation of any slave; but all such debts, obligations and claims shall be held illegal and void.

Section 5. The Congress shall have power to enforce, by appropriate legislation, the provisions of this article.

POLITICAL INQUIRY: *According to the courts' interpretation, the Fourteenth Amendment prohibits discrimination under the law based on a person's race, religion, color, and national origin unless such discrimination is necessary for the government to accomplish a compelling public interest. However, the courts have allowed discrimination based on sex when a government successfully argues that the discrimination is substantially related to the achievement of an important public interest. Argue for or against amending the Constitution so that sex-based discrimination is treated the same as other forms of discrimination.*

Amendment XV (1870)

Section 1. The right of citizens of the United States to vote shall not be denied or abridged by the United States or by any State on account of race, color, or previous condition of servitude.

Section 2. The Congress shall have power to enforce this article by appropriate legislation.

Amendment XVI (1913)

The Congress shall have power to lay and collect taxes on incomes, from whatever source derived, without apportionment among the several States, and without regard to any census or enumeration.

Amendment XVII (1913)

The Senate of the United States shall be composed of two Senators from each State, elected by the people thereof, for six years; and each Senator shall have one vote. The electors in each State shall have the qualifications requisite for electors of the most numerous branch of the State legislatures.

When vacancies happen in the representation of any State in the Senate, the executive authority of such State shall issue writs of election to fill such vacancies: Provided, That the legislature of any State may empower the executive thereof to make temporary appointments until the people fill the vacancies by election as the legislature may direct.

This amendment shall not be so construed as to affect the election or term of any Senator chosen before it becomes valid as part of the Constitution.

Amendment XVIII (1919)

Section 1. After one year from the ratification of this article the manufacture, sale, or transportation of intoxicating liquors within, the importation thereof into, or the exportation thereof from the United States and all territory subject to the jurisdiction thereof for beverage purposes is hereby prohibited.

Section 2. The Congress and the several States shall have concurrent power to enforce this article by appropriate legislation.

Section 3. This article shall be inoperative unless it shall have been ratified as an amendment to the Constitution by the legislatures of the several States, as provided in the Constitution, within seven years from the date of the submission hereof to the States by the Congress.

> The "Prohibition" amendment—making it illegal to manufacture, sell, or transport alcoholic beverages in the United States—was widely disobeyed during the years it was in effect. The Twenty-First amendment repealed this amendment.

Amendment XIX (1920)

The right of citizens of the United States to vote shall not be denied or abridged by the United States or by any State on account of sex. Congress shall have power to enforce this article by appropriate legislation.

> All female citizens meeting their state's minimum age requirement are guaranteed the right to vote.

Amendment XX (1933)

Section 1. The terms of the President and Vice President shall end at noon on the 20th day of January, and the terms of Senators and Representatives at noon on the 3d day of January, of the years in which such terms would have ended if this article had not been ratified; and the terms of their successors shall then begin.

Section 2. The Congress shall assemble at least once in every year, and such meeting shall begin at noon on the 3d day of January, unless they shall by law appoint a different day.

> The first two sections of the Twentieth Amendment establish new starting dates for the president's and vice president's terms of office (January 20) as well as for members of Congress (January 3). Section 2 also decrees that the annual meeting of Congress will begin on January 3 unless Congress specifies a different date.

Section 3. If, at the time fixed for the beginning of the term of the President, the President elect shall have died, the Vice President elect shall become President. If a President shall not have been chosen before the time fixed for the beginning of his term, or if the President elect shall have failed to qualify, then the Vice President elect shall act as President until a President shall have qualified; and the Congress may by law provide for the case wherein neither a President elect nor a Vice President elect shall have qualified, declaring who shall then act as President, or the manner in which one who is to act shall be selected, and such person shall act accordingly until a President or Vice President shall have qualified.

Section 4. The Congress may by law provide for the case of the death of any of the persons from whom the House of Representatives may choose a President whenever the right of choice shall have devolved upon them, and for the case of the death of any of the persons from whom the Senate may choose a Vice President whenever the right of choice shall have devolved upon them.

Section 5. Sections 1 and 2 shall take effect on the 15th day of October following the ratification of this article.

Section 6. This article shall be inoperative unless it shall have been ratified as an amendment to the Constitution by the legislatures of three-fourths of the several States within seven years from the date of its submission.

> Sections 3 and 4 of this amendment establish that if the president elect dies before his or her term of office begins, the vice president elect becomes president. If the president elect has not been selected or is unable to begin the term, the vice president elect serves as acting president until the president is selected or is able to serve.

Amendment XXI (1933)

Section 1. The eighteenth article of amendment to the Constitution of the United States is hereby repealed.

Section 2. The transportation or importation into any State, Territory, or possession of the United States for delivery or use therein of intoxicating liquors, in violation of the laws thereof, is hereby prohibited.

Section 3. This article shall be inoperative unless it shall have been ratified as an amendment to the Constitution by conventions in the several States, as provided in the Constitution, within seven years from the date of the submission hereof to the States by the Congress.

Amendment XXII (1951)

Section 1. No person shall be elected to the office of the President more than twice, and no person who has held the office of President, or acted as President, for more than two years of a term to which some other person was elected President shall be elected to the office of the President more than once. But this Article shall not apply to any person holding the office of President, when this Article was proposed by the Congress, and shall not prevent any person who may be holding the office of President, or acting as President, during the term within which this Article becomes operative from holding the office of President or acting as President during the remainder of such term.

Section 2. This article shall be inoperative unless it shall have been ratified as an amendment to the Constitution by the legislatures of three-fourths of the several States within seven years from the date of its submission to the States by the Congress.

POLITICAL INQUIRY: *Critics of term limits in general argue that they are undemocratic because they may force out of office an official whom the voters want to keep in office as their representative. Other critics of term limits for the president argue that forcing out a popular, successful president during a time of war may be harmful to the nation. Argue for or against eliminating the two-term limit for the presidency.*

Amendment XXIII (1961)

Section 1. The District constituting the seat of Government of the United States shall appoint in such manner as the Congress may direct: A number of electors of President and Vice President equal to the whole number of Senators and Representatives in Congress to which the District would be entitled if it were a State, but in no event more than the least populous State; they shall be in addition to those appointed by the States, but they shall be considered, for the purposes of the election of President and Vice President, to be electors appointed by a State; and they shall meet in the District and perform such duties as provided by the twelfth article of amendment.

Section 2. The Congress shall have power to enforce this article by appropriate legislation.

Amendment XXIV (1964)

Section 1. The right of citizens of the United States to vote in any primary or other election for President or Vice President, for electors for President or Vice President, or for Senator or Representative in Congress, shall not be denied or abridged by the United States or any State by reason of failure to pay any poll tax or other tax.

Section 2. The Congress shall have power to enforce this article by appropriate legislation.

Amendment XXV (1967)

Section 1. In case of the removal of the President from office or of his death or resignation, the Vice President shall become President.

Section 2. Whenever there is a vacancy in the office of the Vice President, the President shall nominate a Vice President who shall take office upon confirmation by a majority vote of both Houses of Congress.

Section 3. Whenever the President transmits to the President pro tempore of the Senate and the Speaker of the House of Representatives his written declaration that he is unable to discharge the powers and duties of his office, and until he transmits to them a written declaration to the contrary, such powers and duties shall be discharged by the Vice President as Acting President.

Section 4. Whenever the Vice President and a majority of either the principal officers of the executive departments or of such other body as Congress may by law provide, transmit to the President pro tempore of the Senate and the Speaker of the House of Representatives their written declaration that the President is unable to discharge the powers and duties of his office, the Vice President shall immediately assume the powers and duties of the office as Acting President.

Thereafter, when the President transmits to the President pro tempore of the Senate and the Speaker of the House of Representatives his written declaration that no inability exists, he shall resume the powers and duties of his office unless the Vice President and a majority of either the principal officers of the executive department or of such other body as Congress may by law provide, transmit within four days to the President pro tempore of the Senate and the Speaker of the House of Representatives their written declaration that the President is unable to discharge the powers and duties of his office. Thereupon Congress shall decide the issue, assembling within forty-eight hours for that purpose if not in session. If the Congress, within twenty-one days after receipt of the latter written declaration, or, if Congress is not in session, within twenty-one days after Congress is required to assemble, determines by two-thirds vote of both Houses that the President is unable to discharge the powers and duties of his office, the Vice President shall continue to discharge the same as Acting President; otherwise, the President shall resume the powers and duties of his office.

Amendment XXVI (1971)

Section 1. The right of citizens of the United States, who are eighteen years of age or older, to vote shall not be denied or abridged by the United States or by any State on account of age.

Section 2. The Congress shall have power to enforce this article by appropriate legislation.

Amendment XXVII (1992)

No law varying the compensation for the services of the Senators and Representatives shall take effect, until an election of Representatives shall have intervened.

> The vice president becomes president if the president resigns or dies.

> The president can nominate a person to fill a vice-presidential vacancy. Congress must approve the nominee. President Richard Nixon appointed and Congress confirmed Gerald Ford to the vice presidency when Vice President Spiro Agnew resigned. When President Nixon resigned, Vice President Ford, who had not been elected, became president. He subsequently appointed and Congress confirmed Nelson Rockefeller to be vice president.

> If the president indicates in writing to Congress that he or she cannot carry out the duties of office, the vice president becomes acting president until the president informs Congress that he or she is again fit to resume the responsibilities of the presidency.

> If the vice president in concert with a majority of cabinet officials (or some other body designated by Congress) declares to Congress in writing that the president is unable to fulfill the duties of office, the vice president becomes acting president until the president claims he or she is again fit for duty. However, if the vice president and a majority of cabinet officials challenge the president's claim, then Congress must decide within three weeks if the president can resume office.

> The Twenty-Sixth Amendment guarantees citizens 18 years of age and older the right to vote.

> Proposed in 1789, this amendment prevents members of Congress from raising their own salaries. Approved salary increases cannot take effect until after the next congressional election.

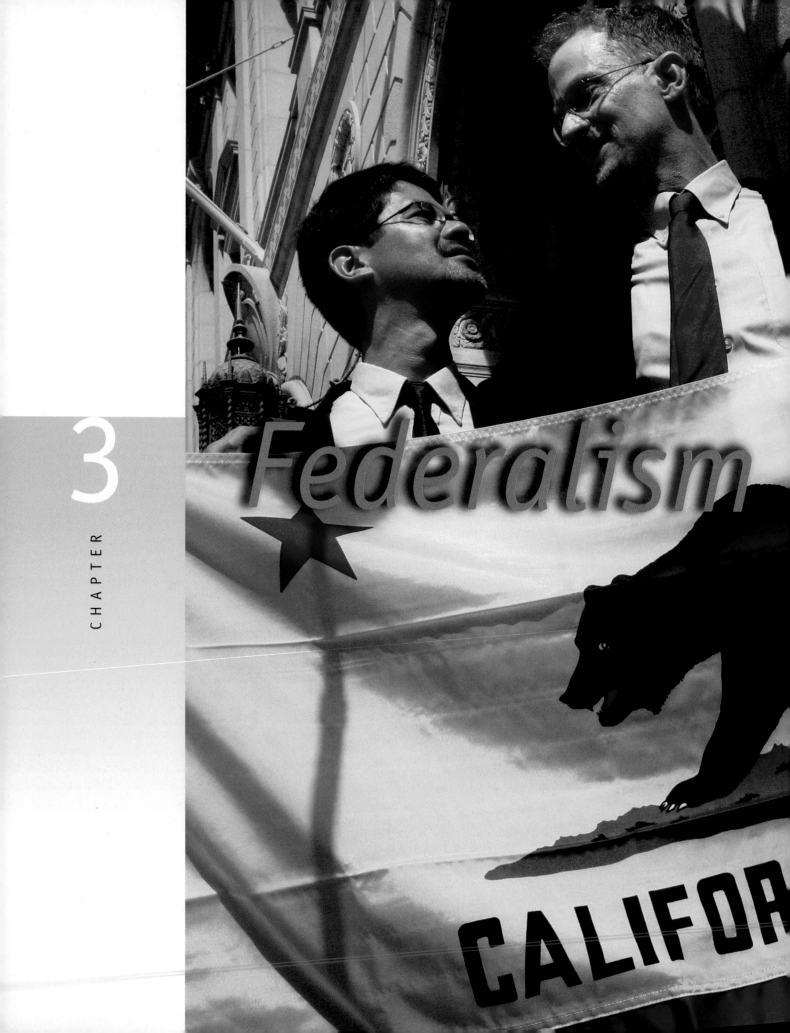

CHAPTER

3

Federalism

CALIFOR

THEN

The newly created national government and the preexisting state governments acted independently as they implemented the innovative federal system of government established in 1789.

NOW

National, state, and local governments challenge one another regularly over the proper interpretation of the Constitution's distribution of power in the federal system.

NEXt

Will Supreme Court justices continue to issue conflicting interpretations of federalism?

Will state and local governments continue their efforts to be laboratories for the creation of effective domestic policies?

Will intergovernmental relations evolve so that government can provide more efficient, effective public service?

This chapter examines the nature and evolution of the constitutional distribution of authority between the national and state governments in the U.S. federal system of government.

FIRST, we take an *overview of the U.S. federal system* and its distinct dual sovereignty.

SECOND, we explore the details of dual sovereignty by considering the *constitutional distribution of authority* between the national and state governments.

THIRD, we focus on the *evolution of the federal system* and see how national and state governments' power relationships have changed over time.

FOURTH, we survey the complex intergovernmental relations that dominate today's federalism: *intergovernmental relations.*

The framers of the Constitution

of the United States balanced their preference for a strong central government with their critics' calls for retaining state government authority over day-to-day matters by creating a system of government with dual sovereignty. That is, the Constitution established a new central government that would coexist with the existing state governments and distributed governing authority to these two levels of government—the national and the state—with each level having ultimate authority over different policy matters and different geographic areas. The framers called this new system of government a *federal system*. Because the federal system was a product of negotiation and compromise, as Chapter 2 explored, the constitutional language that distributes authority between the national and the state governments is not always clear.

Since the 1789 creation of the federal system, the number of governments in the United States has grown, as new states have joined the union and state governments have created local governments to help them serve their states' citizens better. Today, with more than 89,000 distinct governments in the United States—one national, 50 state, and over 89,476 local governments—and given vague constitutional language regarding the proper authority of national and state governments, the courts frequently must interpret the framers' intent with respect to the distribution of authority. Among the conflicts over jurisdiction that have reached the courts are disagreements over which level of government has the authority to set the legal drinking age, to establish gun-free school zones, to legalize the medical use of marijuana, and to determine which votes count in a presidential election.

Wherever you live in the United States, at least four or five governments collect taxes from you, provide services to you, and establish your rights and responsibilities. With so many governments in action, citizens who are interested in influencing public policies have many access points. Yet which government has the authority to address your concerns may not be clear to you. It may not even be clear to government officials. Ultimately, the Constitution, as interpreted by the U.S. Supreme Court justices, determines which government is responsible for which matters.

Even as the wrangling continues over the proper interpretation of the constitutional distribution of authority between governments, the U.S. national, state, and local governments engage every day in collaborative efforts to fulfill the complex, costly needs of the people whom they serve. Such intergovernmental efforts are essential in today's world. But they complicate attempts to clarify which level of government is ultimately responsible for which services and policies.

An Overview of the U.S. Federal System

federal system
a governmental structure with two levels of government in which each level has sovereignty over different policy matters and geographic areas

The U.S. Constitution established an unprecedented government structure characterized by a federal system of governance. A **federal system** has two constitutionally recognized levels of government, each with sovereignty—that is, ultimate governing authority, with no legal superior—over different policy matters and geographic areas. According to the Constitution, the national government has ultimate authority over some matters, and the state governments hold ultimate authority over different matters. In addition, the national government's jurisdiction covers the entire geographic area of the nation, and each state government's jurisdiction covers the geographic area within the state's borders. The existence of two governments, each with ultimate authority over different matters and geographic areas—an arrangement called dual sovereignty—is what distinguishes the federal system of government from the two other most common systems of government, known as unitary and confederal. The American colonists' experience with a unitary system, and subsequently the early U.S. citizens' life under a confederal system (1781–1788), led to the creation of the innovative federal system.

Unitary System

Colonial Americans lived under Great Britain's unitary system of government. Today, the majority of the world's nations, including Great Britain, have unitary governments. In a **unitary system,** the central government is sovereign. It can create other governments (regional governments) and delegate powers and responsibilities to them. The central government in a unitary system can also unilaterally take away any responsibilities it has delegated to the regional governments it creates and can even eliminate the regional governments.

Indeed, under Britain's unitary system of government during the American colonial period, the British Crown (the sovereign government) created colonial governments and gave them authority to handle day-to-day matters such as regulating marriages, resolving business conflicts, providing for public safety, and maintaining roads. As the central government in Britain approved tax and trade policies that harmed the colonists' quality of life, growing public discourse and dissension spurred the colonists to protest. It was the colonists' failed attempts to influence the central government's policies—by lobbying the king's selected colonial governors, sending petitions to the king, and boycotting certain goods— that eventually sparked more radical acts such as the Boston Tea Party and the colonists' declaration of independence from Great Britain.

unitary system
a governmental structure in which one central government has sovereignty, although it may create regional governments to which it delegates responsibilities

Confederal System

When the colonies declared their independence from Great Britain in 1776, each became an independent sovereign state and adopted its own constitution. As a result, no state had a legal superior. In 1777, delegates from every state except Rhode Island met in a convention and agreed to a proposed alliance of the thirteen sovereign state governments. In 1781, the thirteen independent state governments ratified the Articles of Confederation, the first U.S. constitution, which created a confederal system of government.

In a **confederal system,** several independent sovereign governments (such as the thirteen state governments in the American case) agree to cooperate on specified matters while each retains ultimate authority over all other governmental matters within its borders. The cooperating sovereign governments delegate some responsibilities to a central governing body. Each sovereign government selects its own representatives to the central governing body. The sovereign governments retain ultimate authority in a confederal system for the simple reason that they can recall their delegates from the central government at any time and can either carry out or ignore the central government's policies.

As detailed in Chapter 2, the effectiveness of the confederation created by the Articles of Confederation increasingly came into question. In February 1787, the national Congress passed a resolution calling for a constitutional convention "for the sole and express purpose of revising the Articles of Confederation" in order to preserve the Union. Clear-eyed about the failures of the unitary and confederal systems, the colonists decided to experiment with a unique government system—a federal system. The federal system created by the Constitution of the United States has succeeded in preserving the union for over 220 years.

confederal system
a structure of government in which several independent sovereign governments agree to cooperate on specified governmental matters while retaining sovereignty over all other governmental matters within their jurisdictions

Federal System

The state delegates who met in Philadelphia in 1787 drafted a new constitution that created an innovative federal system of government with dual sovereignty. The Constitution's framers established dual sovereignty by detailing a new, sovereign national government for

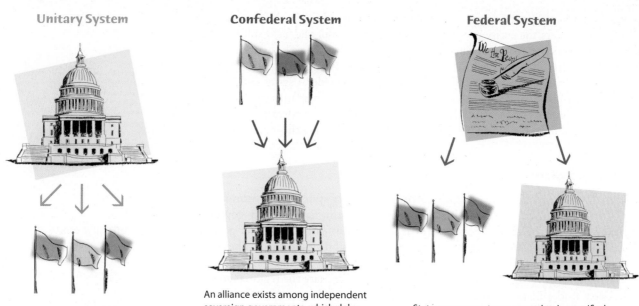

Unitary System	**Confederal System**	**Federal System**
The central government is sovereign, with no legal superior. It may create state governments and delegate legal authority to them. It can also eliminate such governments.	An alliance exists among independent sovereign governments, which delegate limited authority to a central government of their making. The independent sovereign governments retain sovereignty, with no legal superior, over all matters they do not delegate to the central government.	State governments are sovereign in specified matters, and a central (national) government is sovereign in other specified matters. The matters over which each government is sovereign are set forth in a constitution, which is the supreme law of the land. Dual sovereignty is the distinguishing characteristic of a federal system.

POLITICAL INQUIRY

FIGURE 3.1 ■ **Who is sovereign in a unitary system of government? In a confederal system of government? In a federal system of government? Which of the systems of government does the United States have, and why?**

the United States and modifying the sovereignty of the existing state governments. The national government thus created has no legal superior on matters over which the Constitution gives it authority, and the state governments have no legal superior on the matters over which they are granted authority by the Constitution.

Such dual sovereignty does not exist in unitary and confederal systems, where sovereignty is held by one level of government (the central government in a unitary system and the regional governments in a confederal system). Figure 3.1 compares the three types of governing systems. The European Union (EU), or United States of Europe, represents the most recent innovation in governmental systems. See "Global Context" for a look at this new governing system.

The federal system, as it works in the United States today, can be confusing—not only to citizens but also to elected officials and even Supreme Court justices. The confusion occurs because in addition to the one national and fifty distinct state governments that are operating in the country today, more than 89,000 local governments are functioning, even though the Constitution does not mention local governments.

It is state constitutions that authorize states to create local governments. State governments delegate some of their responsibilities to these local governments through legislation and/or the approval of a *charter*, which is a local government's version of a constitution. At the same time, state governments have the authority to take back delegated responsibilities and even to eliminate local governments. Because the state government retains ultimate authority over all the matters it delegates to its local governments and can eliminate its local governments, the relationship between a state government and its local governments is *unitary* (following a unitary system of governmental structure).

INTERGOVERNMENTAL RELATIONS (IGR)   To govern, a government must have the authority to formulate and approve a plan of action, to raise and spend money to finance the plan, and to hire workers to put the plan into action. In the U.S. federal system

GLOBAL CONTEXT

THE UNITED STATES OF EUROPE

Clearly not a unitary system, the European Union (EU) claims to be "more than just a confederation of countries, but . . . not a federal State." The principles, institutions, and power relationships of the EU have developed over the last fifty years through a series of treaties among European nations. The current twenty-seven EU member states have delegated some of their national sovereignty to several shared institutions (each with legislative, executive, and/or judicial functions) through a series of treaties, not in one single document such as the Constitution of the United States.

> **What are some potential future impacts of EU membership— good and bad—for EU member nations?**

Each European country that joins the EU has its own constitution and maintains its national sovereignty— with all inherent powers of sovereignty—in order to further its national interests. (Each state in the United States has its own constitution; however, the Constitution of the United States is the supreme law of the land and distributes sovereignty between the national government and the state governments.) Yet when a country joins the EU, it agrees to follow the decisions of the EU institutions, which focus on the collective interests of European nations.

The roots of the EU reach back to 1951. That year, six countries—Belgium, the Federal Republic of Germany, France, Italy, Luxembourg, and the Netherlands—signed a treaty establishing among themselves a common market for their coal and steel. By the 1960s, these six countries had signed additional treaties in which they expanded their common market to a wide range of goods and services, eliminated import taxes on one another's goods, and established common trade and agricultural policies. The success of those policies soon led to agreement on common social and environmental policies as well. Moreover, additional European countries joined what the world knew as the European Economic Community (EEC).

By 1990, twelve European countries belonged to the EEC, and they turned their attention to negotiating a new treaty to clarify the principles and the institutions of their government system. In 1992, the presidents and prime ministers of the EEC countries signed the Treaty on European Union, better known as the Treaty of Maastricht, for the Dutch city in which it was signed. The Treaty of Maastricht, which took effect in 1993, defines the foundations for the current EU institutions and the relationships among these bodies.

Originally, the collaborative efforts of European countries focused on a common European market for the sale of goods and services, as noted above. Today, however, EU policies range well beyond economic considerations. Indeed, the EU targets a wide range of policy areas, including environmental protection, public health, consumer rights, transportation, education, economic development, and fundamental human rights.

> Traditionally, the number twelve is a symbol of perfection, completeness, and unity. The circle of twelve gold stars on the European Union flag represents solidarity, harmony, and unity among the peoples and nations of Europe.

SOURCE: "Europe in 12 Lessons," *Europa*, http://europa.eu/abc/12lessons/index_en.htm.

---

today, the responsibility for these three elements of any given public policy—the policy *statement,* the policy *financing,* and the policy *implementation*—may rest entirely with one level of government (national, state, or local), or it may be shared in a collaborative effort by two or more of these levels. Political scientists label the collaborative efforts of two or more levels of government working to serve the public **intergovernmental relations (IGR).** The provision of elementary and secondary public education is an example of IGR.

Education is a policy matter that the U.S. Constitution reserves for the states. In all but four states, the state governments have created school districts—which are local-level governments—to provide elementary and secondary education. In providing education, the school districts implement national and state policy, as well as their own policy statements.

intergovernmental relations (IGR)

collaborative efforts of two or more levels of government working to serve the public

For example, Titles VI and IX of the national Civil Rights Act require equal educational opportunities for all children no matter their race, religion, ethnicity, color, or sex. The national Individuals with Disabilities Education Act mandates equal educational opportunity for all children no matter their disabilities. Among other policies, state laws determine what requirements an individual must meet to earn state certification to teach in public schools. State compulsory education laws determine for how many years, or until what grade, children must attend school. School districts determine policies for the day-to-day operations of elementary and secondary schools, including school dress codes, the hours of the school day, and discipline procedures.

All three levels of government provide some funding for elementary and secondary education. School districts collect property taxes from those who own property within the geographic area covered by the district. State governments grant money to each school district to supplement its property tax revenue. On average, state grants to school districts cover about 50 percent of the total cost of elementary and secondary education. Historically, the federal government provided grants to pay for less than 10 percent of elementary and secondary education costs. However, in 2009 the national government designated $4 billion for school reform efforts. Known as the Race to the Top Fund, these federal dollars were given to states to encourage and reward their creation of the conditions for education innovation and reform; their achievement of significant improvement in student outcomes; and their implementation of plans to improve student assessment, teacher effectiveness, and data collection.[1] State and federal grant money comes with rules and regulations that direct the policies and the actions of grant recipients.

School districts hire the personnel—teachers, custodians, coaches, librarians, cafeteria workers, principals, superintendents, and others—who implement national, state, and school district policies. The United States thus delivers the public service of elementary and secondary education through a complex network of intergovernmental relations wherein the three levels of government share policy making and financing, and the school districts dominate policy implementation.

We can measure the scope of IGR today by looking at the distribution of the workers whom national, state, and local governments hire to deliver specific public services. The graphs in Figure 3.2 show some policies that are purely national and several that are truly intergovernmental. Another gauge of the extent of IGR is the percentage of national grant money that state and local governments spend on the delivery of specific services. In 2007, federal grants to state and local governments made up 28 percent of all state and local expenditures.[2]

WHAT A FEDERAL SYSTEM MEANS FOR CITIZENS

For citizens, living in a federal system of government means that their legal rights and liberties and their civic responsibilities vary depending on where they live. The majority of U.S. citizens live under the jurisdiction of at least five governments: national, state, county (called *borough* in Alaska and *parish* in Louisiana), municipal or township, and school district. Each of these governments can impose responsibilities on the people living in its jurisdiction. The most obvious responsibility is to pay taxes. These taxes can include the national personal income tax; state sales and personal income taxes; and county, municipal, township, and school district property taxes. Each government can also guarantee personal liberties and rights. The Constitution lists individual liberties in the Bill of Rights. In addition, every state constitution has its own bill of rights, and some local governments offer further protections to their citizens. For example, some cities and counties prohibit discrimination based on an individual's sexual orientation, yet most states do not, nor does the national government.

Thus, the federal system can be confusing for citizens. It can also be confusing for the many governments created to serve the people. Which government is responsible for what services and policies? Because the Constitution of the United States is the supreme law of the land, it is to the Constitution that we must turn to answer that question. Yet constitutional language is not always clear. As we saw in Chapter 2, the framers hammered out the Constitution through intensive bargaining and compromise that produced a text that is often vague and ambiguous.

Also as discussed in Chapter 2, the U.S. Supreme Court has the authority to determine what the Constitution means and hence what is constitutional. This authority came from the Court's decision in the *Marbury v. Madison* case (1803), in which the justices established the principle of judicial review: the Court's authority to determine whether an action of any government operating within the United States violates the Constitution.[3]

Although the Supreme Court is the final interpreter of the Constitution, the Court's *constructions* (interpretations) have changed over time. For example, it is true that dual sovereignty—and therefore a federal system—still exists in the United States today, but the courts have interpreted the Constitution in such a way that the authority of the national government has expanded significantly over the last 220-plus years. In addition, the determination of which government has ultimate authority over specific matters has become even less clear because of the evolution of a complex arrangement of various levels of government working together to meet the various responsibilities that the Constitution delegates, implies, or reserves to them.

Later in this chapter, we consider this evolution of the U.S. federal system. Before we do, it is useful to examine the constitutional distribution of authority to the national and state governments.

Who Employs the Public Servants?

	National	State	Local
National defense	100%		
Postal service	100%		
Elementary & secondary education	1%		99%
Hospitals	14%	36%	50%
Higher education		81%	19%
Public welfare	2%	44%	55%
Police protection	14%	9%	77%
Streets & highways	1%	42%	57%
Air transportation	48%	3%	47%

POLITICAL INQUIRY

FIGURE 3.2 ■ **What proportion of employees working in the postal service is national? What proportion of employees working in elementary and secondary education is national? What explains the difference in these two cases?**

SOURCE: U.S. Census Bureau, "All Governments—Employment and Payroll by Function: 2006," www.census.gov/compendia/statab/tables/09s0444.pdf.

Constitutional Distribution of Authority

By distributing some authority to the national government and different authority to the state governments, the Constitution creates the dual sovereignty that defines the U.S. federal system. The Constitution specifically lists the several matters over which the national government has ultimate authority, and it implies additional national authority. The Constitution spells out just a few matters over which the state governments have authority. Part of the reason there is a lack of constitutional detail on state authority is that at the time of the Constitution's drafting, the states expected to retain their authority, except for matters that, by way of the Constitution, they agreed to turn over to the newly created national government.

To fulfill their responsibilities to their citizens, both the national and the state governments have the authority to engage in the functions inherent to all sovereign governments. This authority extends to the concurrent powers, the first topic in this section.

Concurrent Sovereign Authority

To function, sovereign governments need the authority to make policy, raise money, establish courts to interpret policy when a conflict arises about its meaning, and implement policy. These authorities are recognized as *inherent* to all governments—they are defining characteristics of governments. In the U.S. federal system, we designate these inherent governing functions as the **concurrent powers** because the national and the state governments hold these powers jointly and each can use them at the same time. For example, national and state governments make their own public policies, raise their own revenues, and spend those revenues to implement their policies. State governments delegate these authorities, in limited ways, to the local governments they create so that they can function as governments. (Figure 3.3 presents the number of local governments in each state.)

concurrent powers

basic governing functions of all sovereign governments, in the United States they are held by the national, state, and local governments and include the authority to tax, to make policy, and to implement policy

Number of Local Governments in Each State

WA 1,845
OR 1,546
ID 1,240
MT 1,273
ND 2,699
MN 3,526
WI 3,120
MI 2,893
NH 545
VT 733
ME 850
MA 861
NY 3,403
SD 1,983
WY 726
NE 2,659
IA 1,954
IL 6,994
IN 3,231
OH 3,702
PA 4,871
RI 134
CT 649
NJ 1,383
DE 338
MD 256
NV 198
UT 599
CO 2,416
KS 3,931
MO 3,723
KY 1,346
WV 663
VA 511
CA 4,344
AZ 645
NM 863
OK 1,880
AR 1,548
TN 928
NC 963
SC 698
TX 4,835
LA 526
MS 1,000
AL 1,185
GA 1,439
FL 1,623
AK 177
HI 19

POLITICAL INQUIRY

FIGURE 3.3 ■ What might explain the range in the number of local governments that exist in the fifty states? Do the states with the largest geographic area have the largest number of local governments? Are there regional patterns? Do states with smaller populations have fewer local governments?

SOURCE: www.census.gov/govs/cog/GovOrgTab03ss.html.

In addition to the inherent governing powers that the national and state governments hold concurrently, in the federal system of dual sovereignty, the national government and the state governments have sovereignty over different matters. We now consider these distinct sovereign powers.

National Sovereignty

The Constitution distributes powers that are (1) enumerated, or specifically listed, and (2) implied for the national government's three branches—legislative, executive, and judicial. For example, Article I of the Constitution enumerates (lists) the matters over which Congress holds the authority to make laws, including interstate and foreign commerce, the system of money, general welfare, and national defense. These matters are **enumerated powers** of the national government. The Constitution also gives Congress **implied powers**—that is, powers that are not explicitly described but may be interpreted to be necessary to fulfill the enumerated powers. Congress specifically receives implied powers through the Constitution's **necessary and proper clause,** sometimes called the **elastic clause** because the national government uses this passage to stretch its enumerated authority. The necessary and proper clause states that Congress has the power to "make all laws which shall be necessary and proper" for carrying out its enumerated powers.

Articles II and III of the Constitution also enumerate powers of the national government. Article II delegates to the president the authority to ensure the proper implementation of national laws and, with the advice and consent of the U.S. Senate, the authority to make treaties with foreign nations and to appoint foreign ambassadors. With respect to the U.S. Supreme Court and the lower federal courts, Article III enumerates jurisdiction over legal cases involving constitutional issues, national legislation, and treaties. The jurisdiction of the Supreme Court also extends to disagreements between two or more state governments, as well as to conflicts between citizens from different states. Figure 3.4 lists the national powers enumerated in Articles I, II, and III of the Constitution.

THE SUPREMACY CLAUSE The country's founders obviously anticipated disagreements over the interpretation of constitutional language and prepared for them by creating the Supreme Court. The Court has mostly supported the national government when states, citizens, or interest groups have challenged Congress's use of the necessary and proper clause to take on new responsibilities beyond its enumerated powers. Unless the Supreme Court finds a national law to be outside of the enumerated or implied powers, that law is constitutional and hence the **supreme law of the land,** as defined by the supremacy clause in Article VI of the Constitution: "This Constitution, and the laws of the United States which shall be made in pursuance thereof; and all treaties made, or which shall be made, under the authority of the United States, shall be the supreme law of the land." State and local governments are thereby obligated to comply with national laws that implement national enumerated and implied powers, as well as with treaties—including treaties with Native American nations.

NATIONAL TREATIES WITH INDIAN NATIONS Throughout U.S. history, the national government has signed treaties with Native American nations, which are legally viewed as sovereign foreign nations. As with all treaties, treaties with Native American nations are

enumerated powers
the powers of the national government that are listed in the Constitution

implied powers
powers of the national government that are not enumerated in the Constitution but that Congress claims are necessary and proper for the national government to fulfill its enumerated powers in accordance with the necessary and proper clause of the Constitution

necessary and proper clause (elastic clause)
a clause in Article I, Section 8, of the Constitution that gives Congress the power to do whatever it deems necessary and constitutional to meet its enumerated obligations; the basis for the implied powers

supreme law of the land
the Constitution's description of its own authority, meaning that all laws made by governments within the United States must be in compliance with the Constitution

NATIONAL POWERS

Punish offenses against the laws of the nation

Lay and collect taxes for the common defense and the general welfare

Coin and regulate money

Establish courts inferior to the U.S. Supreme Court

Raise and support armies

Administer the Capitol district and military bases

Declare war

Organize, arm, and discipline state militias when called to suppress insurrections and invasions

Provide for copyrights for authors and inventors

Regulate interstate and foreign commerce

Regulate the armed forces

Provide and maintain a navy

Establish standard weights and measures

Create naturalization laws

Punish the counterfeiting of money

Punish piracies and felonies on the seas

Develop roads and postal service

Define bankruptcy

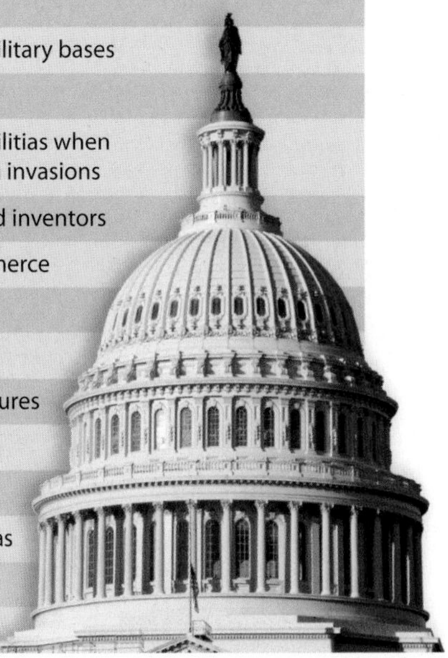

FIGURE 3.4

Enumerated Powers of National Government

supreme law with which the national government and state and local governments must comply. The core issue in the majority of these treaties is the provision of land (reservations) on which the native peoples could resettle after non-Indians took their lands during the eighteenth and nineteenth centuries. Today, the federal government recognizes more than 550 Indian tribes. Although most Native Americans no longer live on reservations—most native peoples have moved to cities—approximately three hundred reservations remain, in thirty-four states.[4] Figure 3.5 indicates the number of federally recognized tribes in each state.

Even though Indian reservations lie within state borders, national treaties and national laws, not state or local laws, apply to the reservation populations and lands. State and local laws, including laws having to do with taxes, crime, and the environment, are unenforceable on reservations. Moreover, Native American treaty rights to hunt, fish, and gather on reservations and on public lands supersede national, state, and local environmental regulations.[5]

With the exception of Native American reservations, state governments are sovereign within their state borders over matters the Constitution distributes to them. What are the matters that fall within state sovereignty?

State Sovereignty

The Constitution specifies only a few state powers. It provides the states with a role in national politics and gives them the final say on formally amending the Constitution. One reason for the lack of constitutional specificity regarding state authority is that the state governments were already functioning when the states ratified the Constitution. Other than those responsibilities that the states agreed to delegate to the newly created federal government through their ratification of the Constitution, the states expected to retain

FIGURE 3.5

Federally Recognized Indian Tribes and Groups

SOURCE: www.ncsl.org/?tabid=13278.

their sovereignty over all the day-to-day matters internal to their borders that they were already handling. Yet the original Constitution did not speak of this sovereignty explicitly.

POWERS DELEGATED TO THE STATES   The state powers enumerated in the Constitution give the states a distinct voice in the composition and priorities of the national government. Members of Congress are elected by voters in their home state (in the case of senators) or their home district (in the case of representatives in the House). Voters also participate in the election of their state's Electoral College electors, who vote for the president and the vice president on behalf of their state, as we saw in Chapter 2. Overall, state voters expect that the officials whom they elect to the national government will carefully consider their concerns when creating national policy. This is representative government in action.

In addition to establishing the various electoral procedures that give voice to state interests in the national policy-making process, the Constitution creates a formal means by which the states can ensure that their constitutional authority is not changed or eliminated without their approval. Specifically, the Constitution stipulates that three-fourths of the states (through votes in either their legislatures or special conventions, as discussed in Chapter 2) must ratify amendments to the Constitution. By having the final say in whether the supreme law of the land will be changed through the passage of amendments, the states can protect their constitutional powers. Indeed, they did just that when they ratified the Tenth Amendment (1791).

POWERS RESERVED TO THE STATES   The Constitution's extremely limited attention to state authority caused concern among citizens of the early American republic. Many people feared that the new national government would meddle in matters for which states had been responsible, in that way compromising state sovereignty. Citizens were also deeply concerned about their freedoms, corresponding to the protections listed in each state constitution's bill of rights. As described in Chapter 2, the states ratified the Bill of Rights, the first ten amendments to the Constitution, in response to those concerns.

The Tenth Amendment asserts that the "powers not delegated to the United States by the Constitution, nor prohibited by it to the states, are *reserved to the states* [emphasis added] respectively, or to the people." This **reserved powers** clause of the Tenth Amendment acknowledged the domestic matters over which the states had exercised authority since the ratification of their own constitutions. These matters included the ordinary, daily affairs of the people—birth, death, marriage, intrastate business, commerce, crime, health, morals, and safety. The states' reserved powers to protect the health, safety, lives, and property of their citizens are referred to as their **police powers.** It was over these domestic matters, internal to each state, that the states retained sovereignty according to the Tenth Amendment. In addition, state courts retained sovereignty over legal cases that involve their state's constitution and legislation (and that do not also raise issues involving the U.S. Constitution). Figure 3.6 summarizes the constitutionally reserved and enumerated powers of the states at the time of the Tenth Amendment's ratification.

The Tenth Amendment's affirmation of state sovereignty is brief and vague, and the Supreme Court continues to this day to resolve conflicts over its interpretation. New cases, leading to fresh interpretations, come before the Court when state governments challenge national laws that the states deem to infringe on their reserved powers but that the national government claims to fulfill its enumerated or implied powers. New interpretations by the Court also arise when the national government or citizens challenge the constitutionality of a state or local government action. Citizens, local

reserved powers
the matters referred to in the Tenth Amendment over which states retain sovereignty

police powers
the states' reserved powers to protect the health, safety, lives, and properties of residents in a state

STATE POWERS

Conduct local, state, and national elections

Establish republican forms of government

Build and maintain infrastructure (roads, bridges, canals, ports)

Administer family laws (e.g., marriage and divorce)

Establish criminal laws (except on the high seas)

Provide education

Tax estates and inheritance

Protect public health and safety

Regulate occupations and professions

Regulate intrastate commerce

Protect property rights

Regulate banks and credit

Establish insurance laws

Regulate charities

Conduct public works

Regulate land use

FIGURE 3.6

Constitutionally Delegated and Reserved State Powers

governments, state governments, and the national government persistently ask the courts to resolve constitutional conflicts in order to protect their liberties, their rights, and, in the case of governments, their sovereignty.

The Supreme Court's Interpretation of National versus State Sovereignty

McCulloch v. Maryland
established that the necessary and proper clause justifies broad understandings of enumerated powers

The landmark case of **McCulloch v. Maryland** (1819) exemplifies a Supreme Court ruling that established the use of the implied powers to expand the national government's enumerated authority.[6] The case stemmed from Congress's establishment of a national bank, and in particular a branch of that bank located in the state of Maryland, which the Maryland state authorities tried to tax. Attorneys for the state of Maryland argued that if the federal government had the authority to establish a national bank and to locate a branch in Maryland, then Maryland had the power to tax the bank. On a more basic level, Maryland's legal counsel asserted that Congress did not have the constitutional authority to establish a national bank, noting that doing so was not an enumerated power. Lawyers for the national government in turn argued that federal authority to establish a national bank was implied and that Maryland's levying a tax on the bank was unconstitutional, for it impinged on the national government's ability to fulfill its constitutional responsibilities by taking some of its financial resources.

The Supreme Court decided in favor of the national government. The justices based their ruling on their interpretation of the Constitution's necessary and proper clause and the enumerated powers of Congress to "lay and collect taxes, to borrow money . . . and to regulate commerce among the several states." The Court said that combined, these powers implied that the national government had the authority to charter a bank and to locate a branch in Maryland. In addition, the Court found that Maryland did not have the right to tax that bank, because taxation by the state would interfere with the exercise of federal authority. In addition to establishing that the necessary and proper clause justifies broad understandings of the enumerated powers, the Court affirmed once and for all that in the event of a conflict between national legislation (the law chartering the national bank) and state legislation (Maryland's tax law), the national law is supreme *as long as* it is in compliance with the Constitution's enumerated and implied powers.

> In 1995, the U.S. Supreme Court ruled the national Gun-Free School Zones legislation unconstitutional and affirmed that the Constitution reserves to the *states* the power to establish gun-free school zones. Notice the bilingual gun-free and drug-free school zone signs at this Phoenix, Arizona, school.

THE POWER TO REGULATE COMMERCE A few years later, in the case of *Gibbons v. Ogden* (1824), the Supreme Court again justified a particular national action on the basis of the implications of an enumerated power.[7] The *Gibbons* case was the first suit brought to the Supreme Court seeking clarification on the constitutional meaning of *commerce* in the Constitution's clause on the regulation of interstate commerce. The Court established a broad definition of commerce: "all commercial intercourse—meaning all business dealings." The conflict in this case concerned which government, New York State or the national government, had authority to regulate the operation of boats on the waterways between New York and New Jersey. The Court ruled that regulation of commerce implied regulation of navigation and that therefore the national government had authority to regulate it, not New York State.

Following the *Gibbons* decision, the national government frequently justified many of its actions by arguing that they were necessary to fulfill its enumerated powers to regulate interstate commerce, and the Court typically agreed. The case of *United States v. Lopez* (1995) is an example, however, of the Court's recent trend of being more critical of Congress's attempts to use the commerce clause to justify a national law.[8] The context for the case is the national Gun-Free School Zones Act of 1990, which mandated gun-free zones within a specified area surrounding schools. The lawyers for Alfonso Lopez, a twelfth-grader charged with violating this national law by bringing a .38-caliber handgun to school, successfully argued that the law was unconstitutional. The Court rejected the national government attorney's argument that the 1990 law was a necessary and proper means to regulate interstate commerce. Instead, the Court found that the law was a criminal statute, for which the state governments, not the national government, have authority.[9]

THE POWER TO PROVIDE FOR THE GENERAL WELFARE Another enumerated power that has expanded through Court interpretation of what the Constitution implies is the power of the national government to provide for the general welfare. The national government's landmark Social Security Act of 1935 was a response to the Great Depression's devastating impact on the financial security of countless Americans. The congressional vote to establish Social Security was overwhelmingly favorable. Yet the constitutionality of this very expansive program, which has become the most expensive national program, was tested in the courts shortly after its passage. In 1937, the Supreme Court had to decide: Was Social Security indeed a matter of general welfare for which Congress is delegated the authority to raise and spend money? Or was Social Security a matter for the state governments to address?[10] The Court found the national policy to be constitutional—a reasonable congressional interpretation, the justices wrote, of the enumerated and implied powers of the national government.

The Supreme Court's decisions in the *McCulloch, Gibbons,* and Social Security cases set precedents for the expansion of national power in domestic policy matters by combining the necessary and proper clause with such enumerated powers as the regulation of commerce and providing for the general welfare. The Court continues today to support Congress's use of the elasticity provided by the implied powers clause to expand its delegated powers. The Court also continues to protect national enumerated powers. Yet Congress does not always get its way, as the justices' decision in the *Lopez* case indicates.

In addition to establishing dual sovereignty and creating two independently operating levels of government, the Constitution enumerates some obligations that the national government has to the states—the topic to which we now turn.

National Obligations to the States

On August 27, 2005, the day before Katrina (a powerful category 3 hurricane) hit the Gulf Coast states, National Hurricane Center director Max Mayfield personally called the governors of Mississippi and Louisiana and the mayor of New Orleans. Mayfield wanted to be sure that these state and local officials understood the severity of the approaching storm.[11] That same day, President George W. Bush declared a national state of emergency for the area, and Mississippi governor Haley Barbour did the same for his state. Louisiana governor Kathleen Blanco had declared a state of emergency for her state the day before. New Orleans mayor Ray Nagin ordered a mandatory evacuation of the city's 485,000 residents.[12] Federal Emergency Management Administration (FEMA) director Michael Brown told state and local officials in the Gulf states that FEMA was ready with all available assistance and was "going to move quick . . . and going to do whatever it takes to help disaster victims."[13]

Even with this apparent readiness at all levels of government, the impact of Katrina's subsequent flooding in New Orleans because of a levee break was devastating: over 1,200 people dead, more than 1 million evacuees, and an estimated $200 billion-plus of damage.[14] The devastation prompted questions about the national government's obligations to local and state governments and to citizens in times of disaster. The Constitution describes several obligations that the national government has to the states, including assistance during times of domestic upheaval (see Table 3.1).

Department of Homeland Security (DHS) secretary Michael Chertoff explained four days after Katrina hit that the national government steps in "to assist local and state authorities. Under the Constitution, state and local authorities have the principal first line of response

> President George W. Bush, New Orleans Mayor Ray Nagin (to the left of the president), and Louisiana Governor Kathleen Blanco (far left, behind the mayor) visit with homeowner Ethel Williams, whose home was devastated by Hurricane Katrina. Federal, state, and local governments, as well as non-profit organizations receiving government funds and charitable donations, worked together to address Katrina's devastation.

TABLE 3.1

National Obligations to the States

The federal government:

- must treat states equally in matters of the regulation of commerce and the imposition of taxes
- cannot approve the creation of a new state from the property of an existing state without the consent of the legislatures of the states concerned
- cannot change state boundaries without the consent of the states concerned
- must guarantee a republican form of government
- must protect states from foreign invasion
- at their request, must protect states against domestic violence

obligation. DHS has the coordinating role, or the managing role. The president has, of course, the ultimate responsibility for all the federal effort here. I want to emphasize the federal government does not supersede the state and local government."[15]

There is no denying the national government's constitutional obligation to assist state and local governments in times of domestic upheaval. Yet does the national government have to wait for state or local officials to ask for help before it takes action? The Constitution is not clear about that question, and to date the courts have not rendered an interpretation on the matter.

State-to-State Obligations: Horizontal Federalism

Just as the Constitution establishes national obligations to the states, it also defines state-to-state obligations. In Article IV, the Constitution sets forth obligations that the states have to one another. Collectively, these state-to-state obligations and the relationships they mandate are forms of **horizontal federalism.** For example, state governments have the right to forge agreements with other states, known as **interstate compacts.** Congress must review and approve interstate compacts to ensure that they do not harm the states that are not party to them and the nation as a whole. States enter into cooperative agreements to provide services and benefits for one another, such as monitoring paroled inmates from other states; sharing and conserving natural resources that spill over state borders, such as water; and decreasing pollution that crosses state borders.

States also cooperate through a procedure called **extradition,** the legal process of sending individuals back to a state that accuses them of having committed a crime, and from which they have fled. The Constitution establishes a state governor's right to request the extradition of an accused criminal. Yet the courts have also supported governors' refusals to extradite individuals.

The Constitution asserts, too, that each state must guarantee the same **privileges and immunities** to all U.S. citizens—that is, citizens from other states who visit or move into the state—that it provides its own citizens. This guarantee does not prohibit states from imposing reasonable requirements before extending rights to visiting or new state residents. For example, states can and do charge higher tuition costs to out-of-state college students. In addition, in many states, new state residents must wait thirty days before they can register to vote. Yet no state can deny new state residents who are U.S. citizens the right to register to vote once they meet a reasonable state residency requirement.

Today, one very controversial state-to-state obligation stems from the full faith and credit clause of Article IV, Section 1, of the Constitution. The **full faith and credit clause** asserts that each state must recognize as legally binding (that is, valid and enforceable) the public acts, records, and judicial proceedings of every other state. For example, states must recognize the validity of out-of-state driver's licenses. Currently, public debate is ongoing about the impact of the full faith and credit clause on same-sex marriage contracts, and hence the constitutionality of the national Defense of Marriage Act (DOMA) of 1996, which allows states to determine whether they will recognize same-sex marriage contracts or same-sex civil union contracts legalized in other states. President Obama's Justice Department is also reviewing the constitutionality of DOMA.

The debates over same-sex marriage and civil unions raise several challenging constitutional questions. Because the Constitution is supreme, answers to those questions will eventually come from the Supreme Court's interpretation of the Constitution. Recently, the Supreme Court ruled that although the Constitution *is* the supreme law, state and local governments can guarantee their citizens more liberties and rights than are found in the Constitution, which guarantees only the required minimum.

> The Justice Department, under the direction of U.S. Attorney General Eric Holder, is tackling a variety of federalism questions as it considers the constitutionality of numerous pieces of state and national legistlation including the Defense of Marriage Act (1996), which allows states discretion in providing "full faith and credit" to same-sex marriage and civil union contracts made in other states.

The New Judicial Federalism

Political scientists use the phrase **new judicial federalism** to describe the practice whereby state judges base decisions regarding citizens' legal rights and liberties on their state constitutions when those laws guarantee more than the minimum rights or liberties enumerated in the U.S. Constitution. In fact, many state and local governments grant more liberties and rights than the Constitution guarantees, and can do so, according to the Supreme Court.

In *Pruneyard Shopping Center and Fred Sahadi v. Michael Robins et al.* (1980), the Court considered the case of a group of politically active high school students who had set up tables in a mall to hand out informational pamphlets and obtain signatures on a petition.[16] The pamphlets and petition dealt with opposition to the United Nations' stand on Zionism—that is, the existence of the Jewish state of Israel. After the owner of the shopping center asked the students to leave his private property, the students sued him on the basis of their belief that the California state constitution specifically protected their freedom of speech and expression, even in a privately owned shopping center. The Supreme Court agreed with the students that California's constitution gave its citizens more freedom of expression than the U.S. Constitution guaranteed, and judged that greater freedom to be constitutional.

New judicial federalism expands the authority of state governments in an era when the Supreme Court is ever more frequently being asked to clarify the constitutional distribution of authority. As we have seen, the delineation among national powers (enumerated and implied) and the states' reserved powers has never been clear. To complicate matters, over the course of U.S. history, national, state, and local governments' interactions have evolved into collaborative efforts whereby the creation, financing, and implementation of a given public policy are shared by two or more levels of government through intergovernmental relations. We now explore the evolution of intergovernmental relations in the U.S. federal system.

Evolution of the Federal System

Evolution is a slow and continuous change, often from the simple to the complex. The federal system established by the Constitution has evolved from a simple system of *dual federalism* to a complex system of intergovernmental relations characterized by *conflicted federalism*.

Evolution has occurred in the power relationship between the national government and the states, the state governments and their local governments, and the national government

horizontal federalism
the state-to-state relationships created by the U.S. Constitution

interstate compacts
agreements between states that Congress has the authority to review and reject

extradition
the return of individuals accused of a crime to the state in which the crime was committed upon the request of that state's governor

privileges and immunities clause
the Constitution's requirement that a state extend to other states' citizens the privileges and immunities it provides for its own citizens

full faith and credit clause
the constitutional clause that requires states to comply with and uphold the public acts, records, and judicial decisions of other states

new judicial federalism
the practice whereby state judges base decisions regarding civil rights and liberties on their state's constitution, rather than the U.S. Constitution, when their state's constitution guarantees more than minimum rights

and local governments. However, our focus here is on the evolution of the dual sovereignty established by the U.S. federal system of government. We first survey four types of federalism, characterized by four different power relationships between the national and the state governments, all of which continue to this day. We then explore various means by which the national government has altered the power relationship between it and the state governments.

Dual Federalism

dual federalism
the relationship between the national and state governments, dominant between 1789 and 1932, whereby the two levels of government functioned independently of each other to address their distinct constitutional responsibilities

Initially, the dual sovereignty of the U.S. federal system was implemented in such a way that the national and state governments acted independently of each other, as in political scientist Deil Wright's coordinate model of intergovernmental relations. (See "Analyzing the Sources.") Political scientists give the name **dual federalism** to this pattern of implementation of the federal system, whereby the national government takes care of its enumerated powers and the states independently take care of their reserved powers. From 1789 through 1932, dual federalism was the dominant pattern of national-state relations. Congresses and presidents did enact some laws that states argued infringed on their powers, and the Courts typically found in favor of the states in those cases. Yet as the 1819 *McCulloch* case shows, sometimes the Court ruled in favor of the national government.

Cooperative Federalism

grant-in-aid (intergovernmental transfer)
transfer of money from one government to another government that does not need to be paid back

A crippling economic depression that reached global proportions, known as the Great Depression, began in 1929. To help state governments deal with the domestic problems spawned by the economic collapse, Congress and President Franklin D. Roosevelt (1933–1945) approved numerous policies, collectively called the New Deal. Through those policies, the independent actions of national and state governments to fulfill their respective responsibilities evolved into cooperative efforts. **Grants-in-aid**—transfers of money from one level of government to another (also known as **intergovernmental transfers**)—became a main mechanism of President Roosevelt's New Deal programs.

The national grants of money offered to the state governments, and eventually also to local governments, during the Great Depression had few specific terms and conditions and did not need to be paid back. State and local governments welcomed the national grants, which assisted them in addressing the domestic matters that fell within their sovereignty while allowing them to make most of the specific program decisions to implement the policy. The era of federalism that began during the Depression, with its growing number of collaborative, intergovernmental efforts to address domestic matters reserved to the states, is the period of **cooperative federalism** (1932–1963), described by Wright's overlapping model. (See "Analyzing the Sources.")

cooperative federalism
the relationship between the national and state governments whereby the two levels of government work together to address domestic matters reserved to the states, driven by the policy priorities of the states

Centralized Federalism

centralized federalism
the relationship between the national and state governments whereby the national government imposes its policy preferences on state governments

By the time of Lyndon Johnson's presidency (1963–1969), a new kind of federalism was replacing cooperative federalism. In this new form of federalism, the national government imposed its own policy preferences on state and local governments. Specifically, in **centralized federalism,** directives in national legislation, including grant-in-aid programs with ever-increasing conditions or strings attached to the money, force state and local governments to implement a particular national policy. Wright's inclusive model comes closest to diagramming centralized federalism. (See "Analyzing the Sources.")

devolution
the process whereby the national government returns policy responsibilities to state and/or local governments

Presidents since Richard Nixon (1969–1974) have fought against this centralizing tendency by proposing to return policy responsibilities (policy making, policy financing, and policy implementation) to state and local governments. Presidents Nixon and Ronald Reagan (1981–1989) gave the name *new federalism* to their efforts to revert such obligations to state and local governments, and today we use the term **devolution** to refer to the return of policy responsibilities to state and local governments.

DEIL WRIGHT'S MODELS OF INTERGOVERNMENTAL RELATIONS IN A FEDERAL SYSTEM

The diagram below presents Deil Wright's models of intergovernmental relations in the United States.* The *coordinate model,* indicates that the relationship between the national government and state governments is one of independence. Each government has autonomy over its functions. The *overlapping model* shows the interdependent relationships among all three levels of government in the United States. Wright argues that the authority pattern in the overlapping model is based on bargaining between the national and the state governments. Finally, the *inclusive model* shows dependent relationships with a hierarchical pattern of authority.

*Deil Wright, *Understanding Intergovernmental Relations,* 3rd ed. © 1988 Wadsworth, a part of Cengage Learning, Inc.

Evaluating the Evidence

① Which of Wright's models do you think the Constitution's framers—the creators of the U.S. federal system—had in mind? Justify your selection.

② Which of Wright's models do you think best presents the relationships among the national, state, and local governments today? Explain.

③ Which model displays the relationships and pattern of authority that you believe will best serve you and your family? Justify your selection.

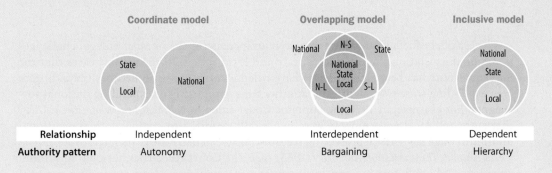

	Coordinate model	Overlapping model	Inclusive model
Relationship	Independent	Interdependent	Dependent
Authority pattern	Autonomy	Bargaining	Hierarchy

Republicans and Democrats (including presidents, members of Congress, and state and local lawmakers) broadly support devolution, but they debate *which elements of the policy-making process* should be devolved: policy creation, financing, and/or implementation. They also butt heads over *which policies* to devolve. The legislation and court decisions that result from these debates make for a complicated coexistence of dual federalism, cooperative federalism, and centralized federalism.

Conflicted Federalism

David B. Walker, a preeminent scholar of federalism and intergovernmental relations, uses the term **conflicted federalism** to describe today's national-state governmental relations, which involve the conflicting elements of dual, cooperative, and centralized federalisms.[17] Efforts to centralize policy making at the national level are evident, as are efforts to decentralize the implementation of national policies to the state and local levels. For some policy matters, the national and state governments operate independently of each other, and hence dual federalism is at work. For most policies, however, intergovernmental efforts are the norm. These efforts may be voluntary and a means to advance state policy priorities (cooperative federalism), or they may be compelled by national legislation (centralized federalism).

conflicted federalism
the current status of national-state relations that involve the conflicting elements of dual, cooperative, and centralized federalisms

> Benjamin Franklin's 1754 cartoon, displaying a rattlesnake cut in eight pieces and the phrase "Join, or Die," emphasized the need for the colonies to work together against threats by Native Americans. During the War for Independence, the cartoon became popular as a symbol of the need for colonies to unite. In 1775, the newly established U.S. Navy first flew the Gadsden Flag, which portrays a coiled rattlesnake with 13 rattles and the phrase "Don't Tread on Me," symbolizing the power and persistence of the united colonies. Today's Tea Party movement members, angered by a national government they perceive to be too involved in their lives and the economy—in violation of the founders' notion of federalism—have adopted the Gadsden Flag as a symbol of their patriotic anger.

The era of conflicted federalism, has seen an increase in the number of legal challenges to national legislation that mandates state and local action. In the various cases that the Supreme Court has heard, the justices have ruled inconsistently, sometimes upholding or even expanding state sovereignty and at other times protecting or expanding national sovereignty. For example, in 1976 the Supreme Court ruled in *National League of Cities v. Usery* that state and local governments were not legally required to comply with the national minimum wage law—hence protecting state authority.[18] Then nine years later, in the *Garcia v. San Antonio Transportation Authority* (1985) case, the Court ruled that national minimum wage laws did apply to state and local government employees—thus expanding national authority.[19]

Another policy matter that has been subject to conflicting Court decisions is the medical use of marijuana. California has fought an up-and-down battle with the national government over medical uses of marijuana. In 1996, California voters approved the Compassionate Use Act, allowing people to grow, obtain, or smoke marijuana for medical needs, with a doctor's recommendation. Then in 2001, the U.S. Supreme Court ruled that the national government could charge people who distributed marijuana for medical use with a crime, even in California, where the state law allowed such activity.[20] The Court interpreted the national supremacy clause to mean that national narcotics laws took precedence over California's law, which California had argued was grounded in the reserved powers of the states. But in 2003, the Court refused to review a case challenging a California law allowing doctors to recommend marijuana use to their patients.[21] As a consequence of the Court's refusal to take on the case, the decision from the lower court prevailed. The lower court's ruling had been that doctors could *not* be charged with a crime for recommending marijuana to patients. To add to the confused legal status of medicinal marijuana in California, the U.S. Supreme Court in 2005 upheld the right of the national government to prosecute people who smoke the drug at the recommendation of their doctors, as well as those who grow it for medical purposes.[22]

The confusion caused by conflicting Court decisions regarding medical marijuana has become even more problematic since October 2009, when President Obama's attorney general announced that the federal government will not prosecute individuals who are dispensing marijuana or who are using it in compliance with state law in one of the states that

has legalized such activities. How did the U.S. federal system evolve from dual federalism to today's conflicted federalism?

Landmarks in the Evolution of Federalism: Key Constitutional Amendments

Understanding the U.S. federal system's evolution from dual federalism to conflicted federalism requires a brief review of the tools the national government uses to expand its authority to direct state and local governments' domestic policies. Although the formal language of the Constitution with regard to the distribution of national and state sovereignty remains essentially as it was in 1791 (when the Tenth Amendment was ratified), three amendments—the Fourteenth, Sixteenth, and Seventeenth—have had a tremendous impact on the power relationship between national and state government. The Civil War, which was a catalyst for the ratification of the Fourteenth Amendment, also influenced the national-state power relationship.

THE CIVIL WAR AND THE POSTWAR AMENDMENTS   The military success of the northern states in the Civil War (1861–1865) meant the preservation of the union—the United States of America. The ratification of the Thirteenth Amendment (1865) brought the legal end of slavery in every state. In addition, the Fourteenth Amendment (1868), which extended the rights of citizenship to individuals who were previously enslaved, also placed certain limits and obligations on state governments.

The Fourteenth Amendment authorizes the national government to ensure that the state governments follow fair procedures (due process) before taking away a person's life, liberties, or pursuit of happiness and that the states guarantee all people the same rights (equal protection of the laws) to life, liberties, and the pursuit of happiness, without discrimination. In addition, the amendment guarantees the privileges and immunities of U.S. citizenship to all citizens in all states. Accordingly, since the Fourteenth Amendment's ratification, Congresses and presidents have approved national laws that direct the states to ensure due process and equal protection. This legislation includes, for example, laws mandating that all government buildings, including state and local edifices, provide access to all persons, including individuals with physical disabilities. In addition, the Supreme Court has used the Fourteenth Amendment to justify extending the Bill of Rights' limits on national government to state and local governments (under incorporation theory, which

Chapter 4 considers). And in *Bush v. Gore* (2000), the Supreme Court used the amendment's equal protection clause to end a controversial Florida ballot recount in the 2000 presidential election.[23]

Conducting elections is a power reserved for the states. Therefore, state laws detail how citizens will cast their votes and how the state will count them to determine the winners. In the 2000 presidential election, Democratic candidate Al Gore successfully challenged, through Florida's court system, the vote count in that state. The Florida State Supreme Court interpreted Florida election law to require the state to count ballots that it initially did not count. In response, Republican candidate George W. Bush challenged the Florida Supreme Court's finding by appealing to the U.S. Supreme Court. Lawyers for candidate Bush argued that Florida's election law violated the Fourteenth Amendment's equal protection clause by not ensuring that the state would treat each person's vote equally. The U.S. Supreme Court found in favor of candidate Bush, putting an end to the vote recount called for by the Florida Supreme Court. Candidate Bush became President Bush. (For more on the 2000 election, see Chapter 9.)

> A Broward County, Florida, election official attempts to determine whether there is a countable vote on this ballot during the 2000 presidential election. The Florida Supreme Court called for a recount of ballots in several counties, but the U.S. Supreme Court stopped the Florida recount, finding that the subjectivity of election officials determining which votes were countable violated the Constitution's equal protection clause.

THE SIXTEENTH AMENDMENT Passage of the Sixteenth Amendment (1913) powerfully enhanced the ability of the national government to raise money. It granted Congress the authority to collect income taxes from workers and corporations without apportioning those taxes among the states on the basis of population (which had been mandated by the Constitution before this amendment).

The national government uses these resources to meet its constitutional responsibilities and to assist state governments in meeting their constitutional responsibilities. Moreover, the national government also uses these resources as leverage over state and local governments, encouraging or coercing them to pursue and implement policies that the national government thinks best. Specifically, by offering state and local governments grants-in-aid, national officials have gained the power to determine many of the policies these governments approve, finance, and implement. For example, by offering grants to the states for highways, the federal government encouraged each state to establish a legal drinking age of 21 years (which we explore later in the chapter).

THE SEVENTEENTH AMENDMENT Before ratification of the Seventeenth Amendment in 1913, the Constitution called for state legislatures to select U.S. senators. By that arrangement, the framers strove to ensure that Congress and the president would take the concerns of state governments into account in national policy making. Essentially, the original arrangement provided the state legislatures with lobbyists in the national policy-making process who would be accountable to the states. Once ratified, the Seventeenth Amendment shifted the election of U.S. senators to a system of popular vote by the citizens in a state.

With that change, senators were no longer directly accountable to the state legislatures' because the latter no longer selected the senators. Consequently, state governments lost their direct access to national policy makers. Some scholars of federalism and intergovernmental relations argue that this loss has decreased the influence of state governments in national policy making.[24]

Further Evolutionary Landmarks: Grants-in-Aid

In 1837, the national government shared its revenue surplus with the states in the form of a monetary grant. But the government did not make a habit of such financial grants-in-aid until the Great Depression of the 1930s. Today, there is growing controversy over the strings attached to the various kinds of grants issued by the federal government.

categorical formula grant
money granted by the national government to state and local governments for a specified program area and in an amount based on a legislated formula

CATEGORICAL GRANTS Historically, the most common type of grant-in-aid has been the **categorical formula grant**—a grant of money from the federal government to state and local governments for a narrow purpose, as defined by the federal government. The legislation that creates such a grant includes a formula determining how much money is available to each grant recipient. The formula is typically based on factors related to the purpose of the grant, such as the number of people in the state in need of the program's benefits. The Census Bureau collects much of the data used in grant formulas through the decennial (occurring every ten years) census, which is mandated by the U.S. Constitution. (More than 400 billion grant dollars will be distributed based on the data collected in the 2010 Census.) Categorical grants come with strings—that is, rules and regulations with which the recipient government must comply.

One typical condition is a matching funds requirement, which obligates the government receiving the grant to spend some of its own money to match a specified percentage of the grant money provided. Matching funds requirements allow the national government to influence the budget decisions of state and local governments by forcing them to spend some of their own money on a national priority, which may or may not also be a state priority, in order to receive national funding.

Since the 1960s, the national government has also offered categorical project grants. Like the categorical formula grant, a **categorical project grant** covers a narrow purpose (program area), but unlike the formula grant, a project grant does not include a formula specifying how much money a recipient will receive. Instead, state and local governments interested in receiving such a grant must compete for it by writing proposals detailing what pro-

The National Decennial Census

THEN (1990)	NOW (2010)
State and local governments played a limited role in updating the Census Bureau address lists for the 1990 Census.	State and local governments are very involved in updating the Census Bureau address lists for the 2010 Census.
State and local governments played a limited role in educating people about, and encouraging people to complete, the Census.	State and local governments, as well as community organizations, are very involved in educating people about, and encouraging people to complete, the Census, with a focus on illegal immigrants.
One in six households received the long Census questionnaire, with 100 questions.	All households receive the same Census questionnaire, with 10 questions.
Respondents were instructed to select one of the listed races to define themselves.	Respondents are instructed to select all relevant races from the list to define themselves.

WHAT'S NEXT?

> Do you think the response rate for the 2010 Census will surpass the response rate of the 2000 Census? Explain your answer.

> Will state and local governments become even more involved in the Census in the future? Explain your answer.

grams they wish to implement and what level of funding they need. A categorical project grant has strings attached to it and typically offers much less funding than a categorical formula grant.

BLOCK GRANTS Another type of formula-based intergovernmental transfer of money, the **block grant,** differs from categorical formula and categorical project grants in that the use of the grant money is less narrowly defined by the national government. Whereas a categorical grant might specify that the money is to be used for a child care program, a block grant gives the recipient government more discretion to determine what program it will be used for within a broad policy area such as assistance to economically needy families with children. When first introduced by the Nixon administration in the 1970s, the block grant also had fewer strings attached to it than the categorical grants. Today, however, the number and the specificity of conditions included in block grants are increasing.

AMERICAN RECOVERY AND REINVESTMENT ACT OF 2009 In February 2009, President Obama and the 111th Congress enacted the American Recovery and Reinvestment Act (ARRA). The goal of the ARRA was to stimulate the nation's economy, which was in the depths of what some have called the Great Recession. The ARRA included

categorical project grant
money granted by the national government to state and local governments for a specified program area; state and local governments compete for these grants by proposing specific projects they want to implement

block grant
money granted by the national government to states or localities for broadly defined policy areas, with fewer strings than categorical grants, and in amounts based on complicated formulas

$499 billion in spending, $280 billion of which went to state and local governments through grants. Most of the money that was quickly distributed to state and local governments was in the form of categorical formula grants for specific government programs related to health, nutrition, and income security, such as unemployment. Where states had more discretion over the use of grant money, they used it to keep people employed or to create new jobs. For example, state and local governments used the grants to keep teachers and police officers on the job. Moreover, they created jobs in the construction industry by hiring private construction firms to do government construction projects. The federal government stimulus money in the form of competitive categorical project grants was distributed more slowly because state and local governments had to prepare proposals that made a case for the federal government to fund their projects. Categorical project grants provided funds for energy efficiency programs, broadband access, high-speed rail transportation projects, and educational reforms.[25]

State and local governments have grown dependent on national financial assistance, and so grants are an essential tool of national power to direct state and local government activity. Although the states welcome federal grant money, they do not welcome the strings attached to the funds.

STATE ATTEMPTS TO INFLUENCE GRANT-IN-AID CONDITIONS

State government opposition to the conditions attached to national grants came to a head in 1923 in the case of *Massachusetts v. Mellon*.[26] In this case, the Supreme Court found the conditions of national grants-in-aid to be constitutional, arguing that grants-in-aid are voluntary cooperative arrangements. By voluntarily accepting the national grant, the justices ruled, the state government agrees to the grant conditions. This 1923 Court decision was essential to the proliferation of national grants in subsequent years and to the evolution of federalism and intergovernmental relations as well. But the Court's decision did not end states' challenges to grant conditions.

In 1987, South Dakota challenged a 1984 national transportation law that penalized states whose legal drinking age was lower than 21 years. The intent of the national law was to decrease "drinking while intoxicated" (DWI) car accidents. States with legal drinking ages lower than 21 years would lose 10 percent of their national grant money for transportation. South Dakota argued that Congress was using grant conditions to put a law into effect that Congress could not achieve through national legislation because the law dealt with a power reserved to the states—determining the legal age for drinking alcoholic beverages.

In its decision in *South Dakota v. Dole*, the Court found that the national government could not impose a national drinking age because setting a drinking age is indeed a reserved power of the states.[27] Yet, the Court ruled, the national government could *encourage* states to set a drinking age of 21 years by threatening to decrease their grants-in-aid for highway construction. In other words, conditions attached to voluntarily accepted grants-in-aid are constitutional. Ultimately, the national policy goal of a 21-year-old drinking age was indeed accomplished by 1988—not through a national law but through a condition attached to national highway funds offered to state governments, funds on which the states are dependent. The national "encouragement" for states to establish 21 years as the legal drinking age is still controversial, as this chapter's "Thinking Critically About Democracy" section highlights.

Over time, the number and specificity of the grant conditions have grown. State and local governments have increasingly lobbied national lawmakers during the policy-making processes that create and reauthorize grants. One goal of this **intergovernmental lobbying** is to limit the grant conditions—or at least to influence them to the states' advantage. In other words, lobbyists for an individual state work to ensure that the conditions, including the grants' formulas, benefit that state. Beyond the efforts of lobbyists hired by individual states, coordinated lobbying on behalf of *multiple* states, municipal governments, and county governments is common.

If a state does not want to comply with a grant condition, then it need not accept the grant. The problem for state and local governments is that they have come to rely on national grant funds. In 2009 and 2010, almost half of state and local revenue came from national grants. However, after the ARRA grant money is distributed, the

> The Constitution reserves to the states the authority to establish the legal drinking age. However, the national government's grant-in-aid for highways requires states to set 21 years as the age when people can legally purchase alcohol, or the states risk losing a percentage of their highway grant dollars.

SHOULD STATE GOVERNMENTS LOWER THE MINIMUM LEGAL DRINKING AGE TO 18?

The Issue: The 1984 National Minimum Drinking Age Act mandated that any state that did not raise its minimum purchase and public possession of alcohol age to 21 years would lose 10 percent of its federal highway grants-in-aid. By 1988, all states had established 21 years as their minimum age for purchasing and public possession of alcohol. (Note that although it is illegal to sell alcohol to a person under the age of 21 in all states, most states allow parents to provide their children with alcohol in the privacy of their own homes.)[28] In 2009, John McCardell Jr., president emeritus of Middlebury College, and 135 college and university presidents issued the Amethyst Initiative. This initiative called on elected officials to support a public debate over the effects of the 21-year-old drinking age. The question, Should state governments lower the drinking age?, fuels the debate.

Yes: The traditional argument for lowering the minimum legal drinking age (MLDA) is that it is not moral or logical for governments to say that at the age of 18 citizens are responsible enough to vote, decide guilt or innocence as a juror in a trial, and take up arms for the nation, but they are not responsible enough to drink a beer. Other supporters of a lower MLDA argue that it will decrease the rate of binge drinking among college students, which has increased among college students, especially women, since the 1980s.

No: According to the National Institutes of Health, "since the early 1980s, alcohol-related traffic fatalities have been cut in half, with the greatest proportional declines among persons 16–20 years old." Moreover, the U.S. Department of Transportation estimates that increasing the drinking age to 21 years prevents 1,000 traffic deaths each year.[29]

Other approaches: McCardell and his supporters are calling on the federal government to provide a waiver of the 10 percent reduction in highway grants-in-aid penalty to states that participate in a pilot alcohol-education program coupled with an MLDA of 18 years. A certified educator, trained to cover alcohol-related legal, ethical, health, and safety issues, would teach the education program. Community involvement, such as attending DWI court hearings and establishing safe-ride programs, would complement in-class instruction. Students who successfully complete the program and pass a required final exam would receive a license entitling them to the same drinking privileges and responsibilities currently guaranteed to those 21 years of age and older.

What do you think?

1. What role, if any, do you think increased car safety (air bags, for example) had in the decrease of alcohol-related traffic fatalities since the early 1980s? Do you think seat-belt laws can explain some of the decrease? What factors, other than the change in MLDA, might help account for the decrease in alcohol-related traffic fatalities?

2. Other than an increase in binge drinking, what negative effects might you attribute to the states lowering MLDA to 18 years?

3. Does the fact that so many people under the age of 21 years drink threaten the legitimacy of the law or the authority of the government? Explain.

---

percentage of state and local revenue coming from the national government will probably decrease to what it was before the Great Recession, about 30 percent.[30] Because the national government has no constitutional obligation to offer grants-in-aid to state or local governments, intergovernmental lobbies persistently lobby Congress to ensure not only favorable grant formulas but also the survival of grants-in-aid on which state and local governments depend. They also lobby to prevent the passage of national laws mandating specific state and local actions.

Federalism's Continuing Evolution: Mandates

In our earlier analysis of the constitutional distribution of sovereignty, we considered specific examples of the Court's expansion of national authority through its decisions in cases involving conflicts over constitutional interpretation. The constitutional clauses most often questioned are

intergovernmental lobbying
efforts by groups representing state and local governments to influence national public policy

- the necessary and proper clause (Article I, Section 9)
- the national supremacy clause (Article VI)
- the general welfare clause (Article I, Section 8)
- the regulation of interstate commerce clause (Article I, Section 8)

With those Court decisions in hand, the national government is able to *mandate* certain state and local government actions. In addition, through a process known as *preemption*, the federal government can take away states' and localities' policy authority and impose its policy choices on state and local governments.

National **mandates** are clauses in national laws, including grants-in-aid, that direct state and local governments to do something specified by the national government. Many mandates relate to ensuring citizens' civil rights and civil liberties, as in the case of the mandate in the Rehabilitation Act of 1973 requiring that all government buildings, including those of state and local authorities, be accessible to persons with disabilities. When the national government assumes the entire cost of a mandate, it is a *funded mandate*. When the state or local government must cover all or some of the cost, it is an *unfunded mandate*.

Also common is the federal government's use of preemption. **Preemption** means that a national policy supersedes a state or local policy because it deals with an enumerated or implied national power. Therefore, people must obey, and states must enforce, the national law even if the state or local government has its own law on the matter.

The Supreme Court typically has supported the federal government's arguments that the national supremacy clause and the necessary and proper clause—coupled with the powers delegated to the national government to provide for the general welfare and to regulate interstate commerce—give the federal government the authority to force state and local governments to implement its mandates. The Court has also supported the national government's argument that it can attach conditions to the grants-in-aid it offers state and local governments, hence forcing those that voluntarily accept national grants to implement policies established by national lawmakers.

Today's Federalism: Intergovernmental Relations

In *Federalist* No. 45, James Madison argued that under the proposed Constitution, the states will retain "a very extensive portion of active sovereignty." More specifically, he notes that

> the powers delegated by the proposed Constitution to the federal government are few and defined. Those which are to remain in the State governments are numerous and indefinite. The former will be exercised principally on external objects, as war, peace, negotiation, and foreign commerce; with which last the power of taxation will, for the most part, be connected. The powers reserved to the several States will extend to all the objects which, in the ordinary course of affairs, concern the lives, liberties, and properties of people, and the internal order, improvement, and prosperity of the State.

How well does today's federalism match Madison's description of the federal system the Constitution would create?

There are signs of the dual federalism that Madison forecasted—the national and state governments acting independently to create, finance, and implement policies to fulfill their distinct constitutional responsibilities. The national government is undeniably the principal actor in the "external objects" of war, diplomacy, and international commerce. The national government creates, finances, and implements policies in these external matters. However, when we consider the internal objects reserved to the states, Madison's dual federalism is harder to find.

Several realities account for today's intergovernmental relations—the complex networks of national, state, and local governments' collaborative efforts—in domestic policy matters. Foremost is the reality that since passage of the Sixteenth Amendment and without a constitutional requirement to balance its budget, the national government is able to acquire the money needed to pay its expenses and a share of the expenses incurred by state and local governments. State constitutions mandate balanced state and local government bud-

mandates
clauses in legislation that direct state and local governments to comply with national legislation and national standards

preemption
constitutionally based principle that allows a national law to supersede state or local laws

gets, which limit the ability of state and local governments to engage in the level of long-term borrowing that the national government can incur. Voters in numerous states have used direct democracy procedures, which provide them the legal right to vote on public policies, to place limits on their state and local governments' abilities to increase taxes as well as increase expenditures. The combination of the national government's greater pool of resources and state governments' taxing and spending constraints help to explain **fiscal federalism**—the large number and size (in dollar value) of national grants-in-aid to state and local governments.

Federal grants may support innovative state and local programs targeting societal problems that face citizens throughout the nation, such as unemployment, poverty, hunger, and housing insecurity during times of severe economic downturns and air, land, and water pollution (cooperative federalism). Federal grants may also encourage state or local governments to change their laws and policies in support of national government priorities or preferences, such as changing their legal drinking age (centralized federalism).

In addition to using its financial resources to support or direct state and local policies, the national government has successfully used its enumerated and implied powers to create and expand its role in domestic policy matters. Supported by the U.S. Supreme Court in its interpretation of constitutionally enumerated and implied powers, and the national supremacy clause, the national government's policies extend to all the objects which, in the ordinary course of affairs, concern lives, liberties, and properties of people, and the internal order, improvement, and prosperity of the states and the local governments that the states create. Through preemption and mandates (funded and unfunded), state and local governments must work with the national government to help finance and implement national policy. Hence, when it comes to domestic matters, intergovernmental relations characterize today's federal system.

Knowing that they can benefit from federal grants, state and local governments perpetually lobby national policy makers in hopes of influencing the policies they will have to implement. At the same time, debates continue over the proper interpretation of the constitutional distribution of powers between the national and the state governments. State and local governments challenge national policies in the courts. The national government challenges state and local policies in the courts. Hence, the conversation about the proper interpretation of the federal system of government created by the U.S. Constitution continues today.

fiscal federalism
the relationship between the national government and state and local governments whereby the national government provides grant money to state and local governments

CONCLUSION

THINKING CRITICALLY ABOUT WHAT'S NEXT FOR FEDERALISM

Until recent decades, the pattern of Supreme Court interpretation of the distribution of constitutional power between the national and the state governments favored an expansion of the national government's enumerated and implied powers in domestic policy matters. However, the last few decades have witnessed inconsistency in the Court's interpretations. The Court protects and even expands national powers in some cases while protecting states' powers in other cases. Will U.S. Supreme Court Justices continue to issue conflicting interpretations of federalism?

Traditionally, state and local governments have been laboratories for domestic policies. Addressing long-term problems, such as poverty, and confronting new problems, such as global warming, while working within fiscal constraints, state and local governments have regularly experimented with innovative policies and programs. Federal grants-in-aid have supported, and sometimes even encouraged, state and local governments to work out solutions to domestic problems. Will state and local governments maintain their efforts to be laboratories for the creation of effective domestic policies?

The reality of federalism, as evidenced by the inadequate response to Hurricane Katrina, can be ineffective and inefficient. Governments can disagree on which government, if any, is responsible for addressing a problem. They may also disagree on what action needs to occur. Moreover, two or more levels of government may decide to act independently of each other, causing overlap in efforts and waste of resources. Will IGR evolve so that government can provide more efficient, effective public service?

Summary

1. An Overview of the U.S. Federal System
Dual sovereignty is the defining characteristic of the United States' federal system of government. Under a federal system, the national government is sovereign over specific matters, and state governments are sovereign over different matters. Today, it is often difficult to differentiate between national sovereignty and state sovereignty.

2. Constitutional Distribution of Authority
The vagueness of the U.S. Constitution's language providing for enumerated and implied national powers, reserved state powers, concurrent powers, and national supremacy has provoked ongoing conflict between the federal government and the states over the proper distribution of sovereignty. The U.S. Supreme Court has the final word on the interpretation of the Constitution—and hence the final say on national and state sovereignty.

3. Evolution of the Federal System
The Supreme Court's interpretations of the Constitution's distribution of authority have reinforced the ability of national officials to compel state and local governments to implement national policy preferences. Mandates and preemption, as well as conditions placed on voluntarily accepted national grants-in-aid, require states to assist in financing and implementing national policies. As a result, relations between the national government and the states have evolved from a simple arrangement of dual federalism to a complex system of intergovernmental relations (IGR).

4. Today's Federalism: Intergovernmental Relations
Federalism's dual sovereignty is clearly seen in the external matters delegated to the national government, such as war, diplomacy, and foreign commerce, but very difficult to identify in the domestic matters reserved to the state governments, which are dominated by intergovernmental relations.

Key Terms

block grant 101
categorical formula grant 100
categorical project grant 101
centralized federalism 96
concurrent powers 88
confederal system 83
conflicted federalism 97
cooperative federalism 96
devolution 96
dual federalism 96
enumerated powers 89
extradition 95
federal system 82

fiscal federalism 105
full faith and credit clause 95
grants-in-aid
    (intergovernmental
    transfers) 96
horizontal federalism 95
implied powers 89
intergovernmental
    lobbying 103
intergovernmental relations
    (IGR) 85
interstate compacts 95
mandates 104

McCulloch v. Maryland 92
necessary and proper clause
    (elastic clause) 89
new judicial federalism 95
preemption 104
police powers 91
privileges and immunities
    clause 95
reserved powers 91
supreme law of the land 89
unitary system 83

For Review

1. In terms of which government is sovereign, differentiate among a unitary system, a confederal system, and a federal system of government.

2. To which level of government does the Constitution distribute the enumerated powers? Implied powers? Concurrent authorities? Reserved powers? Provide several examples of each power and authority.

3. What matters fall within the scope of state sovereignty?

4. Differentiate among dual federalism, cooperative federalism, centralized federalism, and conflicted federalism.

5. How does the national government use grants-in-aid, mandates, and preemption to direct the policy of state and local governments?

6. What do we mean by intergovernmental relations (IGR)? Why is the term a good description of U.S. federalism today?

For Critical Thinking and Discussion

1. Is the federal system of government that provides citizens with the opportunity to elect a large number of officials each year a benefit or a burden for citizens? Explain your answer.

2. Would the amount of money citizens pay for their governments through taxes and fees decrease if there were fewer levels of governments serving them? Defend your answer.

3. Would the quality or quantity of government services decrease if there were fewer levels of government in the United States? Why or why not?

4. Note at least three societal problems you believe the national government can address best (more effectively and efficiently than state or local governments). Discuss why you believe the national government is best suited to address these problems. Do these problems fit in the category of enumerated national powers? Explain your answer.

5. Note at least three societal problems you believe state or local governments can address best (more effectively and efficiently than the national government). Discuss why you believe state or local governments are best suited to address these problems. Do these problems fit in the category of powers reserved to the states? Explain your answer.

MULTIPLE CHOICE: Choose the lettered item that answers the question correctly.

1. The characteristic that distinguishes a federal system of government from both a unitary and a confederal system is
   a. dual sovereignty.
   b. the existence of three levels of government.
   c. sovereignty held by only the central government.
   d. sovereignty held by only the regional governments.

2. The authorities to make policy, raise money, establish courts, and implement policy that are inherent to all governments are examples of
   a. concurrent powers.   c. implied powers.
   b. enumerated powers.   d. reserved powers.

3. The necessary and proper clause of the Constitution establishes the
   a. enumerated powers of the national government.
   b. implied powers of the national government.
   c. implied powers of the state governments.
   d. reserved powers of the state governments.

4. The authority to coin and regulate money, to regulate interstate and foreign commerce, and to make treaties with foreign nations (including Native American nations) are examples of
   a. concurrent powers.   c. implied powers.
   b. enumerated powers.   d. reserved powers.

5. The Supreme Court used implied powers to confirm the national government's authority to establish a national bank, and applied the national supremacy clause to deny state authority to tax branches of the national bank, in the case of
   a. *Gibbons v. Ogden.*   c. *Marbury v. Madison.*
   b. *United States v. Lopez.* d. *McCulloch v. Maryland.*

6. The state-to-state obligations detailed in the Constitution create state-to-state relationships known as
   a. centralized federalism.   c. dual federalism.
   b. cooperative federalism.   d. horizontal federalism.

7. The current debate over states' recognizing same-sex marriage contracts from other states may eventually force the Supreme Court to interpret the Article IV clause that concerns
   a. extradition.   c. interstate compacts.
   b. full faith and credit.   d. privileges and immunities.

8. The powers that the Tenth Amendment to the Constitution establishes are the
   a. enumerated powers.   c. implied powers.
   b. concurrent powers.   d. reserved powers.

9. Political scientists label today's federalism
   a. centralized federalism.
   b. conflicted federalism.
   c. dual federalism.
   d. horizontal federalism.

10. _____ provide(s) state governments with the most discretion over their policy actions (including policy formulation, policy financing, and policy implementation).
    a. National block grants
    b. National categorical grants
    c. National mandates
    d. National preemption

FILL IN THE BLANKS.

11. _____ is the name political scientists give to the collaborative efforts of two or more levels of government working to serve the public.

12. All national, state, and local laws must comply with the Constitution of the United States, for the Constitution is the _____ .

13. The practice whereby state judges base decisions regarding civil rights and liberties on their state constitutions, rather than on the U.S. Constitution, when their state constitution guarantees more than the minimum rights, is labeled _____ .

14. The national government has used the _____ clause of the Constitution, also known as the elastic clause, to stretch its enumerated powers.

15. Beginning in the 1970s, state governments and presidents began to respond to centralized federalism by calling for _____ , which is the return of policy creation, financing, and/or implementation to the state governments.

Answers: 1. a; **2.** a; **3.** b; **4.** b; **5.** d; **6.** d; **7.** b; **8.** d; **9.** b; **10.** a; **11.** Intergovernmental relations; **12.** supreme law of the land; **13.** new judicial federalism; **14.** necessary and proper; **15.** devolution.

RESOURCES FOR RESEARCH AND ACTION

Internet Resources

Bureau of the Census
www.census.gov Access the *Statistical Abstract of the United States* as well as other sources of data about national and state governments at this site.

Council of State Governments
www.csg.org This site is a place where state officials can share information on common problems and possible solutions.

National Conference of State Legislatures
www.ncsl.org/statefed/statefed.htm This site is dedicated to state-federal issues and relationships.

National Governors Association (NGA)
www.nga.org The NGA lobbies the national government on behalf of governors and also provides the governors with opportunities to share information on policies.

Internet Activism

Facebook
www.facebook.com/uscensusbureau Census Bureau Facebook, Blogs, Twitter, YouTube, and other social media channels allow visitors to interact with the agency and others, and encourage visitors to freely comment and give welcomed feedback.

Blog
http://ncsl.typepad.com/the_thicket/federalism/ This National Council of State Legislatures (NCSL) blog focuses on issues of federalism and their impacts on state governments.

Twitter
http://twitter.com/tenthamendment The Tenth Amendment Center works to preserve and protect states' rights and federalism through education about the Tenth Amendment to the U.S. Constitution.

YouTube
www.youtube.com/watch?v=dBdQP-8izDc The national president of Mothers Against Drunk Drivers (MADD) and the founder of Amethyst present two sides of the debate on lowering the minimum drinking age.

Recommended Readings

O'Toole, Laurence J. *American Intergovernmental Relations: Foundations, Perspectives, and Issues,* 3rd ed. Washington, DC: CQ Press, 2000. A collection of readings giving a comprehensive overview of U.S. federalism and intergovernmental relations, covering historical, theoretical, and political perspectives as well as fiscal and administrative views.

Rehnquist, William H. *The Supreme Court: Revised and Updated.* New York: Vintage Books, 2001. A history of the Supreme Court by the deceased chief justice, probing the inner workings of the Court, key Court decisions in the evolution of federalism, and insights into the debates among the justices.

Walker, David B. *The Rebirth of Federalism: Slouching Toward Washington,* 2nd ed. Washington, DC: CQ Press, 2000. Both a history of U.S. federalism and an assessment of the status of U.S. federalism today.

Movies of Interest

When the Levees Broke: A Requiem in Four Acts (2006)
This Spike Lee documentary critically examines the responses of federal, state, and local governments to Hurricane Katrina. Through images of the disaster, interviews with Katrina's victims, and clips of government officials' media interviews, Lee focuses on racial issues and intergovernmental ineptitude—from the poor construction of the levees to the delayed and inadequate federal, state, and local response.

Hoxie: The First Stand (2003)
This documentary presents one of the first integration battles in the South post-*Brown v. Board of Education of Topeka, Kansas.* The opponents are the Hoxie Board of Education, which in the summer of 1955 decided to integrate its schools, and grassroots citizens' organizations that resisted integration through petitions, harassment, and threats of violence against the school board members, their families, and the school superintendent.

Dances with Wolves (1990)
Sent to command the U.S. Army's westernmost outpost in the 1860s, Lieutenant John Dunbar witnesses, as an observer and a participant, the conflicts created in the Dakota Territory as white settlers encroach on territory of the Sioux Indians. Movie critics and historians praised Kevin Costner (the movie's director and lead actor) for correcting the erroneous image of Native Americans presented in classic Hollywood Westerns.

CHAPTER

4

Civil
Liberties

THEN

The Bill of Rights was designed to protect citizens' rights to speak and act without undue monitoring by or interference from the national government; however, Congress soon legislated exceptions to those protections.

NOW

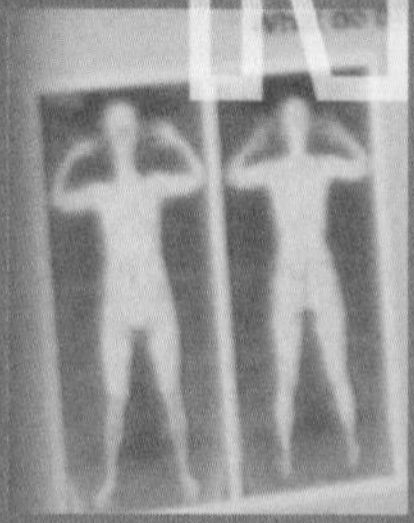

As part of a global war on terrorism, the national government increasingly monitors the words and actions of citizens and others, while people continue to protest and challenge governmental policies.

Will the Supreme Court uphold post-9/11 laws allowing the president to place terrorist suspects under surveillance without a court order?

Will airports and national security agencies further develop and deploy security systems based on methods such as thumbprint and eye-scan technology?

Will the Court uphold post-9/11 laws that require Internet providers to secretly share personal information about their clients with the FBI?

NEXT

The subject of this chapter is civil liberties, the personal freedoms that protect citizens from government interference and allow them to participate fully in social and political life.

FIRST, we discuss the protection of *civil liberties in the American legal system*—including the freedoms protected by the Bill of Rights, the application of those protections to state governments, and the tensions inherent within the Bill of Rights.

SECOND, we explore the *freedoms of speech, assembly, and the press: First Amendment freedoms in support of civic engagement.*

THIRD, we examine how the *freedoms of religion, privacy, and criminal due process* strengthen civil society by encouraging inclusiveness and community engagement.

FOURTH, we consider *freedoms in practice* by looking at *the controversy over the Second Amendment and the right to bear arms.*

FIFTH, we consider the changing nature of *civil liberties in post-9/11 America.*

A strong belief in civil liberties

is deeply embedded in our understanding of what it means to be an American. Civil liberties protect people from government intrusion and allow them to follow their own belief systems. Civil liberties also empower people to speak out against the government, as long as they do not harm others.

Since the nation's founding, political discourse among the people has often focused on the ideals of liberty and freedom. The colonists took up arms against Britain because the king and Parliament refused to recognize their liberties as English citizens—freedoms their counterparts in Great Britain took for granted: freedom of speech and assembly and the right to be free from unrestrained governmental power, especially in the investigation and prosecution of crimes. As scholar Stephen L. Carter noted, by declaring their independence, the colonists engaged in the ultimate act of dissent.[1] Withdrawing their consent to be governed by the king, they created a new government that would tolerate political discourse and disagreement and that could not legally disregard the collective or individual will of citizens.

Ideologies of liberty and freedom inspired the War for Independence and the founding of the new nation.[2] Those rights, though guaranteed, were never absolute. In fact, one of the early acts passed by Congress after the Bill of Rights was the Alien and Sedition Acts (1789), which not only limited immigration but also prohibited certain criticisms of the government. From its origins, the Constitution guaranteed basic liberties, but those protections were tempered by other goals and values, perhaps most importantly by the goal of order and the need to protect people and their property. Following the terrorist attacks of September 11, 2001, the national government enacted laws aimed at protecting American citizens and property from further attack. But those laws have had a dramatic impact on individual freedoms and rights, in some cases overturning decades of legal precedent in the area of civil liberties. Our civil liberties—though protected—have always been threatened, challenged, contested, and defended—especially during a time of war, when they are often most important.

Civil Liberties in the American Legal System

Civil liberties are individual liberties established in the Constitution and safeguarded by state and federal courts. We also refer to civil liberties as *personal freedoms* and often use the concepts of "liberty" and "freedom" interchangeably.

Civil liberties differ from civil rights. **Civil liberties** are constitutionally established guarantees that protect citizens, opinions, and property *against* arbitrary government interference. In contrast, civil rights (the focus of Chapter 5) reflect positive acts of government (in the form of constitutional provisions or statutes) *for* the purpose of protecting individuals against arbitrary or discriminatory actions. For example, the freedom of speech, a liberty established in the First Amendment to the U.S. Constitution, protects citizens against the government's censorship of their words, in particular when those words are politically charged. In contrast, the constitutionally protected right to vote requires the government to step in to ensure that all citizens be allowed to vote, without restriction by individuals, groups, or governmental officials.

civil liberties
constitutionally established guarantees that protect citizens, opinions, and property against arbitrary government interference

The Freedoms Protected in the American System

The U.S. Constitution, through the Bill of Rights, and state constitutions explicitly recognize and protect civil liberties. As Table 4.1 summarizes, the first ten amendments to the Constitution explicitly limited the power of the legislative, executive, and judicial branches of the national government.

The Bill of Rights established the freedoms that are essential to individuals' and groups' free and effective participation in the larger community. Consider how the absence of freedom to speak one's mind or the absence of protection against the arbitrary exercise of police powers might affect the nature and the extent of people's engagement in political and community debates and discussions. Without these protections, citizens could not freely express their opinions through rallies, speeches, protests, letters, pamphlets, public meetings, blogs, e-mail, and other forms of civic engagement. The Constitution's framers, who had been denied these liberties under British rule, saw them as indispensable to forming a new democratic republic.

The meanings of these precious freedoms have shifted over the course of U.S. history, as presidents, legislators, judges, and ordinary citizens have changed their minds about how much freedom the people should have. When Americans have not perceived themselves as being under some external threat, they generally have adopted an expansive interpretation of civil liberties. At those times, citizens tend to believe that the government should interfere as little as necessary in individuals' lives. Accordingly, they strongly support people's right to gather with others and to speak their minds, even when the content of that speech is controversial. When the nation has been under some perceived threat, citizens have often allowed the government to limit protected freedoms.[3] (See "Analyzing the Sources" on page 114.) Limits have also extended to many **due process** protections—legal safeguards that

due process
legal safeguards that prevent the government from arbitrarily depriving citizens of life, liberty, or property; guaranteed by the Fifth and Fourteenth amendments

TABLE 4.1

The Bill of Rights: Limiting Government Power

Amendment I: Limits on Congress	Congress cannot make any law establishing a religion or abridging the freedom of religious exercise, speech, assembly, or petition.
Amendments II, III, IV: Limits on the Executive	The executive branch cannot infringe on the right of the people to bear arms (II), cannot house soldiers in citizens' houses (III), and cannot search for or seize evidence without a legal warrant from a court of law (IV).
Amendments V, VI, VII, VIII: Limits on the Judiciary	The courts cannot hold trials for serious offenses without providing for a grand jury (V), a trial jury (VII), a fair trial (VI), and legal counsel (VI). The accused also have the right to hear the charges against them (VI), to confront hostile witnesses (VI), and to refrain from giving testimony against themselves (V); and they cannot be tried more than once for the same crime (V). In addition, neither bail nor punishment can be excessive (VIII), and no property can be taken from private citizens without "just compensation" (V).
Amendments IX, X: Limits	Any rights not listed specifically in the Constitution for the National Government are reserved to the states or to the people (X), and the enumeration of certain rights in the Constitution should not be interpreted to mean that those are the only rights the people have (IX).

ANALYZING THE SOURCES

BALANCING THE CONSTITUTIONAL TENSION

Two of the leading intellectuals of the Founding Era, Benjamin Franklin and Thomas Jefferson, have interpreted this tension between personal freedom and national security in different ways.

"Those who would give up essential liberty to purchase a little temporary safety deserve neither liberty or safety."

—Benjamin Franklin

"A strict observance of the written laws is doubtless one of the highest duties of a good citizen, but it is not the highest. The laws of necessity, of self-preservation, of serving our country when in danger, are of higher obligation." —Thomas Jefferson

Evaluating the Evidence

① Why is Jefferson easier to believe in times of war and Franklin in times of peace?

② How does the Constitution and its interpretation ensure that both views are kept at the forefront of the American consciousness?

prevent the government from arbitrarily depriving people of life, liberty, or property without adhering to strict legal procedures. In this chapter, we consider not only the historical context of our civil liberties but also recent changes in how Congress, the president, and the courts interpret these liberties.

The Historical Basis for American Civil Liberties: The Bill of Rights

The framers vividly remembered the censorship and suppression of speech that they had suffered under British rule. Colonists had been harshly punished, often by imprisonment and confiscation of their property and even death, if they criticized the British government, through both speech and the publication of pamphlets. The framers understandably viewed liberty as a central principle guiding the creation of a new democratic republic. Federalists such as Alexander Hamilton saw the Constitution itself as a bill of rights because it delegated specific powers to the national government and contained specific provisions designed to protect citizens against an abusive government (see Table 4.2).

The protections listed in Table 4.2 were designed to protect people from being punished, imprisoned, or executed for expressing political beliefs or opposition. However, the Anti-Federalists still stressed the need for a written bill of rights. As we saw in Chapter 2, the ratification of the Constitution stalled because citizens feared that the government might use its expanded powers to limit individual freedoms, particularly those associated with political speech and engagement. The First Amendment, which ensures freedom of religion, the press, assembly, and speech, was essential to political speech and to discourse in the larger society.

The freedoms embodied in the Bill of Rights are broad principles rather than specific prohibitions against governmental action. From the nation's beginnings, the vagueness of the Bill of Rights led to serious disagreement about how to interpret its amendments. For example, the First Amendment's establishment clause states simply that "Congress shall make no law respecting an establishment of religion." Some commentators, most notably Thomas Jefferson, argued that the clause mandated a "wall of separation between church and state" and barred any federal support of religion. Others more narrowly interpreted the clause as barring only the establishment of a national religion or the requirement that all public officials swear an oath to some particular religion. This disagreement about the breadth of the establishment clause is ongoing today, as courts and lawyers continue to try to determine what the proper relationship should be between church and state.

Other freedoms, too, have been subject to differing interpretations, including the First Amendment guarantees of freedom of speech, assembly, and the press. These conflicting interpretations often arise in response to public crises or security concerns. Security concerns also affect the protections offered to those accused of threatening the safety of the nation. For example, the USA PATRIOT Act, passed by Congress almost immediately after the September 11 attacks and amended in 2002, allows law enforcement a good deal of legal leeway. It permits agents to sidestep well-established rules that govern how searches and seizures may be conducted and to restrict criminal due process protections severely, particularly for persons suspected of involvement in organizations thought to have ties to

TABLE 4.2

Citizens' Protections in the Original Constitution

Clause	Protection
Article I, Sec. 9	Guarantee of *habeas corpus*—a court order requiring that an individual in custody be brought into court and told the cause for detention
Article I, Sec. 9	Prohibition of *bills of attainder*—laws that declare a person guilty of a crime without a trial
Article I, Sec. 9	Prohibition of *ex post facto laws*—retroactive laws that punish people for committing an act that was legal when the act was committed
Article III	Guarantee of a trial by jury in the state where the crime was committed

> According to the Supreme Court, public schools cannot sponsor religious activities, including teacher-led school prayer, without violating the First Amendment's establishment clause. Here, students at an Illinois high school bow their heads in student-initiated prayer. Does the ban on prayer in public schools violate the free exercise clause in your view?

Since September 11, 2001, the struggle to balance national security with civil liberties has become more dynamic. Here, demonstrators rally to demand the closure of Guantanamo Bay prison camp and end indefinite detention without charges or trial.

suspected terrorists. Civil liberties advocates worry that fear is causing Americans to give up their most precious freedoms.

Incorporation of the Bill of Rights to Apply to the States

The framers intended the Bill of Rights to restrict the powers of only the *national government*. They did not see the Bill of Rights as applicable to the state governments. In general, there was little public worry that the states would curtail civil liberties, because most state constitutions included a bill of rights that protected the individual against abuses of state power. Further, it was generally believed that because the state governments were geographically closer to the people than the national government, they would be less likely to encroach upon individual rights and liberties.

Through most of early U.S. history, the Bill of Rights applied to the national government, but not to the states. That assumption is illustrated by the case of *Barron v. Baltimore* (1833), in which a wharf owner named Barron sued the city of Baltimore. Barron claimed that the city had violated the "takings clause" of the Fifth Amendment, which bars the taking of private property for public use without just compensation. *Barron* argued that by paving its streets, the city of Baltimore had changed the natural course of certain streams; the resulting buildup of silt and gravel in the harbor made his wharf unusable. The case centered on the idea that the Fifth Amendment protects individuals from actions taken by both the national and the state or local governments. The Supreme Court disagreed, ruling that the Fifth Amendment was restricted to suits brought against the federal government.[4]

In 1868, three years after the Civil War ended, the Fourteenth Amendment was added to the U.S. Constitution. The Fourteenth Amendment reads as if it were meant to extend the protections of the Bill of Rights to citizens' interactions with *state governments:*

> No State shall make or enforce any law which shall abridge the privileges or immunities of citizens of the United States; nor shall any State deprive any person of life, liberty, or property, without due process of law; nor deny to any person within its jurisdiction the equal protection of the laws.

total incorporation
the theory that the Fourteenth Amendment's due process clause requires the states to uphold all freedoms in the Bill of Rights; rejected by the Supreme Court in favor of selective incorporation

selective incorporation
the process by which, over time, the Supreme Court applied those freedoms that served some fundamental principle of liberty or justice to the states, thus rejecting total incorporation

Although this language sounds like an effort to protect citizens' rights and liberties from arbitrary interference by state governments, the Supreme Court rejected the doctrine of **total incorporation:** that is, the application of *all* the protections contained in the Bill of Rights to the states. Instead, beginning with a series of cases decided by the Court in the 1880s, the justices formulated a narrower approach, known as **selective incorporation.**[5] This approach considered each protection individually, one case at a time, for possible incorporation into the Fourteenth Amendment and application to the states. In each case, the justices rejected the plaintiff's specific claims of protection against the state. But the Court held that due process mandates the incorporation of those rights that serve the fundamental principles of liberty and justice, those that were at the core of the "very idea of free government" and that were unalienable rights of citizenship.

Despite those early cases, the Supreme Court continued to embrace the idea that although citizenship meant being a citizen of a state and of the nation as a whole, the Bill of Rights protected citizens only against the national government. As Table 4.3 shows, not until 1925 did the Court gradually begin the process of incorporation, starting with the First Amendment protections most central to democratic government and civic engagement. That year, in the case of *Gitlow v. New York,* the Court held that freedom of speech is "among the fundamental personal rights and 'liberties' protected by the due process clause of the Fourteenth Amendment from impairment by the states."[6] In 1931, in its decision in

Selective Incorporation of the Bill of Rights

TABLE 4.3

Amendment	Liberty	Date	Key Case
I	Freedom of speech	1925	Gitlow v. New York
	Freedom of the press	1931	Near v. Minnesota
	Freedom of assembly and petition	1937	DeJonge v. Oregon
	Freedom to practice religion	1940	Cantwell v. Connecticut
	Freedom from government-established religion	1947	Everson v. Board of Education
II	Right to bear arms	2010	McDonald v. City of Chicago
III	No quartering of soldiers		Not incorporated
IV	No unreasonable searches and seizures	1949	Wolf v. Colorado
	Exclusionary rule	1961	Mapp v. Ohio
V	Right to just compensation (for property taken by government)	1897	Chicago, B&Q RR Co. v. Chicago
	No compulsory self-incrimination	1964	Malloy v. Hogan
	No double jeopardy	1969	Benton v. Maryland
	Right to grand jury indictment		Not incorporated
VI	Right to a public trial	1948	In re Oliver
	Right to counsel in criminal cases	1963	Gideon v. Wainwright
	Right to confront witnesses	1965	Pointer v. Texas
	Right to an impartial jury	1966	Parker v. Gladden
	Right to a speedy trial	1967	Klopfer v. North Carolina
	Right to a jury in criminal trials	1968	Duncan v. Louisiana
VII	Right to a jury in civil trials		Not incorporated
VIII	No cruel and unusual punishments	1962	Robinson v. California
	No excessive fines or bail		Not incorporated

Near v. Minnesota, the Court added freedom of the press, and in 1937 it added freedom of assembly to the list of incorporated protections.[7]

Incorporation progressed further with the landmark case of *Palko v. Connecticut* (1937), in which the Court laid out a formula for defining fundamental rights that later courts have used time and time again in incorporation cases, as well as in due process cases more generally. The justices found that fundamental rights were rooted in the traditions and conscience of the American people. Moreover, if those rights were eliminated, the justices argued, neither liberty nor justice could exist.[8] Judges in subsequent cases have used this formula to determine which Bill of Rights protections should be applied to the states. In case after case, the justices have considered whether such a right is fundamental—that is, rooted in the American tradition and conscience and essential for liberty and justice—and they have been guided by the principle that citizen participation in government and society is necessary for democracy in gauging the importance of each constitutionally protected right.

Over time, the Supreme Court has incorporated most Bill of Rights protections, as Table 4.3 summarizes. Among the few notable exceptions to the trend of incorporation are the Third Amendment's prohibition against the quartering of soldiers in citizens' homes, which has not been an issue since colonial times. The Fifth Amendment's provision for a grand jury indictment, whereby a panel of citizens determines whether or not there is enough evidence for prosecutors to bring a criminal case, runs counter to a trend in state criminal cases away from a reliance on grand juries; a grand jury is not required to guarantee that states adhere to Fifth and Sixth amendment protections during the arrest, interrogation, and trial of criminal defendants. Similarly, the Seventh Amendment's provision of a jury in a civil trial is widely viewed as less important than the Sixth Amendment's guarantee of a jury trial in criminal cases in which life and liberty may be at stake.

Freedoms of Speech, Assembly, and the Press: First Amendment Freedoms Supporting Civic Discourse

Civic discourse and free participation in the political process have certain requirements. As we consider in this section, an individual must be able to express his or her political views through speech, assembly, and petition. The person must also live in a society with a press that is independent of government censorship. Freedom of speech, assembly, petition, and the press is essential to an open society and to democratic rule. These freedoms ensure that individuals can discuss the important issues facing the nation and try to agree about how to address these matters. Scholars have referred to this sharing of contrasting opinions as the **marketplace of ideas.** It is through the competition of ideas—some of them radical, some even loathsome—that solutions emerge. Freedom of the press allows for the dissemination and discussion of these varying ideas and encourages consensus building.

marketplace of ideas
a concept at the core of the freedoms of expression and press, based on the belief that true and free political discourse depends on a free and unrestrained discussion of ideas

The marketplace of ideas enables people to voice their concerns and views freely and allows individuals to reconsider their ideas on important national and local issues. The centrality of the freedom of political expression to the First Amendment reflects the founders' belief that democracy would flourish only through robust discussion and candid debate.

The First Amendment and Political Instability

Over time, the Supreme Court has distinguished between political expression that the First Amendment protects and expression that the government may limit or even prohibit. The government has tried to limit speech, assembly, and the press during times of national emergency, when it has viewed that expression as more threatening than it would be in normal times.

THE TENSION BETWEEN FREEDOM AND ORDER A fundamental tension exists between the Bill of Rights, with its goal of protecting individual freedoms, and the government's central goal of ensuring order. Not even a decade had gone by after the Constitution's ratification when Congress passed the Alien and Sedition Acts (1798). These laws placed the competing goals of freedom and order directly in conflict. The Sedition Act criminalized all speech and writings judged to be critical of the government, Congress, or the president. This was just the first of many times in U.S. history that lawmakers sacrificed free speech and freedom of the press in an effort to ensure national security and order. For example, President Abraham Lincoln attempted to silence political dissidents during the Civil War by mandating that they be tried in military courts, without the due process protections afforded in a civilian court. Lincoln also suspended the writ of **habeas corpus** (Latin, meaning "you have the body"), an ancient right and constitutional guarantee that protects an individual in custody from being held without the right to be heard in a court of law.[9] Again, political dissidents were targeted for indefinite detention without trial. Whenever the nation has perceived itself under attack or threat, pressure has been placed on the government by some citizens to limit individual freedom to ensure societal order, and other citizens have pressured the government to maintain freedom while securing order.

habeas corpus
an ancient right that protects an individual in custody from being held without the right to be heard in a court of law

The struggle for a balance between freedom and order continues today as the United States fights a global war on terrorism. Part of the 1789 Alien and Sedition Acts, known as the Alien Enemies Act, empowered the president to deport aliens suspected of threatening the nation's security or to imprison them indefinitely.[10] After the September 11 terrorist attacks on U.S. soil, President George W. Bush invoked those same powers for enemy combatants, insurgents, and suspected terrorists captured in the United States or abroad. Like President Lincoln, President Bush also argued that military combatants and suspected ter-

THE ELECTION PROTESTS IN IRAN

Neda Agha-Soltan, a 27-year-old musician, became politically engaged for the first time after the 2009 presidential elections in Iran. Four hours after the polls closed on June 12, the Iranian government had announced the reelection of President Mahmoud Ahmadinejad, claiming he had received more than 60 percent of the 40 million paper ballots cast in the election. The leading opposition candidate, Mir-Hossein Mousavi, had been ahead in the polls before the election. During his campaign, he promised to reverse the country's hard-line policies and limits on civil liberties. Under President Ahmadinejad, authorities had curbed Internet access, shut down almost all liberal newspapers, jailed Iranian-American scholars, and kept activists under close surveillance and frequently summoned them for questioning.

How will technology affect the exercise of political liberties in Iran and around the world?

In addition to Mousavi, there had been several other candidates who boasted of substantial followings in the weeks leading to the election. As the outcome of the election was announced, protests erupted across Tehran and spread across the country. Mousavi challenged the outcome and declared himself the winner, suggesting that election irregularities were widespread. Almost immediately young people, women, moderate religious officials, and intellectuals took to the streets to demonstrate their opposition to Ahmadinejad. The police closed the universities in Tehran—detaining over 200 students—and arresting over 170 people in a crackdown on protests. The Supreme Leader Ayatollah Khamenei soon announced support for President Ahmadinejad, despite popular pressure to support a fair election. The Basij, a paramilitary force that supports Khamenei, joined the police and military in attacking and subduing the protesters; they have been accused of invading college dorms at night and destroying property, and they were filmed shooting into crowds.

As part of the crackdown against political protest, the government blocked citizens' cell-phone transmissions and access to such Web sites as Facebook, and they shut down text-messaging services. Despite those measures, messages reached the rest of the world, as protesters posted on international blogs, sent tweets, and downloaded video on YouTube and other sites as evidence of violence against the protesters. Opposition leaders claim that protesters were tortured and raped while in prison. Protesters in their turn attacked police, burned vehicles, and destroyed property.

On June 20th, on her way to a protest, Neda Agha-Soltan was killed as she stood beside her car. She was shot through the heart and died in the street; citizens nearby filmed her death and quickly posted the video on the Internet. Her death became a symbol of the abuses in Iran and inspired a call for continued protest. Because the Ahmadinejad administration had blamed outside forces for instigating rebellion, international journalists were banned from leaving their offices or from reporting stories on the protests. Despite that, over one hundred video clips of a July 20 protest were posted on the Internet. Regardless of governmental crackdown, arrests, and torture, protesting bloggers found ways to post and tweet continuously to the outside world what they were experiencing.

In the months following the election, the Iranian government has reported thirty-six deaths from the protests, but opposition leaders claim that twice as many deaths have resulted from government repression of protest. World humanitarian agencies have repeatedly called for investigation of the civil and human rights abuses resulting from this election. President Ahmadinejad was sworn into office in August 2009.

rorists should be tried in military tribunals and denied the protections of civilian courts, including the right to a speedy and public trial.[11] While the Obama Adminstration has moved to try some detainees in civilian criminal courts,[12] it has also been publicly struggling with the decision to retain Guantánamo detainees indefinitely without trials.[13]

THE HISTORICAL CONTEXT FOR FREE SPEECH LAWS   The Supreme Court's willingness to suppress or punish political speech has changed over time in response to perceived internal and external threats to the nation. During World War I, the Court upheld the conviction of socialist and war protester Charles Schenck for distributing a pamphlet to recently drafted men urging them to resist the draft.[14] For the first time, the Court created through its ruling a test to evaluate such government actions, called the **clear and present danger test.** Under this standard, the government may silence speech or expression only when there is a clear and present danger that such speech will bring about some harm that the government has the power to prevent. In the *Schenck* case, the Court noted that the circumstances of war permit greater restrictions on the freedom of speech than would be allowable during peacetime. The justices ruled that Schenck's actions could endanger the nation's ability to carry out the draft and prosecute the war.

Soon after the *Schenck* case, a majority of the justices adopted a far more restrictive test that made it easier to punish citizens for the content of their speech. This test, known as the **bad tendency test,** was extended in the case of Benjamin Gitlow, who was convicted of violating a New York State criminal anarchy law by publishing pamphlets calling for a revolutionary mass action to create a socialist government.[15] The political context of Gitlow's conviction is revealing: a so-called red scare—fears that the socialist revolution in the Soviet Union would spread to other nations with large populations of workers—was sweeping the nation. Gitlow's lawyer contended that there was no proof that Gitlow's pamphlet created a clear and present danger of a violent uprising. The Court disagreed, however, ruling that any speech that had the tendency to incite crime or disturb the public peace could be silenced.

This highly restrictive test required only that the government demonstrate that some speech may at some time help to bring about harm. The threat did not need to be immediate or even direct. The test sacrificed the freedoms of speech and the press to concerns about public safety and protection of the existing order. The bad tendency test lasted only a short while; by the late 1930s, the Court had reverted to the clear and present danger test, which the justices interpreted more broadly to protect speech and participation. The relative peace and stability of the period between the two world wars is apparent in the Court's handling of speech and press cases, as the justices required government officials to demonstrate that the speech clearly posed a danger to public safety.

Even after the Court reverted to the clear and present danger test, however, it still allowed concerns about national security to control its handling of First Amendment cases. In the wake of World War II, a war of conflicting ideologies emerged between the United States and the Soviet Union. Termed the *Cold War* because it did not culminate in a direct military confrontation between the countries, this development nevertheless created a climate of fear and insecurity in both nations. Concerns about the spread of communism in the United States led to prosecutions of individuals deemed to be sympathetic to communism and socialism under the Smith Act of 1940. This federal law barred individuals from advocating or teaching about "the duty, necessity, desirability, or propriety of overthrowing or destroying any government in the United States by force or violence."

In the most important case of this period, the Supreme Court upheld the conviction of several individuals who were using the writings of German philosophers Karl Marx and Friedrich Engels, along with those of Soviet leaders Vladimir Lenin and Josef Stalin, to teach about socialism and communism.[16] In upholding the convictions, the justices found that although the use of these writings did not pose a risk of imminent danger to the government, it created the *probability* that such harm would result. Because there was a probability that these readings would lead to the destruction of the government, the Court reasoned, the speech could be barred. The seriousness of the evil was key to the test that came out of this ruling, known as the **clear and probable danger test.** Because the government was suppressing speech to avoid the gravest danger, an armed takeover of the United States, the Supreme Court majority ruled that it was justified in its actions—even if the risk or probability of this result was relatively remote.

As the Cold War subsided and concerns diminished about a potential communist takeover of the United States, the Court shifted to a broader interpretation of the First Amendment speech and press protections. Beginning with *Brandenburg v. Ohio* (1969), the Court signaled that it would give more weight to First Amendment claims and less to government concerns about security and order. In this case, the Court considered the convictions of the leaders of an Ohio Ku Klux Klan group who were arrested after they made a speech at a televised rally, during which they uttered racist and anti-Semitic comments and showed guns and rifles. Local officials charged them with violating a state law that banned speech that disturbed the public peace and threatened armed overthrow. In overturning the convictions, the Court reverted to a strict reading of the clear and present danger test. The justices held that government officials had to demonstrate that the speech they sought to silence went beyond mere advocacy, or words, and that it created the risk of imminent disorder or lawlessness.[17]

THE STANDARD TODAY: THE IMMINENT LAWLESS ACTION TEST The *Brandenburg* test, known as both the **imminent lawless action test** and the **incitement test,** altered the clear and present danger test by making it even more stringent. Specifically, after the *Brandenburg* decision, any government in the United States—national, state, or local—trying to silence speech would need to show that the risk of harm from the speech was highly likely and that the harm was imminent or immediate. The imminent lawless action test is the standard the courts use today to determine whether speech is protected from government interference.

Even though the *Brandenburg* test is well established, the issue of whether speech is protected continues to be debated. For example, since the September 11 attacks, public attention has increasingly focused on Web sites operated by terrorists and terrorist sympathizers, especially members of militant Islamic groups. Some of these sites carry radical messages; for example, one site urges viewers to eliminate all "enemies of Allah" by any necessary means and gives instructions on loading weapons. Do First Amendment guarantees protect such sites? What about Web sites that encouraged property damage against offices of the Democratic Party after the health care reform bill passed? Courts examining this question must determine not only whether the speech intends to bring about a bad result—most would agree that intent exists—but also whether the speech incites lawless action that is imminent.

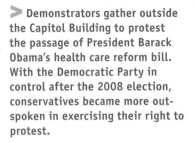

> Demonstrators gather outside the Capitol Building to protest the passage of President Barack Obama's health care reform bill. With the Democratic Party in control after the 2008 election, conservatives became more outspoken in exercising their right to protest.

imminent lawless action test (incitement test)
a standard established in the 1969 *Brandenburg v. Ohio* case whereby speech is restricted only if it goes beyond mere advocacy, or words, to create a high likelihood of imminent disorder or lawlessness

Freedom of Speech

The freedom to speak publicly, even critically, about government and politics is central to the democratic process. Citizens cannot participate fully in a political system if they are unable to share information, opinions, advice, and calls to action. Citizens cannot hold government accountable if they cannot criticize government actions or demand change.

PURE SPEECH VERSUS SYMBOLIC SPEECH The Supreme Court has made a distinction between pure speech that is "just words" and advocacy that couples words with actions. With respect to civic discourse, both are important. When speech moves beyond words into the realm of action, it is considered to be **symbolic speech,** nonverbal "speech" in the form of an action such as picketing or wearing an armband to signify a protest.

Unless words threaten imminent lawless action, the First Amendment will likely protect the speaker. But in civic discourse, words are often combined with action. For example, in the 1960s, antiwar protesters were arrested for burning their draft cards to demonstrate their refusal to serve in Vietnam, and public high school students were suspended from school for wearing black armbands to protest the war. When the two groups brought their cases to the Supreme Court, the justices had to determine whether their conduct rose to the level of political expression and merited First Amendment protection. Together, these cases help to define the parameters for symbolic speech.

In the first of these cases, *U.S. v. O'Brien,* the justices considered whether the government could punish several Vietnam War protesters for burning their draft cards in violation of

symbolic speech
nonverbal "speech" in the form of an action such as picketing, flag burning, or wearing an armband to signify a protest

commercial speech
advertising statements that describe products

the Selective Service Act, which made it a crime to "destroy or mutilate" those cards. The Court balanced the free expression guarantee against the government's need to prevent the destruction of the cards. Because the cards were critical to the nation's ability to raise an army, the Court ruled that the government had a compelling interest in preventing their destruction. Moreover, because the government had passed the Selective Service Act to facilitate the draft and not to suppress speech, the impact of the law on speech was incidental. When the justices balanced the government's interest in making it easy to raise an army against the incidental impact that this law had on speech, they found that the government's interest overrode that of the political protesters.[18]

In contrast, when the Court considered the other symbolic speech case of this era, *Tinker v. Des Moines,* they found that the First Amendment did protect the speech in question. In this case, the justices ruled that the political expression in the form of the students' wearing black armbands to school to protest the Vietnam War was protected.[19] On what basis did the justices distinguish the armbands in the *Tinker* case from the draft cards in the *O'Brien* case? They cited legitimate reasons for the government to ban the burning of draft cards: in a time of war, the cards were especially important to aid in the military draft. But there were no comparable reasons to ban the wearing of armbands, apart from the school district's desire to curb or suppress political expression on school grounds. School officials could not show that the armbands had disrupted normal school activities.[20] For that reason, the Court argued, the symbolic speech in *Tinker* warranted more protection than that in *O'Brien.*

The highly controversial case of *Texas v. Johnson* (1989) tested the Court's commitment to protecting symbolic speech of a highly unpopular nature. At issue was a man's conviction under state law for burning the American flag during the Republican National Convention in 1984 to emphasize his disagreement with the policies of the administration of President Ronald Reagan (1981–1989). The Supreme Court overturned the man's conviction, finding that the flag burning was political speech worthy of protection under the First Amendment.[21] After the *Johnson* decision, Congress quickly passed the Flag Protection Act in an attempt to reverse the Court's ruling. Subsequently, however, in the case of *U.S. v. Eichman* (1990), the Court struck down the new law by the same 5–4 majority as in the *Johnson* ruling.[22]

The decisions in these flag-burning cases were very controversial and have prompted Congress to pursue the only remaining legal avenue to enact flag protection statutes—a constitutional amendment. Indeed, each Congress since the *Johnson* decision has considered creating a flag-desecration amendment. Every other year from 1995 to 2006, the proposed amendment has received the two-thirds majority necessary for approval in the U.S. House of Representatives, but it has consistently failed to achieve the same constitutionally required supermajority vote in the U.S. Senate. Senate opponents of the ban argue that ratification of the amendment would undermine the principles bolstering the meaning of the flag. Although the amendment is still regularly proposed in both houses, in recent years it has not moved from committee consideration to a vote on the floor.

> Here, anti-war demonstrators exercise their right to free speech and assembly, protesting the war in Iraq. Protected speech can be verbal or symbolic, as in the alteration to the American flag below.

NOT ALL SPEECH IS CREATED EQUAL: UNPROTECTED SPEECH

The Supreme Court long ago rejected the extreme view that all speech should be free in the United States. Whereas *political speech* tends to be protected against government suppression, other forms of speech can be limited or prohibited.

The courts afford **commercial speech,** that is, advertising statements, limited protection under the First Amendment. According to the Supreme Court, commercial speech may be restricted as long as the restriction "seeks to implement a substantial government interest, directly advances that interest, and goes no further than necessary to accomplish its objective." Restrictions on tobacco advertising, for example, limit free speech in the interest of protecting the health of society. In 2010, the Supreme Court, in the controversial *Citizens United v. Federal Elections Commission* decision, revised its previous rulings and determined that the First Amendment also protected corporate spending during elections as a form of free speech. Legislation that limits such spending was an unconstitutional banning of political speech.[23]

Other forms of speech, including libel and slander, receive no protection under the First Amendment. **Libel** (written statements) and **slander** (verbal statements) are false statements that harm the reputation of another person. To qualify as libel or slander, the defamatory statement must be made publicly and with fault, meaning that reporters, for example, must undertake reasonable efforts to verify allegations. The statement must extend beyond mere name-calling or insults that cannot be proven true or false. Those who take a legal action on the grounds that they are victims of libel or slander, such as government officials, celebrities, and people involved with specific public controversies, are required to prove that the defendant acted with malice—with knowledge that the statement was false or recklessly disregarded the truth or falsity of the statement.

Obscenity, indecent or offensive speech or expression, is another form of speech that is not protected under the First Amendment. After many unsuccessful attempts to define obscenity, in 1973 the Supreme Court developed a three-part test in *Miller v. California.*[24] The Court ruled that a book, a film, or another form of expression is legally obscene if

- the average person applying contemporary standards finds that the work taken as a whole appeals to the prurient interest—that is, tends to excite unwholesome sexual desire
- the work depicts or describes, in a patently offensive way, a form of sexual conduct specifically prohibited by an antiobscenity law
- the work taken as a whole lacks serious literary, artistic, political, or scientific value

Of course, these standards do not guarantee that people will agree upon what materials are obscene. What is obscene to some may be acceptable to others. For that reason, the Court has been reluctant to limit free speech, even in the most controversial cases.

The Court may also ban speech known as **fighting words**—speech that inflicts injury or results in public disorder. The Court first articulated the fighting-words doctrine in *Chaplinsky v. New Hampshire* (1942). Walter Chaplinsky was convicted of violating a New Hampshire statute that prohibited the use of offensive, insulting language toward persons in public places after he made several inflammatory comments to a city official. The Court, in upholding the statute as constitutional, explained the limits of free speech: "These include the lewd and obscene, the profane, the libelous, and the insulting or fighting words—those which by their very utterance inflict injury or tend to incite an immediate breach of the peace."[25] Thus the Court ruled that, like slander, libel, and obscenity, "fighting words" do not advance the democratic goals of free speech. Cross burning, for example, has been a form of symbolic speech that in the United States has come to represent racial violence and intimidation against African Americans and other vulnerable groups. In 2005, the Supreme Court in *Virginia v. Black* found that a state could ban cross burning when it was used to threaten or attempt to silence other individuals, but that the state law could not assume all cross burnings attempt to communicate that message.

Even the types of "unprotected speech" we have considered enjoy broad protection under the law. Although cigarette ads are banned from television, many products are sold through every media outlet imaginable. Though a tabloid such as the *National Inquirer* sometimes faces lawsuits for the false stories it prints, most celebrities do not pursue legal action because of the high burden of proving that the paper knew the story was false, intended to damage the subject's reputation, and in fact caused real harm. Even though network television is censored for broadcasting objectionable material, the Supreme Court has ruled that the government cannot ban (adult) pornography on the Internet or on paid cable television channels.[26] The Court even struck down a ban on the transmission of "virtual" child pornography, arguing that no real children were harmed in the creation of these photographic or computer-generated images.[27] And, despite continued reaffirmation of the fighting-words doctrine, the Supreme Court has declined to uphold any convictions for fighting words since *Chaplinsky*. In short, the Court is reluctant to do anything that might

libel
false written statements about others that harm their reputation

slander
false verbal statements about others that harm their reputation

obscenity
indecent or offensive speech or expression

fighting words
speech that is likely to bring about public disorder or chaos; the Supreme Court has held that such speech may be banned in public places to ensure the preservation of public order

limit the content of adults' free speech and expression, even when that speech is unpopular or offensive.

Freedom of Assembly and Redress of Grievances

The First Amendment says that people have the freedom to assemble peaceably and to seek redress of (compensation for) grievances against the government; yet, there are limits placed on assembly. As the Supreme Court has considered free assembly cases, it has been most concerned about ensuring that individuals and groups can get together to discuss their concerns and that they can take action in the public arena that advances their political goals.

The Court's stance in free speech cases provides insight into its leanings in cases concerning freedom of assembly. The Court is keenly aware of the need for order in public forums and will clamp down on speech that is intended and likely to incite public unrest and anger. That is one reason the Court has reaffirmed the fighting-words doctrine. Although officials cannot censor speech before it occurs, they can take action to limit speech once it becomes apparent that public disorder is going to erupt. In its rulings, the Court has also allowed content-neutral **time, place, and manner restrictions**—regulations regarding when, where, or how expression may occur. Such restrictions do not target speech based on content, and to stand up in court, they must be applied in a content-neutral manner. For example, people have the right to march in protest, but not while chanting into bullhorns at four o'clock in the morning in a residential neighborhood.

The Court's rulings in these various cases illustrate how the government is balancing the freedom of public assembly against other concerns, notably public safety and the right of an individual to be left alone. The Court is carefully weighing the freedoms of one group of individuals against another and attempting to ensure the protection of free public expression.

time, place, and manner restrictions
regulations regarding when, where, or how expression may occur; must be content neutral

Freedom of the Press

Throughout American history, the press has played a crucial role in the larger debate about political expression. Before the War for Independence, when the British monarchy sought to clamp down on political dissent in the colonies, the king and Parliament quickly recognized the urgency of silencing the press. A free press is essential to democratic ideals, and democracy cannot survive when a government controls the press. The First Amendment's guarantees of a free press ensure not only that American government remains accountable to its constituents but also that the people hear competing ideas about how to deal with matters of public concern. Increasingly, the Internet has become the place where ordinary citizens share their views on important political issues.

Ensuring a free press can complicate the work of government. Consider the challenge presented to the George W. Bush administration when the *New York Times* broke a story in late 2005 that the National Security Agency (NSA) had been using futuristic spy technology against thousands of individuals inside the United States.[28,29] The NSA is responsible for monitoring the communications of foreigners outside U.S. borders and does not have authority to engage in surveillance of Americans in the United States. Moreover, the Fourth Amendment protects American citizens against searches without either a warrant or a court order. Despite claims to the contrary during his campaign, President Obama has not changed that policy and has sided with the Bush Administration in legislation challenging it.[30]

Certain well-established principles govern freedom of the press in the United States. First and foremost, the courts almost never allow the government to engage in prior restraint. **Prior restraint** means censorship—the attempt to block the publication of material that is considered to be harmful. The Supreme Court established this rule against censorship in 1931 in the landmark case of *Near v. Minnesota*. After editor

prior restraint
a form of censorship by the government whereby it blocks the publication of news stories viewed as libelous or harmful

Jay Near wrote a story in the *Saturday Press* alleging that Jews were responsible for corruption, bribery, and prostitution in Minneapolis, a state judge barred all future sales of the newspaper. The Court overturned the state judge's ruling, finding that the sole purpose of the order was to suppress speech. Because freedom of the press has strong historical foundations, the Court concluded, censorship is clearly prohibited.

In the *Near* ruling, the Court recognized, however, that there might be times when governmental officials could limit the publication of certain stories. Specifically, such censorship might be justified under extraordinary circumstances related to ensuring public safety or national security or in cases involving obscenity. In reality, though, the Court has disallowed prior restraint in the vast majority of cases. For example, in the most important case examining the national security exception, *New York Times v. U.S.* (1971), the Court rejected the government's attempt to prevent publication of documents that detailed the history of the United States' involvement in Vietnam. In this case, also known as the *Pentagon Papers* case, the government argued that censorship was necessary to prevent "irreparable injury" to national security. But the Court dismissed that argument, asserting that full disclosure was in the interest of all Americans and that publication of the documents could contribute to the ongoing debate about the U.S. role in the Vietnam War.[31] In their ruling, the justices recognized that some materials are clearly necessary for full and fair discussion of issues facing the nation, whereas others are far less important to political discourse. (The Court, for example, has allowed the government to censor publications that are far less central to public debate, such as obscene materials.)

The Court is far more willing to allow the government to impose constraints on broadcast media than on print media. Why should a distinction be made between print and broadcast media? Probably the most important justification is that only a limited number of channels can be broadcast, and the government is responsible for parceling out those channels. Because the public owns the airwaves, the people may also impose reasonable regulations on those who are awarded licenses to operate broadcast channels.

The Court views the Internet to be more like print media than like broadcast media. Thus far, the Court has signaled its interpretation that the Internet is an enormous resource for democratic forums, one that allows users access to virtually unlimited sites at very low cost (*Reno v. ACLU*, 1997). The Court's fine distinctions are between media that allow more and media that allow less access to individuals and groups to engage in political discourse. The Court's assumption is that print media and the Internet provide relatively cheap and virtually unlimited access and enable people to tap easily into discussions about issues facing the nation. In contrast, broadcast media, with much scarcer channels, represent a much more limited arena for dialogue and thus can reasonably be regulated.

Freedoms of Religion, Privacy, and Criminal Due Process: Encouraging Community and Civic Engagement

The Constitution's framers understood that the government they were creating could use its powers to single out certain groups for either favorable or unfavorable treatment and in that way could interfere with the creation of community—and with citizens' engagement within that community. The founders' commitment to community building and citizens' engagement lies at the heart of several constitutional amendments in the Bill of Rights. Specifically these are the amendments establishing the freedom of religion, the right to privacy, and the right to due process for individuals in the criminal justice system.

The First Amendment and the Freedom of Religion

The religion clauses of the First Amendment—the establishment clause and the free exercise clause—essentially do two things. First, they bar the government from establishing or supporting any one religious sect over another, and second, they ensure that individuals are not hindered in the exercise of their religion. Whereas the establishment clause requires that the government be neutral toward religious institutions, favoring neither one specific religion over others nor all religious groups over nonreligious groups, the free exercise clause prohibits the government from taking action that is hostile toward individuals' practice of their religion. As we now consider, there is tension between these two clauses.

THE ESTABLISHMENT CLAUSE   Stating only that "Congress shall make no law respecting an establishment of religion," the **establishment clause** does little to clarify what the relationship between church and state should be. The Constitution's authors wanted to ensure that Congress could not create a national religion, as a number of European powers (notably France and Spain) had done; the framers sought to avoid that level of government entanglement in religious matters. Further, many colonists had immigrated to America to escape religious persecution in Europe, and although many were deeply religious, uncertainty prevailed about the role that government should play in the practice of religion. That uncertainty, too, is reflected in the brevity of the establishment clause. The question arises, does the clause prohibit the government from simply preferring one sect over another, or is it broader, encompassing any kind of support of religion?

This is a crucial question because religious institutions have always been important forums for community building and engagement in the United States. Americans continue to be a very religious people. In 2009, over 81 percent of Americans surveyed said religion was fairly or very important in their lives.[32] But even given their strong religious affiliations, most Americans believe in some degree of separation between religious organizations and the government. The actual debate has been about how much separation the establishment clause requires.

Over time, scholars and lawyers have considered three possible interpretations of the establishment clause. One interpretation, called separationism, is that the establishment clause requires a *strict separation of church and state* and bars most or all government support for religious sects. Supporters of the strict separationist view invoke the writings of Thomas Jefferson, James Madison, and others that call for a "wall of separation" between church and state.[33] They also point to societies outside the United States in which religious leaders dictate how citizens may dress, act, and pray as examples of what can happen without strict separation.

A second, and more flexible, interpretation allows the government to offer support to religious sects as long as that support is neutral and not biased toward one sect. This interpretation, known as *neutrality* or the *preferential treatment standard,* would permit government support provided that this support extended to all religious groups. The third interpretation is the most flexible and reads the establishment clause as barring only establishment of a state religion. This interpretation, known as *accommodationism,* allows the government to offer support to any or all religious groups provided that this support does not rise to the level of recognizing an official religion.[34]

Which of these three vastly different interpretations of the establishment clause is correct? Over time, the Supreme Court has shifted back and forth in its opinions, usually depending on the kind of government support in question. Overall, the courts have rejected the strictest interpretation of the establishment clause, which would ban virtually any form of aid to religion. Instead, they have allowed government support for religious schools, programs, and institutions if the support advances a secular (nonreligious) goal and does not specifically endorse a particular religious belief.

For example, in 1974, the Court upheld a New Jersey program that provided funds to the parents of parochial school students to pay for bus transportation to and from school.[35] The Court reasoned that the program was necessary to help students to get to school safely and concluded that if the state withdrew funding for any of these programs for parochial school students, it would be impossible to operate these schools. The impact would be the hindrance of the free exercise of religion for students and their parents.

In another landmark case, *Lemon v. Kurtzman* (1971), however, the Court struck down a state program that used cigarette taxes to reimburse parochial schools for the costs of teachers' salaries and textbooks. The Court found that subsidizing parochial schools furthered a process of religious teaching and that the "continuing state surveillance" that would be necessary to enforce the specific provisions of the laws would inevitably entangle the state in religious affairs.[36]

establishment clause
First Amendment clause that bars the government from passing any law "respecting an establishment of religion"; often interpreted as a separation of church and state but increasingly questioned

In the *Lemon* case ruling, the Court refined the establishment clause standard to include three considerations.

- Does the state program have a secular, as opposed to a religious, purpose?
- Does it have as its principal effect the advancement of religion?
- Does the program create an excessive entanglement between church and state?

This three-part test is known as the **Lemon test.** The programs most likely to withstand scrutiny under the establishment clause are those that have a secular purpose, have only an incidental effect on the advancement of religion, and do not excessively entangle church and state.

More recently, the Court upheld an Ohio program that gave vouchers to parents to offset the cost of parochial schooling.[37] The justices ruled that the purpose of the program was secular, not religious, because it was intended to provide parents with an alternative to the Cleveland public schools. Any aid to religious institutions—in this case, mostly Catholic schools—was indirect, because the primary beneficiaries were the students themselves. Finally, there was little entanglement between the church and state, because the parents received the vouchers based on financial need and then were free to use these vouchers as they pleased. There was no direct relationship between the religious schools and the state.

So where the government program offers financial support, the Court has tended to evaluate this program by using either the preferential treatment standard or the accommodationist standard. Where the program or policy involves prayer in the school or issues related to the curriculum, however, the Court has adopted a standard that looks more like strict separationism. Table 4.4 summarizes the Court's decisions in a variety of school-related free exercise and establishment clause cases.

As Table 4.4 illustrates, a series of cases beginning with *Engel v. Vitale* (1962) has barred formalized prayer in the school, finding that such prayer has a purely religious purpose and that prayer is intended to advance religious, as opposed to secular, ideals.[38] For that reason, the Court has barred school-organized prayer in public elementary and secondary schools on the grounds that it constitutes a state endorsement of religion. Student-organized prayer is constitutional because the state is not engaging in any coercion by mandating or encouraging student participation.

Recently, courts have begun to grapple with the decision of some school boards to mandate the inclusion of intelligent design in the curriculum.[39] **Intelligent design** is the assertion that the apparent design in the universe and in living things is the product of an intelligent cause rather than of an undirected process such as natural selection. Though

Lemon test

a three-part test established by the Supreme Court in the 1971 case *Lemon v. Kurtzman* to determine whether government aid to parochial schools is constitutional; the test is also applied to other cases involving the establishment clause

intelligent design

theory that the apparent design in the universe and in living things is the product of an intelligent cause rather than of an undirected process such as natural selection; its primary proponents believe that the designer is God and seek to redefine science to accept supernatural explanations

TABLE 4.4

Religion and Schools: Permissible and Impermissible Activities

Public Funding Not Permitted	Supreme Court Case	Year
Parochial school salaries	*Lemon v. Kurtzman*	1971
Parochial school textbooks	*Lemon v. Kurtzman*	1971
Public Funding Permitted	**Supreme Court Case**	**Year**
Parochial school busing	*Everson v. Board of Education*	1947
Parochial/private school computers	*Mitchell v. Helms*	2000
Public/private school vouchers	*Zelman v. Simmons-Harris*	2002
Public School Activities Not Permitted	**Supreme Court Case**	**Year**
Teacher-led nondenominational prayer	*Engel v. Vitale*	1962
Banning the teaching of evolution	*Epperson v. Arkansas*	1968
Requiring teaching of creationism	*Edward v. Aguillard*	1987
Requiring Ten Commandments posting	*Stone v. Graham*	1980
Official graduation ceremony prayers	*Lee v. Weisman*	1992
Moment of silence for voluntary prayer	*Wallace v. Jaffree*	1985
Student-led prayers using PA system	*Santa Fe School District v. Doe*	2000
Requiring all students to say the Pledge	*W. Virginia Board of Ed. v. Barnette*	1943
Public School Activities Permitted	**Supreme Court Case**	**Year**
Off-campus release-time religion classes	*Zorach v. Clauson*	1952
After-school student-led religion club	*Board of Education of Westside Community Schools v. Mergens*	1990
Use of public school building by religious groups (after hours)	*Lamb's Chapel v. Center Moriches School District*	1993
Public school teachers teaching in parochial schools	*Agostini v. Felton*	1997
Voluntary after-school Bible study	*Good News Club v. Milford Central School*	2001

creationism
theory of the creation of the earth and humankind based on a literal interpretation of the biblical story of Genesis

free exercise clause
First Amendment clause prohibiting the government from enacting laws prohibiting an individual's practice of his or her religion; often in contention with the establishment clause

not stated by its primary proponents, many supporters believe that the designer is God, and they seek to redefine science to accept supernatural explanations.

Advocates of intelligent design claim that unlike **creationism,** which defends a literal interpretation of the biblical story of Genesis, intelligent design is a scientific theory. For that reason, they say, school boards should be permitted to include it in the curriculum, alongside evolution. Opponents claim that intelligent design is just another form of creationism, because it is based upon a belief in a divine being, does not generate any predictions, and cannot be tested by experiment. Mandating that schools teach intelligent design, critics argue, constitutes an endorsement of religion by the state.

THE FREE EXERCISE CLAUSE The tension between the establishment and free exercise clauses arises because the establishment clause bars the state from helping religious institutions, whereas the **free exercise clause** makes it illegal for the government to enact laws prohibiting the free practice of religion by individuals. Establishment clause cases often raise free exercise claims, and so courts must frequently consider whether by banning state aid, they are interfering with the free exercise of religion.

Although free exercise and establishment cases raise many of the same concerns, they are different kinds of cases, whose resolution depends on distinct legal tests. Establishment clause cases typically involve well-established and well-known religious institutions. Because establishment clause cases often center on state aid to religious schools, many involve the Roman Catholic Church, which administers the largest number of private elementary and secondary schools in the country. In contrast, free exercise clause cases tend to involve less mainstream religious groups, among them Mormons, Jehovah's Witnesses, Christian Scientists, and Amish. These groups' practices tend to be less well known—or more controversial. For example, free exercise clause cases have involved the right to practice polygamy, to use hallucinogens, to refuse conventional medical care for a child, and to refuse to salute the flag.

The Supreme Court has refused to accept that the government is barred from *ever* interfering with religious exercise. Free exercise claims are difficult to settle because they require that courts balance the individual's right to free practice of religion against the government's need to adopt some policy or program. First and foremost, the Court has always distinguished between religious beliefs, which government may not interfere with, and religious actions, which government is permitted to regulate. For example, although adults may refuse lifesaving medical care on the basis of their own religious beliefs, they may not refuse medical procedures required to save the lives of their children.[40]

In assessing those laws that interfere with religiously motivated action, the Court has distinguished between laws that are neutral and generally applicable to all religious sects and laws that single out one sect for unfavorable treatment. In *Employment Division, Department of Human Resources v. Smith* (1990), the Court allowed the state of Oregon to deny unemployment benefits to two substance-abuse counselors who were fired from their jobs after using peyote as part of their religious practice. Oregon refused to provide benefits because the two men had been fired for engaging in an illegal activity. The Court concluded that there was no free exercise challenge, because Oregon had good reason for denying benefits to lawbreakers who had been fired from their jobs. The justices concluded that the state was simply applying a neutral and generally applicable law to the men as opposed to singling them out for bad treatment.[41] One consequence of this case was that several states, including Oregon, passed laws excluding members of the Native American Church, who smoke peyote as part of traditional religious rites, from being covered by their controlled-substance laws.

In summary, people are free to hold and profess their own beliefs, to build and actively participate in religious communities, and to allow their religious beliefs to inform their participation in politics and civil society. However, individual *actions* based on religious beliefs may be limited if those actions conflict with existing laws that are neutrally applied in a nondiscriminatory fashion.

The Right to Privacy

So far in this section, we have explored the relationship between civil liberties and some key themes of this book: civic participation, inclusiveness, community building, and community engagement. We now shift our focus somewhat to consider the **right to privacy**, the right of an individual to be left alone and to make decisions freely, without the interference of others. Privacy is a core principle for most Americans, and the right to make decisions, especially about intimate or personal matters, is at the heart of this right. Yet the right to privacy is also necessary for genuine inclusiveness and community engagement, because it ensures that each individual is able to act autonomously and to make decisions about how he or she will interact with others.

The right to privacy is highly controversial and the subject of much public debate. In large part, the reason is that this right is tied to some of the most divisive issues of our day, including abortion, aid in dying, and sexual orientation. The right to privacy is also controversial because, unlike the freedoms of speech, the press, assembly, and religion, it is not explicitly mentioned anywhere in the Constitution. A further reason for the debate surrounding the right to privacy is that the Supreme Court has only recently recognized it.

THE EMERGENT RIGHT TO PRIVACY For more than one hundred years, Supreme Court justices and lower-court judges have concluded that the right to privacy is implied in all the other liberties spelled out in the Bill of Rights. Not until the landmark Supreme Court case *Griswold v. Connecticut* (1965) did the courts firmly establish the right to privacy. The issue in this case may seem strange to us today: whether the state of Connecticut had the power to prohibit married couples from using birth control. In their decision, the justices concluded that the state law violated the privacy right of married couples by preventing them from seeking to access birth control, and the Court struck down the Connecticut prohibition. The Court argued that the right to privacy was inherent in many of the other constitutional guarantees, most importantly the First Amendment freedom of association, the Third Amendment right to be free from the quartering of soldiers, the Fourth Amendment right to be free from unreasonable searches and seizures, the Fifth Amendment protection against self-incrimination, and the Ninth Amendment assurance of rights not explicitly listed in the Bill of Rights. Justice William O. Douglas and his colleagues effectively argued that a zone of privacy surrounded every person in the United States and that government could not pass laws that encroached upon this zone.[42]

In its ruling, the Court asserted that the right to privacy existed quite apart from the law. It was implicit in the Bill of Rights and fundamental to the American system of law and justice. The right to privacy hinged in large part on the right of individuals to associate with one another, and specifically the right of marital partners to engage in intimate association.

In a 1984 case, the Supreme Court ruled that the Constitution protects two kinds of freedom of association: (1) intimate associations and (2) expressive associations.[43] The protection of intimate associations allows Americans to maintain intimate human relationships as part of their personal liberty. The protection of expressive associations allows people to form associations with others and to practice their First Amendment freedoms of speech, assembly, petition, and religion.

> Thirteen-year-old Savanna Redding was suspected of possessing prescription strength ibuprofen and over-the-counter naproxen pills in her public school. Female school officials questioned her, asked her to strip down to her underwear, and then show she had nothing hidden in her underwear. In *Safford v. Redding* (2009), the Court found this "strip-search" to be unreasonable.

THE RIGHT TO PRIVACY APPLIED TO OTHER ACTIVITIES The challenge for the Court since *Griswold* has been to determine which activities fall within the scope of the privacy right, and that question has placed the justices at the center of some of the most controversial issues of the day. For example, the first attempt to extend the privacy right, which raised the question of whether the right protected abortion, remains at least as controversial today as it was in 1973 when the Court decided the first abortion rights case, *Roe v. Wade*.[44] In *Roe* and the many abortion cases the Court has heard since, the justices have tried to establish whether a woman's right to abortion takes precedence over any interests the state may have in either the woman's health or the fetus's life. Over time, the Court has adopted a compromise position by rejecting the view that the right to abortion is absolute and by attempting to determine when states can regulate, or even prohibit, access to abortion. In 1992, the Court established the "undue burden" test, which asks whether a state abortion law places a "substantial obstacle in the path of a woman seeking an abortion before the fetus attains viability."[45] Although the Court used this standard to strike down spousal notification requirements, it has upheld other requirements imposed by some states, including waiting periods, mandatory counseling, and parental consent.

The Court has also stepped gingerly around other privacy rights, such as the right to choose one's sexual partners and the right to terminate medical treatment or engage in physician-assisted suicide. Both of these rights have been presented to the Court as hinging on the much broader right to privacy. With respect to the right to terminate medical treatment, the Court has been fairly clear. Various Court decisions have confirmed that as long as an individual is competent to terminate treatment, the state may not stop him or her from taking this action, even if stopping treatment will lead to the person's death.[46]

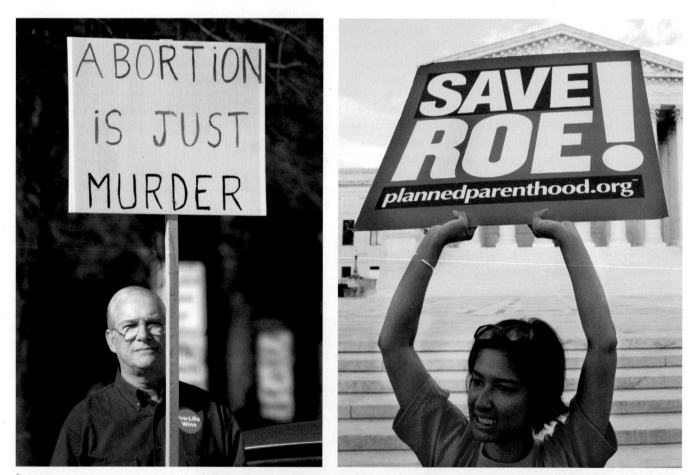

> Public debate over abortion was not settled by the Supreme Court's 1973 decision in *Roe v. Wade*. In this photo taken more than three decades later, pro-life and pro-choice activists in Washington, D.C., hold signs supporting their differing viewpoints. Abortion rights advocates frame the issue in terms of a woman's right to privacy and to control her own body. Abortion rights opponents view abortion as murder and frame the issue in terms of the rights of an unborn child.

The Court has been less clear in its rulings when an incompetent person's right is advanced by another individual, such as a spouse, a parent, or a child. In these circumstances, the Court has accepted the state's argument that before treatment may be terminated, the state may require that the person seeking to end life show that his or her loved one would have wanted that course of action.[47] When a person's wishes are not clear, loved ones may wage legal battles over whether to discontinue life support (see Chapter 14).

In cases involving the right to engage in consensual sexual activities with a partner of one's choosing, the Supreme Court has also employed a less than absolute approach. For many years, the Court allowed states to criminalize homosexual activity, finding that the right to engage in consensual sexual activity did not extend to same-sex partners.[48] In a 2003 case, *Lawrence v. Texas,* the Court changed course by ruling that the right to engage in intimate sexual activity was protected as a liberty right, especially when the activity occurred inside one's home, and that states could not criminalize this activity.[49] Since that decision, rights activists have worked through the courts and state and federal legislatures to secure for same-sex partners the same rights that heterosexual couples enjoy, including benefits provided by group health insurance and marriage. Marriage is regulated by the states, and as Figure 4.1 shows, there is a wide range of state laws pertaining to marriage; many of these laws have only been recently passed. The *Lawrence* decision aside, states are still free

Defense of Marriage Act, constitutional ban or similar

Gay marriage

Civil union or domestic partnership equal in rights to marriage

Legislation or court case pending

Other

* No law on books addressing issue.

** Recognizes all states' same-sex marriages; does not provide them.

POLITICAL INQUIRY

FIGURE 4.1 ▪ STATE MARRIAGE LAWS What regional variations do you see regarding these laws? How would you explain the existence of both a ban on gay marriage and a law protecting civil unions and domestic partnerships in Nevada and Oregon? How does your home state currently address same-sex marriages or civil unions?

Sharing Personal Information on the Internet

WEB SITE	THEN (2003)	NOW (2010)
Facebook	0 active users >	117 million unique users per month
MySpace	0 active users >	42 million unique users per month
Twitter	0 active users >	20 million unique users a month
LinkedIn	0 active users >	13.8 million unique users a month

WHAT'S NEXT?

> Will social-networking Web sites be required to share personal information about their clients, and their clients' Internet behavior, with federal investigators?

> How will our conceptions of privacy (and privacy rights) change as people post increasing amounts of information about themselves on the Web?

> Will the courts continue to protect virtually unlimited speech on the Web?

SOURCE: http://blog.nielson.com/nielsonwire/global/facebook-and-twitter-post-large-year-over-year-gains-in-unique-users. May 4, 2010.

to prohibit a range of sexual activities, including prostitution, child sexual abuse, and sex in public places.[50] In the Court's view, these activities can be prohibited primarily because they are not consensual or do not take place in the home, a place that accords special protection by the privacy right.

The right to privacy remains very controversial. Cases brought under the right to privacy tend to link this right with some other civil liberty, such as the protection against unreasonable search and seizure, the right to free speech, or the protection against self-incrimination. In other words, the privacy right, which the justices themselves created, seems to need buttressing by other rights that the Bill of Rights *explicitly* establishes. The explanation for this development may be the contentiousness of Americans' civic discourse about abortion, aid in dying, and other privacy issues. In short, continuing civic disagreement may have forced the Court to fall back on rights that are well established and more widely accepted.

Public discourse about privacy is constantly evolving as people voluntarily share more and more information about themselves through online networking sites such as Facebook, MySpace, Twitter, and LinkedIn. (See "Then, Now, Next.") Users of such sites and bloggers share stories, photos, and videos of themselves—as well as of others, who may be unaware that they are the subject of a posting, a blog, or a video. Civil libertarians worry about the misuse and theft of personal information in a high-tech society where people's financial, employment, consumer, legal, and personal histories are so easily accessible. Government and law enforcement agencies are still deciding how they may use such materials in criminal investigations. Legal implications remain unclear.

The Fourth, Fifth, Sixth, and Eighth Amendments: Ensuring Criminal Due Process

The last category of civil liberties that bear directly on civic engagement consists of the criminal due process protections established in the Fourth, Fifth, Sixth, and Eighth amendments. Does it surprise you that so many of the Bill of Rights amendments focus on the rights of individuals accused of crimes? The context for this emphasis is the founders' concern with how the British monarchy had abused its power and used criminal law to impose its will on the American colonists. The British government had used repeated trials, charges of treason, and imprisonment without bail to stifle political dissent. The founders therefore wanted to ensure that there were effective checks on the power of the federal government, especially in the creation and enforcement of criminal law. As we have seen, the Bill of Rights amendments were incorporated to apply to the states and to their criminal codes through the process of selective incorporation. Thus, criminal due process protections are the constitutional limits imposed on law enforcement personnel.

These four amendments together are known as the **criminal due process rights** because they establish the guidelines that the government must follow in investigating, bringing to trial, and punishing individuals who violate criminal law. Each amendment guides the government in administering some facet of law enforcement, and all are intended to ensure justice and fairness in the administration of the law. Criminal due process is essential to guarantee that individuals can participate in the larger society and that no one person is singled out for better or worse treatment under the law. Like the First Amendment, due process protects political speech and freedom. Without these liberties, government officials could selectively target those who disagree with the laws and policies they advocate.

Moreover, without these rights, there would be little to stop the government from using criminal law to punish those who want to take action that is protected by the other amendments we have examined in this chapter. For example, what good would it do to talk about the freedom of speech if the government could isolate or punish someone who spoke out critically against it without having to prove in a public venue that the speech threatened public safety or national security? The criminal due process protections are essential to ensuring meaningful participation and engagement in the larger community and to safeguarding justice and fairness.

THE FOURTH AMENDMENT AND THE PROTECTION AGAINST UNREASONABLE SEARCHES AND SEIZURES

The Fourth Amendment requires police to get a warrant before engaging in a search and guides law enforcement personnel in conducting criminal investigations and in searching an individual's body or property. It has its roots in colonial history—specifically, in the British government's abuse of its law enforcement powers to prosecute and punish American colonists suspected of being disloyal.

The Fourth Amendment imposes significant limits on law enforcement. In barring police from conducting any unreasonable searches and seizures, it requires that they show probable cause that a crime has been committed before they can obtain a search warrant. The warrant ensures that police officers can gather evidence only when they have probable cause. Further, a judicially created ruling known as the **exclusionary rule** compels law enforcers to carry out searches properly. Established for federal prosecutions in 1914, the exclusionary rule forbids the courts to admit illegally seized evidence during trial.[51] This rule was extended to state court proceedings in the Supreme Court decision *Mapp v. Ohio* (1961).[52] In this case, the Court overturned an Ohio court's conviction of Dollree Mapp for the possession of obscene materials. Police had found pornographic books in Mapp's apartment after searching it without a search warrant and despite the defendant's refusal to let them in. Critics of the exclusionary rule note that securing a warrant is not always necessary or feasible and that guilty people sometimes go free because of procedural technicalities. They argue that reasonable searches should not be defined solely by the presence of a court-ordered search warrant.[53]

What are "reasonable" and "unreasonable" searches under the Fourth Amendment? Over time, the U.S. Supreme Court has established criteria to guide both police officers and judges hearing cases. In the strictest definition of reasonableness, there is a warrant: where there is no warrant, the search is considered to be unreasonable. However, the Supreme Court has ruled that even without a warrant, some searches would still be reasonable. In 1984, for example, the Court held that illegally obtained evidence could be admitted at trial if law enforcers could prove that they would have obtained the evidence legally anyway.[54]

In another case the same year, the Court created a "good faith" exception to the exclusionary rule by upholding the use of evidence obtained with a technically incorrect warrant, because the police officer had acted in good faith.[55]

More broadly, a warrantless search is valid if the person subjected to it has no reasonable expectation of privacy in the place or thing being searched. From colonial times to the present, the assumption has been that individuals have a reasonable expectation of privacy in their homes. Where there is no reasonable expectation of privacy, however, there can be no unreasonable search, and so the police are not required to get a warrant before conducting the search or surveillance. Since the 1990s, the Court has expanded the situations in which there is no reasonable expectation of privacy and hence no need for a warrant. For example, there is no reasonable expectation of privacy in one's car, at least in those areas that are in plain view, such as the front and back seats. There is also no expectation of privacy in public

criminal due process rights
safeguards for those accused of crime; these rights constrain government conduct in investigating crimes, trying cases, and punishing offenders

exclusionary rule
criminal procedural rule stating that evidence obtained illegally cannot be used in a trial

places such as parks and stores, because it is reasonable to assume that a person knowingly exposes his or her activities to public view in those places. The same is true of one's trash: because there is no reasonable expectation of privacy in the things that one discards, police may search this material without a warrant.[56]

In instances where there is a reasonable expectation of privacy, individuals or their property may be searched if law enforcement personnel acquire a warrant from a judge. To obtain a warrant, the police must provide the judge with evidence that establishes probable cause that a crime has been committed. Further, the warrant must be specific about the place to be searched and the materials that the agents are seeking. These requirements limit the ability of police simply to go on a "fishing expedition" to find some bit of incriminating evidence.

As society changes, expectations of privacy change as well. For example, technological innovation has given us e-mail and the Internet, and Fourth Amendment law has had to adapt to these inventions. Is there a reasonable expectation of privacy in our communications on the Internet? This is an important question, especially in light of citizens' heightened concerns about terrorism and white-collar crime.

THE FIFTH AND SIXTH AMENDMENTS: THE RIGHT TO A FAIR TRIAL AND THE RIGHT TO COUNSEL The Fifth and Sixth amendments establish the rules for conducting a trial. These two amendments ensure that criminal defendants are protected at the formal stages of legal proceedings. Although less than 10 percent of all charges result in trials, these protections have significant symbolic and practical importance, because they hold the state to a high standard whenever it attempts to use its significant power to prosecute a case against an individual.

The Fifth Amendment bars **double jeopardy** and compelled self-incrimination. These safeguards mean, respectively, that a person may not be tried twice for the same crime or forced to testify against himself or herself when accused of a crime. These safeguards are meant to protect people from persecution, harassment, and forced confessions. A single criminal action, however, can lead to multiple trials if each trial is based on a separate offense.

The Sixth Amendment establishes the rights to a speedy and public trial, to a trial by a jury of one's peers, to information about the charges against oneself, to the confrontation of witnesses testifying against oneself, and to legal counsel. The protection of these Fifth and Sixth Amendment liberties is promoted by the **Miranda rights,** based on the Supreme Court decision in *Miranda v. Arizona* (1966).[57] In the *Miranda* case, the Court outlined the requirement that "prior to questioning, the person must be warned that he has a right to remain silent, that any statement he does make may be used against him, and that he has a right to the presence of an attorney, either retained or appointed." Later cases have created some exceptions to *Miranda* (see Table 4.5).

Together, the Fourth, Fifth, and Sixth amendments ensure the protection of individuals against abuses of power by the state, and in so doing they promote a view of justice that the community widely embraces. Because these rights extend to individuals charged with violating the community's standards of right and wrong, they promote a broad sense of inclusiveness—a respect even for persons who allegedly have committed serious offenses, and a desire to ensure that the justice system treats all people fairly.

The Court has considered the community's views in reaching its decisions in cases brought before it. For example, through a series of Supreme Court cases culminating with *Gideon v. Wainwright* (1963), the justices interpreted the right to counsel to mean that the government must provide lawyers to individuals who are too poor to hire their own.[58] The justices adopted this standard because they came to believe that the community's views of fundamental fairness dic-

---

double jeopardy

the trying of a person again for the same crime that he or she has been cleared of in court; barred by the Fifth Amendment

Miranda rights

criminal procedural rule, established in the 1966 case *Miranda v. Arizona,* requiring police to inform criminal suspects, on their arrest, of their legal rights, such as the right to remain silent and the right to counsel; these warnings must be read to suspects before interrogation

---

TABLE 4.5

Cases Weakening Protection Against Self-Incrimination

Year	Case	Ruling
1986	*Moran v. Burbine*	Confession is not inadmissible because police failed to inform suspect of attorney's attempted contacts.
1991	*Arizona v. Fulminante*	Conviction is not automatically overturned in cases of coerced confession if other evidence is strong enough to justify conviction.
1994	*Davis v. U.S.*	Suspect must unequivocally and assertively state his right to counsel to stop police questioning.

tated this result. Before this decision, states had to provide attorneys only in cases that could result in capital punishment.

**THE EIGHTH AMENDMENT: PROTECTION AGAINST CRUEL AND UN-
USUAL PUNISHMENT** The meaning of *cruel* and *unusual* has changed radically since the Eighth Amendment was ratified, especially with regard to the imposition of capital punishment—the death penalty. Moreover, Americans have always disagreed among themselves about the death penalty itself. Throughout the country's history, citizens and lawmakers have debated the morality of capital punishment as well as the circumstances under which the death penalty should be used. Central to the public debate have been the questions of which crimes should be punished by death and how capital punishment should be carried out.

Generally, the Court has supported the constitutionality of the death penalty. An exception was the landmark case *Furman v. Georgia* (1972), in which, in a 5–4 decision, the Court suspended the use of the death penalty.[59] Justices Brennan and Marshall believed the death penalty to be "incompatible with evolving standards of decency in contemporary society." The dissenting justices argued in turn that capital punishment had always been regarded as appropriate under the Anglo-American legal tradition for serious crimes and that the Constitution implicitly authorized death penalty laws because of the Fourteenth Amendment's reference to the taking of "life." The majority decision came about as a result of concurring opinions by justices Stewart, White, and Douglas, who focused on the arbitrary nature with which death sentences had been imposed. The Court's decision forced the states and the national legislature to rethink their statutes for capital offenses to ensure that the death penalty would not be administered in a capricious or discriminatory manner.[60] Over time, the courts have also interpreted the Eighth Amendment as requiring that executions be carried out in the most humane and least painful manner. Public discourse and debate have strongly influenced thinking about which methods of execution are appropriate.

Recent studies, however, suggest that states' administration of the sedative sodium pentothal has left individuals conscious and in agony but paralyzed and thus unable to cry out while they are dying. But in 2008, the Supreme Court ruled in a 7–2 decision that lethal injection does not constitute cruel and unusual punishment,[61] paving the way for ten states, which had halted lethal injections pending the case's outcome, to resume executions. The 2008 decision of *Baze v. Rees* marked the first time the Supreme Court reviewed the constitutionality of a method of execution since 1878, when the Court upheld Utah's use of a firing squad.[62]

In that early ruling, the Court said the Constitution prohibits executions that involve torture, such as burning alive or drawing and quartering an individual, as well as other infliction of "unnecessary cruelty" that the justices did not define. As Figure 4.2 on page 136 demonstrates, states have greatly differed in their interpretation of a constitutionally legitimate means of execution. In the recent case, lawyers for the Kentucky inmates argued that the state is violating that standard by using drugs that pose a risk of extreme pain if something goes wrong and by failing to provide adequate safeguards. But in its decision in 2008, the Court ruled that there is no Eighth Amendment requirement that a government-sanctioned execution be pain free, only that it does not involve a "substantial" or "objectively intolerable" risk of serious harm—a risk greater than possible alternatives.

Freedoms in Practice: Controversy Over the Second Amendment and the Right to Bear Arms

The fierce debate today over gun control illustrates much about the nature of political discourse and citizen action in the United States. Americans disagree about how to interpret the Second Amendment of the Constitution, but they do agree to have their disputes settled through laws and court rulings rather than armed conflict. Private citizens and political interest groups use their First Amendment freedoms of speech and assembly to voice their opinions about the place of guns in society. They also work behind the scenes to influence elected officials through campaign contributions and lobbying (see Chapter 7). At the heart of this debate is the question of the role of guns in creating a safe and free society.

States with and without the Death Penalty

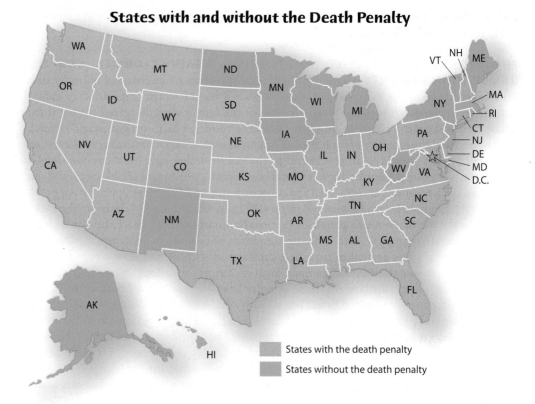

States with the death penalty

States without the death penalty

Nationwide Murder Rates, 2008
per 100,000 People

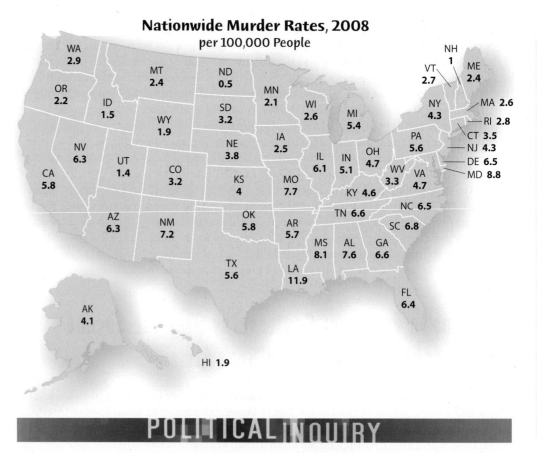

POLITICAL INQUIRY

FIGURE 4.2 ■ **STATE LAWS REGARDING CAPITAL PUNISHMENT** What relationship do you see between the two maps? Are states with death penalties likely to have higher or lower murder rates than states without death penalties? What might this mean for public policy decisions?

Competing Interpretations of the Second Amendment

Americans disagree about the purpose and the contemporary significance of the Second Amendment, which reads

> A well regulated Militia, being necessary to the security of a free State, the right of the people to keep and bear Arms, shall not be infringed.

Some people argue that the amendment gives individual citizens the right to bear arms, free from government control.[63] On the opposing side, others stress that the Second Amendment's original purpose was to ensure that state militias could back the government in maintaining public order.[64] These people suggest that the right to bear arms is thus a group right subject to regulation by Congress and the states.[65] The unorganized militia has not been activated since before the Civil War, and the government now has adequate weapons to defend the nation, these critics say.

States differ widely in the degree to which citizens have access to guns. Some states allow residents to carry concealed weapons for personal protection, but others do not. In 1976, Washington, D.C., passed the nation's toughest gun control laws, including a ban on handguns, rifles, and automatic weapons, except for individuals with a special permit—mostly police and security guards. In a 2008 ruling, the Supreme Court ruled in a 5–2 decision that "the right of the people to keep and bear arms" is not limited to state militias but, rather, is a part of "the inherent right of self-defense," striking down the district's handgun ban.[66] In 2010, the Court ruled that the Fourteenth Amendment incorporates the Second Amendment to the states, requiring them to respect these rights in state law.[67]

Citizens Engaged: Fighting for a Safer Nation

This disagreement over the Second Amendment's meaning is reflected in the actions of ordinary citizens and organized interest groups. For example, the Million Moms and the Second Amendment Sisters are two interest groups with clashing views on the issue of gun control. The Million Moms see stronger gun control laws as a way to prevent the alarmingly high number of U.S. deaths of young people from gun violence, an estimated ten deaths per day.[68] The Second Amendment Sisters believe that guns are a woman's best tool for self-defense and give her the ability to protect herself and her family.[69] Both groups have joined vocally in the public debate, exercising their freedom of speech and assembly to influence opinions about guns in the United States. They disagree over how best to protect themselves and their families in a dangerous world. Each group struggles to interpret the Second Amendment to fit its members' own understandings of social needs and problems today.

> The Second Amendment Sisters and the Million Mom March represent women on different sides of the gun control debate. What are your views on gun control?

Civil Liberties in Post-9/11 America

Public discussion about the proper balance between individual freedom and public safety is not limited to gun control policies. Debate has intensified as the nation struggles with the aftermath of the September 11, 2001 terrorist attacks and the continuing global war on terror. Citizens and government leaders are rethinking their beliefs about the proper scope of government power. Over the course of U.S. history, liberty and security have coexisted in a state of tension.

In the wake of September 11, this tension has become more acute, as the federal, state, and local governments have taken certain actions that directly intrude upon individual freedoms. The government argues these actions are necessary to protect life and property. But civil libertarians shudder at what they see as unprecedented violations of individual freedoms and rights.

Perceived Intrusions on Free Speech and Assembly

Although the tension between liberty and order has been clear since the origins of our republic, this conflict has become more intense in recent years. For instance, the Foreign Intelligence Surveillance Act (FISA) of 1978, which empowers the government to conduct secret searches where necessary to protect national security, significantly broadened the powers of law enforcement agencies to engage in investigation. Agencies must go before a designated court, the Foreign Intelligence Surveillance Act Court, to justify a secret search. Civil libertarians are concerned about the FISA court's concealed location and sealed records, as well as its judicial proceedings, in which the suspect is never told about the investigation and probable cause is not required to approve surveillance or searches of any person suspected of having some link to terrorism.

Following September 11, 2001, a number of government agencies engaged in the surveillance of political groups in the United States. In late 2005, the media exposed a program by the Bush administration and the National Security Administration (NSA) to target U.S. civilians for electronic surveillance without judicial oversight. Members of the Bush administration claimed that they had monitored only communications where one party was suspected of links to terrorism and was currently overseas. Beginning in 2005, however, the American Civil Liberties Union (ACLU) issued a series of reports demonstrating that the Federal Bureau of Investigation (FBI) spied not only on people suspected of taking part in terrorist plots but also on individuals involved in peaceful political activities.[70] In one instance, the FBI monitored the organizers of an antiwar protest who had gathered at a Denver bookstore, and agents compiled a list with the descriptions and license plates of cars in the store's vicinity. In 2009, the ACLU filed a lawsuit challenging the constitutionality of the 2008 FISA Amendment Act, which increased the ability of the federal government to engage in the warrantless surveillance of American citizens.[71] The ACLU has released similar reports describing the Pentagon's database of peaceful war protesters.[72]

The ACLU and other critics of the domestic surveillance program have argued that the federal government is targeting political protest, not

POLITICAL INQUIRY

A CHOICE BETWEEN FREEDOM AND SECURITY What message is the cartoonist trying to convey? Do you think citizens must choose between freedom and security? Explain. Do you support the central provisions of the USA PATRIOT Act and the NSA wiretapping program? Why or why not? Do such programs increase security or threaten liberty? Explain.

SOURCE: By Clay Bennett. Reproduced with permission from the October 29, 2001 issue of The Christian Science Monitor (www.CSMonitor.com). © 2001 The Christian Science Monitor.

domestic terrorism plots. Opponents of the policy warn that the FBI and other agencies are infringing upon free speech, assembly, and expression. But employees of the NSA and the Department of Justice have defended the government's expanded investigation and enforcement activities, claiming that the threats to national security are grave and that the government must be given the power it needs to protect against these dangers.[73]

Perceived Intrusions on Criminal Due Process

Even though several years have passed since September 11, 2001, concern lingers about another terrorist attack on U.S. soil, and many Americans are willing to accept some infringement on their freedoms if it makes them safer. These citizens assume that criminal activity may be afoot and that the surveillance is not being used to target groups that are politically unpopular or critical of the administration. Much of the debate about the surveillance activities of the FBI and other groups centers on the distinction between criminally active groups and politically unpopular groups. How do we know which groups the federal government is using its powers to investigate?

To what extent must administration officials provide evidence of criminal intent before placing a suspect under surveillance? Since September 11, 2001, the laws that govern domestic spying have been modified in such a way that the government has much more leeway in conducting searches and investigations, even where there is no proof of criminal activity.

The terrorism of September 11 led to important shifts in U.S. policy. One example is the USA PATRIOT Act, which Congress passed six weeks after the attacks with little debate in either the House or the Senate.[74] This law, reauthorized in 2005, allows the FBI and other intelligence agencies to access personal information and records without getting permission from, or even informing, targeted individuals. Much of the data come from private sources, which are often ordered to hand over their records. For example, the USA PATRIOT Act authorized the FBI to order Internet service providers to give information about their clients to the FBI. The USA PATRIOT Act also empowered intelligence agencies to order public libraries to hand over records of materials that the targeted individuals borrowed or viewed.

On July 28, 2007, President Bush called on Congress to pass legislation to reform the FISA in order to ease restrictions on the surveillance of terrorist suspects in cases where one party or both parties to the communication are located overseas. The Protect America Act of 2007, signed into law on August 5, 2007, essentially legalized ongoing NSA practices.[75] Under the act, the U.S. government may wiretap without FISA court supervision any communications that begin or end in a foreign country. The act removes from the definition of "electronic surveillance" in FISA any surveillance directed at a person reasonably believed to be located outside the United States. This means that the government may listen to conversations without a court order as long as the U.S. attorney general approves the surveillance. Supporters stress that flexibility is needed to monitor the communications of suspected terrorists and their networks. Critics, however, worry that the law is too vague and provides the government with the ability to monitor any group or individual it opposes, regardless of whether it has links to terrorism. In 2009, the Inspectors General of the Department of Defense, the Department of Justice, the CIA, the NSA, and the Office of the Director of National Intelligence revealed that the surveillance program had a much larger scope than previously believed. The report also demonstrated conflict within the Obama and Bush administrations as to how helpful the information obtained through these measures was in combating terrorism.[76]

Although many Americans are concerned about domestic surveillance, especially in situations where it targets political speech and expression, these laws remain on the books, and this surveillance likely will continue. For the time being, the line between suspected criminal activity and purely political expression remains blurred. Civic discourse about how to balance liberty and national security continues to evolve as Americans consider how much freedom they should sacrifice to protect public safety.

In addition to conversations about search and surveillance procedures, the nation is struggling with larger questions about the rights of detainees accused of conducting or supporting terrorist activities. Some political commentators argue that the torture of these individuals is appropriate in specific situations.[77] They point to a "ticking time bomb" scenario, in which the torture of a single suspect known to have information about the location of a nuclear bomb would be justified in order to save thousands or millions of innocent lives. Critics of this logic note that information obtained through torture is unreliable and not worth the price of violating our moral codes. Further, they argue that if the United States legalizes torture, Americans will lose their standing as a moral society and alienate potential allies in the war against terror.[78]

In response to the criticism of torture, Congress and the president passed the Detainee Treatment Act of 2005, which bans cruel, inhuman, or degrading treatment of detainees in U.S. custody, but provides significant exceptions to the definition of torture, such as waterboarding (the practice of pouring water over the nose and mouth while the victim is strapped to an inclined board to induce the sensation of drowning.)[79] Despite this legislation, questions remain. For example, in 2006 various media outlets reported the practice of **rendition,** which involves the transfer of custody of suspected terrorists to other nations for imprisonment and interrogation. Critics saw the practice as an attempt to circumvent U.S. law, which requires due process and prohibits torture. Former secretary of state Condoleezza Rice denied that U.S. officials transfer suspects to places where they know these individuals will be tortured.[80] But according to a February 2007 European Parliament report, the CIA conducted 1,245 flights over European territory between 2001 and April 2006, many of them to destinations where suspects could face torture.[81] The Obama Adminstration continued the policy of rendition but pledged to closely monitor the treatment of the incarcerated to ensure that they were not tortured.[82] Unquestionably, the global war on terror has caused U.S. citizens and public officials to reconsider the boundaries of acceptable behavior as they balance the need to protect the civil liberties of the accused with the desire to prevent terrorist attacks. Events such as the attempted 2009 Christmas airplane attack increase the tension between liberty and order.

rendition
transfer of suspected terrorists to other nations for imprisonment and interrogation; this practice circumvents U.S. law, which requires due process and prohibits torture

Discrimination Against Muslim Americans

Immediately after September 11, members of the Bush administration said repeatedly that the war on terror was not a war on immigrants or a war on Islam. Despite assurances, civil libertarians and leaders in the Muslim American community criticized administration policies targeting Muslims. Among these were policies allowing racial profiling of Arab and Muslim men; the use of secret evidence in national security cases; widespread FBI interviews of Muslims; raids of Muslim homes, schools, and mosques; the special registration and fingerprinting of Muslims from specific Arab nations; and the detention and deportation of many Arab and Muslim nationals without the right to legal representation.[83]

President Obama's administration has faced similar criticism for its policies. In response to critics, in March 2010 President Obama appointed the legal director of the American-Arab Anti-Discrimination Committee, Nawar Shora, to the Transportation Security Administration as a senior adviser to the office reviewing civil rights and liberties.[84] Members of these presidential administrations have explained aggressive policing in Muslim communities as a way to catch would-be terrorists and to cause them to delay or abandon their plans. Critics have argued that the policies deny Muslims due process and violate their civil liberties, as well as cause officials to ignore non-Muslim terrorist potentials. As American-born Muslims continue to participate in "home-grown" terrorism, this tension between liberty and security will only intensify.

Critics contend that administration policies have violated Muslims' freedoms of speech, religion, and association as law enforcers monitor their words, religious ceremonies, and organizational ties and as Muslims have become targets of government interrogation and even detention. In a government profiling program designed to catch would-be terrorists, race, age, and national origin, too, can lead to interrogation. Many in the executive branch argue that they are required to do whatever they can to protect U.S. citizens from another terrorist strike. Critics worry that racial and religious profiling will alienate the 7 million Muslim citizens and will, in fact, jeopardize officials' ability to gather valuable intelligence. (See "Thinking Critically About Democracy.") The nation's struggles to balance the demands of freedom and order are clearly illustrated in the ongoing conversation about how to protect personal liberty while ensuring national security.

SHOULD U.S. AUTHORITIES USE ETHNIC PROFILING IN THE INTEREST OF NATIONAL SECURITY?

The Issue: In light of the ongoing terrorist threat, should airport security and law enforcement officials practice ethnic and religious profiling to prevent a hijacking or a terrorist attack?

Yes: The most serious threat we face as a nation is the threat posed by militant Islamic fundamentalists. Militant Islam, or fundamentalism, is a radical ideology that teaches its adherents to apply the laws of Islam, the Shari'a, to all people by creating Islamic states.

Given the nature of the threat, it makes sense for police seeking suspects after a terrorist attack to search mosques rather than churches or synagogues and to question pedestrians who appear to be Middle Eastern or wear head scarves. To avoid an attack, it also makes sense to focus on the people most likely to threaten our safety. Heightened scrutiny for young Middle Eastern men fitting the profile of al-Qaeda recruits is reasonable. Should we require an 85-year-old grandmother from Wisconsin to remove her shoes at the airline gate simply because we just asked a 25-year-old single man from Saudi Arabia to do the same? Common sense tells us that we can more efficiently use resources by concentrating our attention on those who are most likely to pose a risk.

Although profiling may inconvenience law-abiding Muslims, they must be willing to endure mild inconvenience for the larger goal of saving lives. Indeed, integrationist Muslims who seek to live successfully within the U.S. constitutional framework react with fear and loathing when Islamist extremists commit acts of terror in the name of Islam.*

No: Racial, ethnic, and religious profiling is inefficient, counterproductive, and morally wrong. Race and ethnic appearance are poor predictors of behavior. First, it is difficult to determine a person's religion by appearance alone. People from the Middle East have a wide range of skin tones and facial features. They include Christians and Jews as well as Muslims. Cases of mistaken identity are widespread. Many of those who found themselves the victims of anti-Muslim hate crimes after September 11 included numerous non-Muslims such as Chaldeans, Hindus, and Sikhs. More important, focusing on race and ethnicity keeps security officials' attention on a set of surface details that tell us little about a person and that draw officers' attention away from what is much more important and concrete: behavior.

Focusing on ethnic appearance can cause us to miss genuine threats. John Walker Lindh, a 20-year-old white Californian, fought with the Taliban in Afghanistan. Does an 85-year-old Middle Eastern grandmother deserve closer scrutiny than a 25-year-old white American man who has just bought a one-way ticket and looks nervous and sweaty?

Subjecting all Muslims or Middle Easterners to intrusive questioning, stops, or searches will harm our enforcement and detection efforts. First, profiling will drain enforcement efforts away from the close observation of suspicious behavior. Second, profiling will alienate law-abiding Muslims whose cooperation is critical for effective information gathering and counterterrorist intelligence. Alienating law-abiding Muslims by treating them like terrorist suspects will ultimately harm our ability to gather information about real terrorist threats.

We must find effective ways to secure the nation without giving up what is best about our country. Enacting discriminatory policies that take away individual liberty destroys the values for which we are fighting.**

Other approaches: The issue of ethnic profiling is more complicated than proponents and opponents often indicate in their arguments. In some cases, law enforcement use ethnic profiling based on specific threats. But law enforcement officials need to recognize that ethnic profiling limits their ability to detect terror suspects who may not fit the mold of the stereotypical terrorist—including women.

What do you think?

① Should airport security officers pay greater attention to passengers who appear to be Middle Eastern or Muslim? Why or why not?

② Should the FBI use ethnic or religious profiling to select people to interview as part of its counterterrorism efforts?

③ Will profiling strengthen or weaken our intelligence-gathering efforts? Explain.

④ Is racial, ethnic, or religious profiling ever justified? If so, in what cases? If not, why not?

*For a fuller exposition of this argument, see Daniel Pipes, "Fighting Militant Islam, Without Bias," *City Journal*, November 2001.

**For a fuller exposition of this argument, see David A. Harris, "Flying While Arab, Immigration Issues, and Lessons from the Racial Profiling Controversy." Testimony before the U.S. Commission on Civil Rights (October 12, 2001).

At the core of the U.S. political and legal system lies a strong belief in individual liberties and rights. This belief is reflected in the Bill of Rights, the first ten amendments to the Constitution. The freedoms therein are at the heart of civic engagement and ensure that individuals can freely participate in the political and social life of their communities. But these freedoms are also malleable, and at times the government has starkly limited them, as when officials perceive a threat to national security.

The inevitable tension between freedom and order is heightened in a post-9/11 world. Americans and their government struggle to protect essential liberties while guarding the nation against future terrorist attacks. This tension between national security and personal freedom is reflected in contemporary debates over free speech, political protest, and due process.

Do antiwar protests threaten the nation's success in Iraq? Will airports and national security agencies further develop and deploy security systems based on methods such as thumbprint and eye-scan technology? Should the government be able to track citizens' phone calls and e-mail messages? Should security officials profile Muslims and Arabs? Is torture ever justifiable? Will the Court uphold new laws that require Internet providers to secretly share personal information about their clients with the FBI? Those are the questions we confront in a post-9/11 world as we struggle to maintain the commitment to liberty that defines our nation while preserving the nation itself.

Summary

1. Civil Liberties in the American Legal System
The U.S. Constitution—and more specifically, the Bill of Rights, the first ten amendments—protects individuals against the unrestrained exercise of power by the federal government. The framers intended the Bill of Rights to ensure that individuals could engage freely in political speech and civic discourse in the larger society. Although the Bill of Rights was initially interpreted as imposing limits only on the national government, over time the Supreme Court has interpreted most of its protections as applying to the state governments as well.

2. Freedoms of Speech, Assembly, and the Press: First Amendment Freedoms Supporting Civic Discourse
Civic engagement is possible only in a society that fully protects civil liberties. Some of the civil liberties guaranteed in the Bill of Rights relate specifically to political participation and discourse. Most importantly, the freedoms of speech, assembly, petition, and the press empower individuals to engage actively and freely in politics and public life. These freedoms have always existed in a state of tension with the goal of national security; in times of crisis or instability, the judicial system has interpreted them narrowly.

3. Freedoms of Religion, Privacy, and Criminal Due Process: Encouraging Community and Civic Engagement
Other Bill of Rights freedoms encourage inclusiveness and community building, ensuring that individuals can be fully engaged in the social life of the nation. The freedom of religion, right to privacy, and criminal due process protections ensure that no one individual or group may be singled out for either favorable or unfavorable treatment.

4. Freedoms in Practice: Controversy Over the Second Amendment and the Right to Bear Arms
Historical context is crucial to our understanding of the freedoms protected by the Bill of Rights. Americans actively disagree about the proper interpretation of the Second Amendment and about the role of guns in maintaining a free and safe society.

5. Civil Liberties in Post-9/11 America

The tension between liberty and security, always present in U.S. political culture, has become more acute since the terrorist attacks of September 11, 2001. In the wake of those attacks, federal and state law enforcement officials have limited the speech, assembly, and petition rights of some American citizens and nationals and have curtailed the due process protections of those suspected of engaging in or supporting domestic and international terrorism.

Key Terms

bad tendency test 120
civil liberties 112
clear and present danger test 120
clear and probable danger test 120
commercial speech 122
creationism 128
criminal due process rights 133
double jeopardy 134
due process 113

establishment clause 126
exclusionary rule 133
fighting words 123
free exercise clause 128
habeas corpus 118
imminent lawless action test (incitement test) 121
intelligent design 127
Lemon test 127
libel 123
marketplace of ideas 118
Miranda rights 134

obscenity 123
prior restraint 124
rendition 140
right to privacy 129
selective incorporation 116
slander 123
symbolic speech 121
time, place, and manner restrictions 124
total incorporation 116

For Review

1. What are civil liberties? How do civil liberties differ from civil rights? Why do we protect civil liberties?

2. How does the First Amendment support civic discourse?

3. What protections does the Bill of Rights provide to those accused of committing a crime?

4. What are the two sides of the issue of Second Amendment rights? How has the Supreme Court interpreted this right?

5. How have the terrorist attacks of September 11, 2001, affected civil liberties in the United States?

For Critical Thinking and Discussion

1. Under what circumstances should the government be allowed to regulate or punish speech?

2. Should Congress pass a constitutional amendment banning flag burning? Why or why not?

3. Under what circumstances should government be able to punish people for practicing their religious beliefs?

4. Should the government be allowed to search people and property without a warrant based on probable cause that a crime was committed? Explain.

5. Do you believe that the USA PATRIOT Act and the NSA domestic surveillance program make the nation safer? Why or why not?

6. Will giving up liberty to enhance security protect the nation against terrorists, or will it destroy the fundamental values upon which the nation was founded? Defend your position.

MULTIPLE CHOICE: Choose the lettered item that answers the question correctly.

1. Civil liberties
   a. are protected only in Article III of the U.S. Constitution.
   b. entitle all citizens to equal protection of the laws.
   c. protect individuals against an abuse of government power.
   d. did not exist until the twenty-first century.

2. Which of the following is protected by the U.S. Constitution and the courts?
   a. slander
   b. libel
   c. fighting words
   d. symbolic speech

3. Teacher-led prayer in public schools is prohibited by
   a. the establishment clause.
   b. the free exercise clause.
   c. the due process clause.
   d. the equal protection clause.

4. The right to privacy was first established in the case
   a. *Griswold v. Connecticut.*
   b. *Roe v. Wade.*
   c. *Lemon v. Kurtzman.*
   d. *Miller v. California.*

5. Criminal defendants' rights to legal counsel and a jury trial are protected by the
   a. First Amendment.
   b. Second Amendment.
   c. Fourth Amendment.
   d. Sixth Amendment.

6. Critics of the USA PATRIOT Act charge that the law violates the
   a. Second Amendment.
   b. Fourth Amendment.
   c. Eighth Amendment.
   d. Tenth Amendment.

7. Police would most likely be required to use a warrant if they wanted to collect evidence from
   a. a house.
   b. the back seat of a car.
   c. a school locker.
   d. a prison cell.

8. According to the Supreme Court, burning the U.S. flag is a form of
   a. hate speech.
   b. libel.
   c. symbolic speech.
   d. treason.

9. Citizens' disagreement about how to interpret the Eighth Amendment is reflected in the current debate over
   a. school vouchers.
   b. intelligent design.
   c. "virtual" child pornography.
   d. lethal injection.

10. The Second Amendment protects U.S. citizens'
    a. free speech.
    b. freedom from self-incrimination.
    c. freedom of religion.
    d. freedom to bear arms.

FILL IN THE BLANKS.

11. _____ refers to the process by which the Supreme Court has applied to the states those provisions in the Bill of Rights that serve some fundamental principle of liberty or justice.

12. _____ set guidelines that the government must follow in investigating, bringing to trial, and punishing those accused of committing a crime.

13. Under the _____ , evidence obtained illegally cannot be used in a trial.

14. The Fifth Amendment protection against _____ ensures that criminal defendants cannot be tried again for the same crime when a court has already found them not guilty of committing that crime.

15. Speech that is likely to bring about public disorder or chaos and which may be banned in public places to ensure the preservation of public order is called _____ .

Answers: 1. c; 2. d; 3. a; 4. a; 5. d; 6. b; 7. a; 8. c; 9. d; 10. d; 11. Selective incorporation; 12. criminal due process rights; 13. exclusionary rule; 14. double jeopardy; 15. fighting words.

Internet Resources

Center for Democracy and Technology
www.cdt.org The effect of new computer and communications technologies on American civil liberties is the subject of this site.

Public Broadcasting Station
www.npr.org/news/specials/patriotact/patriotactprovisions .html PBS provides a summary of controversial provisions of the USA PATRIOT Act, including major arguments for and against each provision.

Internet Activism

The American Civil Liberties Union
www.aclu.org/blog/ The American Civil Liberties Union (ACLU) is a national organization with state affiliates that consistently supports the interest of liberty when challenged by security interests. Go to the Web site to follow the ACLU blog and engage in the subsequent discussion over the appropriate protection of constitutional rights from infringement by federal, state, and local governments.

Twitter
http://twitter.com/acuconservative The American Conservative Union is one of the oldest conservative interest groups in the country and engages the debate between liberty and security from a conservative perspective.

Facebook: Epic.org
www.facebook.com/group.php?gid=20774297052 The Electronic Privacy Information Center focuses public attention on the political issues surrounding privacy and civil liberties emerging from rapidly changing technologies.

Recommended Readings

Baker, Thomas E., and John F. Stack. *At War With Civil Rights and Civil Liberties.* Rowan & Littlefield Publishers, 2005. A collection of essays written by constitutional law scholars, as well as Supreme Court Justice Breyer and Attorney General John Ashcroft, that demonstrate the difficulty of balancing liberty with security in a time of war.

Bollinger, Lee C., and Geoffrey R. Stone, eds. *Eternally Vigilant: Free Speech in the Modern Era.* Chicago: University of Chicago Press, 2002. Drawing on the work of legal scholars, an examination of the philosophical underpinnings of free speech, with a highlighting of the history of contentious free speech disputes.

Carroll, Jamuna, ed. *Privacy.* Detroit, MI: Greenhaven Press, 2006. An edited volume of point-counterpoint articles exploring a wide variety of issues, including counterterrorism measures, Internet privacy, video surveillance, and employee monitoring.

Fisher, Louis. *The Constitution and 9/11: Recurring Threats to America's Freedoms.* Lawrence, KA: University Press of Kansas. This book, written by one of the nation's foremost experts on separation of powers, surveys the historic responses to threats to national security by the branches of the federal government and then evaluates the current challenges to the constitutional law of national security after 9/11.

Spitzer, Robert J. *The Politics of Gun Control,* 4th ed. Washington, DC: CQ Press, 2007. Analysis of the gun control debate in the United States, including its history, the constitutional right to bear arms, the criminological consequences of guns, citizen political action, and the role and impact of American governing institutions.

Movies of Interest

Rendition (2007)
When an Egyptian terrorism suspect "disappears" on a flight from Africa to Washington, D.C., his American wife and a CIA analyst struggle to secure his release from a secret detention (and torture) facility somewhere outside the United States.

Good Night and Good Luck (2005)
This film examines the conflict between veteran journalist Edward R. Murrow and Senator Joseph McCarthy as Murrow attempts to investigate and discredit McCarthy's tactics in investigating and destroying Communist elements in the federal government and larger society.

Enemy of the State (1998)
This film depicts the adventures of an attorney entangled in a web of national politics when a reporter friend accidentally records the murder of a senator. Unaware that he is in possession of the reporter's video, the attorney becomes the target of a National Security Agency investigation that nearly succeeds in destroying his personal and professional life.

The Siege (1998)
After the U.S. military abducts an Islamic religious leader, New York City becomes the target of escalating terrorist attacks. As the bombings continue, the U.S. government responds by declaring martial law, detaining Muslim men, and sending U.S. troops into the streets of New York City.

The People Versus Larry Flynt (1996)
This film documents the economic success, courtroom battles, and personal challenges of *Hustler* magazine publisher Larry Flynt. Flynt is obnoxious and hedonistic in ways that offend and anger "decent people," even as he fights to protect freedom of speech for all.

CHAPTER

5

Civil Rights

THEN

African Americans, women, Native Americans, Latinos, and other groups struggled to achieve equality in the United States.

NOW

Groups of citizens continue to struggle for their civil rights, including Asian Americans, lesbians and gay men, and citizens with disabilities.

NEXT

What other groups of legally disadvantaged citizens will fight for their civil rights?

What criteria will the U.S. Supreme Court use in deciding cases concerning sex-based discrimination?

How will the state of the economy and threats of terrorism shape the issues and the demands at the forefront of future civil rights battles?

This chapter examines the struggle by various groups for equality under the law.

FIRST, we look at *the meaning of equality under the law.*

SECOND, we trace the history of *slavery and its aftermath* in the United States, noting how promises of equal protection for African Americans have often fallen short.

THIRD, we consider the evolution of the African American *civil rights movement.*

FOURTH, we examine *the government's response to the civil rights movement.*

FIFTH, we look at *the movement for women's civil rights,* including the lengthy struggle to obtain suffrage and the continuing battle for equal treatment under the law.

SIXTH, we provide an overview of several *other civil rights movements:* Native American, Latino and Asian American citizens; citizens with disabilities; and lesbian, gay, bisexual, and transgendered citizens.

SEVENTH, we discuss the controversy over *affirmative action* and consider the question *is it constitutional?*

civil rights
the rights and privileges guaranteed to all citizens under the equal protection and due process clauses of the Fifth and Fourteenth amendments; the idea that individuals are protected from discrimination based on characteristics such as race, national origin, religion, and sex

inherent characteristics
individual attributes such as race, national origin, religion, and gender

Although the Declaration of

Independence claims that all men are created equal and are endowed with the natural rights of life, liberty, and the pursuit of happiness, neither the Articles of Confederation nor the Constitution as initially ratified guaranteed that the government would treat or protect all men equally. Indeed, those constitutions did *not* guarantee nonwhite men or women of all races and colors the same legal rights that they guaranteed to white men. For example, African American men and women had no legal rights and were bought and sold as property until 1865, when the Thirteenth Amendment to the Constitution made such enslavement illegal. The Constitution did not guarantee American women the right to sue, nor did it protect married women's right to own property, until well into the nineteenth century. Many Americans experienced unequal treatment under the law throughout U.S. history.

Fast-forward to today. When asked what principles or ideals they hold most dear, many Americans will mention equality. Yet, even today, not all people in the United States are treated equally under the law. Moreover, people disagree strongly on the meaning of "equal protections of the law," which has been a stated constitutional guarantee since 1868, when the states ratified the Fourteenth Amendment to the U.S. Constitution.

Disagreement about what constitutes "equal treatment" is at the heart of many past and current struggles for equality. Does equal treatment mean that the government must ensure that all people have equal opportunities to pursue their happiness? Does it bar all differential treatment by the government and its officials, or are there certain situations in which it is acceptable for the government to treat people differently to fulfill its mission (establish justice, ensure domestic tranquility, provide for the common defense, protect the general welfare, and secure the blessings of liberty)?

In this chapter, we examine the concept of equality under the law. We focus on how groups of citizens that were originally deprived of equal protection of their liberties and pursuit of happiness have been able to expand their rights in numerous areas, including voting rights and equal access to educational and employment opportunities, to housing, and to public accommodations.

The Meaning of Equality Under the Law

Although the issue of protecting civil liberties was in the forefront at the nation's founding, as we discussed in Chapter 4, the issue of guaranteeing civil rights reached the national agenda much later.[1] When we talk about **civil rights** in the United States, we mean the rights and privileges guaranteed by the government to all *citizens* under the equal protection and due process clauses of the Fifth and Fourteenth amendments and the privileges and immunities clause of the Fourteenth Amendment. These rights are based on the idea that the government should protect individuals from discrimination that results from inherent characteristics. **Inherent characteristics** are individual characteristics that are part of a person's nature, such as race, religion, national origin, and sex.

The Constitution imposes constraints (civil liberties) and responsibilities (civil rights) on governments, which includes government officials and employees, but *not* on private individuals or organizations. However, governments can write laws that prohibit private individuals and organizations from infringing on civil liberties and civil rights. For example, the national government enacted the Civil Rights Act of 1964, which prohibited private businesses and organizations from discriminating in hiring decisions based on the inherent characteristics of race, color, religion, national origin, and sex.

Most people agree that no government, private individual, or organization should treat people differently because of these inherent characteristics. The courts have determined that treating citizens differently based on their inherent characteristics is unfair, arbitrary, and in most situations illegal. However, people and even government officials, including judges, disagree about whether the list of inherent characteristics should include characteristics such as age, physical and mental disabilities, and sexual orientation. For example, should the government guarantee same-sex couples the same right to marry, and hence have the same legal benefits of marriage, as it guarantees to heterosexual couples? Moreover, there are debates over if and when the government should allow differential treatment in order for it to fulfill its mission.

As we explored in Chapter 4, no civil liberty is absolute; there are situations in which the government may infringe on an individual's liberty. For example, the government may infringe on an individual's freedom of speech if it views her speech as violating the imminent lawless action test (or incitement test); the risk of harm from the speech is

Fighting for Their Rights: How Groups and Issues Change

THEN (1960s AND 1970s)	NOW (2011)
African Americans, women, Native Americans, and Latinos fought for equal treatment under the law.	Asian citizens, citizens with disabilities, and lesbian, gay, bisexual, and transgendered citizens fight for equal treatment under the law.
Key strategies included nonviolent civil disobedience, protests, and seeking remedy through the justice system.	Protest and lawsuits remain important strategies, but today's activists also focus on petitioning Congress and state legislatures in attempts to pass legislation.
Important issues included equal access to schools, public accommodations, voting rights, and equal pay.	Important issues include spousal rights for gays and lesbians, voting rights, and immigration policy.

WHAT'S NEXT?

> What groups will begin to seek ways of achieving their civil rights?

> How will new technologies change the strategies and tactics that civil rights activists use?

> What important issues will be at the forefront of the civil rights agenda in the future?

highly likely and the harm is imminent or immediate. Civil rights are also not absolute. The national courts have established "tests" that the government uses to determine when unequal protection under the law (that is, differential or discriminatory treatment) is legal.

Today, the courts use three tests—*strict scrutiny, heightened scrutiny,* and *ordinary scrutiny*—to determine when unequal treatment is legal. Which test the court uses depends on the inherent characteristic that is the basis for differential treatment. For example, courts view race, ethnic origin, and religion to be **suspect classifications,** meaning that judges will assume that the laws treating individuals differently because of these inherent characteristics are unconstitutional and violate the equal protection clauses. When the courts hear a challenge to laws with suspect classifications, they use the **strict scrutiny test,** which means that the government must show that the differential treatment is necessary for it to achieve a compelling public interest for which it is responsible. Using the strict scrutiny test in *Loving v. Virginia* (1967), the Supreme Court determined that laws barring interracial marriage violated the Constitution because there was no compelling public interest for which the government was responsible; hence, the laws were not necessary for a compelling public interest.[2] Therefore, today it is illegal to deny interracial couples the right to marry.

The courts do not consider the inherent characteristic of sex to be a suspect classification, and therefore laws that allow differential treatment of women and men do not need

suspect classifications
distinctions based on race, religion, and national origin, which are assumed to be illegitimate

strict scrutiny test
the guidelines the courts use to determine the legality of suspect classification-based discrimination; on the basis of this test, discrimination is legal if it is a necessary means by which the government can achieve a compelling public interest

heightened scrutiny test (intermediate scrutiny test)
the guidelines used most frequently by the courts to determine the legality of sex-based discrimination; on the basis of this test, sex-based discrimination is legal if the government can prove that it is substantially related to the achievement of an important public interest

ordinary scrutiny test (rational basis test)
on the basis of this test, discrimination is legal if it is a reasonable means by which the government can achieve a legitimate public interest

to pass the strict scrutiny test when challenged. Instead, the courts apply the **heightened scrutiny** test (also known as the **intermediate scrutiny test**) in sex-based discrimination cases, which requires the government to show that the sex-based differential treatment is substantially related to an important public interest for which the government is responsible. The heightened scrutiny test is a weaker test, making it easier for the government to justify sex-based discrimination than discrimination based on race, religion, or ethnic origin. Therefore, today women in the military do not have the same opportunities in combat roles (and hence combat-related benefits) as military men do.

The weakest test the courts use when determining if a law allowing discriminatory treatment is legal is the **ordinary scrutiny test** (also called the **rational basis test**). Using the ordinary scrutiny test, courts require governments to show that the differential treatment is a rational means to achieve a legitimate public interest for which the government is responsible. State governments have established minimum ages for numerous legal rights, such as the right to marry, the right to get a driver's license, and the right to purchase alcoholic beverages. Many states have also established a retirement age (a maximum age) for state judges. These are areas of life where the courts, applying the ordinary scrutiny test, have determined age-based discrimination to be legal. Differential treatment based on age is a reasonable way to achieve some legitimate public interests. Can you determine what the public interests are in each of these age-based differential treatment situations?

For most of our nation's history, the law not only allowed unequal treatment for different racial, ethnic, and religious groups as well as for men and women, but also *required* this unequal treatment for a majority of the population. Women were not granted the right to vote until 1920, and they faced a wide variety of discriminatory practices. Ethnic and religious groups also faced widespread discrimination, some as a matter of law. For example, more than 120,000 people of Japanese ancestry were forcibly interned in camps during World War II. More recently, following the terrorist attacks of September 11, 2001, the federal government has detained thousands of Arabs and Arab Americans in prisons without providing any criminal due process protections. But probably the most blatant example of discrimination in U.S. history is slavery. This practice was protected under the law, and slaves were considered to be the property of their owners. They had no protection under the law and could be treated in any way their owners saw fit.

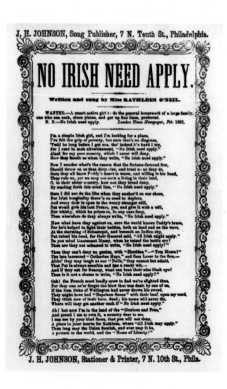

> Historically, people have encountered discrimination because of their ethnicity, race, or gender. In some places, Irish citizens were barred from applying for jobs, African Americans attending theaters were forced to use separate entrances (here with the ironic promise of "good shows in comfort"), and help-wanted ads were segregated based on gender.

Slavery and Its Aftermath

When it was first written, the Constitution implicitly endorsed the unequal and discriminatory treatment of African Americans.[3] Some of the most important provisions of the new constitution treated people of African descent as property, allowing states to continue to permit them to be enslaved. Although the movement to abolish slavery was in its early stages in 1787, the year the Constitution was completed, by the early to mid-1800s, it had gained significant momentum in the North, largely because of the activism of various religious and humanitarian groups.[4]

Slavery in the United States

Most African Americans today are the descendants of Africans who were forcibly brought to the New World. In 1619, twenty Africans arrived in Jamestown as *indentured servants,* workers with a fixed term of service. But by the mid-1600s, slavery began to replace indentured servitude.

OPPOSITION TO SLAVERY Many chafed at the hypocrisy of those who sought freedom and equality but kept slaves. Among the first to challenge slavery were former slaves, who staged both peaceful protests and armed insurrections throughout the late 1700s and early 1800s. These activists successfully rallied support in the North for the gradual abolition of slavery by 1804. They argued forcefully against the injustice of the slave system, moving the opponents of slavery to action by their horrifying firsthand accounts of the treatment of slaves.

Despite those arguments, the U.S. Congress, wary of the divisiveness caused by the slavery issue, sought to balance the antislavery position of the abolitionist states with the proslavery sentiments of the slaveholding states. One such attempt was the Missouri Compromise, passed by Congress in 1820. The compromise regulated slavery in the newly acquired western territories: slavery was prohibited north of the 36°30′ north parallel, except within the state of Missouri.

The abolitionists, including organizations such as the American Anti-Slavery Society, objected to the efforts of Congress to accommodate the slaveholding states and called for the emancipation of all slaves. Members of the American Anti-Slavery Society were actively engaged in **civil disobedience,** which is nonviolent refusal to comply with laws or government policies that are morally objectionable. Specifically, American Anti-Slavery Society members actively supported the Underground Railroad, a series of safe houses that allowed escaping slaves to flee to the northern states and Canada. Between 1810 and 1850, an estimated 100,000 people escaped slavery through the Underground Railroad (see Figure 5.1 on page 152). But in 1850, the U.S. Congress—in an attempt to stall or prevent the secession, or separation, of southern states from the Union—passed the Fugitive Slave Act. The law required federal marshals to return runaway slaves or risk a $1,000 fine (over $20,000 in today's dollars); private citizens who harbored or abetted runaway slaves could be imprisoned for six months and fined $1,000. Passage of this law meant that "conductors" on the Underground Railroad operated in clear violation of the statute, risking their own livelihoods and property.

THE CIVIL WAR ERA Abolitionists were bolstered in their efforts when Harriet Beecher Stowe's popular book *Uncle Tom's Cabin* was published in 1852. Vividly depicting the harsh reality of slavery in the United States, this work inspired many to actively challenge slavery. By the late 1850s, the widespread distribution of *Uncle Tom's Cabin,* as well as the trial and execution of John Brown, a white abolitionist who tried to ignite a slave insurrection in Harpers Ferry, in what was then Virginia and is now West Virginia, had convinced many northerners that slavery was immoral.

Yet the U.S. Supreme Court ruled otherwise. In 1857, Dred Scott, an African American enslaved by a surgeon in the U.S. Army, sued for his freedom, arguing that because he had lived in both a free state (Illinois) and a free territory (the Wisconsin Territory, now Minnesota),

civil disobedience
active, but nonviolent, refusal to comply with laws or governmental policies that are morally objectionable

he had become a free man and as such he could not be re-enslaved when he moved to Missouri. (Figure 5.1 shows states that did and did not allow slavery at that time.) The Supreme Court rejected Scott's claim and in *Dred Scott v. Sandford* ruled that the Missouri Compromise of 1820 was unconstitutional because the U.S. Congress lacked the authority to ban slavery in the territories.[5] It also ruled that Scott was not a U.S. citizen, asserting that slaves were property rather than citizens with **standing to sue,** or the legal right to bring lawsuits in court. Although the *Dred Scott* decision appeared to be a victory for slaveholding states, it was also pivotal in mobilizing the abolitionist movement and swaying public opinion in favor of a war to prevent secession and to bring about emancipation.

Certain that their way of life was under siege and alarmed by the election of Abraham Lincoln as president in 1860, the southern states decided that they should secede from the union. By May 1861, eleven southern states had declared their independence and created the Confederate States of America. A long and bloody civil war followed as the North fought to bring the southern states back into the union.

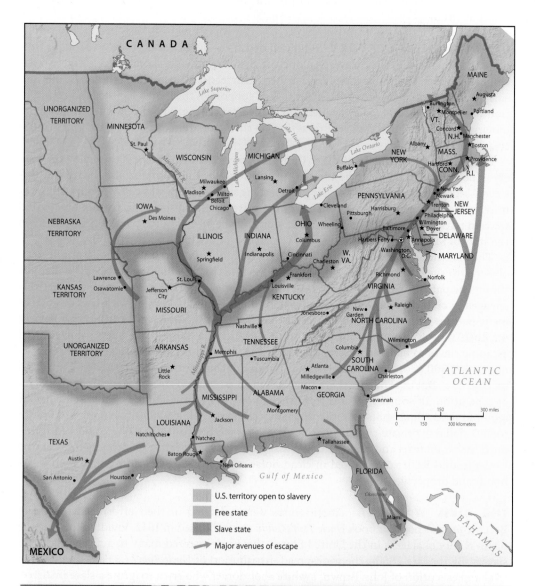

POLITICAL INQUIRY

FIGURE 5.1 ■ ROUTES TO FREEDOM ON THE UNDERGROUND RAILROAD Why did many escaping slaves use routes that followed the Mississippi River or the Atlantic coast? Which northern cities were important "stations" on the Underground Railroad? Why was legislation such as the Fugitive Slave Act ultimately powerless to stop this movement?

One of the most important turning points of the Civil War was the Emancipation Proclamation, issued by Abraham Lincoln in April 1862. This order abolished slavery in the states that had seceded from the Union. The Union army and navy were charged with implementing the order. The proclamation had several purposes: it decreed that the abolition of slavery was a goal of the war, and by doing so it effectively prevented Britain and France from intervening in the war on the southern side, because those countries had both renounced the institution of slavery. When the South finally surrendered in April 1865, it did so knowing that its economic way of life, which depended on slave-based plantation farming, was over. At the end of the war, nearly 4 million slaves in the United States were freed. The states then ratified three constitutional amendments to codify the victories won on the battlefield:

- the Thirteenth Amendment (1865), which ended slavery throughout the United States and prohibited it in the future
- the Fourteenth Amendment (1868), which defines *citizens* as "all persons born or naturalized in the United States" and mandates the same privileges and immunities for all citizens and due process and equal protection for all people
- the Fifteenth Amendment (1870), which decrees that every man has the right to vote, regardless of color

Reconstruction and the First Civil Rights Acts

After the North won the war and Lincoln was assassinated in April 1865, members of Congress and others in government disagreed about the best way to proceed in the South. Many Republicans thought that the South should be stabilized and quickly brought back into the political fold. Like Lincoln, these moderates endorsed a plan that would enable the southern states to be quickly represented in Congress. Others, however, took a more radical view and argued that all those who had ever supported the Confederacy should be kept out of national and state politics. As the 1860s drew to a close, many of these more radical Republicans had come to power and had strictly limited the people in southern states who could participate in politics. As a result of their activities, during the **Reconstruction era** between 1866 and 1877—when the institutions and the infrastructure of the South were rebuilt—freed slaves, who could easily say they had never supported the Confederacy, made up a sizeable portion of both the electorate and the candidate pool in the southern states. Federal troops provided protection that facilitated their participation. During this decade, African American voters made the most of their position in the South and elected a substantial number of other African Americans to legislative offices in the local, state, and federal governments. In some places, such as South Carolina, African American legislators outnumbered whites, giving them a majority during the Reconstruction years.

Between 1865 and 1875, Congress passed a series of laws designed to solidify the rights and protections outlined in the Thirteenth, Fourteenth, and Fifteenth amendments. Congress needed to spell out the rights of African Americans because of the pervasiveness of **Black Codes,** laws passed immediately after the Civil War by the confederate states that limited the rights of "freemen," or former slaves. These codes prevented freemen from voting, owning property, or bringing suit. To remedy that situation, Congress passed laws that sought to negate the Black Codes. One law, the Civil Rights Act of 1866, extended the definition of *citizen* to anyone born in the United States (including freemen) and granted all citizens the right to sue, own property, bear witness in a court of law, and enter into legal contracts. The Enforcement Act of 1870 bolstered the Fifteenth Amendment by establishing penalties for interfering with the right to vote. The Civil Rights Act of 1872, also known as the Anti–Ku Klux Klan Act, made it a federal crime to deprive individuals of their rights, privileges, or immunities protected by the Constitution. Although the Reconstruction-era Congress sought to remedy the new forms of inequality that emerged after the Civil War, its efforts would be short-lived.

Backlash: Jim Crow Laws

In 1877, the inauguration of President Rutherford Hayes (1877–1881) brought the Reconstruction era to a decisive end, almost immediately rolling back the gains African Americans had achieved in education and political participation. Under Hayes, the federal troops that

Reconstruction era
the time after the Civil War between 1866 and 1877 when the institutions and infrastructure of the South were rebuilt

Black Codes
laws passed immediately after the Civil War by the confederate states that limited the rights of "freemen" (former slaves)

GLOBAL CONTEXT

MODERN FORMS OF SLAVERY

On December 10, 1948, the United Nations General Assembly adopted the Universal Declaration of Human Rights, which promoted "universal respect for and observance of human rights and fundamental freedoms." The Declaration includes the following statement: "No one shall be held in slavery or servitude: slavery and the slave trade shall be prohibited in all their forms." When Americans think of slavery, they think of our nation's own historical experience with the institution of slavery: slave ships, plantation life, and the Civil War. It surprises many that in the twenty-first century, slavery still exists. As former United Nations Secretary General Kofi Annan has observed:

✳ What can governments do to prevent modern-day slavery?

> Nearly every day, there are shocking reports of men, women and children who are exploited, denied their basic rights and their dignity and deprived of a better future, through both ancient and modern forms of slavery.
>
> Slavery and trafficking, and related practices such as debt bondage, forced prostitution and forced labour, are violations of the most fundamental human rights: the right to life; the right to dignity and security; the right to just and favourable conditions of work; the right to health; and the right to equality. These are rights that we all possess—irrespective of our sex, our nationality, our social status, our occupation or any other characteristic.*

Women and children, particularly in Asia but also in countries of the former Soviet Union, are sometimes forced to be part of prostitution rings that operate in those countries as well as in Western democracies. In some countries, young women who respond to help-wanted ads for international work as nannies or domestic servants are essentially kidnapped and forced to work as prostitutes. Often, traffickers advertise in the help-wanted sections of local newspapers, offering high-paying jobs as models, domestic servants, hotel maids, nannies, or shop clerks in Western nations and promising to help secure the required visa applications and work permits.

Traffickers rely on people's desire for a better life as a lure. Once victims are out of their homeland, they may be raped and forced into prostitution. Frequently, traffickers will confiscate the victim's identification and travel permits (often forgeries), withhold food or shelter unless the victim complies, and use the threat of imprisonment by authorities or the threat of harm to the victim's family at home as a means of ensuring compliance. The U.S. Department of State estimates that 800,000–900,000 people annually are trafficked across international borders worldwide, including an estimated 20,000 people who are brought into the United States.

*Secretary-General Kofi Annan, message on the occasion of the International Day for the Abolition of Slavery, December 2, 2003.

Jim Crow laws
laws requiring strict separation of racial groups, with whites and "nonwhites" required to attend separate schools, work in different jobs, and use segregated public accommodations, such as transportation and restaurants

de jure segregation
segregation mandated by law

had protected African Americans from physical reprisals were withdrawn. State and local governments throughout the South mandated racial segregation by enacting what came to be known as **Jim Crow laws.** These laws required the strict separation of racial groups, with whites and "nonwhites" going to separate schools, being employed in different jobs, and using segregated public accommodations, such as transportation and restaurants. **De jure segregation,** legally mandated separation of the races, became the norm in much of the South.

The idea behind the Jim Crow laws was that whites and nonwhites should occupy separate societies and have little to do with each other. Many whites feared that racial mixing would result in interracial dating and marriage, which would inevitably lead to the decline of their superior position in society; thus in many southern states, miscegenation laws, which banned interracial marriage, cohabitation, or sex, were passed and severe penalties imposed for those who violated them. Interracial couples who married risked losing their property and even their liberty, since heavy fines and jail sentences were among the penalties for breaking those laws.

State and local governments in the South also found creative ways to prevent African Americans from exercising their right to vote. They relied on several tactics:

- The **white primary** was a primary election in which only white people were allowed to vote. Because Democrats dominated politics so heavily in the post–Civil War South, the only races that really mattered were the primary races that determined the Democratic nominees. But Southern states restricted voting in these primaries to whites only.
- The **literacy test** determined eligibility to vote. Literacy tests were designed so that few voters would stand a chance of passing the exam administered to African American voters, whereas the test for white voters was easy to pass. Typically, white voters were exempt from literacy tests because of a grandfather clause (see below).
- A **poll tax,** a fee levied for voting, often presented an insurmountable obstacle to poor African Americans. White voters were often exempt from poll taxes because of a grandfather clause.
- The **grandfather clause** exempted individuals from conditions on voting (such as poll taxes or literacy tests) if they themselves or their ancestor had been eligible to vote before 1870. Because African Americans did not have the right to vote in southern states before the Civil War, the grandfather clause was a mechanism to protect the voting rights of whites.

These laws were enforced not only by government agents, particularly police, but by nongovernmental groups as well. Among the most powerful of these groups was the Ku Klux Klan (KKK). During the late 1800s and into the 1900s, the Klan was dreaded and hated throughout the southern states, and it used its powers to threaten and intimidate those African Americans and whites who dared to question its core principle: that whites are in every way superior to African Americans. The Klan's particular brand of intimidation, the burning cross and the lynching noose, was reviled throughout the southern and border states, but few could dispute the power the Klan wielded in those areas.

Governmental Acceptance of Discrimination

The federal government too had seemingly abandoned African Americans and the quest for equality under the law. In the *Civil Rights Cases* of 1883, the Supreme Court ruled that Congress lacked the authority to prevent discrimination by private individuals and organizations. Rather, Congress's jurisdiction, the Court claimed, was limited to banning discrimination in official acts of state or local governments. The Court also declared that the Civil Rights Act of 1875, which had sought to mandate "full and equal enjoyment" of a wide variety of facilities and accommodations, was unconstitutional.

In 1896, the Court struck what seemed to be the final blow against racial equality. In 1890, Louisiana passed a law that required separate accommodations for blacks and whites on railroad trains. Several citizens of New Orleans sought to test the constitutionality of the law and enlisted Homer Plessy, who was one-eighth African American (but still considered "black" by Louisiana state law) to serve as plaintiff. The choice of Plessy, who could pass for white, was intended to show the arbitrary nature of the statute. On June 7, 1892, Plessy boarded a railroad car designated for whites only. Plessy was asked to leave the whites-only car, and he refused. He was then arrested and jailed, charged with violating the state law. In 1896, the U.S. Supreme Court heard ***Plessy v. Ferguson,*** in which Plessy's attorneys argued that the Louisiana state law violated the **equal protection clause** of the Fourteenth Amendment, which states that no state shall "deny to any person within its jurisdiction the equal protection of the laws."

In a 7–1 decision, the Court rejected Plessy's arguments, claiming that segregation based on race was not a violation of the equal protection clause. Rather, the court made this argument:

> We consider the underlying fallacy of the plaintiff's argument to consist in the assumption that the enforced separation of the two races stamps the colored race with a badge of inferiority. If this be so, it is not by reason of anything found in the act, but solely because the colored race chooses to put that construction upon it.[6]

In its decision, the Court created the **separate but equal doctrine,** declaring that separate but equal facilities do not violate the Fourteenth Amendment's equal protection clause. Under this doctrine, the Court upheld state laws mandating separation of the races in schools

white primary
a primary election in which a party's nominees for general election were chosen but in which only white people were allowed to vote

literacy test
a test to determine eligibility to vote; designed so that few African Americans would pass

poll tax
a fee for voting; levied to prevent poor African Americans in the South from voting

grandfather clause
a clause exempting individuals from voting conditions such as poll taxes or literacy tests if they or their ancestor had voted before 1870, thus sparing most white voters

Plessy v. Ferguson
1896 Supreme Court ruling creating the separate but equal doctrine

equal protection clause
the Fourteenth Amendment clause stating that no state shall "deny to any person within its jurisdiction the equal protection of the laws"

separate but equal doctrine
established by the Supreme Court in *Plessy v. Ferguson,* it said that separate but equal facilities for whites and nonwhites do not violate the Fourteenth Amendment's equal protection clause

and all public accommodations such as businesses, public transportation, restaurants, hotels, swimming pools, and recreational facilities. The only condition the Court placed on these segregated facilities was that the state had to provide public facilities for both whites and nonwhites. The Court paid little attention to whether the school systems or public accommodations were comparable in quality. As long as the state had some kind of facilities in place for both whites and nonwhites, the segregation was permitted. This doctrine would become the legal backbone of segregationist policies for more than five decades to come.

The Civil Rights Movement

In the early decades of the twentieth century, African Americans continued their struggle for equal protection of the laws. Though the movement for civil rights enjoyed some early successes, the century was nearly half over before momentous victories by civil rights activists finally began to change the status of African Americans in revolutionary ways. These victories were the result of strong leadership at the helm of the movement, the effective strategies used by activists, and a national government that was finally ready to fulfill the promise of equality embodied in the Declaration of Independence.

Fighting Back: Early Civil Rights Organizations

In the early years of the twentieth century, the political climate was open to reform, with activists in the Progressive movement calling for an end to government corruption, reforms to labor laws, the protection of children from abusive labor practices, and an expansion of rights, including the right of women to vote and the civil rights of African Americans (see Chapter 8 for more on the Progressive movement). In 1909, W. E. B. Du Bois (an influential African American writer and scholar, who is today acknowledged as the father of social science) joined with Oswald Garrison Villard (publisher of the *New York Evening Post*, an influential newspaper, and grandson of the abolitionist leader William Lloyd Garrison) to form the National Association for the Advancement of Colored People (NAACP). One of the targets of the NAACP for the next several decades was the separate but equal doctrine, which remained in place through the first half of the twentieth century.

Citing the lack of graduate schools, law schools, and medical schools for African Americans, the NAACP argued that the states had violated the equal protection clause by failing to make such schools available to African Americans. During the 1930s, lawsuits brought by the NAACP in several states ended discriminatory admissions practices in professional schools.[7] Momentum in the movement for equality continued to grow, fueled in part by the growing political activism of African American soldiers returning home after fighting against fascism abroad during World War II. Many of these soldiers began to question why they were denied freedom and equality in their own country, and they mobilized for civil rights in their communities. Though the Court had not yet overturned the separate but equal doctrine, by 1950 the U.S. Supreme Court had ruled that segregating classrooms, dining rooms, or library facilities in colleges, universities, and professional schools was unconstitutional.

Taking cues from those court decisions, by the 1950s the NAACP and other groups had changed their tactics. Instead of arguing that states had to provide equivalent schools and programs for African Americans and whites, these groups began to argue that segregation itself was a violation of the equal protection clause. But it was not until 1954 that the U.S. Supreme Court struck down the separate but equal doctrine, finding it inherently unequal and therefore unconstitutional.

The End of Separate but Equal

In the fall of 1951, Oliver Brown, a welder at the Santa Fe Railroad yard in Topeka, Kansas, sought to have his daughter Linda enrolled in the third grade in an all-white public school seven blocks from their home. The act was not accidental; it was the calculated first step in an NAACP legal strategy that would result in sweeping changes to the nation's public school system, effectively shattering the segregated school system dominant in the South.[8] The Browns lived in an integrated neighborhood in Topeka, and Topeka schools were segregated, as allowed (but not required) under Kansas state law. Oliver Brown spoke with a Topeka attorney and with the Topeka NAACP, which persuaded him to join a lawsuit against the Topeka Board of Education. Brown agreed and was directed to attempt to register Linda at the all-white public school. Linda was denied admission.

The stand taken by Oliver Brown and the other plaintiffs was not in vain. Thurgood Marshall, who would go on to become the first African American to sit on the U.S. Supreme Court, argued the case, and in a unanimous decision in 1954 the Supreme Court ruled in **Brown v. Board of Education of Topeka** that segregated schools violate the equal protection clause of the Fourteenth Amendment. In one stroke, the Court concluded that "separate but equal" schools were inherently unequal, because they stamped African American children with a "badge of racial inferiority" that stayed with them throughout their lives.

In a second case the following year (sometimes called the second Brown decision or Brown II), the court grappled with the issue of how the first *Brown* decision should be implemented—recognizing that many southern states would be reluctant to enforce the decision unless they were made to do so. In its decision, the justices called on the states to dismantle the segregated school system "with all deliberate speed" but left it to local officials to determine how to achieve a desegregated system. Many have criticized the Court's unwillingness or inability to provide more concrete guidelines to local and state officials, contending that the Court's failure to act ultimately undermined the impact of the *Brown* opinion. Nevertheless, the Court's decision in this case signaled both a new era in civil rights law and a governmental climate favorable to changing centuries-long inequalities in American society.[9]

> *Brown v. Board of Education,* the Supreme Court case that resulted in orders to desegregate all public schools, was brought by the father of Linda Brown, here shown in her segregated classroom (front, center). The strategy and plans for this monumental case were developed by the best legal and political minds of the civil rights movement.

Brown v. Board of Education of Topeka
the 1954 Supreme Court decision that ruled that segregated schools violated the equal protection clause of the Fourteenth Amendment

Rosa Parks's Civil Disobedience on a Montgomery Bus

In December 1955, a now-legendary woman named Rosa Parks was on a bus returning home from work as a seamstress at a Montgomery, Alabama, department store. In Montgomery and throughout the South, buses were segregated, with white riders boarding in the front and sitting front to back and African American riders sitting back to front.[10] The bus driver asked the 43-year-old African American woman to give up her seat for a white man; Parks refused and was arrested for violating a local segregation law. (See "Analyzing the Sources" on page 158.)

The Montgomery chapter of the NAACP, of which Parks and her husband were active members, had sought a test case to challenge the constitutionality of the state's Jim Crow laws. Parks agreed to participate in the case, and her arrest came at a pivotal time in the civil rights movement. Activists were buoyed by the *Brown* decision. Momentum favored the civil rights activists in the South, and their cause was bolstered when civil rights and religious leaders in Montgomery chose a 27-year-old preacher relatively new to the city to lead a bus boycott to protest Parks's arrest and the segregated public facilities. His name was Martin Luther King Jr.[11]

Dr. Martin Luther King Jr. and the Strategy of Civil Disobedience

The year-long bus boycott garnered national media attention and King became a national symbol for the civil rights movement. King's leadership skills were put to the test during the year-long battle: He was arrested. His home was bombed. Death threats were made against

ANALYZING THE SOURCES

A FAMOUS IMAGE FROM THE CIVIL RIGHTS ERA

Chances are you have seen this famous photograph before. It is a powerful image. Rosa Parks is the African American woman who refused to obey the law requiring her to give up her seat for a white man and move to the back of the bus. Her refusal and subsequent arrest were the catalyst for a 381-day bus boycott in Montgomery, Alabama, a boycott that ended when the Supreme Court ruled that Montgomery's segregated bus law was unconstitutional. This photo of Parks sitting on a bus in front of a white man was taken a month later.

Evaluating the Evidence

① The man sitting behind Rosa Parks is Nicholas Chriss, a reporter who was working for United Press International at the time the photograph was taken. Who do you think most people looking at this photograph assume that he is? Who did you think he was when you first saw the image?

② Journalists and civil rights advocates, who wanted to create a dramatic, lasting image of the landmark Court decision, had to talk Rosa Parks into having the picture taken. Do you think the photo's impact would be diminished if more people knew about its origin?

③ What is your opinion of the ethics of using a staged photograph such as this one? Can a staged photograph accurately depict a historic event? Why or why not?

him. But for 381 days, the buses of Montgomery remained virtually empty, representing a serious loss in revenue to the city and causing the NAACP to be banned in the state of Alabama. African Americans walked to and from work, day in and day out, for over a year. White employers drove some domestic servants to and from work. Finally, in December 1956, the U.S. Supreme Court ruled that segregated buses were unconstitutional.[12] The bus boycott was a success on many fronts: its righteousness was confirmed by the Supreme Court, the protests garnered national media attention and evoked public sympathy, and the civil rights movement had gained an articulate leader who was capable of unifying and motivating masses and who had an effective strategy for challenging the racism of American society. King advocated protesting government-sanctioned discrimination through civil disobedience and peaceful demonstrations. African American students, as well as white students and other civil rights activists from throughout the country, used the tactics of civil disobedience, including boycotts, sit-ins, and marches, to challenge the policies of segregation. One such demonstration was held in August 1963, in which hundreds of thousands of black and white Americans heard King deliver his famous "I Have a Dream" speech in the shadow of the Lincoln Memorial. (You can view the speech on YouTube at www.youtube.com/watch?v=PbUtL_0vAJk.)

One famous series of marches occurred in early March 1965 from Selma to Montgomery, Alabama. On Sunday, March 7, about six hundred civil rights activists began a march out of Selma, protesting the policies of intimidation and violence that prevented African Americans from registering to vote. The demonstrators, led by John Lewis (now a Democratic member of Congress from Georgia), walked only six blocks to the Edmund Pettus bridge, where law enforcement officials, including Alabama State Troopers and members of the sheriff's office of Dallas County, Alabama, were waiting.[13] When the peaceful protesters attempted to cross the bridge, law enforcement officers brutally attacked them, using tear gas, bull whips, and night sticks. Dubbed Bloody Sunday, the march and the beatings were televised nationally and were instrumental in swaying public opinion in favor of civil rights. The marches sparked a renewed focus on the lack of voting rights for African Americans and ultimately helped to pressure Congress to pass the Voting Rights Act in 1965.[14]

King, who was not present at the Bloody Sunday march, returned to Selma to lead another march on the following Tuesday. When law enforcement officers again confronted the marchers at the bridge, King asked his followers to kneel in prayer and then turn around and return to their starting point. Critics charged that King was giving in to law enforcement and questioned his nonviolent tactics.[15] Differences over the use of nonviolent civil disobedience generated divisions within the civil rights movement,[16] with the more militant leaders such as Stokely Carmichael and Malcolm X advocating more aggressive tactics.[17]

Although the violence used against protesters generated positive opinions of the civil rights movement, another form of violence, urban riots, eroded feelings of goodwill toward the movement. For five days in 1965, rioting in the Watts neighborhood of Los Angeles resulted in thirty-four deaths, more than 1,000 injuries, and over 4,000 arrests. Though the immediate cause of the violence was an altercation between white police officers and an African American man who had been arrested for drunk driving, the frustration and anger that spilled over had long been brewing in this poor, predominantly African American neighborhood.

On April 4, 1968, Martin Luther King was in Memphis, Tennessee, in support of African American sanitation workers who were striking for equal treatment and pay with white workers. Standing on a balcony at the Lorraine Motel, King was killed by an assassin's bullet. Heartbreak, hopelessness, and despair followed King's assassination—a feeling manifested in part by further rioting in over one hundred cities. Many Americans, both black and white, objected to the looting depicted in nightly news broadcasts. But those who sympathized with the rioters noted that because of the accumulated injustices against African Americans, the government and the rule of law had lost legitimacy in the eyes of those who were rioting.

> Dr. Martin Luther King Jr. delivers his "I Have a Dream" speech to close to 300,000 people participating in the August 28, 1963 March on Washington. The march supported proposed civil rights legislation and the end of segregation. Dr. King was awarded the Nobel Peace Prize in 1964.

The Government's Response to the Civil Rights Movement

The civil rights movement is credited not only with ending segregation in public schools but also with the desegregation of public accommodations such as buses, restaurants, and hotels and with promoting universal suffrage. As a result of the movement, Congress passed the 1965 Voting Rights Act, which aggressively sought to counter nearly one hundred years of disenfranchisement, as well as the 1964 Civil Rights Act, which bars racial discrimination in accommodations and private employment, and the 1968 Civil Rights Act, which prohibits racial discrimination in housing.

> Two young college students help a Mississippi woman register to vote during the Freedom Summer of 1964. In that summer, thousands of civil rights activists encouraged and assisted African Americans in the Deep South to register to vote. During the Freedom Summer more than 1,000 civil rights volunteers were arrested, close to 100 were beaten by angry mobs and police officers, and at least 3 black volunteers were murdered in response to their efforts to register African American voters.

The Civil Rights Act of 1964

Simultaneously expanding the rights of many Americans and providing them with important protections from discrimination, the Civil Rights Act of 1964 includes provisions that mandate equality on numerous fronts:

- It outlaws arbitrary discrimination in voter registration practices within the states.
- It bans discrimination in public accommodations, including hotels, restaurants, and theaters.
- It prohibits state and local governments from banning access to public facilities on the basis of race, religion, or ethnicity.
- It empowers the U.S. Attorney General to sue to desegregate public schools.
- It bars government agencies from discrimination, and imposes the threat of the loss of federal funding if an agency violates the ban.
- It establishes a standard of equality in employment opportunity.

The last part of the act, Title VII, which establishes the equality standard in employment opportunity, provides the legal foundation for a body of law that regulates fair employment practices. Specifically, Title VII bans discrimination in employment based on inherent characteristics—race, national origin, religion, and sex. Title VII also established the Equal Employment Opportunity Commission (EEOC), a government body that still administers Title VII today.

Other Civil Rights Legislation in the 1960s

Although the Civil Rights Act of 1964 sought to address discrimination in access to public accommodations, employment, and education, many civil rights leaders believed that further legislation was necessary to protect the voting rights of African Americans in the South because they had been so systematically intimidated and prevented from participating.[18] In some southern counties, less than a third of all eligible African Americans were registered to vote, whereas nearly two-thirds of eligible white voters were registered in the same counties.

During the summer of 1964, thousands of civil rights activists, including many college students, worked to register black voters in southern states where black voter registration was dismal. Within months, a quarter of a million new voters had been added to the voting rolls. However, because of violent attacks on thousands of civil rights activists and the murders of three black activists in Mississippi in the summer of 1964, Congress determined that it needed to enact a federal law to eliminate discriminatory local and state government registration and voting practices. The Voting Rights Act of 1965 (VRA) banned voter registration practices, such as literacy tests. Moreover, the VRA mandated federal intervention in any county in which less than 50 percent of eligible voters were registered.

One component of the VRA provided for periodic review of some of its tenets. After a specified period of time, Congress must pass and the president must sign an extension of the law to have those requirements remain in effect. In 2006, President George W. Bush (2001–2009) signed legislation extending the VRA for twenty-five years.

In 1968, in the aftermath of Martin Luther King's murder on April 4, Congress passed and President Lyndon Johnson signed an additional piece of civil rights legislation. The Civil Rights Act of 1968 sought to end discriminatory practices in housing, including mortgage lending and the sale or rental of housing. The act also banned the practice of **steering,** in which realtors would steer African American families to certain neighborhoods and white families to others. National civil rights laws enacted since the 1960s have made de jure segregation and discrimination in housing and credit opportunities illegal. However, **de facto segregation,** the segregation caused by the tendency of people to live in neighborhoods with others of their own race, religion, or ethnic group, still prevails in many communities throughout the United States today.

steering

the practice by which realtors steered African American families to certain neighborhoods and white families to others

de facto segregation

segregation caused by the fact that people tend to live in neighborhoods with others of their own race, religion, or ethnic group

Impact of the Civil Rights Movement

The culmination of many acts of resistance by individuals and groups, the civil rights movement has had a momentous impact on society by working for the laws and rulings that bar discrimination in employment, public accommodations, education, and housing. The movement has also had a profound impact on voting rights by establishing the principle that the laws governing voter registration and participation should ensure that individuals are permitted to vote regardless of their race. As shown in Figure 5.2, as a result of the Voting Rights Act, in Mississippi, for example, the percentage of African Americans registered to vote jumped from 7 percent in 1965 to 72 percent in 2006, and then to 82 percent in 2008. Today, in some states, including Georgia, Mississippi, and South Carolina, a greater percentage of African Americans are registered than whites. In addition, all states, especially those in the

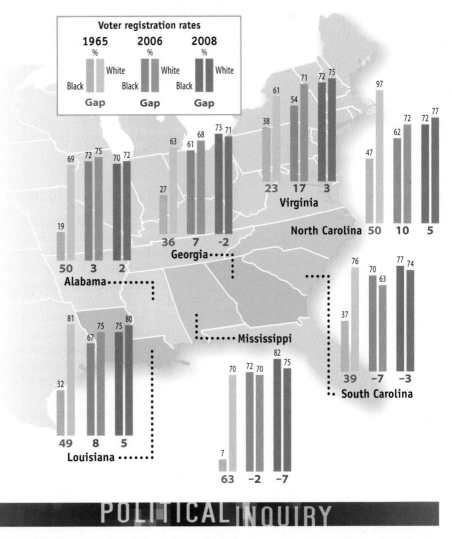

Voter Registration Rates 1965, 2006, and 2008

POLITICAL INQUIRY

FIGURE 5.2 ■ In view of the profound impact of the Voting Rights Act, as indicated by the data presented here, has the act outlived its usefulness? What might be some reasons for continuing the act? For discontinuing it? In which states was the voter registration for black citizens in 2008 substantially larger than it was in 2006? What might explain these large increases in black citizen voter registration in 2008?

SOURCE: www.usdoj.gov/crt/voting/intro/intro_c.htm; Table 4b, Reported Voting and Registration of the Voting-Age Population, by Sex, Race and Hispanic Origin, for States: November 2006, www.census.gov/hhes/www/socdemo/voting/publications/p20/2006/tables.html; Table 4b, Reported Voting and Registration of the Voting-Age Population, by Sex, Race and Hispanic Origin, for States: November 2008, www.census.gov/hhes/www/socdemo/voting/publications/p20/2008/tables.html.

South, have seen an increase in the number of African Americans elected to serve in offices at the state, county, and municipal levels and in school districts. Indeed, more African Americans serve in elected office in Mississippi than in any other state, and all southern states boast among the highest numbers of African American elected officials.[19]

In addition to having a profound impact on race relations and civil rights law, the civil rights movement soon came to be regarded by other groups as a model of political engagement. Ethnic minorities, women, persons with disabilities, and gays and lesbians have adopted many tactics of the movement in their own quest to secure their civil rights.

The Movement for Women's Civil Rights

As already noted, the pronouncement in the Declaration of Independence that "all men are created equal" initially applied only to white men, and usually only to those who owned property. Not only did the concept of equal protection of the laws not apply to nonwhite male citizens, until the Civil War amendments to the Constitution and subsequent pieces of national legislation such as the Voting Rights and Civil Rights acts, it also did not apply to female citizens—white or nonwhite. Like African American men, women had to wait until the Constitution was amended and civil rights legislation was adopted, in response to the women's rights movement, for equal protection of the laws.

Advocates for women's civil rights began their efforts in the mid-1800s, initially focusing on gaining the right to vote for women citizens. That endeavor, the first wave of the women's rights movement, won suffrage for women in 1920. The cause of women's civil rights was rejuvenated in the 1960s, when the second wave of the movement began. This second wave continues today.

The First Wave of the Women's Rights Movement

The segregation of the women delegates at the 1840 World Anti-Slavery Conference in London was a defining moment for the first wave of the U.S. women's rights movement. Forced to sit in the balcony behind a drawn curtain, Lucretia Mott and Elizabeth Cady Stanton recognized that without improving their own legal and political status, women were not going to be successful in fighting for the legal rights of other groups of people.

In 1848, Mott and Stanton organized a meeting at Seneca Falls, New York, to talk about the lack of legal rights of U.S. citizens who happened to be born female. At the end of the convention, the participants signed the Declaration of Sentiments. This Declaration, modeled after the Declaration of Independence, listed many rights and opportunities that the law did not guarantee women, including the right to vote, educational and employment opportunities equal to those of white men, and married women's rights to own property as well as legal standing to sue. At the end of the convention, the participants signed the Declaration of Sentiments (see Appendix D).

Clearly, John Adams and the other architects of the Constitution had ignored Abigail Adams's request to her husband and his colleagues to "remember the ladies" when they created the new system of government. Adams warned her husband that not only would women not feel bound to obey laws in which they had no say but also the ladies would "foment a rebellion" if they were not provided a voice in government.

The signatories of the Declaration of Sentiments began Adams's forecasted rebellion. The document they signed insisted "that [women] have immediate admission to all rights and privileges which belong to them as citizens of these United States." For those women and men who joined this new movement for women's civil rights, the right to vote became the focal point. They recognized that this right was the foundational right that would enable women to win the other rights and privileges of citizenship.

Because the Constitution initially reserved for the states the authority to determine who had the right to vote as well as to be employed and obtain the best possible education, many of the initial battles for women's rights took place at the state level of government. Eventually, as the national government's responsibilities expanded through court interpretations of the Constitution, especially the Fourteenth Amendment, the federal government's role in guaranteeing civil rights expanded.

STATE-LEVEL RIGHTS Even after ratification of the Fourteenth Amendment (1868) guaranteeing equal protection of the laws for all people and the same privileges and immunities to all citizens, women's educational and work opportunities were limited by social norms as well as state laws. Education for girls prepared them to be good wives and mothers, not to be economically independent. By the late 1800s, a few colleges began to admit women, and several women's colleges were established. Yet most colleges did not offer women the same educational opportunities as men, and women who graduated and aspired to a career were limited in two ways. First, by choosing a career, these educated women gave up the possibility of marriage. They were not legally banned from marriage, but societal norms prevented them from having both a career and a husband. Second, their career choices were limited: teaching, the developing professions of nursing and social work, or missionary work.

In 1873, Myra Bradwell challenged women's limited career choices when she sued the state of Illinois over its refusal to let her practice law.[20] She argued that the Fourteenth Amendment's privileges and immunities clause protected her right to earn a living in a career of her choice. In this case, the Supreme Court found that women's God-given destiny was to "fulfill the noble and benign offices of wife and mother" and that allowing women to practice law would impinge on that destiny. The *Bradwell* case established the precedent for the Court to justify allowing women to be treated differently from men (sex-based discrimination) if the different treatment was deemed a *rational* means by which the government could fulfill a *legitimate* public interest. In the *Bradwell* case, the Court applied the *ordinary scrutiny* test, deeming it legitimate for the government to protect the role of women as wives and mothers, and to accomplish that protection, it was rational to deny them equal employment opportunities.

In 1875, another women's rights case came before the Supreme Court. In this case, Virginia Minor of Missouri (actually her husband, because she, like all married women, did not have standing to sue) challenged the constitutionality of the Missouri law that guaranteed the right to vote only to male U.S. citizens. In this case, *Minor v. Happersett,* the Court acknowledged that women were citizens, yet it also decreed that state governments established voting rights, not the U.S. Constitution.[21] Therefore, the justices argued that the Fourteenth Amendment's privileges and immunities clause did not give women rights not established in the Constitution, hence it did not extend to women the right to vote. Although by 1875 some local governments (school districts specifically) had extended voting rights to women, no state other than New Jersey had ever given women the right to vote. Women who owned property in New Jersey had the right to vote for a brief period between the end of the War for Independence and 1807, when it was taken away in response to the lobbying of politicians and professional men.

THE NINETEENTH AMENDMENT TO THE CONSTITUTION The American Women's Suffrage Association (AWSA), directed by Lucy Stone, had been leading the battle to extend the right to vote to women in the states since 1869. Also since 1869, the National Women's Suffrage Association (NWSA), directed by Susan B. Anthony and Elizabeth Cady Stanton, had been fighting to extend to women all rights of citizenship, including but not limited to the right to vote. Unlike the AWSA, the NWSA focused its suffrage battle on the federal level, specifically on amending the U.S. Constitution. In 1890, frustrated by their lack of success in the battle to extend suffrage to women, the AWSA and the NWSA joined forces, creating the National American Women's Suffrage Association (NAWSA). The NAWSA focused its efforts on amending the U.S. Constitution.

In 1916, Alice Paul founded the National Women's Party, which adopted more radical tactics than the NAWSA had been willing to use in its fight for suffrage. Noting the lack of support on the part of national officials for suffrage, Paul's organization called on voters in the 1916 election not to vote for candidates who opposed women's suffrage, including President Wilson, who was running for reelection. In 1917, after President Wilson was reelected, Paul and other suffragists chained themselves to the White House fence and called

> A line of women rally for women's suffrage in New York City in 1915. After the Supreme Court determined in 1875 that the Fifteenth Amendment (1870) did not guarantee women the right to vote, suffragists mobilized to win the vote for women.

on Wilson to support the suffrage amendment. Arrested, jailed, and force-fed when they engaged in a hunger strike, the women gained media attention, which in turn brought national attention to their struggle for suffrage and the president's opposition. After several months and persistent media pressure, President Wilson called on the House and the Senate to approve the women's suffrage amendment.

By June 1919, the House and the Senate approved what was to become the Nineteenth Amendment. In 1920, Tennessee became the thirty-sixth state to ratify the amendment, and it was added to the Constitution. The Nineteenth Amendment prohibited the national and state governments from abridging or denying citizens the right to vote on account of sex. The right to vote was extended to another group of citizens in 1971 when the states ratified the Twenty-sixth Amendment. This amendment guarantees citizens 18 years of age and older the right to vote. However, college students and civil rights advocates have raised concerns about lack of equal protection of voting rights for college students living away from their parents.

> Alice Paul designed this pin and presented it to the many suffragists arrested and imprisoned for picketing in front of the White House for women's suffrage between 1917 and 1919. The pin, a replication of a prison gate, calls attention to the injustice of being "jailed for freedom."

The Second Wave of the Women's Rights Movement

After the Nineteenth Amendment was added to the Constitution, the push for women's rights ceased to be a mass movement. Women were still organized in groups and lobbied the government for women's civil rights, but the many women's organizations were no longer working collectively toward one agreed-upon goal, such as the right to vote. Another mass women's movement did not arise until the 1960s. Several factors account for the mobilization of the second wave of the women's movement in the

1960s, which focused this time on the plethora of rights related to the social, economic, and political status of women, many of the same rights originally demanded in the Declaration of Sentiments.

By the 1960s, large numbers of women were working outside the home in the paid labor force. Working women talked with one another about their work and family lives and came to recognize common concerns and problems, including discrimination in educational opportunities, employment opportunities, and pay; lack of child care; domestic violence; the problem of rape, for which *they* were often blamed; and their inability to obtain credit (borrow money) without having a male cosign on the loan. Women recognized that as a class of citizens they did not have equal protection of the laws.

In 1961, at the prodding of Esther Peterson, the director of the Women's Bureau in the Department of Labor, President John F. Kennedy (1961–1963) established a Commission on the Status of Women, chaired by Eleanor Roosevelt. In 1963, the commission reported that women in the United States were discriminated against in many areas of life, including education and employment. In its report, the commission argued that women needed to pursue lawsuits that would allow the Supreme Court to interpret properly the Fourteenth Amendment's equal protection clause, hence prohibiting discrimination against women.

By the mid-1960s, the women's rights movement was rejuvenated with a second wave of mass activity. The goal of this second wave was equal legal rights for women. The means to achieve that goal included public demonstrations, legislation, litigation, and an as yet unsuccessful attempt to enact the Equal Rights Amendment (ERA), which had been written by Alice Paul and first introduced in Congress in 1923.

FEDERAL LEGISLATION AND WOMEN'S RIGHTS In 1955, Edith Green (D-Oregon) introduced into Congress the first piece of national legislation written specifically to protect women, the Equal Pay Act. Enacted into law in 1963, the Equal Pay Act prohibited employers from paying women less than men were paid for the same job, which was the standard employment practice at the time. Indeed, beginning with school boards in the mid-1800s and the federal Mint during the Civil War, governments had hired women specifically because they could pay them less than men.

The 1964 Civil Rights Act as initially drafted prohibited discrimination in education, employment, and public accommodations based on race, ethnicity, and religion. Yet because of congressional women's efforts, Title VII of the proposed act was rewritten to

> Members of the Business and Professional Women (an advocacy and educational organization that has promoted women's equity since 1919) and Representative Catherine May (R-Washington), one of the thirteen women serving in Congress at the time, surround President John Kennedy as he signs the Equal Pay Act in 1963. President Barack Obama is surrounded by six of the ninety women serving in Congress in 2009, including Nancy Pelosi, the Speaker of the House of Representatives, as he signs the Lilly Ledbetter Fair Pay Act, which remedies loopholes in the Equal Pay Act. Ledbetter, standing to the left of the president, sued her employer after learning that—over a period of nineteen years—her pay was lower than that of her male coworkers who were doing the same job. Her failed discrimination lawsuit fueled the bill's passage.

prohibit discrimination in all personnel decisions based on *sex* as well as the other inherent characteristics. Initially, the EEOC, the federal agency responsible for monitoring Title VII implementation, did not take sex-based discrimination complaints seriously. Women serving on state committees on the status of women responded by establishing the National Organization for Women (NOW) in 1966. NOW's initial statement of purpose is modeled on the requests of the 1848 Seneca Falls Declaration of Sentiments, demonstrating the continued lack of progress toward the goal of women's equality under the law.[22]

To take advantage of Title VII's promise of equal employment opportunities, women needed to pursue educational opportunities on an equal basis with men. Yet Title VI of the 1964 Civil Rights Act does not prohibit sex-based discrimination in institutions that receive federal funds, including educational institutions. By 1972, women's rights advocates won an amendment to the 1964 Civil Rights Act, Title IX, which prohibits sex-based discrimination in educational institutions receiving federal funds.

The Equal Pay Act, Title VII, and Title IX are landmark pieces of national legislation that provide equal protection of the law for women. At the same time that Congress was enacting laws prohibiting sex-based discrimination, the courts were reinterpreting the equal protection clause of the Fourteenth Amendment.

WOMEN'S RIGHTS AND THE EQUAL PROTECTION CLAUSE   In 1971, in the case of *Reed v. Reed,* the Supreme Court for the first time in history used the equal protection clause of the Fourteenth Amendment to find a law that discriminated against women unconstitutional.[23] In the *Reed* case, the Supreme Court found that an Idaho state law giving automatic preference to men to administer the estate of a deceased person who had not named an administrator was not a rational means to fulfill a legitimate government interest. Hence, using the ordinary scrutiny test established in the 1873 *Bradwell* case, the court ruled this discriminatory treatment of women was unconstitutional.

Then, in 1976, the Supreme Court developed a new test for the legality of sex-based discrimination. Oklahoma law allowed women 18 years of age to buy beer with 3.2% alcohol content. Yet men in Oklahoma had to be 21 years of age to purchase 3.2% beer. Men challenged the law, asking the Court to decide if this sex-based discrimination was constitutional. In this case, *Craig v. Boren,* the Court established the heightened scrutiny test for sex-based discrimination cases: different treatment is legal if it is substantially related to an important government interest.[24] The Court used this test in the *Craig* case to find the Oklahoma law unconstitutional. The Court also used the heightened scrutiny test in the 1996 *U.S. v. Virginia* case.[25] In this case, the Court found the male-only admission policy of the Virginia Military Institute unconstitutional. Justice Ruth Bader Ginsburg noted in her opinion that the state of Virginia had not shown that this discriminatory admissions policy was substantially related to the important government objective of training soldiers.

Today, courts sometimes use the ordinary scrutiny test and other times the heightened scrutiny test when deciding sex-based discrimination cases as well as other non–race-based discrimination cases. Proponents of an ERA argue that the strict scrutiny test, which is used in race-, religion-, and ethnic-based discrimination cases, should also be used in sex-based discrimination cases and that this will not happen until the Constitution is amended to explicitly guarantee equality of rights under the law whether a person is a man or a woman.

THE PROPOSED EQUAL RIGHTS AMENDMENT   During the 1970s, as the Supreme Court was reinterpreting the implications of the Fourteenth Amendment for sex-based discrimination, lobbying for the Equal Rights Amendment increased. In 1972, Congress approved the ERA, which states that "equality of rights under the law shall not be denied or abridged by the United States or by any State on account of sex." Finally, forty-nine years after it was first introduced in Congress, the ERA was sent to the states for ratification.

Opponents of the ERA argued it was a duplication of the Fourteenth Amendment and therefore was not needed. Opponents also claimed that passage of the amendment would make women subject to the military draft; would lead to the integration of all single-sex institutions, including schools and public bathrooms; and would result in the legalization of and public funding for all abortions. Moreover, they argued that the ERA was not needed because Congress was passing laws that guaranteed women equal protection in employment and education. Whether or not the claims of its opponents were accurate, they were successful in defeating the ERA, which had not been ratified by enough states by the deadline of 1982.

The first wave of the women's rights movement won the vote through constitutional amendment. The second wave successfully expanded women's civil rights through litigation and legislation. Yet many women's rights advocates argue that women still battle inequities, including unequal pay, sexual harassment, and the glass ceiling (aspiring to higher-level jobs but being unable to win them). Although the situation for women has greatly improved, some argue, not all women have benefited equally from gains in women's rights. Nonwhite women have two characteristics that can lead to discriminatory treatment: gender and color, necessitating a struggle for equal protection on two fronts: the women's rights movement and the civil rights movements of their racial group. We now explore the struggles of several other groups of citizens for equal civil rights.

Other Civil Rights Movements

Today, discriminatory treatment is still a reality for many groups of citizens. The civil rights acts notwithstanding, discrimination in employment, education, housing, and due process still occurs. Moreover, battles for civil rights continue. Unfortunately, we cannot discuss all the civil rights movements that have occurred or are ongoing in the United States. Therefore, we will explore the civil rights battles of just a few groups of citizens: Native Americans; Hispanic Americans; Asian Americans; citizens with disabilities; and lesbian, gay, bisexual, and transgendered people. The hard-fought victories and aspirations of these groups offer an overview of both the history and the breadth of contemporary civil rights movements.

Native Americans' Rights

At first, the fledgling nation recognized the native residents of the land that became the United States as members of sovereign and independent nations with inherent rights. The federal government entered into more than 370 treaties with Native American tribes between 1778 and 1870.[26] Most of those treaties promised land to tribes that agreed to move, and almost all those promises were empty, with the government reneging on most of the agreements. In addition, in 1830, Congress passed the Indian Removal Act, which called for the forced relocation of all native peoples to lands west of the Mississippi. In the end, most Native Americans were dispossessed of their lands and wound up living on reservations. The federal government treated Indians as subhumans, relegating them to second-class status, as they had African Americans.

Until Congress passed the Indian Citizenship Act in 1924, Native Americans had virtually no rights to U.S. citizenship, and even the laws that allowed immigrants to become citizens did not apply to Native Americans. The Indian Rights Association, founded in 1882 and active in lobbying Congress and the state legislatures until the 1930s, was one of the most important of the early groups that actively campaigned for full suffrage for native peoples, in the belief that enfranchisement would help to "civilize" them. The early 1900s also saw the founding of the Society of American Indians and the American Indian Defense Association, both of which fought for citizenship for Native Americans and then for their civil rights. However, for more than forty years after passage of the Indian Citizenship Act, the basic rights enumerated in the Bill of Rights were not granted to Native Americans. In the 1960s, Indian activists became more radical, occupying government

> Elouise Cobell watches Deputy Secretary of the Interior David Hayes testify during a Dec. 17, 2009, Senate Indian Affairs Committee hearing in Washington, D.C., on a multi-billion dollar lawsuit in which Cobell, a member of the Blackfeet Nation of Montana was the lead plaintiff. In the suit, which took 13 years to make its way through the courts, Cobell accused the federal government of mismanaging funds held in trust for Native Americans since 1887. The settlement reached in 2009 awarded Native Americans $3.4 billion in reparations, but the Senate has yet to approve it, delaying payment to half a million Native Americans.

buildings, picketing, and conducting protests. In 1968, the American Indian Movement (AIM) was founded. In the same year, Congress passed the Indian Civil Rights Act, which ensured that Native Americans would have the full protection of the Bill of Rights both on and off their reservations. Although this law had significant symbolic impact, it lacked an enforcement mechanism, and so native peoples continued to be deprived of basic due process protections and equal education and employment opportunities. The National Indian Education Association (NIEA), founded in 1969, continues to confront the lack of quality educational opportunities for Native Americans and the loss of native culture and values.

During the 1970s, Native American organizations began a new effort to force the federal government to honor treaties granting Indians fishing and hunting rights as well as rights to the natural resources buried in their lands. Indians in New York, Maine, and elsewhere sued for land taken from them decades or even a century ago in violation of treaties. Starting with the 1975 Indian Self-Determination and Education Assistance Act, the national government has enacted laws that support greater autonomy for Indian tribes and give them more control of their assets.

The 1988 Indian Gaming Regulatory Act is the best known of the federal laws enacted to support Indian self-determination. This law authorizes Indian tribes to establish gaming operations on their property and requires them to negotiate compacts with the states in which their lands are located. The compacts typically include a profit-sharing understanding that requires the Indian tribe to give a proportion of its profits to the state government and possibly to contiguous local governments. The act mandates that the money made through gaming operations be used for education, economic development, infrastructure (for example, roads and utilities), law enforcement, and courts. By 2009, the National Indian Gaming Commission, the independent agency that regulates Indian gaming, reported that more than 240 of the federally recognized 562 Indian tribes operate more than four hundred casinos and bingo halls in twenty-eight states. The gross revenues for these gaming activities totaled $26.7 billion in 2008.[27] Clearly, one goal of the Gaming Act was to generate resources that would increase the educational and employment opportunities on Indian reservations.

Even with gaming profits, however, the prospects for many Native Americans today remain bleak. According to race and ethnic relations scholars Joe R. Feagin and Clairece Booher Feagin, "Native Americans have endured the longest Depression-like economic situation of any U.S. racial or ethnic group."[28] They are among the poorest, least educated U.S. citizens. Moreover, congressional testimony and materials submitted to support reauthorization of the Voting Rights Act in 2005 documented a pattern of continued discrimination against Native Americans in their right to vote in several states, including Arizona and South Dakota.[29] Like many other groups of U.S. citizens with characteristics that identify them as non–white European descendants, Native Americans continue to fight in the halls of government, in the courtrooms, and in the public arena for their constitutionally guaranteed rights and privileges.

Citizens of Latin American Descent

U.S. citizens of Latin American descent (Latinos) include those whose families hail from Central America, South America, or the Caribbean. Latinos are the largest minority group in the United States, making up almost 16 percent of the total U.S. population. Sixty percent of this Latino population is composed of natural-born U.S. citizens.[30] Latinos make up a large percentage of the population of several states, including New Mexico, California, Texas, Arizona, and Florida.

Sixty-three percent of the voting-age Hispanic population were citizens and 59 percent of this group were registered voters in 2008. In the 2008 presidential election, 84 percent of Hispanic registered voters voted, constituting almost 8 percent of the voters.[31] So far, the elections that have occurred in the twenty-first century have been followed by numerous lawsuits claiming that individual citizens, organized groups, and local governments have prevented eligible Latino voters from voting. For example, in 2006 the national government sued Philadelphia's city government for failing to assist voters effectively—specifically

Spanish-speaking voters—who had limited-English proficiency. Limited-English proficiency continues to cause problems with access to voting and equal educational and employment opportunities for many U.S. citizens, including Latino citizens. We focus here on U.S. citizens of Mexican origin—the largest Latino population in the United States today.

EARLY STRUGGLES OF MEXICAN AMERICANS In 1846, because of land disputes sparked by white immigrants from the United States encroaching on Mexican territory, the United States declared war on Mexico. By the terms of the 1848 Treaty of Guadalupe Hidalgo, which ended the war, Mexico ceded territory to the United States for $15 million. The Mexican landowners living within this ceded territory had the choice of staying on their land and remaining in what was now the United States or relocating to Mexico. According to the treaty, those Mexicans who stayed on their land would become U.S. citizens, and their civil rights would be protected. Although nearly 77,000 Mexicans chose to do so, and became U.S. citizens, their civil rights were *not* protected.[32] Thus began a long and continuing history of discrimination against U.S. citizens of Mexican descent.

At the turn of the twentieth century, Mexican Americans organized to protest the various forms of discrimination they were experiencing, which included segregated schools, inequities in employment opportunities and wages, discrimination by law enforcement officers, and barriers to their voting rights such as poll taxes and English-only literacy tests. In 1929, several Mexican American organizations combined to create the League of United Latin American Citizens (LULAC).[33]

In 1945, LULAC successfully challenged the segregated school systems in California, which provided separate schools for Mexican children that were of poorer quality than the schools for white children. In this case, *Mendez v. Westminister*, the federal court set an important precedent by using the Fourteenth Amendment to guarantee equal educational opportunities.[34] In 1954, the U.S. Supreme Court followed this lower court's precedent when it ended legal race-based segregation in public schools throughout the nation in the *Brown v. Board of Education of Topeka* case.

THE CHICANO MOVEMENT In addition to the women's rights movement and the civil rights movement for African American rights, the 1960s witnessed the birth of the Chicano Movement, the mass movement for Mexican American civil rights. The Chicano Movement was composed of numerous Latino organizations focusing on a variety of issues, including rights to equal employment and educational opportunities. One of the most widely recognized leaders in the Chicano Movement was Cesar Chavez.

Cesar Chavez began his civil rights work as a community organizer in 1952, encouraging Mexican Americans to vote and educating them about their civil rights. In the early 1960s, Chavez, along with Jessie Lopez and Dolores Huerta, founded the Agricultural Workers Organizing Committee (AWOC) and the National Farm Worker Association (NFWA). Under Chavez's leadership, the AWOC and the NFWA merged to form the United Farm Workers (UFW) in 1966. The UFW organized successful protests and boycotts to improve working conditions and pay for farmworkers.[35]

The activism of Mexican American workers inspired others to call for additional civil rights protections, including access to equal educational opportunity. In 1968, Mexican American high school students in East Los Angeles staged a walkout to protest high dropout rates of Latino students and the lack of bilingual education, Mexican American history classes, and

> Cesar Chavez began his civil rights work as a community organizer in 1952 by encouraging Mexican Americans to vote and use their civil rights. Together with Dolores Huerta, he founded the United Farm Workers. From the early 1960s until his death in 1993, Chavez was the leading voice for and organizer of migrant farmworkers in the United States. Today, Huerta is the most prominent Chicana labor leader in the country, developing leaders and advocating for the rights of immigrant workers, women, and children.

Mexican American teachers. Though the student walkout did not lead to many immediate changes in the school system, it drew national attention, empowered the students, and inspired other protests.

Until 1971, Latinos were not legally considered a racial minority group, and therefore antidiscrimination laws, such as the 1964 Civil Rights Act, did not apply to them. In the landmark case *Corpus Christi Independent School District v. Cisneros*[36] (1971), the Supreme Court upheld a lower court's ruling that Latinos are a racial minority group; therefore, they are covered by laws protecting the rights of minority groups.[37]

EMPLOYMENT DISCRIMINATION AND OTHER CIVIL RIGHTS ISSUES

Since the 1986 Immigration Reform and Control Act went into effect, organizations that work to protect the rights of Latinos and other minority citizens have been receiving increasing numbers of complaints about employment discrimination. Under this act, employers who hire undocumented immigrant workers are subject to sanctions. To comply with this law, some employers refuse to hire—and thus discriminate against—any applicants for whom English is a second language and any who look Latino under the assumption that all such people could be undocumented immigrants. This means that employers are violating the equal employment rights of Latino citizens in many cases, for they are mistakenly assuming they are undocumented immigrants.

Today, U.S. citizens of Mexican descent continue to experience violations of their civil rights. LULAC, along with the Mexican American Legal Defense and Education Fund (MALDEF; founded in 1968), and other organizations continue to fight for laws that will provide due process and equal protection, equal access to education, and other civil rights for Latino citizens and immigrants. They also work to educate Latinos about their rights and empower them to engage in the political process. Through the efforts of these and other groups, Hispanic voter registration and turnout has significantly increased in recent elections. Moreover, according to the National Association of Latino Elected and Appointed Officials (NALEO), the number of Latinos elected to local, state, and national positions has grown by almost 40 percent in the last decade. Latino elected officials are serving in all levels of government in all regions of the nation.[38]

Citizens of Asian Descent

Asian American citizens come from, or have ancestors from, a number of different countries with diverse cultures, religions, histories, and languages. Today, the largest percentage of Asian Americans have Chinese origins, followed by those of Filipino, Asian Indian, Vietnamese, Korean, and Japanese ancestry. Large numbers of immigrants from Japan came to the United States around the turn of the twentieth century, but it was not until the 1940s that the flow of immigrants from other Asian countries began to increase, beginning with the Philippines. In the 1960s, the number of immigrants from Korea and India began to increase significantly, and in the 1970s—as the Vietnam War ended—immigrants from Vietnam began to arrive in large numbers. Today, 5 percent of the U.S. population is of Asian descent. The largest Asian American populations live in California, New York, Hawaii, Texas, New Jersey, and Illinois.[39]

Like other U.S. citizens with non–white European ancestry, Asian Americans have had to fight continually for their civil rights, specifically for equal protection under the law and particularly for equal access to educational and employment opportunities as well as citizenship. Asian immigrants and Asian Americans created organizations to fight for citizenship and equal protection of the law, such as the Japanese American Citizens League (JACL; founded in the 1930s). One successful result of those efforts was the 1952 Immigration and Nationality Act, which allowed Asian immigrants to become citizens for the first time. Before passage of this law, only U.S.-born children of Asian immigrants could be citizens.

INTERNMENT OF JAPANESE AMERICANS DURING WORLD WAR II
As noted previously, one of the most egregious violations of the civil rights of tens of thousands of Asian American citizens occurred during World War II when Americans of Japanese an-

cestry were forced to move to government-established camps. Under President Franklin Roosevelt's Executive Order 9066, over 120,000 Japanese Americans, two-thirds of whom were native-born U.S. citizens, were relocated from the West Coast of the United States after Japan's attack on Pearl Harbor. During that same period, the federal government also restricted the travel of Americans of German and Italian ancestry who were living on the West Coast (the United States was also fighting against Germany and Italy), but those citizens were not relocated. Many relocated Japanese Americans lost their homes and businesses.

The JACL fought for decades to obtain reparations for the citizens who were interned and for the repeal of a section of the 1950 Internal Security Act that allowed the government to imprison citizens deemed enemy collaborators during a crisis. Congress repealed the section of the 1950 law targeted by the JACL, and in 1987 President Ronald Reagan (1981–1989) signed a bill providing $1.2 billion in reparations.

CONTEMPORARY ISSUES FOR ASIAN AMERICANS   During the 1960s and 1980s, the number of organizations and coalitions pressing for the civil rights of Asian Americans grew as large numbers of new immigrants from Asian countries arrived in the United States in response to changes in U.S. immigration laws. During the 1960s, Asian Americans on college campuses organized and fostered a group consciousness about the need to protect their civil rights. During the 1980s, Asian American organizations began to pay more attention to voting rights as well as to hate crimes and employment discrimination. Then in 1996, numerous organizations, each representing Asian Americans with ancestry from one country, joined to form the National Council of Asian Pacific Americans (NCAPA), which presses for equal protection of the law for all Asians.

With the exception of Korean Americans and Vietnamese Americans, Asian Americans have the highest median income compared with the population as a whole.[40] Asian Americans are also twice as likely as the population as a whole to earn a bachelor's degree or higher.[41] Moreover, Asian Americans are better represented in professional and managerial positions than any other racial or ethnic group, including white Americans. Yet like women, Asian American citizens appear to hit a glass ceiling, for they are not represented in the very top positions in the numbers that their high levels of educational achievement would seem to predict. Therefore, those advocating for Asian American civil rights are increasingly concentrating their efforts on discrimination in employment. Professor Don T. Nakanishi, an expert on Asian Americans, points out that Asian Americans are becoming "more organized, more visible and more effective as participants and leaders in order to advance—as well as to protect—their individual and group interests, and to contribute to our nation's democratic processes and institutions."[42] Today, more than 2,000 Asian Americans serve as elected or appointed officials in all levels of government throughout the nation.

> Before 1952, foreign-born Asian immigrants could not become U.S. citizens; however, children born in the United States to Asian immigrants were citizens by birth. Today, both the biological and the adopted children of U.S. citizens who are born abroad acquire automatic citizenship. For example, for children adopted from Asian countries, such as the young girl in this photo, U.S. citizenship is acquired automatically once the adoption process is completed.

Citizens with Disabilities

The civil rights movements of the 1960s and 1970s made society more aware of the lack of equal protection of the laws for diverse groups of citizens, including people with disabilities. The first law to mandate equal protection for people with physical and mental disabilities was the 1973 Rehabilitation Act, which prohibited discrimination against people with disabilities in federally funded programs. In 1990, people with disabilities achieved a

> Access to public transportation is key to education and employment opportunities, independence, and full community engagement for people with disabilities. The 1990 Americans with Disabilities Act prohibits discrimination against and sets specific requirements to accommodate transportation for people with disabilities on publicly and privately funded transportation systems.

significant enhancement of this earlier victory in their fight to obtain protection of their civil rights. The Americans with Disabilities Act (ADA), enacted in that year, extends the ban on discrimination against people with disabilities in education, employment, health care, housing, and transportation to all programs and organizations, not just those receiving federal funds. The ADA defines a disability as any "physical or mental impairment that substantially limits one or more of the major life activities of the individual." The ADA does not enumerate every disability that it covers, resulting in much confusion over which conditions it covers and which it excludes.

A series of U.S. Supreme Court rulings in the late 1990s and early 2000s narrowed the interpretation of "disability," which decreased the number of people benefiting from the ADA. For example, the Court determined that if an individual can take an action to mitigate an impairment (such as taking medication to prevent seizures), then the impairment is not a disability protected by the ADA. In response, disability advocates, including the National Coalition of Disability Rights and the ADA Watch, successfully lobbied Congress to propose an act restoring the broader interpretation of the term "disability" and, hence, increasing the number of people benefiting from the ADA. The Americans with Disabilities Act Amendments of 2008 went into effect in January 2009. The act applies to the equal protection guaranteed in the Rehabilitation Act (1973) and the ADA (1990). It does not change the written definition of "disability" that is in the ADA, but it does broaden what "substantially limits" and "major life activities" mean, and no longer considers actions taken to mitigate impairments as relevant to determining if employers and educational institutions must accommodate a person's mental or physical disability in public facilities and housing.[43]

There is no question that the ADA has enhanced the civil rights of citizens with disabilities. Before the ADA was enacted, people with disabilities who were fired from their jobs or denied access to schools, office buildings, or other public places had no recourse. Cities were under no obligation to provide even the most reasonable accommodations to people with disabilities who sought employment or the use of public transportation systems. And employers were under no obligation to make even the most minor modifications to their workplaces for employees with disabilities. For example, if a qualified job applicant was wheelchair bound, an employer did not have to consider installing ramps or raising desks to accommodate the wheelchair but could simply refuse to hire the individual. The ADA changed that situation by requiring employers and governmental organizations to make it possible for people with disabilities to participate meaningfully in their communities through reasonable accommodations.

Lesbian, Gay, Bisexual, and Transgendered Citizens

Lesbian, gay, bisexual, and transgendered people (people whose gender identity cannot be categorized as male or female)—a group often referred to with the abbreviation LGBT or GBLT—also actively seek equal civil rights. Some of the specific rights that LGBT persons have organized to fight for include employment rights, housing rights, and marriage rights. Though the 1970s and 1980s saw some successes in these civil rights battles, there was some backlash in the 1990s and early in the twenty-first century. In this section, we focus on the rights of lesbians and gay men.

THE GAY PRIDE MOVEMENT Several LGBT civil rights organizations were founded after the Stonewall Rebellion. In June 1969, groups of gay men and lesbians clashed violently with police in New York City, in a protest over the routine harassment by law enforcement of members of the lesbian and gay community. This influential conflict, which started at the Stonewall bar, marked the first time that members of this community acted collectively and in large numbers to assert their rights. Shortly after this event, in 1970, Lambda Legal, a national organization fighting for full recognition of the civil rights of LGBT citizens, was founded. Within a few years, gays and lesbians began to hold gay pride marches throughout the country, and many new groups such as the Human Rights Campaign and the National Gay and Lesbian Task Force, began advocating for LGBT rights.

As a result of organized educational and lobbying efforts by the gay community, during the 1980s a number of state and local governments adopted laws prohibiting discrimination in employment, housing, public accommodations, and employee benefits—that is, guaranteeing equal protection of some laws—for LGBT persons. In 1982, Wisconsin was the first state to prohibit such discrimination. Yet during the same decade, numerous states had laws on the books prohibiting sex between mutually consenting adults of the same sex, typically in the form of antisodomy laws. In the 1986 case of *Bowers v. Hardwick,* the U.S. Supreme Court upheld Georgia's antisodomy law.[44] In 2003, another lawsuit challenging the constitutionality of a state antisodomy law came before the Supreme Court in the case of *Lawrence v. Texas.*[45] This time, the Court overturned the 1986 *Bowers* decision, finding that the Fourteenth Amendment provides due process and equal protection for sexual privacy and therefore the Texas law was unconstitutional.

Advocates for the rights of LGBT persons hoped this 2003 ruling would lead to federal protections of LGBT citizens' civil rights. But there is still no federal law prohibiting LGBT-based discrimination in employment, housing, or public accommodations. In contrast to the lack of federal legislation, today twenty states and the District of Columbia have antidiscrimination laws guaranteeing equal access to employment, housing, and public accommodations regardless of sexual orientation. Twelve states also prohibit gender identity discrimination.[46]

BACKLASH AGAINST THE MOVEMENT FOR LGBT CIVIL RIGHTS On the other side of the issue, in 1992, opponents of civil rights for LGBT persons succeeded in placing on the ballot in Colorado a proposed law that would prohibit all branches of the state government from adopting any law or policy making it illegal to discriminate against gay men, lesbians, bisexuals, or transgendered people. In 1996, the U.S. Supreme Court, in *Romer v. Evans,* found the state law to be unconstitutional.[47] The parties who filed the suit challenging the law included the Boulder school district; the cities of Denver, Boulder, and Aspen; and the County of Denver.

Another civil rights battle for lesbians and gays is over the issue of marriage rights. The Hawaii state Supreme Court ruled in 1993 that it was a violation of the Hawaii state constitution to deny same-sex couples the right to marry. Opponents of same-sex marriage succeeded in their subsequent efforts to get a state constitutional amendment banning same-sex marriage on the ballot, and in 1996 the majority of Hawaiian voters approved it. The conflict over same-sex marriage that began in Hawaii quickly spread to other states. According to Lambda Legal, by early 2010, four states (Connecticut, Iowa, Massachusetts, and Vermont) and the District of Columbia allowed same-sex couples to marry. Ten states provide equal protection for some state-based rights to same-sex couples through civil union or registered domestic partnership (non-marriage status) laws. In addition, several states respected marriages and non-marriage statuses that same-sex couples enter into in the other states that allow them. The effect of these state laws is that "as of 2009, roughly one-third of the same-sex couples in the United States resided in a jurisdiction offering them at least some form of state-level legal protection."[48] However, the 1996 national Defense of Marriage Act states that the federal government does not recognize same-sex marriages, or civil unions, legalized by any state and that states do not need to recognize same-sex marriages that were legalized in other states.

> On the presidential campaign trail, Barack Obama promised to work for advances in the civil rights of gay and lesbian citizens. However, before his first year in office was over, gay rights activists marched in Washington, D.C. to protest President Obama's lack of action on their behalf.

Though the LGBT community is winning some of its civil rights battles in a growing number of states, in many areas the battle has just begun. For example, in the area of family law, issues involving adoption rights and child custody as well as divorce and property rights are now battlegrounds. In addition, hate crimes continue to be a problem for members of the LGBT community as well as for citizens (and noncitizens) with non-white European ancestry (see "Thinking Critically About Democracy").

The national government enacted its first hate crime law in 1969. Since then, it has expanded the inherent characteristics for which the law guarantees protection. Today, under federal law, a **hate crime** is a crime in which the offender is motivated in part or entirely by her or his bias against the victim because of the victim's actual or perceived race, color, religion, nationality, ethnicity, gender, sexual orientation, gender identity, or disability. Forty-five states and the District of Columbia also have hate crime laws, but the inherent characteristics covered by those laws vary. Although all the state laws cover race, religion, and ethnicity, and most cover gender, sexual orientation, and disability, only a handful also cover gender identity.[49]

> The federal government began collecting data on hate crimes in the 1990s, highlighting the increasing incidence of such crimes. Today, hate crimes motivated by racial prejudice are the most commonly reported.

Affirmative Action: Is It Constitutional?

Laws reinforcing constitutional guarantees by prohibiting discriminatory treatment are the most common objectives of civil rights battles. Nevertheless, in the 1960s the federal government also began implementing policies aimed at reinforcing equal access to employment by mandating recruitment procedures that actively sought to identify qualified minority men for government positions. This policy of **affirmative action** was extended to women in employment and then to educational opportunities. However, affirmative action policies have been and continue to be very controversial.

How Affirmative Action Works

In 1961, President John F. Kennedy (1961–1963) used the term *affirmative action* in an executive order regarding the hiring and employment practices of projects performed by private contractors that were financed with federal funds. The order did more than prohibit race-based discrimination. It required that employers receiving federal funds take affirmative action to ensure that their hiring and employment practices were free of racial discrimination. In 1965, President Lyndon B. Johnson (1963–1968) extended Kennedy's affirmative action order to include the inherent characteristics of race, color, religion, and national origin. Then in 1967, Johnson again extended affirmative action to include women.

Today, affirmative action policies cover such processes as hiring, training, and promoting. Private companies, nonprofit organizations, and government agencies that receive federal government contracts worth at least $50,000 are required by law to have an affirmative action plan for their workers and job candidates.

Affirmative action does not require organizations to hire unqualified candidates, nor does it require the hiring of a qualified minority candidate over a qualified nonminority candidate. Affirmative action does require that an organization make intentional efforts to diversify its workforce by providing equal opportunity to classes of people that have been historically, and in many cases are still today, subject to discrimination. It focuses attention on an employer's history of personnel decisions. If over the years an employer with an affirmative action plan does not hire qualified underutilized workers (women and minority men), it will appear to many that the employer is discriminating and is violating Title VII of the Civil Rights Act. However, critics of affirmative action argue that it discriminates against Caucasians, and they have questioned whether the way it is applied to personnel policies as well as to college admissions policies is constitutional.

In the 1970s, institutions of higher education began to adopt intentional efforts to expand educational opportunities for both men and women from various minority groups. In addition, colleges and universities use affirmative action to ensure a student body that is diverse in race, color, economic status, and other characteristics. These institutions believe

hate crime
a crime committed against a person, property, or society, where the offender is motivated, in part or in whole, by his or her bias against the victim because of the victim's race, religion, disability, sexual orientation, or ethnicity

affirmative action
in the employment arena, intentional efforts to recruit, hire, train, and promote underutilized categories of workers (women and minority men); in higher education, intentional efforts to diversify the student body

SHOULD HATE CRIMES BE PUNISHED MORE SEVERELY THAN OTHER CRIMES?

The Issue: In October 2009, President Obama signed the Matthew Shepard and James Byrd Jr. Hate Crimes Prevention Act. This act expands coverage of the federal hate crime laws by adding sexual orientation, gender, gender identity, and disability to the list of characteristics already covered in the laws: race, color, religion, national origin, and ethnicity. Now those found guilty of committing a crime and having been motivated by bias against their victims because of one of these characteristics will have their punishment increased. Is this type of law just? Is it constitutional?

Yes: Hate crime laws further a compelling government interest. Crimes motivated by hate for a person because of an immutable characteristic are crimes against a whole group of people, not just that individual. When a Muslim is assaulted because he or she is a Muslim, fear spreads throughout the Muslim community, for any member of the community could be next. Hate crimes are intended to intimidate the victim and incite fear in all people like the victim. Hate crimes threaten domestic tranquility in a way that other crimes do not because hate crimes breed retaliatory hate crimes. The harm to public order and tranquility caused by hate crimes requires an additional punishment that indicates society will not tolerate people acting on their biases. Increased punishment may also deter others from committing hate crimes.

No: Hate crime laws violate the principle that all people are created equal. Enhancing punishment for hate crimes sends the message that some people are worth more than other people. If you commit a crime against any person, you might find the government arguing that you were motivated by your prejudice, and therefore the crime was a hate crime and you should be punished more severely. Valuing some victims more by punishing the perpetrators of crimes against them more harshly creates—rather than heals—divisions in society. Assault is assault. Does it really matter what motivated the criminal?

Other approaches: Many states have laws that make it a punishable crime to commit a *breach of the peace:* an act or a behavior that seriously endangers or disturbs public peace and order or that results in community unrest or a disturbance. A legal act can disrupt the public peace and lead to a charge of breaching the peace. For example, although burning the American flag is legal, if you burn it during a Memorial Day Parade in clear view of war veterans and a scuffle ensues, you can be charged with the crime of breach of the peace in many jurisdictions. Any *illegal* act that creates community unrest, no matter what motivated the offender, should therefore result in the additional charge of breach of the peace.

What do you think?

① Do you think that increased punishment for those found guilty of a crime motivated by hate will deter future hate crimes? Explain.

② Some opponents of hate crime laws argue that they will lead to limits on free speech. Do you think this concern is valid? Explain.

---

that having students on campus from a wide variety of backgrounds enhances all students' educational experience and best prepares them to function successfully in a nation that is increasingly diverse. Yet like affirmative action in personnel policies, affirmative action in college admission policies has been controversial.

Opposition to Affirmative Action

In the important *Bakke* decision in 1978, the U.S. Supreme Court found unconstitutional the University of California at Davis's affirmative action plan for admission to its medical school.[50] The UC Davis plan set aside sixteen of the one hundred seats in its first-year medical school class for minorities (specifically, African Americans, Latinos, Asian Americans, and Native Americans). Justice Powell noted in his opinion that schools can take race into consideration as one of several factors for admission but cannot use it as the sole consideration, as Alan Bakke argued UC Davis had done.

Ward Connerly, chairman of the American Civil Rights Institute (ACRI) argues, "There can be no middle ground about the use of race. This is not an area where one can fudge or cheat just a little bit. Either we permit the use of 'race' in American life or we don't. I say,

'We don't!'"[51] Connerly is leading the battle against affirmative action in admissions and employment procedures. Connerly founded the ACRI in 1997, one year after his successful effort to have California voters repeal their state's affirmative action policies in college admissions and employment. After anti–affirmative action victories in Washington (1998) and Michigan (2006), the ACRI has targeted Arizona, Colorado, Missouri, Nebraska, and Oklahoma for similar efforts.[52]

Opponents have challenged affirmative action in the courts as well as through legislative processes and statewide ballot measures. In two cases involving the University of Michigan in 2003, the U.S. Supreme Court upheld the *Bakke* decision that universities can use race as a factor in admissions decisions, but not as the overriding factor. Using the strict scrutiny test, the Court said in the *Grutter v. Bollinger* case that the school's goal of creating a diverse student body serves a *compelling public interest:* a diverse student body enhances "cross-racial understanding . . . breaks down racial stereotypes . . . and helps students better understand persons of different races."[53]

In 2007, however, the Supreme Court found unconstitutional two school districts' policies of assigning students to elementary schools based on race to ensure a diverse student body.[54] The majority of justices argued that those policies violated the equal protection clause of the Fourteenth Amendment. Chief Justice Roberts, writing for the majority, argued that governments should not use laws to remedy racial imbalances caused by economic inequalities, individual choices, and historical biases (de facto imbalances). He stated that such laws put in place discrimination that the Court found unconstitutional in the *Brown* case back in 1954. The justices who dissented from the majority opinion noted that today's policies are trying to ensure inclusion of minorities, not create segregation of, and hence cause harm to, minorities. The dissenters view policies that take race into account to ensure inclusion and balance as necessary means to achieving the compelling public good gained by a diverse student body.

Are affirmative action policies aimed at ensuring equal educational and employment opportunities for women and minority men constitutional, or do they violate the equal protection clause of the Fourteenth Amendment? The answer to that question depends on

POLITICAL INQUIRY

This cartoon suggests a number of the factors that colleges consider when making admissions decisions. Why is membership in a minority group controversial, whereas other factors—such as the ability to play a certain sport or being the son or daughter of a graduate—are not? In the future, how can colleges achieve the goals of a diverse campus and a fair admissions process?

how the majority of the members of the Supreme Court interpret the Fourteenth Amendment. Today, for an affirmative action policy for minority men to be constitutional, the government must pass the strict scrutiny test by showing that affirmative action is necessary to achieve a compelling public interest. In the case of affirmative action for women, the government must pass the heightened scrutiny test by showing that the policy is substantially related to the government's achievement of an important public interest.

CONCLUSION

THINKING CRITICALLY ABOUT WHAT'S NEXT IN CIVIL RIGHTS

For most of U.S. history, the law allowed, and in some cases even required, discrimination against people based on inherent characteristics such as race, ethnicity, and sex. This discriminatory treatment meant that the U.S. government did not guarantee all citizens equal protection of their civil rights. The long and continuing battles for civil rights of African Americans, Native Americans, and women are only part of the story. Latinos, Asian Americans, citizens with disabilities, and LGBT citizens are all currently engaged in political, legal, and civic activities aimed at guaranteeing equal protection of their civil rights. Numerous other groups are working to gain their civil rights as well. These include older Americans, poor Americans, and children born in the United States to parents who are in the country illegally. (The Fourteenth Amendment extends citizenship, and hence civil rights, to these children.) What other groups of legally disadvantaged citizens will fight for their civil rights?

The courts have the final determination of what rights are granted equal protection under the Fourteenth Amendment. The courts also determine if there are situations in which government does not have to guarantee equal protection. For the latter determinations, the courts use one of three scrutiny tests—ordinary scrutiny, heightened scrutiny, or strict scrutiny. Currently, advocates for women's rights criticize the courts' use of the heightened scrutiny test in sex-based discrimination cases. They believe that the courts should apply, instead, the strict scrutiny test which they use in cases of discrimination based on race, religion, and ethnic origin. What criteria will the U.S. Supreme Court use in deciding cases concerning sex-based discrimination in the future?

History tells us that an unhealthy economy, with high levels of unemployment and inflation and without real improvements in wages, as well as perceived threats to national security that are attributed to one ethnic, religious, or racial group, often trigger increased violations of civil rights and therefore new civil rights battles. How will the state of the economy and threats of terrorism shape the issues and the demands at the forefront of future civil rights battles?

Summary

1. The Meaning of Equality Under the Law
The Fourteenth Amendment guarantees all people equal protection of the laws. However, courts use one of three tests—ordinary scrutiny, heightened scrutiny, or strict scrutiny—to determine when discriminatory treatment is a legal means by which the government can fulfill its responsibility to a public interest.

2. Slavery and Its Aftermath
One legacy of slavery in the United States was a system of racial segregation. Under that system, both the states and the federal government condoned and accepted a structure of inherent inequality for African Americans in nearly all aspects of life, and they were forced to use separate facilities, from water fountains to educational institutions.

STUDY NOW

3. The Civil Rights Movement

Through the efforts of the early and modern civil rights organizations such as the NAACP, chinks appeared in the armor of the segregationists. The strategy of using the justice system to right previous wrongs proved instrumental in radically changing the nation's educational system, especially with the key *Brown v. Board of Education* decision in 1954, in which the Supreme Court ruled against segregation. In other arenas, such as public accommodations, and housing, Dr. Martin Luther King's leadership and strategy of nonviolent civil disobedience proved instrumental in winning victories in both legislatures and the court of public opinion.

4. The Government's Response to the Civil Rights Movement

The government responded to the demands for equal rights for African Americans with an important series of laws that attempted to secure fundamental rights, including voting rights and rights to employment, public accommodations, housing, and equal pay.

5. The Movement for Women's Civil Rights

The 1848 Seneca Falls Convention, which produced the Declaration of Sentiments, was the beginning of the first wave of the women's rights movement in the United States. This first wave focused on winning for women the right to vote, which was accomplished by the ratification of the Nineteenth Amendment in 1920. The second wave of the women's rights movement began in the 1960s with women organizing and lobbying for laws guaranteeing them equality of rights. The efforts of the second wave continue today.

6. Other Civil Rights Movements

In addition to African Americans and women, numerous other groups of U.S. citizens have battled for, and continue to fight for, equal treatment under the law. These groups include Native Americans, Latino and Asian American citizens, citizens with disabilities, and lesbian, gay, bisexual, and transgendered citizens. They seek equal employment opportunities, educational opportunities, housing, voting rights, and marriage rights, among others.

7. Affirmative Action: Is It Constitutional?

Since 1866, the national government has enacted civil rights laws that have prohibited discrimination. In a 1961 executive order, President John F. Kennedy introduced the nation to a proactive policy of intentional actions to recruit minority male workers, which he labeled *affirmative action*. President Lyndon B. Johnson extended affirmative action to women. Institutions of higher education also adopted the concept of affirmative action in their admissions policies. Affirmative action has been controversial, however, and a review of recent Supreme Court cases indicates that the constitutionality of affirmative action is in question.

Key Terms

affirmative action 174

Black Codes 153

Brown v. Board of Education of Topeka 157

civil disobedience 151

civil rights 148

de facto segregation 161

de jure segregation 154

equal protection clause 155

grandfather clause 155

hate crime 174

heightened scrutiny test (intermediate scrutiny test) 150

inherent characteristics 148

Jim Crow laws 154

literacy test 155

ordinary scrutiny test (rational basis test) 150

Plessy v. Ferguson 155

poll tax 155

Reconstruction era 153

separate but equal doctrine 155

standing to sue 152

steering 161

strict scrutiny test 149

suspect classifications 149

white primary 155

For Review

1. What is meant by *suspect classification?*

2. What tactics did whites in the South use to prevent African Americans from achieving equality before the civil rights era?

3. What strategy did the early civil rights movements employ to end discrimination?

4. What civil rights did the 1964 Civil Rights Act protect for minority, male citizens but not for female citizens?

5. Why did those fighting for women's civil rights begin their work by concentrating their efforts on state governments rather than on the national government?

6. Other than color and sex, what inherent (immutable) characteristics have been used as a basis for discriminatory treatment of citizens?

7. Explain how an approach to improving access to employment and educational opportunity based on affirmative action differs from an approach based on civil rights legislation.

For Critical Thinking and Discussion

1. Is it constitutional to deny any citizen the equal protection of marriage laws; is denying gay men and lesbians the right to marry a necessary means to a compelling public interest? Explain.

2. Today, more women than men are in college pursuing their bachelor's degrees. Is it legal for schools to give preference to male applicants by accepting men with lower SAT scores and high school grade-point averages than women, to maintain sex balance in the student body? Explain.

3. Many organizations fighting for civil rights protections include in their name the phrase "legal defense and education fund." What do you think explains the common two-pronged focus of these organizations?

4. What would be the effect of using the strict scrutiny test to determine the legality of sex-based discrimination? Would sex-based affirmative action pass the test? Explain.

MULTIPLE CHOICE: Choose the lettered item that answers the question correctly.

1. The idea that individuals are protected from discrimination on the basis of race, national origin, religion, and sex is called
   a. civil liberties.
   b. civil rights.
   c. natural rights.
   d. unalienable rights.

2. Individual attributes such as race, national origin, religion, and sex are called
   a. unalienable rights.
   b. inherent characteristics.
   c. indiscriminatory qualities.
   d. civil rights categories.

3. Laws that required the strict separation of racial groups, with whites and "nonwhites" attending separate schools, working in different jobs, and using segregated public accommodations such as transportation and restaurants are called
   a. Fred Samuels laws.
   b. Sally Hemmings laws.
   c. Jim Crow laws.
   d. Abraham Lincoln laws.

4. An election in which a party's nominees were chosen but in which only white people were allowed to vote is called
   a. a general election.
   b. a run-off primary.
   c. an uncontested primary.
   d. a white primary.

5. A mechanism that exempted individuals from conditions on voting (such as poll taxes or literacy tests) if they or their ancestor had been eligible to vote before 1870 is called
   a. a poll tax.
   b. a white primary.
   c. the grandfather clause.
   d. a literacy test.

6. Unlike sex-based discrimination, race-based discrimination must pass the
   a. heightened scrutiny test.
   b. ordinary scrutiny test.
   c. strict scrutiny test.
   d. ultimate scrutiny test.

7. Initially the courts interpreted which amendment in such a way that women were told they were citizens but that they had no constitutional right to vote?
   a. Thirteenth Amendment
   b. Fourteenth Amendment
   c. Fifteenth Amendment
   d. Nineteenth Amendment

8. What right does Title IX protect for women?
   a. equal access to credit
   b. equal access to educational opportunities
   c. equal access to employment opportunities
   d. suffrage

9. In what decade was the ERA ratified and added to the U.S. Constitution?
   a. 1920s
   b. 1970s
   c. 1980s
   d. It has not been ratified and added to the U.S. Constitution.

10. Today, citizens of what descent experience the highest educational and income level compared with the nation as a whole?
    a. African
    b. Asian
    c. Mexican
    d. Native American

FILL IN THE BLANKS.

11. _____ was the period between 1866 and 1877 when the institutions and infrastructure of the South were rebuilt after the Civil War.

12. The legal right to bring lawsuits in court is called _____ .

13. To pass the strict scrutiny test, differential treatment must be _____ for the government to achieve a _____ public interest.

14. During World War II, the federal government relocated citizens of _____ descent to internment camps.

15. The ADA is the _____ .

Answers: 1. b, 2. b, 3. c, 4. d, 5. c, 6. c, 7. b, 8. b, 9. d, 10. b, 11. Reconstruction, 12. standing to sue, 13. necessary, compelling, 14. Japanese, 15. Americans with Disabilities Act.

RESOURCES FOR RESEARCH AND ACTION

Internet Resources

American Democracy Now Web site
www.mhhe.com/harrison2e Consult the book's Web site for study guides, interactive activities, simulations, and current hotlinks for additional information on civil rights.

Equal Employment Opportunity Commission
www.eeoc.gov/facts/qanda.html This federal government site offers a list of federal laws relevant to equal employment opportunities and includes answers to the most frequently asked questions regarding equal employment laws.

Leadership Conference on Civil Rights/Leadership Conference on Civil Rights Education Fund
www.civilrights.org Founded by the LCCR and the LCCREF, this site seeks to serve as the "online nerve center" for the fight against discrimination in all its forms.

Internet Activism

YouTube
Invite your friends to join you in a critique of the evolution of race relations. Begin by viewing Dr. Martin Luther King's 1963 "I Have a Dream Speech" (www.youtube.com/watch?v=PbUtL_0vAJk) and presidential candidate Barack Obama's 2008 talk on race relations (www.youtube.com/watch?v=pWe7wTVbLUU).

Twitter
http://twitter.com/lambdalegal Lambda Legal is a national organization committed to achieving full recognition of the civil rights of lesbians, gay men, transgendered people, and those with HIV through litigation, education, and public policy work.

Blog
www.splcenter.org/blog/ The Southern Poverty Law Center is a nonprofit civil rights organization dedicated to fighting hate and bigotry and is known internationally for tracking and exposing the activities of hate groups.

Facebook
www.facebook.com/NationalNOW The National Organization for Women (NOW) stands against all oppression, recognizing that racism, sexism, and homophobia are interrelated, that other forms of oppression, such as classism and ableism, work together with these three to keep power and privilege concentrated in the hands of a few.

Recommended Readings

Branch, Taylor. *Parting the Waters: America in the King Years.* New York: Simon and Schuster, 1989. A Pulitzer Prize-winning book focusing on the civil rights movement from 1954 to 1963.

Feagin, Joe R., and Clairece Booher Feagin. *Racial and Ethnic Relations.* Upper Saddle River, NJ: Prentice Hall, 2003. A comprehensive look at the immigration of Africans, Asians, Europeans, Latin Americans, and Middle Easterners to the United States and the history of relations between Native Americans and the U. S. government.

Harrison, Brigid. *Women in American Politics: An Introduction.* Belmont, CA: Wadsworth, 2003. *American Democracy Now* coauthor Brigid Harrison introduces the study of women's participation in American politics, including their historic and contemporary participation in political groups, as voters, and in government.

Herr, Stanley S., Lawrence O. Gostin, and Harold Hongju Koh. *The Human Rights of Persons with Disabilities: Different but Equal.* Oxford: Oxford University Press, 2003. A collection of essays explaining how Article I of the Universal Declaration of Human Rights defines the standard for rights for people with disabilities.

Rosenberg, Gerald. *The Hollow Hope: Can Courts Bring About Social Change?* Second ed. Chicago: The University of Chicago Press, 2008. Rosenberg supports his argument that Congress, the White House, and civil rights activists—not the courts—bring about social change by reviewing the evolution of federal policy in the areas of desegregation, abortion, and the struggle for LGBT rights.

Movies of Interest

Bury My Heart at Wounded Knee (2007)
Based on Dee Brown's book of the same name, this HBO made-for-television movie chronicles ordeals of Sioux and Lakota tribes as the U.S. government displaces them from their lands.

Iron Jawed Angels (2004)
The little-known story of the tensions between the young, militant women's suffrage advocates, led by Alice Paul, and the older, more conservative advocates, such as Carrie Chapman Catt. The details of the suffrage battle during wartime, with a popular president opposed to women's suffrage, are well presented in this made-for-television movie.

Malcolm X (1992)
Based on the book *The Autobiography of Malcolm X* (as told to Alex Haley), this Spike Lee film stars Denzel Washington as black power movement leader Malcolm X. The film depicts the struggle in the 1960s between the black nationalists, such as Malcolm X and the activists who advocated more peaceful means, such as Martin Luther King Jr.

Mississippi Burning (1989)
Gene Hackman and Willem Dafoe portray FBI agents sent into Mississippi in 1964 to investigate the disappearance of two civil rights workers.

6

CHAPTER

Political Socialization and Public Opinion

THEN

Families and schools were the most important influences on children as they developed their political views.

NOW

Families and schools remain influential, but the media have been enormously important in developing the political views of the Millennial Generation.

NEXT

How will technology affect the socialization of new generations of Americans?

How will polling organizations find ways to harness the power of the Internet to predict political behavior accurately?

How can pollsters measure opinions of "cell-onlys"—potential respondents who own only cell phones?

In this chapter, we consider the ways in which people become socialized to politics, and explain the influence of various agents of socialization. We consider how public opinion is measured and take a look at how Americans currently view their governmental institutions.

FIRST, we examine the process of *political socialization* and how it can lead to *civic participation*.

SECOND, we consider the different *agents of socialization*, including family, the media, schools, churches, peers, community and political leaders, and demographic characteristics.

THIRD, we look at ways of *measuring public opinion*.

FOURTH, we focus on *what Americans think about politics*.

The process of developing in-

formed opinions about issues begins with the process of political socialization. Through socialization, we acquire our basic political beliefs and values. Through political socialization, we come to value the attributes of our own political culture. We also develop our ideological outlook and perhaps even begin to identify with a particular political party. Though the process of political socialization begins in early childhood, throughout our lives, institutions, peers, and the media continue to influence our views.

Political socialization is a key component in the process of creating an engaged citizenry. Psychologist Steven Pinker once noted that ". . . no matter how important learning and culture and socialization are, they don't happen by magic."[1] Joe Zavaletta, director of the Center for Civic Engagement at the University of Texas at Brownsville, would agree with Pinker's assertion: "Democracy is not magic. Why we expect our kids to magically become engaged citizens when they turn 18 when they haven't practiced . . . doesn't make any sense."[2]

Through the process of socialization, individuals acquire the ideology and the perspective that shape their political opinions. Though seemingly simple, public opinion is a fundamental building block on which American democracy rests. When we discuss public opinion, we often do so in the context of various public opinion polls that ask respondents everything from whether they approve of the president's job performance to how many sugars they take in their skim milk lattes. Political scientist V. O. Key Jr. wrote, "To speak with precision of public opinion is a task not unlike coming to grips with the Holy Ghost."[3] Key was referring to the nebulous nature of public opinion, which changes from day to day, is sometimes difficult to pinpoint, and is open to subjective interpretation. The glut in the number of "latest polls" has perhaps made us forget that the act of voting is itself simply the act of expressing one's opinion. Indeed, the word *poll* means to gauge public opinion as well as the location where one casts a ballot.

Public opinion is one of the ways citizens interact with their government. Through public opinion surveys, people express their policy priorities ("What do you think is the country's most important problem?") and their approval or disapproval of both government officials ("Do you approve or disapprove of the way the president is handling his job?") and the policies they create ("Do you agree or disagree with President Obama's decision to increase the number of troops in Afghanistan?") Much of the literature bemoaning the decline of civic involvement is based on public opinion research. But studies of civic involvement reveal that public opinion is the starting point for many forms of informed participation—participation that begins when individuals learn about an issue and choose to express their views on it using a variety of media.

Political Socialization and Civic Participation

How do we acquire our political views? Though an infant would be hard pressed to evaluate the president's job performance, of course, children begin to acquire political opinions at an early age, and this process continues throughout adulthood. As noted above, the process by which we develop our political values and opinions is called **political socialization.** As we develop our political values, we form the bedrock of what will become our political ideology. As this ideology emerges, it shapes how we view most political subjects: what side we take on public issues, how we evaluate candidates for office, and what our opinions on policies will be.

political socialization
the process by which we develop our political values and opinions throughout our lives

Although many tend to think that political socialization occurs as people approach voting age, in reality this process begins at home in very early childhood. Core tenets of our belief system—including our political ideology, our beliefs about people of different races and sexes, even our party identification—are often firmly embedded before we have completed elementary school.

A key aspect of political socialization is whether children are socialized to participate in politics. Simply put, civically engaged parents often have civically engaged children. Parents who engage in active forms of participation, such as volunteering on a campaign, and passive forms, such as watching the nightly news or reading a newspaper, demonstrate to children what matters to them. Parents who change the channel to a *Monk* rerun during an important presidential news conference are also socializing their children to their values. Children absorb the political views of their parents as well: a parent's subtle (or sometimes not so subtle!) comments about the president, a political news story, or a policy debate contribute to a child's political socialization by shaping that child's views.

The Process of Political Socialization

The beliefs and values we learn early in life also help shape how we view new information. Although events may change our views, we often choose to perceive events in a way that is consistent with our earlier beliefs. For example, people's evaluation of which candidate "won" a debate often strongly coincides with their party identification. Thus, the process of political socialization tends to be cumulative.

Historically, most social scientists have agreed that family and school have the strongest influence on political socialization. Our families teach us that it is—or is not—valuable to be an informed citizen and coach us in the ways in which we should participate in the civic life of our communities. For example, if your mother is active in Republican Party politics in your town, you are more likely to be active in the party than someone whose parents are not involved in a local party. Is your father active in charitable organizations such as the local food bank? He might ask you to run in a 5K race to raise money to buy food for the upcoming holiday season. Schools also influence our political socialization by teaching us shared cultural values. And in recent times, the omnipresent role that the media play in everyday life warrants their inclusion as one of the prime agents of political socialization.

> Children are socialized to the views of their parents at a very early age. Here a young boy attending an environmental rally holds a placard expressing "his" views. What opinions were you socialized to as a young child?

Participating in Civic Life

Does the process of socialization matter in determining whether individuals are active in civic life? Studies indicate that socialization does matter in a number of ways. First, children whose parents are active in politics or in their community are more likely to be active themselves. Schools also play an important role in socializing young people to become active in civic life—high school and college students are more likely to participate than young people of the same age who are not attending school. Research also indicates that socialization actually *generates* participation. People who have been socialized to participate in civic life are more likely to volunteer for a charitable or a political organization in their communities when they are invited to do so.

From our families and schools we also learn the value of becoming informed. Parents and schools, along with the media and the other agents of socialization that are discussed in the next section, provide us with important information that we can use to make decisions about our political actions. People who lack political knowledge, by contrast, tend not to be actively involved in their communities.[4] In fact, research indicates that when young people use any source of information regularly, including newspapers, radio, television, magazines, or the Internet, they are more likely to engage in all forms of civic participation. There is also a strong link between being informed and voting behavior. According to the results of one survey that measured civic engagement among young people, "youth who are registered to vote are more informed than their nonregistered peers. Eighty-six percent of young registered voters answered at least one of the knowledge questions (measuring political knowledge) correctly as opposed to 78 percent of youth who are not registered to vote."[5]

Agents of Socialization

agents of socialization
the individuals, organizations, and institutions that facilitate the acquisition of political views

Learning, culture, and socialization occur through **agents of socialization,** the individuals, organizations, and institutions that facilitate the acquisition of political views. Among the most important agents of socialization are the family, the media, schools, churches, peers, and political and community leaders. Our political views are also shaped by who we are: our race, ethnicity, gender, and age all influence how we become socialized to political and community life.

Family Influences on Activism and Attitudes

Family takes one of the most active roles in socializing us to politics and influencing our political views and behaviors. We learn whether our family members value civic activism by observing their actions and listening to their views. By example, parents show children whether community matters. The children of political activists are taught to be engaged citizens. They may see their parents attend city council meetings, host Democratic or Republican club meetings in their home, or help local candidates for office by volunteering to campaign door-to-door on a weekend afternoon. Other parents may teach different forms of political engagement—some young children might attend protests or demonstrations with their parents. Others might learn to boycott a particular product for political reasons. When political activists discuss their own involvement, they often observe that "politics is in my blood." In reality, political activism is passed from one generation to the next *through example.*

In other homes, however, parents are not involved in politics or their communities. They may lack the time to participate in political activities, or they may fail to see the value of doing so. They may have a negative opinion of people who participate in politics, constantly making comments like "all politicians are corrupt," "they're just in it for themselves," or "it's all about ego." Such opinions convey to children that politics is not valued and may in fact be frowned upon. A parent's political apathy need not necessarily sour a son or a daughter on politics or civic engagement permanently, however. Instead, first-generation activists often point to external influences such as school, the media, friends, and public policies, any of which can cause someone to become involved in civic life, regardless of family attitudes.

Our families influence not only whether or not we are civically active participants in the political process but also what we believe. While parents or older siblings may discuss specific issues or policies, their attitudes and outlook also shape children's general political attitudes and ideology. Children absorb their parents' beliefs—whether their parents think the government should have a larger or smaller role in people's lives, whether they value equality between the sexes and the races, whether they consider people in government to be trustworthy, and even specific opinions they have about political leaders. In fact, we can see evidence of how strongly parents' views are transmitted to their children in one of the best predictors of the results of presidential elections: each election year, the *Weekly Reader,* a current events magazine that many school districts subscribe to, conducts a nonrandomized poll of its readers. Since 1956, the first- through twelfth-grade student poll has correctly predicted the outcome of every presidential election. Children know for whom their parents will vote and mimic that behavior in their responses to the poll.

The Media's Ever-Increasing Role in Socialization

An almost ever-present fixture in the lives of young Americans today, the media contribute to the political socialization of Americans in many ways. Television, radio, the Internet, and various forms of electronic entertainment and print media help shape Americans' political perspectives. First, the media, especially television, help shape societal norms. The media impart norms and values on children's shows such as *Sesame Street, Barney,* and *Dora the Explorer,* which teach about racial diversity and tolerance. For example, Barney's friends include children with and without disabilities. These shows and others reflect changing societal standards and values. The media also reinforce core democratic values. Television programs such as *American Idol* or *The Biggest Loser,* or Sirius/XM Radio's *20on20,* incorporate the principle of voting: viewers decide which contestant stays or goes, or listeners pick which songs are played.

Second, the media also help determine the national agenda. Whether they are covering the war in Afghanistan, sex-abuse scandals, global climate change, or congressional policy debates, the media focus the attention of the American public. This attention may then have spillover effects as people demand action on a policy issue. We will see in Chapter 7, for example, how media coverage of the Tea Party movement propelled that organization's policy priorities to the forefront of the national political scene during the 2010 congressional elections.

Third, the media educate the public about policy issues. Local and national news programs, newsmagazine shows, and even comedies such as *The Colbert Report* and *The Daily Show with Jon Stewart* (yes, they really are comedies, *not* news programs) inform viewers about current events, the actions of policy makers, and public policy challenges in communities, states, and the nation.

Finally, the media, particularly television, can skew people's perception of public policy priorities and challenges. The oft-quoted saying "if it bleeds, it leads" demonstrates the attention that most local news stations focus on violence. Although crime rates have dropped since the 1970s, the reporting of crime, particularly violent crime, on nightly news broadcasts has increased. Even national news broadcasts and talk shows fall prey to the tendency to emphasize "visual" news—fires, floods, auto accidents, and plane crashes. Although these stories are important to those involved, they have very little long-term impact on society as a whole. But because they pique viewer interest more effectively than, say, a debate in Washington or in a state capital, news programs devote more time to them. Internet news sources also cover these dramatic events, but the sheer number of Internet news sites and blogs makes it more likely that at least some of them will also cover more important news, and people interested in political events and debates can find Internet news sources that cover such events and issues.

Schools, Patriotism, and Civic Participation

As early as kindergarten, children in the United States are socialized to believe in democracy and express patriotism. Schools socialize children to the concept of democracy by making the idea tangible for them. On Election Day, children might vote for their favorite snack and wait for the results at the end of the day. Or they might compare different kinds of apples or grapes, or different books, and then vote for a favorite. Lessons such as these introduce children to processes associated with democracy at its most basic level: they learn about comparing attributes, choosing a favorite, voting, and winning and losing.

Children also are taught patriotism as they recite the Pledge of Allegiance every day, sing patriotic songs, and learn to venerate the "founding fathers," especially George Washington and other American heroes, including Abraham Lincoln, Dr. Martin Luther King Jr., and

> Reciting the Pledge of Allegiance is one way schools socialize children to express patriotism.

John F. Kennedy. Traditionally, elementary and high schools in the United States have emphasized the "great men in great moments" form of history, a history that traditionally concentrated solely on the contributions of men in formal governmental or military settings. Increasingly, however, the curriculum includes contributions by women, African Americans, and other minorities.

Education also plays a pivotal role in determining *who* will participate in the political affairs of the community. Research indicates that higher levels of education are associated with higher levels of political activism. In a book on civic voluntarism, authors Sidney Verba, Kay Schlozman, and Henry Brady write, "Well-educated parents are more likely to also be politically active and to discuss politics at home and to produce children who are active in high school. Growing up in a politicized household and being active in high school are associated with political engagement."[6]

Churches: The Role of Religion

The impact of church and religion in general on one's political socialization varies a great deal from individual to individual. For some people, religion plays a key, defining role in the development of their political beliefs. For others, it is irrelevant.

For many years, political scientists have examined the impact religious affiliation—whether one is Catholic or Jewish, Protestant or Muslim—has on political preferences. For example, religion is related to how people view various issues, especially the issue of abortion. (See "Thinking Critically About Democracy.") But more recent analysis shows that a better predictor of the impact of religion on voting is not so much the religion an individual practices but, rather, how regularly he or she practices it. In general, it seems that those who regularly attend religious services are more likely to share conservative values—and support Republican candidates in general elections.

Research also shows that this relationship between frequency of church attendance and identification with the Republican Party is particularly strong among white Protestants, but less so among Catholics, who are generally more Democratic, and among African Americans. African American voters are even more likely than Catholics to vote for a Democratic candidate but are also likely to have high levels of religiosity, as measured by frequency of attending services.

Figure 6.1 shows the breakdown in party affiliation by religiosity. The results are based on respondents' assessment of the importance of religion in their lives and their frequency of church attendance. Notice in Figure 6.1 that a large proportion of highly religious people (34 percent of Americans, not shown in the figure) are Republicans or lean Republican in voting. Party identification is

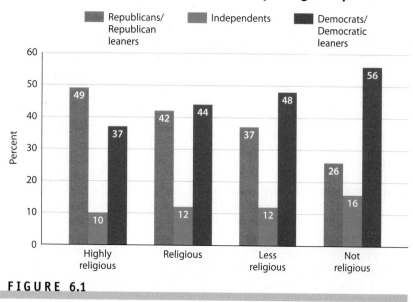

Party Identification, by Religiosity

- Republicans/Republican leaners
- Independents
- Democrats/Democratic leaners

FIGURE 6.1

Party Identification, by Religiosity

SOURCE: www.gallup.com/poll/124649/Religious-Intensity-Remains-Powerful-Predictor-Politics.aspx.

SHOULD ABORTION BE LEGAL?

The Issue: In the 1973 decision *Roe v. Wade,* the Supreme Court legalized abortion, essentially ruling that abortion would be legal in the first trimester of pregnancy, that states could regulate it in the second trimester (for example, by requiring that abortions be performed in a hospital), and that states had the power to ban abortion in the third trimester. Since that time, several other cases have influenced public policy on this issue, with the Court granting states more powers to regulate the circumstances surrounding abortion. Many states now require a mandatory waiting period before obtaining an abortion and/or parental consent for minors who wish to have an abortion. The Court has also struck down some proposed regulations, including a requirement that women notify their spouses before having an abortion.

Abortion is one of the most divisive issues in the United States, and public opinion on this issue has changed very little since the decision in *Roe v. Wade* was announced in 1973. About a quarter of Americans believe that abortion should be legal under any circumstances; 53 percent believe that it should be legal under certain circumstances, and 22 percent think it should be illegal in all circumstances.* As the accompanying figure shows, in 2009, for the first time a small majority (51 percent) of Americans called themselves "pro-life," while 42 percent consider themselves "pro-choice." Although individuals tend to hold very strong views on the abortion issue, very few people base their vote for a candidate solely on that candidate's position on the abortion issue. The divisiveness on this issue is heightened because those who hold different positions on the abortion issue also differ on other issues as well. Consider the stances articulated below, which typify views people express on this issue.

Yes: Women are the ones affected by a pregnancy, and they should be able to make decisions about their own bodies, without interference from the government—the "pro-choice" stance. Therefore, abortion should be legal under all circumstances until the point of viability. Women should be able to choose abortion, in consultation with their doctors, up to the time when the fetus can survive outside the womb, and there should be no restrictions on a woman's options.

No: Life begins at the moment of conception, and a fetus is another human life, as worthy of protection from the law as any other human being—the "pro-life" stance. We need to value life at every stage. Abortion should be illegal except to save the life of the mother; no other exceptions should be allowed. Doctors and others who perform abortions should be subject to criminal prosecution.

Other approaches: Abortion should be legal, but states should be allowed to place various restrictions on abortion. Parents should be notified when their underage daughters are seeking the procedure, for example, and states can require providers to inform women about alternatives such as adoption or make them wait twenty-four hours before performing the procedure. In other words, the goal should be to make abortion "legal but rare."

What do you think?

① Do you consider your view to be pro-choice or pro-life, or do you favor another approach? Do you think that abortion should be legal or illegal under all circumstances, or legal but with restrictions?

② Have you ever based, or would you ever base, your vote solely on a candidate's position on abortion? Why or why not?

③ Think about your own socialization process—how did family, church, peers, and events shape your views on this issue?

*"Abortion: Gallup's Pulse of Democracy: Guidance for Lawmakers," www.galluppoll.com/content/?ci=1576&pg=1.

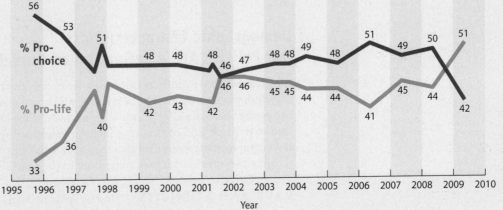

With respect to the abortion issue, would you consider yourself to be pro-choice or pro-life?

Source: www.gallup.com/poll/118399/More-Americans-Pro-Life-Than-Pro-Choice-First-Time.aspx.

nearly evenly divided among the religious (18 percent of Americans), with 42 and 44 percent identifying themselves as Republicans/Republican leaners and Democrats/Democratic leaners, respectively. Among the less religious (32 percent of the population), a large proportion (48 percent) identify themselves as Democrats/Democratic leaners, as do a majority (56 percent) of the not religious (16 percent of the population). Though there is a strong link between religiosity and political party, the differences between the proclivities of religious and nonreligious voters are applicable only to white voters—as discussed later in this chapter, African Americans are likely to be Democrats no matter how religious they are. And although religious Latinos are more likely to be Republican, by and large, majorities of Latinos identify as Democrats. Nonetheless, the relationship between religiosity and party identification is an important factor in American politics, particularly to the extent that religiosity shapes political views on social issues—abortion, or gay marriage, say—and renders them moral imperatives for voters, rather than mere opinions.

Peers and Group Norms

Friends, neighbors, coworkers, and other peers influence political socialization. Through peers, we learn about community and the political climate and values of the area in which we live. For example, your neighbors might inform you that a particular member of the city council is a strong advocate for your neighborhood on the council, securing funds for recreational facilities or increased police protection in your area. Or a coworker might let you know what your member of Congress is doing to help save jobs in the industry in which you work. Much research indicates that the primary impact of peers is to reinforce our already-held beliefs and values, however. Typically, the people with whom you are acquainted are quite similar to you. Although diversity exists in many settings, the norms and values of the people you know tend to be remarkably similar to your own.

Political and Community Leaders: Opinion Shapers

Political and community leaders also help socialize people and influence public opinion. Positions advocated by highly regarded government leaders hold particular sway, and the president plays an especially important role in shaping Americans' views. For example, President Obama's prioritization of health care reform propelled it to become a higher priority for many average Americans. But the role of political leaders in influencing public opinion is not limited to the national stage. In your city, chances are that the views of community leaders—elected and not—influence the way the public perceives local policies. Perhaps the fire or police chief endorses a candidate for city council, or the popular football coach for the Police Athletic League makes the funding of a new football field a policy priority in your town. Often we rely on the recommendations and priorities of well-respected leaders who have earned our trust.

Demographic Characteristics: Our Politics Are a Reflection of Ourselves

Who we are often influences our life experiences, which shape our political socialization and therefore what we think. The racial and ethnic groups we belong to, our gender, our age and the events that have shaped our lives, and where we live all play a role in how we are socialized to political and community life, our values and priorities, and even whom we vote for. Demographic characteristics also shape our levels of civic involvement and may even help determine the ways in which we contribute to the civic life of our communities and our nation.

RACE AND ETHNICITY   Whites, African Americans, Latinos, and Asian Americans prefer different candidates, hold different political views, and have different levels of civic involvement. Among the most salient of these differences are the candidate preferences of African Americans, who strongly support Democratic candidates over Republicans. But

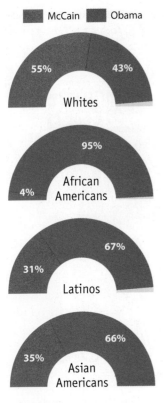

McCain   Obama

55%   43%
Whites

95%
African Americans
4%

67%
31%
Latinos

66%
35%
Asian Americans

FIGURE 6.2

Support of the 2008 Presidential Candidates by Racial Group

SOURCE: The Gallup Poll, Candidate Support by Race, www.gallup.com/poll/108040/Candidate-Support-Race .aspx, and Jane Junn, Taeku Lee, S. Karthick Ramakrishnan, and Janelle Wong, the National Asian American Survey, *Asian Americans and the 2008 Election,* www.naasurvey.com/assets/NAAS-National-report.pdf; www.cnn.com/ELECTION/2008/results/polls/USP00p1.

Figure 6.2 shows that in 2008, President Obama won majorities from Latinos, Asian Americans, and particularly African Americans, 95 percent of whom voted for President Obama. This proportion exceeds the share of the African American vote that Democratic presidential candidates have garnered in recent years, which has averaged 84 to 90 percent. The 43 percent of the white vote that President Obama won exceeds the 41 percent that John Kerry received in 2004, and the average of 39 percent of white votes that Democratic candidates have received since 1964.

This breakdown of 2008 voter preferences is not unique but, rather, reflects well-established differences in party affiliation and ideology between racial and ethnic minorities and whites. But there are also significant differences even within racial and ethnic groups.[7] Table 6.1 shows how the various categories of Latinos differ in terms of party identification. As the table shows, Latinos who identify themselves as Puerto Rican are very likely to be Democrats, while roughly half of all other ethnic Latino groups are likely to be Democrats.

Party affiliation among ethnic groups within the Asian American community also varies somewhat, as Figure 6.3 shows. In general, about 60 percent of all Asian Americans are registered Democrats. South Asians are most likely to be Democrats, and majorities of Chinese and Koreans are Democrats as well. A quarter to a third of all Korean, Southeast Asian, Filipino, and Chinese Americans are unaffiliated with either party.

White, African American, Latino, and Asian American youth also differ significantly in their levels of civic engagement as well as in how young people in these groups connect with their communities. Trends reported in *The Civic and Political Health of the Nation: A Detailed Look at How Youth Participate in Politics and Communities* include the following:

■ African American youth are the most politically engaged racial or ethnic group. They are the most likely to vote, belong to political groups, make political contributions, display buttons or signs, canvass voters, and contact the media about political issues.

■ Asian Americans are more likely to have been active in their communities. They are more apt to work to solve community problems, volunteer, engage in boycotts, sign petitions, and raise charitable contributions.

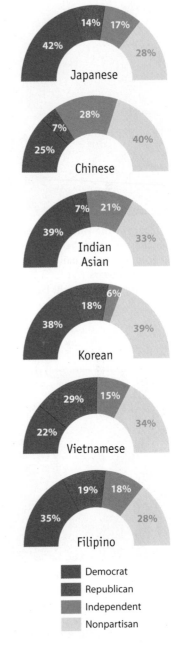

14%   17%
42%   28%
Japanese

28%
7%   40%
25%
Chinese

7%   21%
39%   33%
Indian Asian

6%
18%
38%   39%
Korean

29%   15%
22%   34%
Vietnamese

19%   18%
35%   28%
Filipino

■ Democrat
■ Republican
■ Independent
■ Nonpartisan

FIGURE 6.3

Asian Americans' Party Affiliation by Ethnic Group

SOURCE: Jane Junn, Taeku Lee, S. Karthick Ramakrishnan, and Janelle Wong, the National Asian American Survey, *Asian Americans and the 2008 Election,* www .naasurvey.com/assets/NAAS-National-report.pdf.

Latino Party Identification by National Origin, 2008

TABLE 6.1

	Republican	Democratic	Independent
Puerto Rican	11	61	24
Mexican	18	50	22
Cuban	20	53	26
Other	12	52	24

SOURCE: "Changing Faiths: Latinos and the Transformation of American Religion." © 2006 Pew Hispanic Center, a Pew Research Center project. <http://www.pewhispanic.org>www.pewhispanic.org

> Members of the Millenial Generation are more likely to volunteer than are members of any other age group. Here, Rice University freshman Chris Keller (center) uses a nail gun as Karen Lin (right), Larissa Ikelle (left), and Thurston Spears (far left) help assemble frames at a Habitat for Humanity warehouse that will be used to build low-cost homes in Houston.

> Latinos are the most likely Millenials to engage in political protest. Susan Peralta rallies against a 2010 Arizona immigration reform bill in downtown Phoenix.

> Eleanor Smeal, president of the Feminist Majority and a former president of the National Organization for Women, coined the term "gender gap" after the 1980 presidential election. Smeal noticed that in poll after poll women favored Democratic incumbent Jimmy Carter over Republican challenger Ronald Reagan. Was there a gender gap in the 2008 presidential election?

■ Young Latinos are the least likely to be active in politics or their communities, but they are most likely to have engaged in political protests. One-quarter of Latinos (more than twice the proportion of any other group) have protested, primarily in immigration rights demonstrations. The lack of civic involvement may arise from barriers to participation—including the fact that many Latino youths in the United States are not citizens, which would bar them from voting. The slogan of many immigration reform marches, "Hoy marchamos! Mañana votamos!" (Today we march! Tomorrow we vote!) may be a promise of increased political participation among young Latinos in the future.

■ Young white people are moderately likely to engage in many community and political activities. They are more likely than other groups to run, walk, or bike for charity, and they are also more likely to be members of a community or political group. Of the groups of young people considered here, they are the least likely to protest, the least likely to contribute money to a political cause, and the least likely to persuade others to vote.[8]

GENDER Public opinion polls and voting behavior indicate that men and women have very different views on issues, have different priorities when it comes to public issues, and often favor different candidates, particularly in national elections. This difference in men's and women's views and voting preferences is called the **gender gap,** the measurable difference in the way women and men vote for candidates and in the way they view political issues. Eleanor Smeal, who at the time was president of the National Organization for Women, first noticed the gender gap. In the 1980 presidential election, Democratic incumbent Jimmy Carter lost to Republican challenger Ronald Reagan, but Smeal noticed that in poll after poll, women favored Carter.

Since that watershed 1980 election, the gender gap has been a factor in every subsequent presidential election: women voters are more likely than men to favor Democratic candidates. President Bill Clinton, first elected in 1992, had the smallest gender gap that year, with women voters favoring him by only 4 percent. Four years later, when he ran for reelection, he had the largest gender gap to that point, with women voters favoring him by 11 percent. In the 2008 presidential election, the gender gap continued to favor the Democratic nominee, with women voters favoring Barack Obama over John McCain by 7 percent. The presence of Alaska Governor Sarah Palin as the Republican vice presidential nominee appeared not to have swayed vast numbers of women voters.

Voting turnout patterns increase the effect of the gender gap. Women in most age groups—except those under age 25—are more likely to vote than their male counterparts. In addition, on average women also live longer than men, so older women constitute an important voting bloc. The difference in women's candidate preferences and their higher likelihood of voting means that the gender gap is a political reality that any candidate seeking election cannot ignore.

Young men and women also differ in their level of civic engagement, in the ways in which they are involved with their communities, and in their perspectives on the government. While majorities of young men and women believe it is their *responsibility* (rather than their choice) to get involved to make things better for society, how they choose to get involved varies by gender. As Figure 6.4 shows, women in particular are more likely to participate in certain forms of community activism, such as volunteering and running, walking, biking, or engaging in other fund-raising activities for charity. Men and women are about equally likely to work on solving a community problem, such as volunteering for a nonprofit mediation service that helps negotiate disputes between neighbors. Men are more likely than women to choose formal political forms of activism, such as voting, persuading others to vote, and contributing money to political campaigns.

Women's and men's opinions also differ on public policy issues, though often in unexpected ways. On the one hand, there is very little difference of opinion between men and women on the issue of abortion. On the other hand, men's and women's views on the optimal role of government vary greatly: 66 percent of young women believe that government should do more to solve problems (versus 60 percent of young men), whereas only 27 percent of women believe that government does too many things better left to businesses and individuals, as opposed to 35 percent of men.[9] Women are also more likely to believe that the United States is at risk of another terrorist attack since

> Women's formal participation in government has increased significantly in the past generation, yet there remain differences in how men and women vote and participate in politics. Hawaii state Senate President Colleen Hanabusa (D), a candidate for Hawaii's 1st Congressional District seat (left), and volunteer Sharon Worthington (right), review the phone database at Hanabusa's 2010 campaign headquarters.

gender gap
the measurable difference in the way women and men vote for candidates and in the way they view political issues

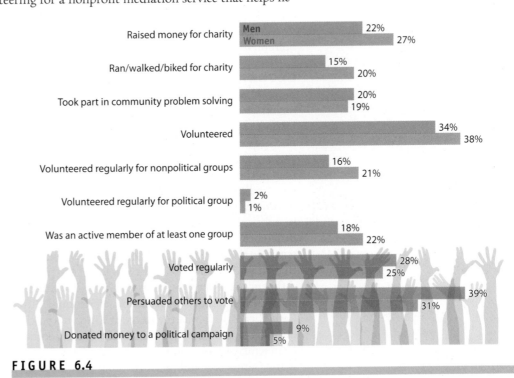

Participation in Civic Activities Among Young Men and Women

Men
Women

Raised money for charity — 22% / 27%
Ran/walked/biked for charity — 15% / 20%
Took part in community problem solving — 20% / 19%
Volunteered — 34% / 38%
Volunteered regularly for nonpolitical groups — 16% / 21%
Volunteered regularly for political group — 2% / 1%
Was an active member of at least one group — 18% / 22%
Voted regularly — 28% / 25%
Persuaded others to vote — 39% / 31%
Donated money to a political campaign — 9% / 5%

FIGURE 6.4

Participation in Civic Activities Among Young Men and Women

SOURCE: Karlo Barrios Marcelo, Mark Hugo Lopez, and Emily Hoban Kirby, *Civic Engagement Among Young Men and Women* (College Park, MD: Circle: The Center for Information and Research on Civic Learning and Engagement, 2007).

September 11, 2001 and they are less likely to feel safe from terrorism. Women, too, are more likely to believe that going to war in Iraq was a mistake, and they were more likely to have reached that conclusion earlier than men were. When it comes to domestic priorities, men and women are equally likely to cite jobs and the economy as high priorities, but women are more likely to consider health care a priority. Men are about 10 percent more likely to favor the death penalty than are women.[10] Do the different life experiences of women and men help to explain some of their policy preferences, and hence their candidate preferences?

AGE AND EVENTS   Differences in the candidates voters prefer—party, gender, the age of the candidates themselves—are one reflection of age and political opinions. People's opinions are also influenced by the events they have lived through and by their political socialization; an epic event may lead to a widespread change in political views. The **generational effect** (sometimes called the *age-cohort effect*) is the impact of a significant external event in shaping the views of a generation. Typically, generational effects are felt most strongly by young people. As a result of the attacks that occurred on September 11, 2001, people who were under age 30 on that day might place a heightened priority on keeping the United States safe in the face of a new kind of threat, for instance. Other key events that have shaped the socialization of a generation include the Great Depression and World War II for the oldest Americans and the war in Vietnam and the changes in society that occurred during the 1960s for the Baby Boom Generation born between 1946 and 1964. The major events that occur while we grow up affect our socialization by shaping our viewpoints and our policy priorities.

One of the strongest examples of the generational effect is the Great Depression. The oldest Americans, who came of age during the era of Democratic president Franklin Roosevelt's New Deal social programs, remain most likely to vote Democratic. But often the impact of events is not immediately apparent. Political scientists continue to measure the effects of the September 11, 2001, terrorist attacks and the subsequent war on terror on the views of the generation socialized to politics during the first decade of the twenty-first century. In the 2008 presidential election, young voters strongly preferred Senator Barack Obama over Republican candidate Senator John McCain. But was this difference in candidate preference a result of the generational effect? Will the Americans who grew up in the wake of those attacks be more patriotic than their parents? Will they resist a militaristic foreign policy throughout their lifetimes? These types of questions will interest public opinion researchers in the decades to come.

GEOGRAPHIC REGION   Since the nation's founding, Americans have varied in their political attitudes and beliefs and how they are socialized to politics, depending on the region of the United States from which they come. These differences stem in part from historical patterns of immigration: Irish and Italian immigrants generally settled in the northeastern seaboard, influencing the political culture of Boston, New York, Philadelphia, and Baltimore. Chinese immigrants, instrumental in building the transcontinental railroad in the nineteenth century, settled in California and areas of the Pacific Northwest and have had a major impact on the political life of those areas.

Among the most important regional differences in the United States is the difference in political outlook between those who live in the Northeast and those in the South. The differences between these two regions predate even our nation's founding. During the Constitutional Convention in 1787, northern and southern states disagreed as to the method that should be used to count slaves for the purposes of taxation and representation. The differences between these two regions were intensified in the aftermath of the Civil War—the quintessential manifestation of regional differences in the United States. Since the Republican Party was the party of Lincoln and the North, the South became essentially a one-party region, with all political competition occurring *within* the Democratic Party. The Democratic Party dominated the South until the later part of the twentieth century, when many Democrats embraced the civil rights movement (as described in Chapter 5). Differences in regional culture and political viewpoints between North and South remain. Today, in national elections, Republicans tend to carry the South, the West, and most of the Midwest, except for large cities in these regions. Democrats are favored in the Northeast, on the West Coast, and in most major cities.

---

generational effect
the impact of an important external event in shaping the views of a generation

Religious Affiliation in Geographic Regions of the United States

TABLE 6.2

MOST PROTESTANT STATES		MOST CATHOLIC STATES		MOST JEWISH STATES		MOST NONRELIGIOUS STATES	
State	**Percentage of Population**	**State**	**Percentage of Population**	**State**	**Percentage of Population**	**State**	**Percentage of Population**
Alabama	76	Rhode Island	52	New York	7	Oregon	18
West Virginia	75	Massachusetts	48	New Jersey	6	Idaho	17
Mississippi	75	New Jersey	46	Massachusetts	4	Washington	16
Tennessee	72	Connecticut	46	Florida	4	Colorado	15
South Carolina	71	New York	40	Maryland	4	Maine	14
Arkansas	70	New Hampshire	38	Connecticut	3	California	14
North Carolina	70	Wisconsin	34	Vermont	3	New Hampshire	13
Georgia	68	Louisiana	33	California	3	Nevada	13
Oklahoma	67	New Mexico	32	Nevada	3	Arizona	12
Kentucky	65	Vermont	32				

SOURCE: Jeffrey M. Jones, "Tracking Religious Affiliation, State by State," June 22, 2004, http://www.gallup.com/poll/12091/tracking-religious-affiliation-state-state.aspx#1.

Table 6.2 illustrates one factor that contributes to these differences in regional political climate: religious affiliation. Although differences in religious affiliation are often a function of people's heritage, church membership can alter the political culture of a region through the perpetuation of values and priorities. As Table 6.2 shows, the South is much more Protestant than other regions of the United States. Not surprisingly, Republicans dominate in this area, particularly among religious Protestants, born-again Christians, and Evangelicals (see the discussion of the influence of churches on political socialization on pages 188–190). Catholics and Jews tend to dominate in the Northeast along the East Coast; both groups are more frequently supporters of the Democratic Party. People without a religious affiliation, who tend to value independence and have negative views of governmental activism, tend to live in the West and vote Republican. We can discern many of the similarities and differences between the political beliefs of members of these various demographic groups because of the increasingly sophisticated and accurate ways in which we can measure public opinion.

Measuring Public Opinion

Public opinion consists of the public's expressed views about an issue at a specific point in time. Public opinion and ideology are inextricably linked because ideology is the prism through which people view all political issues; hence their ideology informs their opinions on the full range of political issues. Indeed, the growing importance of public opinion has even led some political scientists, such as Elizabeth Noelle-Neumann, to argue that public opinion itself is a socializing agent in that it provides an independent context that affects political behavior.[11] Though we are inundated every day with the latest public opinion polls on television, on the Internet, in magazines, and even on podcasts, the importance of public opinion is not a new phenomenon in American politics.

As early as the War for Independence, leaders of the Continental Congress were concerned with what the people thought. Popular opinion mattered because support was critical to the success of the volunteer revolutionary army. As discussed in Chapter 2, after the thirteen colonies won their independence, public opinion was an important concern of political and economic leaders during the early years of the new nation. The dissatisfaction

public opinion
the public's expressed views about an issue at a specific point in time

of ordinary people troubled by debt caused Shays's Rebellion in Massachusetts in 1786–87, which led to a shift in the thinking of the elites who came together in Philadelphia the following May to draft the new Constitution. And once the Constitution was drafted, *The Federalist Papers* were used as a tool to influence public opinion and generate support for the new form of government.

Public opinion is manifested in various ways: demonstrators protesting on the steps of the state capitol; readers of the local newspaper writing letters to the editor on behalf of (or against) a proposal before the city council; citizens communicating directly with government officials, perhaps by telling their local city council member what they think of the town's plan to develop a recreational center or by calling their member of Congress to indicate their opinion of a current piece of legislation. One of the most important ways public opinion is measured is through the act of voting, discussed in Chapter 9. But another important tool that policy makers, researchers, and the public rely on as an indicator of public opinion is the **public opinion poll**, a survey of a given population's opinion on an issue at a particular point in time. Policy makers, particularly elected officials, care about public opinion because they want to develop and implement policies that reflect the public's views.[12] Such policies are more likely to attract support from other government leaders, who are also relying on public opinion as a gauge, but they also help ensure that elected leaders will be reelected because they are representing their constituents' views.[13]

public opinion poll
a survey of a given population's opinion on an issue or a candidate at a particular point in time

The Origins of Public Opinion Polls

In his book *Public Opinion,* published in 1922, political writer Walter Lippmann stressed both the importance of public opinion for policy makers and the value of measuring it accurately. Lippman's thought informed a generation of public opinion researchers, who in turn shaped two divergent areas of opinion research: marketing research, used by businesses to increase sales, and public opinion research, used to measure people's opinions on political issues.

Among the first efforts to gauge public opinion were attempts to predict the outcomes of presidential elections. In 1916, the *Literary Digest,* a popular magazine similar in format to today's *Reader's Digest,* conducted its first successful **straw poll**, a poll conducted in an unscientific manner to predict the outcome of an election. (The term comes from the use of natural straw to determine which way the wind is blowing; so too does a straw poll indicate how the winds of public opinion are blowing.) Between 1920 and 1932, *Literary Digest* correctly predicted the winner of every presidential race by relying on its subscribers to mail in postcards indicating their vote choice. The 1936 presidential election between Democrat Franklin Roosevelt and Republican governor Alfred M. "Alf" Landon of Kansas centered on one issue, however: the government's role in responding to the Great Depression. In effect, the election was a mandate on Roosevelt's New Deal policies. The *Literary Digest* poll predicted that Landon would defeat Roosevelt by 57 to 43 percent, but Roosevelt won that election by a landslide, receiving nearly 63 percent of the popular vote.

straw poll
a poll conducted in an unscientific manner, used to predict election outcomes

Where did the *Literary Digest* go wrong? The greatest error the magazine committed was to use an unrepresentative sample to draw conclusions about the wider voting public. The straw poll respondents were selected from a list of subscribers to the magazine, automobile owners, and people listed in telephone directories. At the height of the Depression, this sample excluded most members of the working and middle classes. And class mattered in the 1936 election, with Roosevelt deriving his support primarily from poor, working-class, and middle-class voters. *Literary Digest* had committed what Lippmann termed an error of the casual mind: "to pick out or stumble upon a sample which supports or defies its prejudices, and then to make it the representative of a whole class."[14] Notice the similarity between *Literary Digest*'s faulty straw poll and many of today's voluntary Internet polls—self-selected respondents often differ dramatically in their views from those of the broader public, thus resulting in poll results that sometimes do not accurately reflect public opinion.

Although the 1936 election destroyed the credibility of the *Literary Digest* poll, it was also the watershed year for a young Princeton-based public opinion researcher named George Gallup. Gallup's entry in political public opinion research was driven in part by a desire to help his mother-in-law, Ola Babcock Miller, win election as Iowa's secretary of state, the

INTERNATIONAL OPINION OF THE UNITED STATES

Many Americans' patriotism and national pride result in the unflagging view that the United States is the best country in the world, but that view is not supported by the opinions of citizens of other nations. Indeed, by and large, many throughout the world have a negative view of the United States. The British Broadcasting Company (BBC) regularly conducts international polls gauging sentiment throughout the world regarding people's views of countries' influence. Respondents are asked to evaluate whether each one of fourteen nations, including the United States, has a positive or a negative influence in the world.

Why do so many nations view the United States negatively? Why are the negatively-ranked nations viewed so poorly?

One poll of residents of twenty countries indicates predominantly negative views of the United States. So although many people's opinions of the United States improved slightly after the election of Barack Obama, more countries have predominantly negative views of America (twelve of twenty), than predominantly positive views (five of twenty). As shown in the accompanying figure, among the nations where the United States enjoys the most favorable ratings are the Philippines (80 percent favorable), Ghana (76 percent), Nigeria (65 percent), and Italy (55 percent), and the region of Central America (64 percent). The United States is most negatively viewed in Germany and Russia (at 65 percent each), Turkey (63 percent), and China (58 percent).

Which countries enjoy the most favorable status? Germany (61 percent positive), Canada (59 percent), the United Kingdom (58 percent), Japan (57 percent), and France (52 percent) all enjoy majority favorable opinions. Israel (52 percent negative), North Korea (51 percent negative), Pakistan (56 percent negative), and Iran (58 percent negative) are the least favorably viewed nations.

SOURCE: www.worldpublicopinion.org/pipa/pdf/feb09/BBCEvals_Feb09_rpt.pdf.

Views of the United States' Influence by Country, January 2009
(by Percent)

Country	% Mainly positive	% Mainly negative
USA	60	31
Canada	38	55
Central America	64	23
Chile	42	42
*Mexico	12	54
Italy	55	31
United Kingdom	41	45
France	36	53
Spain	32	56
Germany	18	65
Russia	7	65
Egypt	40	48
Turkey	21	63
Ghana	76	11
Nigeria	65	30
Philippines	80	13
India	43	20
China	34	58
*Indonesia	33	43
Australia	32	56
Japan	28	29
**Average of 20 tracking countries	40	43

Sample profile has changed.
** *Does not include views of subject country.*
The gap between "mainly positive" and "mainly negative" in this chart represents "Depends," "Neither/neutral," and "DK/NA."

first woman elected to that position. In 1935, Gallup founded the American Institute of Public Opinion, which would later become the Gallup Organization. Gallup gained national recognition when he correctly predicted the outcome of the 1936 election, and scientific opinion polls, which rely on the random selection of participants rather than their own self-selection, gained enormous credibility during this era.

Gallup's credibility suffered a substantial setback, however, after the presidential election of 1948 between Democrat Harry S Truman and Republican Thomas E. Dewey. That year, the "big three" polling organizations, Gallup, Roper, and Crossley, all concluded their polls in October, and all predicted a Dewey victory. By ending their efforts early, the polls missed the swing of third-party voters back to Harry S Truman's camp in the final days of the campaign. The organizations didn't anticipate that many voters would switch back to the Democratic nominee, who wound up winning the presidency. During his administration, Truman would sometimes offer a good-natured barb at the pollsters who had prematurely predicted his demise, and George Gallup responded in kind: "I have the greatest admiration for President Truman, because he fights for what he believes. I propose to do the same thing. As long as public opinion is important in this country, and until someone finds a better way of appraising it, I intend to go right ahead with the task of reporting the opinions of the people on issues vital to their welfare."[15]

How Public Opinion Polls Are Conducted

In politics, public opinion polls are used for many reasons.[16] Political scientist Herbert Asher noted, "Polling plays an integral role in political events at the national, state, and local levels. In any major event or decision, poll results are sure to be a part of the news media's coverage and the decision makers' deliberations."[17] In addition, public opinion polls help determine who those decision makers will be: candidates for public office use polls to determine their initial name recognition, the effectiveness of their campaign strategy, their opponents' weaknesses, and how potential voters are responding to their message. Once elected to office, policy makers often rely on public opinion polls to gauge their constituents' opinions and to measure how well they are performing on the job.

population
in a poll, the group of people whose opinions are of interest and/or about whom information is desired

The process of conducting a public opinion poll consists of several steps. Those conducting the poll first need to determine the **population** they are targeting for the survey—the group of people whose opinions are of interest and about whom information is desired. For example, if your neighbor were considering running for the U.S. House of Representatives, she would want to know how many people recognize her name. But she would be interested only in those people who live in your congressional district. Furthermore, she would probably narrow this population by looking only at those people in the district who are registered to vote. She might even want to narrow her target population further by limiting her survey to likely voters, perhaps those who have voted in past congressional elections.

The sponsor of any poll, whether a candidate, a political party or group, or a news organization, needs to determine what information is desired from survey respondents. Sometimes this information is relatively clear—news media organizations track presidential approval ratings each month, for example. But other times this process might be more complex. Polling organizations construct polls carefully to ensure that the questions actually measure what the client wants to know. Pollsters also recognize that many factors, including question design and question order, influence the responses. For example, this chapter's "Analyzing the Sources" provides data on how Americans identify themselves ideologically:

ANALYZING THE SOURCES

EXAMINING AMERICANS' IDEOLOGY

This graph shows the trend over time regarding Americans' self-described ideology. In all the surveys, respondents were asked to describe their political views as very conservative, conservative, moderate, liberal, or very liberal. Very conservative/conservative and very liberal/liberal responses have been consolidated.

How would you describe your political views?

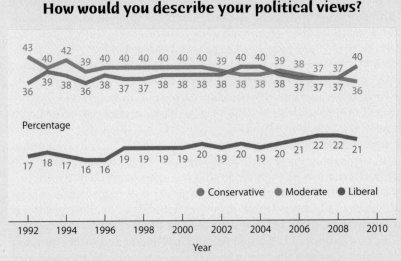

SOURCE: www.gallup.com/poll/124958/Conservatives-Finish-2009-No-1-Ideological-Group.aspx.

Evaluating the Evidence

① What does the graph indicate about how most people identify themselves now? Why do you think this is the case?

② Why do the 2009 data stand out? Are the 2009 data consistent with those of previous years?

③ The data come from a national sample of U.S. citizens. How would the data vary in your state? In your community?

5 percent of Americans identify themselves as very liberal, 16 percent as liberal, 36 percent as moderate, 31 percent as conservative, and 9 percent as very conservative. But other Gallup surveys have indicated that when pollsters changed the term "liberal" to "progressive" in half of the surveys sent to respondents, those who received the questionnaire with the "progressive" alternative responded quite differently. In general, people were more likely to identify themselves as moderates or as progressives when that terminology was used.[18] This simple change in terminology indicates that Americans may be more likely to identify themselves as "conservative" when the opposing term "liberal" is used rather than when the opposing term "progressive" is used.

SAMPLING   Once the target population is determined and the survey measurement instrument, or poll, is designed, pollsters then must select a sample that will represent the views of this population. Because it is nearly impossible to measure all the opinions of any given population, pollsters frequently rely on **random sampling,** a scientific method of selection in which each member of the population has an equal chance at being included in the sample. Relying on random sampling helps to ensure that the sample is not skewed so that one component of the population is overrepresented. To demonstrate this point, suppose the dean of students asks your class to conduct a public opinion survey that will measure whether students believe that parking facilities are adequate at your school. In this case, the population you need to measure is the entire student body. But clearly how you

random sampling
a scientific method of selection for a poll in which each member of the population has an equal chance at being included in the sample

conduct the sampling will affect the responses. If you ask only students in your 8:00 a.m. American Government class, you might find that they have little trouble parking because the campus is not crowded at that hour. If you ask students who attend classes only during peak hours, you might get different, yet not necessarily representative, views as well, since these students may have more difficulty parking than average. How then would you obtain a random sample? The best way would be to ask the registrar for a list of all students, determine your sample size, randomly select every nth student from the list, contact each nth student, and ask for his or her views.

Researchers have noted, however, that one problem with polls is that even those conducted using random samples may not provide the accurate data needed to illuminate political opinions and behaviors. Part of the problem is that randomization can go only so far. One standard method for conducting telephone surveys is to use random-digit dialing of telephones.[19] Many polling organizations still exclude cellular lines from their population.[20] But even those that include cell phone subscribers face a high rate of nonresponse because of the nearly universal use of caller ID, and the transportable nature of cell phones that makes their owners unwilling to participate in surveys.[21] But today, 20 percent of the U.S. population relies exclusively on cell phones and has no landline phone.[22] How might cell phone users be different from those who use only landlines? People who rely exclusively on landlines are likely to be older than "celly-onlys." Indeed, one study found that 33 percent of young adults aged 18–29 years lived in celly-only households.[23] And some individuals who eliminate landlines from their homes do so in order to save money. In fact, in 2008, adults living in poverty were nearly twice as likely to rely on cell phones exclusively, compared with those with higher incomes.[24] So, by eliminating cell phone users from a potential sample, pollsters eliminate individuals who may be poorer or more concerned with the economy than those who pay to keep a landline.

One way pollsters attempt to address these types of concerns is through the use of a **quota sample,** a more scientifically sophisticated method of sampling than random sampling. A pollster using this method structures the sample so that it is representative of the characteristics of the target population. Let's say that your mother is running for mayor of your town, and you would like to conduct a poll that measures opinions of her among various constituencies. From census data, you learn that your town is 40 percent white, 35 percent African American, 20 percent Latino, and 5 percent Asian. Therefore, at a citywide event, you structure your sample so that it reflects the proportions of the population. With a sample of 200 voters, you would seek to include 80 white respondents, 70 African Americans, 40 Latinos, and 10 Asians. Pollsters routinely rely on quota sampling, though often they may not ask participants about their demographic characteristics until the end of the poll.

Another method used to address problems in sampling is **stratified sampling,** in which the national population is divided into fourths and certain areas within these regions are selected as representative of the national population. Although some organizations still rely on quota sampling, larger organizations and media polls now use stratified sampling, the most reliable form of random sample. Today, nearly every major polling organization relies on U.S. census data as the basis of their four sampling regions. Stratified sampling is the basis for much of the public opinion data used by political scientists and other social scientists, in particular the General Social Survey (GSS) and the National Election Study.

SAMPLING ERROR   As we have seen, to accurately gauge public opinion, pollsters must obtain an accurate sample from the population they are polling. A sample need not be large to reflect the population's views. In fact, most national polling organizations rarely sample more than 1,500 respondents; most national samples range from 1,000 to 1,500. To poll smaller populations (states or congressional districts, for example), polling organizations routinely use samples of between 300 and 500 respondents.

The key is having a sample that accurately reflects the population. Let's say that your political science instructor offers extra credit if you attend a weekly study group. The group initially convenes immediately after your regular class session. At the conclusion of the study group, the leader asks if this is a convenient time for everyone to meet. Since everyone present has attended the study group, chances are that the time is more convenient for them than it is for those students who did not attend—perhaps because they have another class immediately after your political science class, or they work during that time period,

quota sample
a method by which pollsters structure a sample so that it is representative of the characteristics of the target population

stratified sampling
a process of random sampling in which the national population is divided into fourths and certain areas within these regions are selected as representative of the national population

or they have child care responsibilities. In other words, the composition of the sample—in this case, the students in the study group—will skew the responses to this question. Similarly, if a poll is administered to a nonrepresentative sample of a population, the responses will not accurately reflect the population's views.

In selecting a representative sample, pollsters need to pay particular attention to the time of day a poll is administered: afternoons yield a disproportionate number of mothers with small children and retirees, and evenings may yield more affluent individuals who do not do shift work. And today's telephone technology presents pollsters with even more obstacles. As we have seen, many potential respondents, particularly young people, have opted out of telephone landlines in favor of cell phones, making them a subset of the population that is more difficult for pollsters to reach. People with caller ID or both cell and landlines frequently screen out unknown numbers or those of survey research companies.

Internet polls present their own set of obstacles, including the ability of some individuals to complete surveys (or vote for their favorite reality show contestant) repeatedly.[25] Nonetheless, market research firms, public opinion polling organizations, and even political candidates are increasingly relying on the Internet as a survey research tool.[26] Some organizations, such as the Harris Poll Online, offer "memberships": poll respondents can earn rewards for completing surveys that help the organization create a representative sample of their target population.

To adjust for problems with sampling, every poll that relies on a sample has a **sampling error** (sometimes called a **margin of error**), which is a statistical calculation of the difference in results between a poll of a randomly drawn sample and a poll of the entire population. Most polls have a sampling error of ±3 percentage points ("plus or minus three percentage points"). This means 3 percentage points should be added and subtracted from the poll results to find the range for the population.

THEN NOW NEXT

Public Opinion Polling

THEN (1970s)	NOW (2011)
Telephone polls replaced mail-in and door-to-door polling because most American households had landlines.	Internet polls are at the cutting edge of public opinion research, but anonymity and multiple responses from the same person can damage a poll's accuracy.
Early telephone polls overrepresented the views of homemakers and retirees, who were more likely to answer the phone during the day.	The accuracy of telephone polls is affected by the difficulty of reaching people who use only cell phones or who screen calls using caller ID.
Pollsters remedied nonrepresentative sampling through quota sampling.	Pollsters rely on stratified sampling to ensure the most representative sample of the population they are targeting.

WHAT'S NEXT?

> How will technologies such as YouTube and social-networking sites such as Facebook shape polling in the future?

> How might pollsters overcome the obstacles associated with Internet polls, in particular, anonymous respondents giving false answers or responding to the same poll multiple times?

> How will cell phones and text messaging change the process of measuring public opinion in the future?

sampling error
also called *margin of error;* a statistical calculation of the difference in results between a poll of a randomly drawn sample and a poll of the entire population

Types of Political Polls

Today, the process of measuring political opinions has evolved drastically from the days of the *Literary Digest*'s straw poll or even George Gallup's first successful predictions of the results of presidential elections.[27] Political candidates, parties, and news organizations rely on several types of polls, depending on their goals and objectives. These include tracking polls, push polls, and exit polls.

■ **Tracking polls** measure changes in public opinion over the course of days, weeks, or months by repeatedly asking respondents the same questions and measuring changes in opinion. Since the 1992 presidential election, tracking polls have been an important tool, particularly for presidential candidates seeking to glean information

tracking polls
polls that measure changes in public opinion over the course of days, weeks, or months by repeatedly asking respondents the same questions and measuring changes in their responses

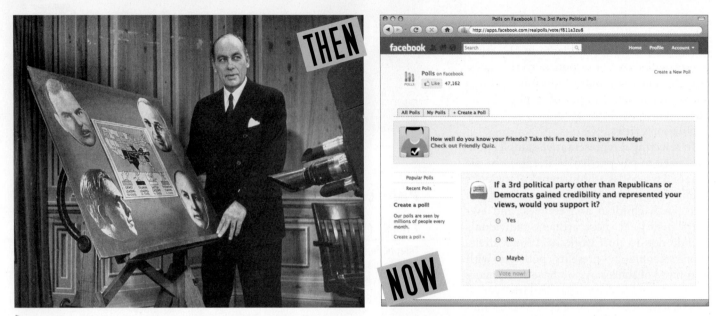

> Pollsters, including Dr. George Gallup, used the latest technology of the times to measure public opinion. In the photo on the left, Gallup discusses Americans' political views on a CBS-Television series called America Speaks in 1948. Today's technologies are again revolutionizing how public opinion is measured. Internet polling is one facet of this revolution.

about how campaign strategy has affected public opinion. Tracking polls are useful in indicating the effectiveness of the media strategy, the success of a day's worth of campaigning, or whether the campaign has gotten its message across in the most recent news cycle.

push polls

a special type of poll that both provides information to campaigns about candidate strengths and weaknesses and attempts to skew public opinion about a candidate

■ **Push polls** are a special type of poll that both provides information to campaigns about candidate strengths and weaknesses and attempts to skew public opinion about a candidate. At their best, push polls help gauge voter priorities so that a campaign can better target its message. The campaign can then determine whether to accentuate that message. But push polls have an unsavory reputation because some campaigns and organizations have used them to smear an opponent. Doing so in the hypothetical structure of push polls enables one campaign to make often baseless accusations against an opponent without having to substantiate the charges. For example, in the 2010 Republican primary for Utah's Senate seat between then-Senator Robert Bennett and one of his challengers, Mike Lee, who had the backing of Tea Party activists, a group unaffiliated with Lee's campaign used a push poll against Bennett. In the conservative state, a push poll asked if it would make a difference if the respondent knew that Bennett introduced a bill that would provide federal funds for abortions and if they knew that Bennett supported "health care to homosexuals."

exit polls

polls conducted at polling places on Election Day to project the winner of an election before the polls close

■ **Exit polls** are conducted at polling places on Election Day to project the winner of an election before the polls close. News organizations frequently sponsor exit polls, which help them predict the outcome of gubernatorial, congressional, and presidential elections. Because of exit polls, news organizations can frequently predict the outcome of a given election shortly after the polls have closed. Exit polls also provide the media, candidates, and political parties with information about why voters voted the way they did.

What Americans Think About Politics

Public opinion research is the means by which individuals can convey their opinions and priorities to policy makers. Consequently, polls connect Americans to their government.[28] Through public opinion polls, whether conducted by campaigns or media organizations, government officials come to know and understand the opinions of the masses.[29] Through polls, leaders learn what issues are important to people, which policy solutions they prefer, and whether they approve of the way government officials are doing their jobs.[30] The role of opinion polls in shaping citizens' involvement with their government is also circular: polls play a pivotal role in shaping public opinion, and the results of polls, frequently reported by the media, provide an important source of information for the American public.

The Most Important Problem

Several polling organizations routinely ask respondents to identify (either from a list or in their own words) what they view as "the most important problem" facing the country. Since April 2008, "the economy" has been most frequently cited as the most important problem, with fully 72 percent of those surveyed in 2010 identifying it as their top concern, as shown in Figure 6.5.[31] Not surprisingly, until November 2007, the war in Iraq was the top issue, with about a third of Americans—34 percent—citing it as the most important problem. By April 2008, only 23 percent named the war in Iraq as the most important problem. Until that time, Iraq had consistently been named the top problem for the four previous years. Interestingly, however, the percentage of Americans who were concerned about the situation in Iraq was not as high as it was for other wars, as reflected in the results of previous surveys conducted during earlier armed conflicts. For example, 56 percent of respondents identified the Korean War as the most important problem in September 1951, and 62 percent named the Vietnam War as the top problem in January 1967.[32] In general, other problems Americans identify as important include the state of the economy, gas prices, health care, immigration, and terrorism.

Figure 6.5 shows the proportion of people who responded "the economy" when asked "What do you think is the most important problem facing this country today?" From 2001 through 2008, comparatively smaller proportions of respondents identified the economy as the most important problem. During that time, other issues, including the wars in Iraq and Afghanistan, dominated the public psyche. But as the recession hit in 2008, increasing numbers identified the economy as important, peaking at over 80 percent in early 2009. As the recovery started in 2010, decreasing proportions were naming the economy as the most important problem, declining from 72 percent in February to 63 percent in April.

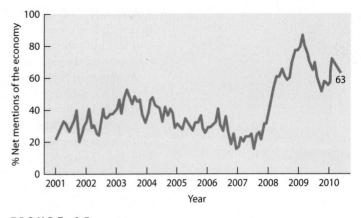

FIGURE 6.5

Percentage of Americans Mentioning the Economy as the Nation's Most Important Problem

SOURCE: Frank Newport, "U.S. Satisfaction at 15%, Lowest Since 1992," April 14, 2008, www .gallup.com/poll/106498/US-Satisfaction-15-Lowest-Since-1992.aspx.

Public Opinion About Government

Analysts of public opinion, government officials, and scholars of civic engagement are all concerned with public opinion about the government at all levels, in particular about the institutions of the federal government. For decades, public opinion researchers have measured the public's trust in government by asking survey respondents to rate their level of trust in the federal government's ability to handle domestic and international policy matters and to gauge their amount of trust and confidence in the executive, legislative, and judicial branches of government.

The responses to these questions are important for several reasons. First, although these measures indicate public opinion about institutions rather than individuals, individual officeholders nonetheless can use the data as a measure of how well they are performing their jobs. Lower levels of confidence in the institution of the presidency, for example, tend to parallel lower approval ratings of specific presidents.[33] Second, trust in government is one measure of the public's sense of efficacy, their belief that the government works for people like them, as discussed in Chapter 1. If people trust their government, they are more likely to believe that it is responsive to the needs of citizens—that it is working for people like them.

As indicated by the results of a Gallup poll that tracks trust in government over time, the public's trust in the ability of the federal government to handle both international affairs and domestic problems has in general declined over the years, but has experienced a slight rebound since 2009. Many analysts attribute the decline to widespread dissatisfaction with both foreign policy as it relates to the war in Iraq and the economic downturn, and attribute the rebound to the optimism fostered by the election of a president, Barack Obama, and the slow uptick in the economy.

As shown in Figure 6.6, the public's trust in government to handle international problems reached a record high immediately after the September 11, 2001, terror attacks, with 83 percent of those surveyed indicating a great deal or a fair amount of trust. The public's trust in government to handle international problems then steadily declined from 2004 through 2007, reaching a nadir of 51 percent in 2007, as the war in Iraq dragged on. The effect of President George W. Bush's "surge strategy" in Iraq and then the optimism generated by the election of President Obama account for a temporary increase in optimism, but as the war in Afghanistan drags on trust declines again, hitting 57 percent in late 2010.

The public's trust in the government's ability to handle domestic matters also peaked in 2001, as shown in Figure 6.7, which indicates the percentage of people who trust the government to handle domestic problems. Notably, a significant dip in the assessment of the government's ability to handle domestic matters occurred in 2005, immediately after Hurricane Katrina devastated parts of Louisiana, Mississippi, and other southern states. The drop in confidence that begins in 2005 reflects the widely perceived ability of the government to manage this crisis. By 2007, worries about the economy dominated the public's thinking, and trust in government to handle domestic problems dropped to 47 percent, a figure that rivals the record low confidence levels of 51 to 49 percent seen in the period between 1974 and 1976, following the Watergate scandal. An uptick registers in 2009, coinciding with Barack Obama's assuming the presidency. But that trust declines to 46 percent in 2010. This decline in trust was viewed by many analysts as a repudiation of both the president's handling of the economy and his health care plan.

The public's trust in specific institutions has also been affected by the September 11, 2001, terror attacks, the subsequent weariness with the war in Iraq, and the optimism following Barack Obama's election as president As Figure 6.8 shows, for example, trust in the executive branch hit a near-record mark in 2002, when fully 72 percent of Americans

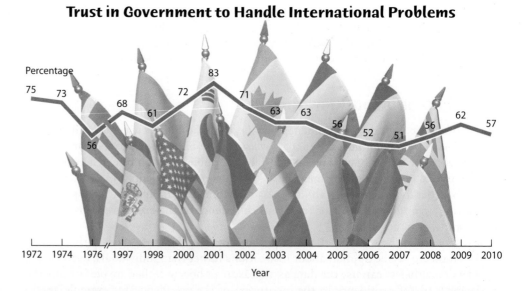

Trust in Government to Handle International Problems

Percentage

75 73 68 72 83 71 63 63 56 52 51 56 62 57 56 61 56

1972 1974 1976 1997 1998 2000 2001 2002 2003 2004 2005 2006 2007 2008 2009 2010

Year

POLITICAL INQUIRY

FIGURE 6.6 ■ **As you can see, public trust in the government's ability to deal with international problems has increased since 2008. Why do you think this is the case? Why was public trust comparatively low from 2003 through 2008?**

SOURCE: Jeffrey M. Jones, "Trust in Government," The Gallup Poll, www.gallup.com/poll/5392/Trust-Government.aspx.

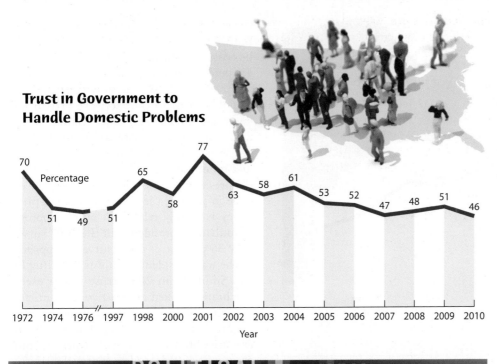

Trust in Government to Handle Domestic Problems

Percentage

70
51
49
51
65
58
77
63
58
61
53
52
47
48
51
46

1972 1974 1976 1997 1998 2000 2001 2002 2003 2004 2005 2006 2007 2008 2009 2010

Year

POLITICAL INQUIRY

FIGURE 6.7 ▆ What impact does the state of the economy have on the public's trust in the government's ability to handle domestic problems? What can you infer about the state of the economy in May 1972? In September 2004? In September 2010?

SOURCE: Jeffrey M. Jones, "Trust in Government," The Gallup Poll, www.gallup.com/poll/5392/Trust-Government.aspx.

Trust in the Executive Branch of Government

Percentage

73
40
58
62
63
64
65
63
72
60
58
52
46
43
42
61
49

Nixon Ford Clinton G. W. Bush Obama

1972 1974 1976 1997 1998 1999 2000 2001 2002 2003 2004 2005 2006 2007 2008 2009 2010

Year

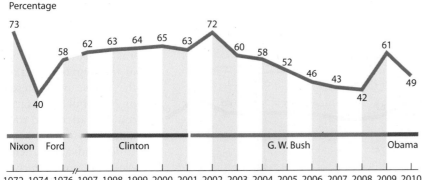

POLITICAL INQUIRY

FIGURE 6.8 ▆ As the graph shows, the public's trust in the executive branch declined steeply (from 73 percent to 40 percent in two years) during the Nixon presidency as a result of the Watergate scandal. The decline during George W. Bush's presidency was more gradual, from 72 percent to 42 percent in six years. Was this decline partly to be expected for any second-term president? How has President Obama fared in trust since becoming president in 2009?

SOURCE: Jeffrey M. Jones, "Trust in Government," The Gallup Poll, www.gallup.com/poll/5392/Trust-Government.aspx.

Trust in the Legislative Branch of Government

Percentage

71 68 61 54 61 57 68 65 67 63 60 62 56 50 47 45 36

1972 1974 1976 1997 1998 1999 2000 2001 2002 2003 2004 2005 2006 2007 2008 2009 2010

Year

POLITICAL INQUIRY

FIGURE 6.9 ▨ Trust in the legislative branch plummeted from 62 percent in 2005 to 47 percent in 2010. What factors can explain that trend? Why do you believe that trust in both the executive and the legislative branches was low from 2006 to 2008, even though those branches were controlled by different political parties?

SOURCE: Jeffrey M. Jones, "Trust in Government," The Gallup Poll, www.gallup.com/poll/5392/Trust-Government.aspx.

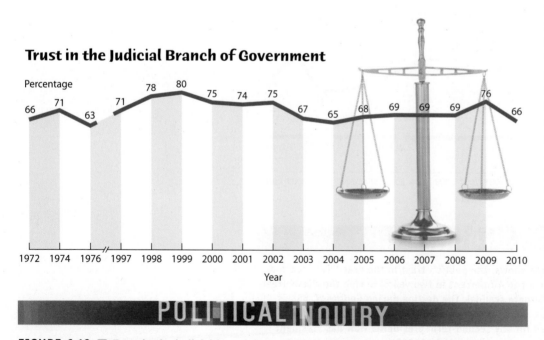

Trust in the Judicial Branch of Government

Percentage

66 71 63 71 78 80 75 74 75 67 65 68 69 69 69 76 66

1972 1974 1976 1997 1998 1999 2000 2001 2002 2003 2004 2005 2006 2007 2008 2009 2010

Year

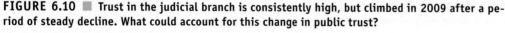

POLITICAL INQUIRY

FIGURE 6.10 ▨ Trust in the judicial branch is consistently high, but climbed in 2009 after a period of steady decline. What could account for this change in public trust?

SOURCE: Jeffrey M. Jones, "Trust in Government," The Gallup Poll, www.gallup.com/poll/5392/Trust-Government.aspx.

voiced a great deal or a fair amount of trust. But then, in 2007, as Figure 6.8 shows, public trust in the executive branch dropped to 43 percent, marking a 9-percentage-point decline from 2005. The only time the level of public trust in the executive branch was lower (at 40 percent) since Gallup began measuring trust in institutions was in 1974, at the height of the Watergate scandal and just months before Richard Nixon resigned the presidency.[34] As previously noted, the decline in trust in the institution of the presidency is closely related to public approval of individual presidents: in the 2007 survey, only 36 percent of those surveyed approved of the way President Bush was handling his job. Similarly, in 2009, trust in the executive branch spiked up to 61 percent, mirroring Barack Obama's higher approval ratings during that time. By 2010, public trust in the executive branch declined to 46 percent, mirroring the president's low approval rating.

For example, in 2009, 61 percent of those surveyed expressed trust in the executive branch, but only 45 percent expressed trust in the legislative branch. But this is not always the case. Take 2007, for example. As shown in Figure 6.9, trust in the legislative branch also declined to 50 percent from 62 percent in 2005. Before 2006, part of this decline of trust could be attributed to the public's dissatisfaction with the Republican Congress's consent to Bush administration policies concerning Iraq. From 2006 through 2010, increasing dissatisfaction with the Democrats in Congress was apparent, culminating in the Republican takeover of the House of Representatives in 2010. Public dissatisfaction could be attributed to the economic downturn.

The judicial branch of government consistently scores higher in levels of public trust than the other two branches. Figure 6.10 shows that confidence in the judiciary typically hovers between 65 and 75 percent, sometimes climbing into the high 70s (or even 80 percent in 1999). The judiciary's lowest rating came in 1976, when there was widespread dissatisfaction with government as a whole in the aftermath of the Watergate scandal.

The process of political socialization is quite different from what it was even a generation ago. Although some agents of socialization such as families, peers, and churches remain important, other agents, particularly the media, are more pervasive and influential than ever before. Although television and radio have played a part in socializing the average 40-year-old in 2011, today's young people are almost constantly bombarded by various forms of media, which may influence their viewpoints, priorities, behaviors, and opinions.

Technology has also drastically changed the way public opinion is measured. The advent of the computer alone—from powerful mainframes to personal computers—has revolutionized the data collection process; today computers facilitate near-instant access to polling data. They also provide the means to generate and survey increasingly representative samples to gauge the public's views with a high degree of accuracy. How will the pervasiveness of cell phones revolutionize the process of public opinion polling?

The catch-22, however, has been the pervasiveness of public opinion polls. People's opinions are solicited by every kind of survey from cheesy Internet polls to reputable polling organizations. As a result, the public has become poll weary, dubious of the value of the pollster's next set of questions. Will increasing weariness with Internet polling result in less representative samples? How might pollsters overcome this challenge?

But technology has provided—and will continue to provide—ways to solve the problems that technology itself has generated in accurately measuring public opinion. Stratified samples and other increasingly sophisticated microsampling techniques have improved the ability of reputable pollsters to gauge public opinion. And pollsters are incorporating new technologies, including text messaging and cell phone surveys, as they work to develop new ways to accurately measure and convey the public's views to candidates, to policy makers, and, through the media, to the public itself.

Summary

1. Political Socialization and Civic Participation

Political socialization begins at home in very early childhood, when our political ideology, our beliefs about people of different races and sexes, and even our party identification can be firmly embedded, and the beliefs and values we learn early help shape how we view new information as we age. One key aspect of political socialization is whether children are socialized to participate in the civic and political life of their communities. Families, schools, and media all contribute to whether and how people participate.

2. Agents of Socialization

Among the agents of socialization—including family, the media, schools, churches, peers, community and political leaders, and demographic characteristics—the most important are the family and the media. Family shapes our political values and ideology from childhood and has a strong impact on our political perspective. The media now rival the family in the influence that they have in shaping our views and informing our opinions. A person's level of religiosity is actually a more important influence than his or her actual belief structure so that, in general, very religious people of all faiths have more in common with one another than with less religious people of the same faith. Demographic characteristics—including race and ethnicity, gender, age, and geographic region—not only contribute to how we are socialized to political and community life and our values and priorities but also influence the candidates we vote for.

3. Measuring Public Opinion

The measurement of public opinion has evolved and become increasingly complex and reliable when done scientifically, though the proliferation of questionable straw polls on the Internet, similar to the initial attempts to predict presidential elections in the early twentieth century, still offers dubious results to the gullible. In measuring public opinion, reputable pollsters identify the target population, design an accurate measure, select a sample, and administer the poll. Through various methods of sampling, pollsters attempt to select a subset of the population that is representative of the population's views. Different types of polls, including tracking polls, push polls, and exit polls, are used for different purposes in political campaigns.

4. What Americans Think About Politics

Americans identify the state of the economy as the "most important problem," replacing the war in Iraq as their top concern. Polls also indicate that their overall satisfaction with the direction the country is headed in is low. Among the three branches of government, people's trust in both the presidency and Congress is at near-record lows, while trust in the judiciary remains relatively stable.

Key Terms

agents of socialization 186

exit polls 202

gender gap 193

generational effect 194

political socialization 185

population 198

public opinion 195

public opinion poll 196

push polls 202

quota sample 200

random sampling 199

sampling error (margin of error) 201

stratified sampling 200

straw poll 196

tracking polls 201

For Review

1. How are political socialization and civic participation linked?

2. Explain in detail the agents of socialization. How does each agent influence an individual's political views over a lifetime?

3. What demographic characteristics contribute to how individuals view politics?

4. How did public opinion polls evolve historically?

5. Explain how public opinion polls are conducted.

6. What factors have an impact on what Americans perceive as the "most important problem"?

7. Describe the most recent trend regarding Americans' trust in government.

For Critical Thinking and Discussion

1. Were you brought up in a family in which joining groups was important? Do your parents belong to any interest groups? Do you? If not, why do you think that is the case?

2. How have your demographic characteristics—your age, the area of the country in which you were raised—contributed to the formation of your political views? How relevant are the generalities described in the chapter to your own experience and beliefs?

3. What do you think is the "most important problem" facing the United States? Is it a problem discussed in this book? Is it one shared by your classmates?

4. What factors influence how satisfied you feel about the direction of the country?

5. Which branch of government do you trust the most? Why?

MULTIPLE CHOICE: Choose the lettered item that answers the question correctly.

1. The public's expressed views about an issue at a specific point in time are called
   a. public opinion.
   b. time frame analysis.
   c. time tracked sample.
   d. stratified sample.

2. Agents of socialization *do not* include
   a. pets.
   b. peers.
   c. churches.
   d. the media.

3. A majority of which of the following demographic groups did not support Barack Obama's candidacy for the presidency?
   a. Latinos
   b. women
   c. whites
   d. Asians

4. The impact of an important external event in shaping the views of a generation is called
   a. the age-cohort effect.
   b. the generational effect.
   c. the lifetime effect.
   d. both (a) and (b).

5. A poll conducted in an unscientific manner, used to predict election outcomes, is called
   a. an exit poll.
   b. a tracking poll.
   c. a push poll.
   d. a straw poll.

6. In a poll, the group of people whose opinions are of interest and/or about whom information is desired is called the
   a. quota sample.
   b. target sample.
   c. population.
   d. bull's-eye group.

7. A method by which pollsters structure a sample so that it is representative of the characteristics of the target population is called a
   a. quota sample.
   b. target sample.
   c. population.
   d. bull's-eye group.

8. Polls that measure changes in public opinion over the course of days, weeks, or months by repeatedly asking respondents the same questions and measuring changes in their responses are called
   a. exit polls.
   b. tracking polls.
   c. push polls.
   d. straw polls.

9. A special type of poll that both provides information to campaigns about candidate strengths and weaknesses and attempts to skew public opinion about a candidate is called
   a. an exit poll.
   b. a tracking poll.
   c. a push poll.
   d. a straw poll.

10. Polls conducted at polling places on Election Day to determine the winner of an election before the polls close are called
    a. exit polls.
    b. tracking polls.
    c. push polls.
    d. straw polls.

FILL IN THE BLANKS.

11. The process by which we develop our political values and opinions throughout our lives is called _____ .

12. The measurable difference in the way women and men vote for candidates and in the way they view political issues is called the _____ .

13. A survey of a given population's opinion on an issue or a candidate at a particular point in time is called a _____ .

14. A scientific method of selection for a poll in which each member of the population has an equal chance at being included in the sample is called _____ .

15. A process of random sampling in which the national population is divided into fourths and certain areas within these regions are selected as representative of the national population is called _____ .

Answers: 1. a; 2. a; 3. c; 4. d; 5. d; 6. c; 7. a; 8. b; 9. c; 10 a; 11. political socialization; 12. gender gap; 13. public opinion poll; 14. random sampling; 15. stratified sampling.

RESOURCES FOR RESEARCH AND ACTION

Internet Resources

Annenberg National Election Studies
www.electionstudies.org   The ANES Web site contains a plethora of information on American public opinion as well as a valuable user guide that can help acquaint you with using the data. It also provides a link to other election studies, including some cross-national studies at www.electionstudies.org/other_election_studies.

The Gallup Organization
www.galluppoll.com   You will find both national and international polls and analysis on this site.

The Roper Center
www.ropercenter.uconn.edu   This Web site features the University of Connecticut's Roper Center polls, the General Social Survey, presidential approval ratings, and poll analysis.

Zogby International
www.zogby.com   For a wide variety of political, commercial, and sociological data, go to this site.

Internet Activism

Twitter
@poll—demonstrates both the power and the limitations of polls relying on new technologies.

Facebook
Friend "Gallup" or search "poll application" to add an application that enables you to create polls for your Facebook page.

Recommended Readings

Bishop, George F., and Stephen T. Mockabee. *Taking the Pulse of Public Opinion: Leading and Misleading Indicators of the State of the Nation.* New York: Springer Publishing, 2010. This analytical work examines how psychology and the media influence well-established public opinion indicators.

Fiorina, Morris P. *Culture War: The Myth of a Polarized America.* New York: Pearson Longman, 2006. A critical view of the notion that the United States is divided along ideological lines. Fiorina asserts that Americans are generally moderate and tolerant of a wide variety of viewpoints.

Jamieson, Kathleen Hall. *Electing the President, 2008.* Philadelphia: University of Pennsylvania, 2008. A fascinating "insider's view" of how public opinion shaped the 2008 presidential campaigns by the director of the Annenberg National Election Studies.

Page, Benjamin I., and Robert Y. Shapiro. *The Rational Public: Fifty Years of Trends in Americans' Policy Preferences.* Chicago: University of Chicago, 1992. An analysis of the policy preferences of the American public from the 1930s until 1990. The authors describe opinion on both domestic and foreign policy.

Traugott, Michael W., and Paul J. Lavrakas. *The Voter's Guide to Election Polls,* 4th ed. New York: Chatham House, 2008. A user-friendly approach, written in question-and-answer format, that helps beginners understand the polling process and how to interpret public opinion data.

Welch, Susan, Lee Sigelman, Timothy Bledsoe, and Michael Combs. *Race and Place: Race Relations in an American City* (Cambridge Studies in Public Opinion and Political Psychology). Cambridge: Cambridge University Press, 2001. An analysis of the impact of residential changes on the attitudes and behavior of African Americans and whites.

Movies of Interest

Lions for Lambs (2007)
Directed by Robert Redford and starring Redford, Meryl Streep, and Tom Cruise, this film about a platoon of U.S. soldiers in Afghanistan demonstrates the influence educational socialization can have on individuals.

Wag the Dog (1997)
A classic Barry Levinson film featuring a spin-doctor (Robert De Niro) and a Hollywood producer (Dustin Hoffman) who team up eleven days before an election to "fabricate" a war in order to cover up a presidential sex scandal.

CHAPTER

7

Interest Groups

THEN

Individuals joined voluntary organizations to achieve goals of value to their members and to influence the direction of society and government.

NOW

Organization and money are crucial predictors of how successfully an interest group will influence policy.

NEXT

Will digital fund-raising, organizing, and communicating strengthen the clout and efficacy of interest groups?

Will expanding Web-based activism change the face of *who* participates in interest groups?

Will digital group activism have unintended negative consequences?

In this chapter, we survey the composition, power, and strategies of interest groups in the United States. We explore the development of interest groups over time and analyze what makes an interest group successful.

FIRST, we examine *the value of interest groups* as tools of citizen participation.

SECOND, we consider the questions of *who joins interest groups, and why.*

THIRD, we examine *how interest groups succeed.*

FOURTH, we look at various *types of interest groups.*

FIFTH, we focus on *interest group strategies.*

SIXTH, we probe the intersection of *interest groups, politics, and money:* specifically, *the influence of political action committees.*

interest groups
organizations that seek to achieve some of their goals by influencing government decision making

social capital
the many ways in which our lives are improved by social connections

Organizations that seek to

achieve their goals by influencing government decision making are called **interest groups.** Also called *special interests,* interest groups differ from political parties in that interest groups do not seek to control the government, as parties do. Interest groups simply want to influence policy making on issues. Interest groups are more important in the political process of the United States than anywhere else in the world.[1] Their strong role is partly due to the number of interest groups that attempt to influence U.S. policy.

Take just one issue—the environment, say—and chances are that you or someone in your class is a member of one of the almost two hundred organizations concerned with the environment, conservation, or ecology in the United States.[2] The multitude of interest groups focused on any given issue is an important component of how government policy is formulated. Interest groups shape the policy process by helping determine which issues policy makers will act on and which options they will consider in addressing a problem.

When we think of interest groups, the typical images that come to mind are of wealthy lobbyists "schmoozing" with easily corrupted politicians. Although that may sometimes be the case, interest groups do not require the leadership of the rich and well connected to be effective. But today, using new technologies such as the social networking Web sites Facebook and Twitter, the organized effort of people from all walks of life can influence policy making. Although moneyed interests may dominate politics, interest groups play a crucial role in leveling the political playing field by providing access for organized "average" people.

The Value of Interest Groups

The nineteenth-century French historian and writer Alexis de Tocqueville, author of the influential work *Democracy in America,* dubbed Americans "a nation of joiners" in 1835, and his analysis still rings true today.[3] Indeed, estimates indicate that about 80 percent of all Americans belong to some kind of voluntary group or association, although not every group is an interest group.[4] The key role interest groups would play in politics was foreseen by the founders—James Madison acknowledged the idea that people with similar interests would form and join groups to prompt government action. He believed that the only way to cure "the mischiefs of faction" was by enabling groups to proliferate and compete with one another.[5]

Yet despite this heritage, some contemporary scholars argue that Americans today are increasingly staying at home. Political scientist Robert Putnam, author of *Bowling Alone: The Collapse and Revival of American Community,* found a marked decrease in the number of people who belong to interest groups and other types of clubs and organizations. These organizations, Putnam argues, are essential sources of **social capital,** the relationships that improve our lives by giving us social connections with which to solve common problems. Putnam demonstrates that social capital improves individual lives in very concrete ways: those with a greater number of social ties live longer, happier, and healthier lives. But social capital also improves communities, and even larger polities, because it stimulates individuals to communicate and interact with their government. Efficacy increases, because when people are engaged and communicate with government officials, government responds by meeting their needs more effectively. This response in turn creates the feeling among individuals that government listens to people like them. And when government responds, it becomes more likely that those affected will try to influence government decisions again.[6]

Critics of Putnam's work have noted that although the number of people belonging to the kinds of groups Putnam analyzed may be declining, people are engaged in other types of groups and clubs and enjoy various forms of group recreation.[7] For example, it is unlikely that you are a member of a gardening club such as those that Putnam researched. (But if you are, good for you!) Yet it is likely that you belong to an online community such as MySpace or Facebook. Such communities facilitate social relationships and may even provide the opportunity for participants to solve community problems. And although people may be less likely to entertain friends and relatives in their homes today (another activity Putnam measured), they are *more likely* to socialize with friends and relatives over meals in restaurants. So even if Putnam is correct in his analysis that we are no longer socially engaged the way Americans used to be, we may still be engaged—but through different channels and in different settings.

> Can a conversation over a skim latte create social capital? People may not be joining gardening clubs, but are they really less connected than in the past? Or are their connections just different?

Political scientist E. E. Schattschneider has written, "Democracy is a competitive political system in which competing leaders and organizations define the alternatives of public policy in such a way that the public can participate in the decision-making process."[8] One of the key types of competitive organizations Schattschneider was describing is interest groups. Schattschneider and other political scientists study and assess the value that interest groups provide in American democracy. This value centrally includes interest groups' usefulness in channeling civic participation—serving as a point of access and a mechanism by which people can connect with their government. Political scientists also explore interest groups, on the one hand, as valuable avenues by which people can influence the policy process and, on the other hand, as resources for policy makers. In this section, we consider various perspectives on the role of interest groups in a democracy, the diverse value that interest groups confer, and the drawbacks of interest groups.

Interest Groups and Civic Participation

Scholars who study civic engagement acknowledge the significant ways in which interest groups channel civic participation. Interest groups afford a way for people to band together to influence government as a *collective force*. Interest groups also seek to involve *individuals* more actively in the political process by encouraging them to vote and to communicate their views one-on-one to their elected officials. In addition, interest groups assist in the engagement of *communities* by providing a forum through which people can come together and form an association. Importantly, too, interest groups offer an alternative means of participation to individuals who are disenchanted with the two-party system. By taking part in interest groups, individuals, acting together, perform important roles in the polity not only by communicating their viewpoints to policy makers but also by providing a medium that other people can use to express their opinions.

Pluralist Theory Versus Elite Theory

An interest group can represent a wide variety of interests, as in the case of a community Chamber of Commerce that serves as an umbrella organization for local businesses. Alternatively, an interest group can restrict itself to a narrower focus, as does the Society for the Preservation and Encouragement of Barbershop Quartet Singing. Scholars who support

THEN NOW NEXT

How Group Participation Has Changed in the United States

THEN (1960s)	NOW (2011)
Individuals joined bowling leagues, civic associations, and community service organizations.	People join Internet-based organizations and use social-networking sites to keep in touch with others who share their personal and public interests.
Many people entertained and socialized a great deal at home.	People are more likely to visit with friends and relatives in restaurants, cafés, and other public settings, as well as online through "virtual visits."
Groups used traditional activities to communicate their interests to policy makers, including letter writing and lobbying.	Groups rely on traditional activities but also increasingly use new technologies to communicate with members, to fund-raise, and to lobby policy makers.

WHAT'S NEXT?

> What new media technologies and strategies might shape how interest groups organize and mobilize members in the future?

> Are there *negative* consequences to relying on the Internet as an organizing tool? What obstacles will some Internet-based organizations face in mobilizing their supporters around a given issue?

> In what ways will technology change how policy makers are influenced in the future?

pluralist theory
a theory that holds that policy making is a competition among diverse interest groups that ensure the representation of individual interests

elite theory
a theory that holds that a group of wealthy, educated individuals wields most political power

pluralist theory emphasize how important it is for a democracy to have large numbers of diverse interest groups representing a wide variety of views.[9] Indeed, pluralists view the policy-making process as a crucial competition among diverse groups whose members attempt to influence policy in numerous settings, including agencies in the executive branch of government, Congress, and the courts.[10] Pluralists believe that interest groups are essential players in democracy because they ensure that individual interests are represented in the political arena *even if some individuals opt not to participate.* Like some of the founders, pluralists argue that individuals' liberties can be protected only through a proliferation of groups representing diverse competing interests, so that no one group dominates.

Pluralists believe, moreover, that interest groups provide a structure for political participation and help ensure that individuals follow the rules in participating in civic society. Following the rules means using positive channels for government action rather than extreme tactics such as assassinations, coups, and other forms of violence. Pluralists also stress that groups' varying assets tend to counterbalance one another. Pluralists contend that this is frequently the case with many policy debates. And so although an industry association such as the American Petroleum Institute, an interest group for the oil and natural gas industry, may have a lot of money at its disposal, an environmental group opposing the industry, such as Greenpeace, may have a large membership base from which to launch grassroots activism.

Proponents of elite theory dispute some claims of pluralist theory. In particular, elite theorists point to the overwhelming presence of elites as political decision makers. According to **elite theory,** a ruling class composed of wealthy, educated individuals wields most of the power in government and also within the top universities, corporations, the military, and media outlets. (See "Thinking Critically About Democracy.") Elite theorists claim that despite appearances that the political system is accessible to all, elites hold disproportionate power in the United States. They also emphasize that elites commonly use that power to protect their own economic interests, frequently by ensuring the continuation of the status quo. And so though nonelites represented by interest groups may occasionally win political victories, elites control the direction of major policies. But elite theorists posit that there is mobility into the elite structure. They emphasize that (in contrast to the situation in aristocracies) talented and industrious individuals from nonelite backgrounds can attain elite status in a democracy, often through education. This mobility, they say, gives the political system an even greater façade of accessibility.

Although these theories offer competing explanations for the role and motivation of interest groups in the United States, many political scientists agree that aspects of both theories are true: elites do have disproportionate influence in policy making, but that power is

THINKING CRITICALLY ABOUT DEMOCRACY

SHOULD CORPORATIONS AND LABOR UNIONS BE ABLE TO SPONSOR UNLIMITED CAMPAIGN ADVERTISEMENTS?

The Issue: During the 2008 Democratic primary, a non-profit conservative interest group, Citizens United, produced a critical film about then–presidential candidate Hillary Clinton. The group sought to have commercials promoting its film aired on television but was prevented from doing so because a federal court ruled that the commercials violated provisions of the Bipartisan Campaign Reform Act of 2002, which banned corporations, labor unions, and other organizations from independent expenditures designed to influence the outcome of an election.

The case wound its way to the U.S. Supreme Court, which had to decide whether collective entities such as labor unions and corporations enjoy the same rights as individuals when it comes to electioneering speech—that is, do these organizations have the same right to unlimited speech (in the form of paid campaign commercials) that individuals do?

Yes: In fact, the Supreme Court ruled that corporations and labor unions do enjoy these same rights. Many conservatives argue that organizations, including corporations, consist of individuals who form associations, and that the Constitution protects not only free speech but also freedom of association.

In writing the opinion of the Court, Justice Anthony Kennedy noted, "If the First Amendment has any force, it prohibits Congress from fining or jailing citizens, or associations of citizens, for simply engaging in political speech."*

No: Critics of the decision argue that it facilitates unmitigated corporate influence in political campaigns. Saying that organizations and corporations share in the protected rights that individuals enjoy detracts from their protection as individual human rights.

In addition, many liberal critics argue that enabling these organizations to spend freely to influence campaigns will have a detrimental effect on campaigns. In his criticism of the decision, President Barack Obama called it "a major victory for big oil, Wall Street banks, health insurance companies and the other powerful interests that marshal their power every day in Washington to drown out the voices of everyday Americans."**

Other approaches: In light of the Supreme Court's ruling in *Citizens United v. the Federal Election Commission,* some groups maintain that voters need to be increasingly skeptical of claims made by organizations and corporations about political candidates. In effect, some interest groups recognize that corporations and labor unions are only as powerful as average Americans enable them to be. The availability of technology provides a medium for average citizens to get both information and their own opinions out in the public arena, thus potentially mitigating the effect of the influence of associations.

What do you think?

① Do you believe that enabling corporations and labor unions to purchase unlimited independent expenditure ads is a protected right?

② What will be the effect of this decision, in your view?

③ How can average Americans get their opinions about candidates heard? How can they find out whether allegations made by associations are accurate?

*www.nytimes.com/2010/01/22/us/politics/22scotus.html.

**Ibid.

---

checked by interest groups. Undisputed is that interest groups are an essential feature of American democracy and provide an important medium through which individuals can exercise some control over their government.

Key Functions of Interest Groups

Many Americans join interest groups, and yet interest groups have a generally negative reputation. For example, it has been said of many a politician that he or she is "in the pockets of the special interests." This statement suggests that the politician is not making decisions based on conscience or the public interest but, rather, has been "bought." This notion is closely linked to the ideas held by elite theorists, who argue that elites' disproportionate share of influence negatively affects the ability of the "average Jill or Joe" to get the

The Value of Interest Groups   217

government to do what she or he wants it to. Yet despite the criticisms frequently leveled by politicians, pundits, and the populace about interest groups' efforts to influence government, they serve several vital functions in the policy-making process in the United States:

- *Interest groups educate the public about policy issues.* Messages from interest groups abound. For example, thanks to organizations such as Mothers Against Drunk Drivers (MADD), most people are aware of the dangers of drinking and driving. In educating the public, interest groups often provide a vehicle for civic discourse, so that genuine dialogue about policy problems and potential solutions is part of the national agenda.

- *Interest groups provide average citizens with an avenue of access to activism.* Anyone can join or form an interest group. Although wealthy and well-educated people are most likely to do so, interest groups can speak for all kinds of people on all kinds of issues. Historically in the United States, groups have been significant forces for advocates of civil rights for African Americans[11] as well as for supporters of equal rights for women,[12] gays and lesbians, and ethnic minorities. Even you and your fellow students can form an interest group. At Swarthmore College, a small number of students formed the Genocide Intervention Network, a group concerned about the genocide in Darfur that became a full-fledged interest group.

- *Interest groups mobilize citizens and stimulate them to participate in civic and political affairs.* Some people are "turned off" by politics because they feel that neither the Democratic nor the Republican party represents their views. In these cases, interest groups, with their typically narrower area of focus, can sometimes fill the void. Moreover, interest groups nurture community involvement by encouraging the formation of local chapters of larger interest groups. They support public education activities by private citizens. And interest groups not only can facilitate the ongoing conversation of democracy between people and their government officials but also encourage voting.

- *Interest groups perform electoral functions.* By endorsing and rating candidates and advertising their positions, interest groups provide voters with cues as to which candidates best represent their views. Interest groups also mobilize campaign volunteers and voters. These activities facilitate informed civic participation.

- *Interest groups provide information and expertise to policy makers.* The private sector often has greater resources than the public sector and can be a source of meaningful data and information for policy makers on pressing social issues.

- *Interest groups can protect the common good.* The federal government is structured so that only one individual (the president) is elected from a national constituency. Interest groups can work to protect the nation's interest as a whole rather than just the needs of a specific constituency.

- *Interest groups are an integral part of the government's system of checks and balances.* Interest groups often "check" one another's influence with competing interests, and they can similarly check the actions of policy makers.

The Downside of Interest Groups

Despite the valuable functions of interest groups, certain criticisms of these organizations are valid. Interest groups do contribute to the appearance of (and sometimes the reality of) corruption in the political system. Indeed, there are various criticisms of the "interest group state." Former president Jimmy Carter bemoaned the influence of special interests, saying that they are "the single greatest threat to the proper functioning of our democratic system," and former president Ronald Reagan charged that interest groups are "placing out of focus our constitutional balance."[13]

Another criticism is that interest groups and their political action committee (PAC) fund-raising arms (which we consider briefly later in this chapter and in more detail in Chapter 9) make money a vital force in American politics. By contributing large sums of money to political campaigns, interest groups' PACs make campaigns expensive and often lopsided; candidates without well-stuffed campaign war chests have a difficult, if not impossible, task in challenging those who receive large PAC contributions. Money also changes the nature of campaigns, making them less engaging for citizens on a grassroots level and more reliant on the mass media. These concerns have been exacerbated by a 2010 U.S. Supreme Court ruling that enables corporations and labor unions to spend money freely on political ads supporting or targeting candidates for federal office, and allows corporations and unions to buy issue advertisements even in the last days of political campaigns. Critics, including President Obama, say these rule changes will increase the importance of money in political campaigns and will enable corporations to exert greater influence over the electoral process.

Interest groups, moreover, are faulted with strengthening the advantages enjoyed by incumbents. Most interest groups want access to policy makers, regardless of these elected officials' party identification. Realizing that the people already in office are likely to be reelected, interest groups use their resources disproportionately to support incumbent candidates. Doing so increases incumbency advantage even further by improving the odds against a challenger.

Finally, although the option to form an interest group is open to any and all activists and would-be activists, elites are more likely to establish and to dominate interest groups than are nonelites. This fact skews the policy process in favor of elites. Interest group activism is much more prominent among the wealthy, the white, the upper-middle class, and the educated than among the poor, the nonwhite, the working class, and the less educated. Although Internet-based interest groups have been particularly effective in attracting young people and others not traditionally drawn to such organizations, many of the most effective national interest groups remain dominated by traditional interest-group populations.

Who Joins Interest Groups, and Why?

People are not all equally likely to join or form interest groups, and this reality has serious consequences for the ability of interest groups to represent everyone's views. Political scientists agree that income and education tend to be the best predictors of interest group membership. That said, enormous diversity exists in the types of people who choose to join or form interest groups.

Patterns of Membership

Interest group participation is related to three demographic characteristics: income, social class, and education. People with higher incomes are more likely to participate in interest groups than those with lower incomes. Also, many surveys show that those who identify themselves as upper-middle or middle class are more likely to join interest groups than those who self-identify as lower-middle or working class. Similarly, higher education levels are a strong predictor of interest group participation. But interest group participation also frequently reflects one's occupation: people tend to belong to associations related to their work.

INTEREST GROUP PARTICIPATION BASED ON OCCUPATION There are several reasons for interest group membership patterns, some of which, as we shall see, are interconnected. For example, people with higher incomes have more disposable income to spend on membership dues for organizations. They are also likely to have occupations in which interest group activity is useful (or even required, as in some professional fields such as the law).

Doctors and lawyers, for example, are likely to be members of professional associations such as the American Medical Association (AMA) and the American Bar Association. These organizations give incentives for membership, such as accreditation of qualified professionals. They also confer benefits by providing various services to members and by attempting to influence government policy on members' behalf. The AMA accredits qualified physicians, promotes opportunities for continuing education to members, and lobbies the government on policy issues related to health care. For example, during the debate over the 2010 health care reform legislation, the AMA sponsored television ads opposing a 21 percent cut in Medicare payments to physicians, and urged viewers to call their senator asking them to "fix the Medicare access problem."[14]

Workers such as teachers and tradespeople are likely to belong to labor unions.[15] Many labor unions are influential in local politics, generating grassroots support for candidates through their membership base. A few of the national labor unions, especially the National Education Association (NEA), the largest teachers' union in the country, and the American Federation of Labor-Congress of Industrial Organizations (AFL-CIO), an organization of many different labor unions, are strongly influential in national politics.

Executives in business and industry are likely to be members of industry-specific and general business organizations that advocate on behalf of their members. All of these professional associations, labor unions, and business organizations are types of interest groups.

INTEREST GROUP PARTICIPATION AND SOCIAL CLASS Differentiating the influence of income from that of class can be difficult when examining the impact of social class on the likelihood of joining an interest group. But in general, people who identify themselves as working class are less likely to have been socialized to participate in interest groups, with the important exception of labor unions, which historically have been most likely to organize working-class occupations. As we considered in Chapter 6, an important predictor of political participation (and interest group participation, specifically) is whether a person learns to take part and join from a young age. If your mother participated in your town's historical preservation society, and your father attended meetings of the local Amnesty International chapter, you are likely to view those behaviors as "what people do" and do them yourself. If you come from a working-class family, you are generally less likely to see your parents engage in these participatory behaviors, rendering you similarly less likely to participate. Although scholars trace much of the lack of participation of working-class people to how they are socialized, the overlapping occurrence of working-class status and lower income is also a factor.[16] That is, working-class people are likely to have lower incomes and less job security than their middle-class counterparts. Thus they may not be able to afford membership dues and contributions to interest groups or may not have access to child care that would allow them to attend meetings. Their lower likelihood of owning a computer limits their chances of taking an active role in Internet-based groups. Or they may simply lack the leisure time to participate.

INTEREST GROUP PARTICIPATION AND EDUCATION Educational attainment also has a strong impact on whether a person will join an interest group. One recent study surveyed 19- to 23-year-olds and found that those who were college students were more than twice as likely to join a politically motivated interest group as their age-group peers who did not attend college.[17] Individuals with higher education levels are more likely to be informed about issues and more willing to invest the time and energy in joining an interest group that represents their views. They may also be more likely to understand how important interest groups are in shaping public policy.

College students are among the most avid participants in Internet-based activist groups. But "belonging" to these groups varies a great deal (not unlike the situation in "real-world" interest groups). A member of an Internet-based interest group may play a highly active role—communicating with other members regularly, attending rallies and other campus events, and taking concrete actions such as signing an Internet petition and participating in a protest. Or members may be more passive: they may limit their activity to reading the regular e-mails from the group that inform them of issues and events, and may only occasionally participate. Or they may be members of a group in name only. But this phenomenon is not unique to Internet-based groups. Many interest groups are dominated by a cadre of committed activists supported by "sometimes-activists." And nearly every group has a contingent of "members" who signed up mainly for the free T-shirt, tote bag, or umbrella.

Motivations for Joining Interest Groups

Some people may join an interest group for the benefits they can gain. Others may gravitate to a group sponsoring a particular cause. Still others may become members of a group for the simple reason that they want to meet new people. Recognizing that

solidary incentives
motivation to join an interest group based on the companionship and the satisfaction derived from socializing with others that it offers

purposive incentives
motivation to join an interest group based on the belief in the group's cause from an ideological or a moral standpoint

individuals have various motivations for joining, interest groups typically provide a menu of incentives for membership. As Figure 7.1 shows, for example, the National Association for the Advancement of Colored People (NAACP) offers a wide range of motivations for people to join the group. In doing so, the NAACP, like many other interest groups, attempts to attract as many members as possible.

SOLIDARY INCENTIVES Some people join interest groups because they offer **solidary incentives**—the feeling of belonging, companionship, friendship, and the satisfaction derived from socializing with others. Solidary incentives are closely linked to Robert Putnam's idea of social capital: both solidary incentives and social capital are related to the psychological satisfaction derived from civic participation. For example, a person might join the Sierra Club because she wants to participate in activities with other people who enjoy hiking or care deeply about wilderness protection. Your uncle might join the National Rifle Association because he likes to compete in shooting contests and wants to get to know others who do the same.

PURPOSIVE INCENTIVES People also join interest groups because of **purposive incentives,** that is, because they believe in the group's cause from an ideological or a moral standpoint. Interest groups pave the way for people to take action with like-minded people. And so you might join People for the Ethical Treatment of Animals (PETA) because you strongly object to animal abuse and want to work with others to prevent cruelty to animals. A friend who is passionately pro-life might join the National Right to Life Committee (NRLC), whereas your pro-choice cousin might join NARAL Pro-Choice America (formerly the National Abortion Reproductive Rights Action League).

The Internet is a particularly effective forum for attracting membership through purposive incentives. Accessible anyplace and anytime, the Internet provides resources for you to join an interest group even during a bout of insomnia at 3:00 a.m. Suppose a conversation earlier in the day got you thinking anew about the brutal genocidal conflict in Darfur. In those dark predawn hours, you can google "save Darfur" and within seconds have a variety of access points for becoming civically engaged by participating in an interest group. Some interest groups may ask you to contribute money; others may urge you to sign an online petition or to call the White House to make your opinions known. You may follow other interest groups on Twitter, enabling you to learn about demonstrations sponsored by other groups right on your college campus and in your community. You may even find out about state and national

FIGURE 7.1 ■ **SOLIDARY, PURPOSIVE, AND ECONOMIC INCENTIVES TO JOIN AN INTEREST GROUP** What is the NAACP, and what does this interest group advocate? What solidary incentives does the membership appeal described in this figure mention? What purposive and economic incentives does it describe?

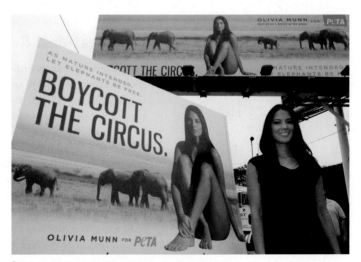

> Interest groups often rely on celebrities to advance their issue positions. Here, actor and TV host Olivia Munn stands beside her image on a PETA billboard targeting the use of elephants and other animals in circuses. Celebrities Demi Moore, Darren Aronofsky, Jennie Garth, and Kyra Sedgwick have all publicly condemned circuses that use animals.

Who Joins Interest Groups, and Why? **221**

demonstrations. The media contacts provided by online interest groups make it easy for you to write a letter to an editor, attempting to convince others of your views. Just learning about the wide variety of activities available can make you feel that you are "doing something" about a cause you believe in.

ECONOMIC INCENTIVES   Many people join interest groups because of material or **economic incentives;** that is, they want to support groups that work for policies that will provide them with economic benefits. For example, the National Association of Police Organizations lobbies Congress concerning many appropriations measures that could affect its membership, including bills that would provide or increase funding for Community Oriented Policing Services (COPS) programs, bulletproof vests, and overtime pay for first responders to disasters.

Nearly all corporate and labor interest groups offer economic incentives to their members. They sometimes do so by advocating for policies that support business or labor in general, such as policies focused on the minimum wage, regulations concerning workplace conditions, and laws governing family leave or health coverage.

Other interest groups offer smaller-scale economic benefits to members. Many Americans over age 50 join the American Association of Retired Persons (AARP) because of the discounts members receive on hotels, airfares, and car rentals. Other organizations provide discounts on health insurance, special deals from merchants, or low-interest credit cards.

Most people join and remain in interest groups for a combination of reasons. A person may initially join an interest group for purposive incentives and then realize some solidary benefits and remain in the group because of the friendships formed. Or someone may join a professional association for the economic benefits but then develop rewarding social networks. Many individuals who join and stay in interest groups do so because of overlapping incentives.

How Interest Groups Succeed

Given that interest groups attempt to influence all kinds of policies, why are some interest groups better at getting what they want than others? Political scientists agree on various factors that influence whether an interest group will succeed. These factors include the interest group's *organizational resources,* the tools it has at its disposal to help achieve its goals; and its *organizational environment,* the setting in which it attempts to achieve those goals. (See "Global Context.")

Organizational Resources

The effectiveness of interest groups in influencing government policy often depends on the resources they use to sway policy makers.[18] Interest groups rely on two key types of resources: membership, the people who belong to a given group; and financial resources, the money the group can spend to exert influence.

HOW MEMBERSHIP AFFECTS SUCCESS   A large membership enhances an interest group's influence because policy makers are more likely to take note of the group's position. The age-old concept of "strength in numbers" applies when it comes to interest groups. The sheer number of a group's membership is often an important factor in forcing policy makers, the media, and the public to pay attention to an issue. Among the largest U.S. interest groups is the American Association of Retired Persons (AARP), which boasts a membership of more than 35 million people. This vast size gives the organization incredible clout and historically has made policy makers unwilling to take on any issue that would unleash the wrath of AARP's formidable membership. For example, for years many economic analysts have suggested increasing the age at which people become eligible to receive Social Security. They reason that the average life span has risen significantly since the eligibility age was set, and that people are working longer because they remain healthier

AMNESTY INTERNATIONAL

On many college campuses throughout the United States, you may find a college chapter of the human rights organization Amnesty International. The group strives to protect human rights by informing the public about violations of human rights, and has attempted to exert pressure on governments and on political and corporate organizations. The group especially seeks to protect those whose rights of freedom of speech and religion have been violated, and political dissidents who have been imprisoned and tortured. The organization familiar to many throughout the United States is part of a much larger international network. In fact, Amnesty International boasts 2.2 million members in 150 countries.

How can international organizations help protect human rights?

In the autumn of 1960, two Portuguese students raised their wineglasses in a toast to "freedom," and were arrested and sentenced to seven years in prison. (Portugal was then under the dictatorial rule of António Salazar.) When British lawyer Peter Benenson learned of the students' plight in 1961, he wrote an article for the newspaper *The Observer,* and so began the organization that has sought to ensure the protection of human rights internationally for decades—Amnesty International. Its goals, according to the Amnesty International Web site, are as follows:

We believe human rights abuses anywhere are the concern of people everywhere.

So, outraged by human rights abuses but inspired by hope for a better world, we work to improve people's lives through campaigning and international solidarity.

Our mission is to conduct research and generate action to prevent and end grave abuses of human rights and to demand justice for those whose rights have been violated.*

In their pursuit of these goals, Amnesty International members have relied on diverse strategies. Whereas student members may conduct letter-writing campaigns, campus vigils, and protests to call attention to the violations of human rights, the organization uses other tactics, including

- sending experts to talk with victims
- observing trials
- interviewing local officials
- meeting with human rights activists
- monitoring global and local media
- publishing detailed reports
- informing the news media
- publicizing their concerns in documents, leaflets, posters, advertisements, newsletters, and Web sites**

*www.amnesty.org/en/who-we-are/about-amnesty-international.
**www.amnesty.org/en/who-we-are/faq#how-ai-works.

> Since 1961, Amnesty International has sought to protect human rights throughout the world. Here, members of the organization stage a protest in front of the Chinese Embassy in Tokyo, Japan, after China executed a Japanese man for drug smuggling in 2010. The sign at right reads "China is supposed to be a generous nation."

longer. But this potential policy solution has long simmered on the back burner. The reason? Politicians in Congress and the White House have not wanted to incur the disapproval of the AARP's members, who would widely oppose increasing the eligibility age and might respond by voting unsympathetic officials out of office. While he was Speaker of the House of Representatives, Dennis Hastert (R-Illinois) remarked that he took "the AARP very seriously"—as had Newt Gingrich when he was Speaker before—and that "Republicans had been courting AARP for some time, listening to them, engaging in a give-and-take dialogue that none of the capital's pundits even suspected was going on."[19]

But size is not the only important aspect of an interest group's membership. The *cohesion* of a group, or how strongly unified it is, also matters to participants and to policy makers.[20] For example, the Human Rights Campaign (HRC) lobbies for federal legislation to end discrimination on the basis of sexual orientation and provides research to elected officials and policy makers on issues of importance to people who are gay, lesbian, bisexual, or transgender. The HRC has a membership of about 600,000, but because the organization limits its advocacy to issues affecting gay, lesbian, bisexual, and transgender people, it is an extremely cohesive association.

Another significant aspect of an interest group's membership is its *intensity*. Intensity is a measure of how strongly members feel about the issues they are targeting. Certain kinds of organizations, including pro-life interest groups such as the National Right to Life Committee, environmental groups such as the Sierra Club and Greenpeace, and animal rights groups such as People for the Ethical Treatment of Animals (PETA), are known for sustaining high levels of intensity. These organizations are more adept at attracting new members and younger members than are older, more entrenched kinds of groups. These newer, youthful members are a significant force behind the persistence and intensity of these groups.

The *demographics* of a group's membership also may increase its success. Members who know policy makers personally and have access to them mean greater influence for the group.[21] Other demographic attributes also matter. Members who are well educated, geographically dispersed (because they can influence a broader network of policy makers than a geographically consolidated membership), or affluent tend to have more influence. Policy makers perceive these attributes as important because the groups' membership is more likely to lobby and to contribute financial resources on behalf of the organization's cause.

HOW FINANCIAL RESOURCES AFFECT SUCCESS For an interest group, money can buy power.[22] Money fuels the hiring of experienced and effective staff and lobbyists, who communicate directly with policy makers, as well as the undertaking of initiatives that will increase the group's membership. Money also funds the raising of more money.[23] For example, the Business Roundtable represents the interests of 150 chief executive officers of the largest U.S. companies, including American Express, General Electric, IBM, and Verizon. In 2009, it spent over $13 million lobbying the president, Congress, and several cabinet departments for policies that would benefit its member corporations, their shareholders, and their member corporations' 10 million employees. Issues of concern to the Business Roundtable include policies such as Securities and Exchange Commission rules, laws concerning corporate ethics, and reform to the nation's class action lawsuit regulations. In the aftermath of the 2010 U.S. Supreme Court decision that enables corporations and labor unions to spend their resources targeting or supporting specific candidates for office, including individuals running for Congress and the presidency, many critics believe that the financial resources of an organization will play an even greater role in determining the group's success in the future.

political action committee (PAC)
a group that raises and spends money to influence the outcome of an election

Sometimes interest groups form a separate entity, called a **political action committee (PAC),** whose specific goal is to raise and spend money to influence the outcome of elections. (See Chapter 9 for a detailed discussion of PACs.) Interest groups use PACs to shape the composition of government; that is, they contribute money to the campaigns of favored candidates, particularly incumbents who are likely to be reelected.[24] That is just one specific example of the influence that interest groups' money has on politics. Interest groups representing the economic concerns of members—business, industry, and union groups—generally tend to have the greatest financial resources for all these activities.[25]

Organizational Environment

The setting in which an interest group attempts to achieve its goals is the *organizational environment*. Key factors in the organizational environment include its leadership and the presence or absence of opposition from other groups.[26]

LEADERSHIP   Strong, charismatic leaders contribute to the influence of an interest group by raising public awareness of the group and its activities, by enhancing its reputation, and by making the organization attractive to new members and contributors. An example of a dynamic leader who has increased his interest group's effectiveness is James P. Hoffa, the son of powerful Teamsters Union president Jimmy Hoffa, who disappeared without a trace in 1975. He has served since 1999 as the president of the Teamsters Union, which primarily represents unionized truck drivers. The younger Hoffa—a graduate of the University of Michigan Law School—is lauded by many teamsters as an intelligent, energetic, and charismatic leader whose skills have increased the size and power of the union.

OPPOSITION   The presence of opposing interest groups can also have an impact on an interest group's success. When an interest group is "the only game in town" on a particular issue, policy makers are more likely to rely on that group's views. But if groups with opposing views are also attempting to influence policy, getting policy makers to act strongly in any one group's favor is more difficult. Consider this example: Hotel Employees and the Restaurant Employees International Union supported increasing the minimum wage, but the National Restaurant Association, which advocates for restaurant owners, opposed a minimum wage hike, arguing that the higher wage would cut into restaurant owners' profits or limit its members' ability to hire as many employees as before. In the face of such opposing interests, policy makers are often more likely to compromise than to give any one group exactly what it wants.

Although each of these factors—organizational resources and the organizational environment—influences how powerful an interest group will be, no single formula determines an interest group's clout. Sometimes an interest group has powerful advocates in Congress who support its cause. Other times, a single factor can prove essential to an interest group's success.

Types of Interest Groups

A wide variety of political interest groups exercise their muscle on virtually every type of policy question, from those concerning birth (such as what is the minimum hospital stay an insurance company must cover after a woman gives birth?) to matters related to death (such as what are the practices by funeral directors that should be banned by the government?). Despite the broad range of issues around which interest groups coalesce, political scientists generally categorize interest groups by what kinds of issues concern them and who benefits from the groups' activities. For example, some interest groups focus primarily on economic decisions that affect their members. Other interest groups pursue ideological, issue-based, or religion-based goals. Yet others lobby for benefits for society at large, and still others advocate on behalf of foreign interests.

Economic Interest Groups

When economic interest groups lobby government, the benefits for their members can be direct or indirect. In some cases, the economic benefits flow directly from the government to the interest group members, as when an agricultural interest group successfully presses for *subsidies,* monies given by the government to the producers of a particular crop or product, often to influence the volume of production of that commodity. For example, in 2008 the finance, insurance, and real estate sector spent nearly $460 million on federal lobbying efforts. These same industries were among the prime beneficiaries of both federal government bailouts and the 2009 economic stimulus package.

In other instances, economic interest groups lobby for or against policies that, though not directly benefiting their members, have an indirect impact on the interest group's membership. That was the case when many unions, including the AFL-CIO, lobbied against the creation of private Social Security accounts, fearing that this privatization would result in a decrease in Social Security retirement benefits for their members.

CORPORATE AND BUSINESS INTERESTS   Large corporate and smaller business interest groups are among the most successful U.S. pressure groups with respect to their influence on government. These groups typically seek policies that benefit a particular company or industry. For example, the Motion Picture Association of America (MPAA) represents the seven major U.S. manufacturers and distributors of movies and television programs. The MPAA lobbies policy makers (often by hosting prerelease screenings of films and lavish dinner receptions) with the goal of securing the passage of antipiracy laws, which aim to prevent the illegal copying of movies and to penalize individuals who sell them. This advocacy benefits the group's members and their employees, because antipiracy laws help to ensure that any copies of movies sold are legal and thus profitable for MPAA members.

umbrella organizations
interest groups that represent collective groups of industries or corporations

Certain industries' associations are stand-alone organizations, such as the National Association of Realtors and the National Beer Wholesalers Association. But industry and business groups also commonly advocate for policies using **umbrella organizations,** which are interest groups representing groups of industries or corporations. Examples of umbrella business organizations include the Business Roundtable, which represents the chief executive officers (CEOs) of 150 large corporations, and the U.S. Chamber of Commerce, a federation of local chambers of commerce that represents about 3 million large and small businesses.

Often corporate and business groups compete against labor groups. This rivalry is a natural result of having different constituencies. Typically, corporate interests advocate on behalf of the company owners, stockholders, and officers, whereas labor unions champion employees' interests.

LABOR INTERESTS   Like corporate interest groups, labor interest groups include both national labor unions and umbrella organizations of unions. The AFL-CIO, an umbrella organization made up of more than fifty labor unions, is among the nation's most powerful interest groups, although its influence has waned over the past several decades as union membership has declined generally. During the 1950s and 1960s, nearly 35 percent of all U.S. workers were union members. By 1983, membership had decreased to about 20 percent, and today about 12 percent of all U.S. workers belong to unions. In part, this decline stems from changes in the U.S. economy, with many highly unionized manufacturing jobs being replaced by less unionized service sector jobs. Given the drop in union membership, labor interest groups' influence has also waned, although the unions' reduced clout is in part due to a lack of cohesion among labor union members.

Like corporate and business interest groups, labor unions pursue policies that benefit their members, although these are frequently at odds with the positions of corporate and business interest groups. And like corporate and business interest groups, labor unions sometimes press for policies that primarily benefit their own members, and at other times they promote policies that benefit all union workers and sometimes even non-union workers. For example, in 2007 the AFL-CIO successfully lobbied Congress for an increase in the federal minimum wage, which benefited the members of many unions whose contracts are based on federally mandated minimum wages but also many non-union workers who are paid the minimum wage.

AGRICULTURAL INTERESTS   Of all types of U.S. interest groups, agricultural interest groups probably have the most disproportionate amount of influence given the small number of farmers and farmworkers in the country relative to the general population. And because agricultural producers in the United States are also very diverse, ranging from small farmers to huge multinational agribusinesses, it is not surprising to see divergent opinions among people employed in the agricultural sector.

The largest agricultural interest group today is the American Farm Bureau Federation (AFBF), which grew out of the network of county farm bureaus formed in the 1920s. With more than 5 million farming members, the AFBF is one of the most influential interest groups in the United States, primarily because of its close relations with key agricultural policy makers. It takes stands on a wide variety of issues that have an impact on farmers, including subsidies, budget and tax policies, immigration policies that affect farmworkers, energy policies, trade policies, and environmental policies. For example, when President Obama sought to end direct subsidies to farmers with sales of over $500,000 as part of his 2010 budget proposal, the opposition by agricultural interest groups, including the AFBF, killed the proposal in Congress.

In addition to large-scale, general agricultural interest groups such as the AFBF, there is an industry-specific interest group representing producers for nearly every crop or commodity produced in the agricultural sector. Table 7.1 shows that corn producers are among the most effective groups in securing subsidies for their growers. Between 1995 and 2006, more than 1.5 million corn farmers across the United States received in excess of $56 billion in government subsidies. Table 7.1 reveals as well that the producers of several other crops—wheat, cotton, soybeans, and rice—have managed to secure subsidies of more than $10 billion each from 1995 to 2006.

TRADE AND PROFESSIONAL INTERESTS Nearly every professional occupation—doctor, lawyer, engineer, chiropractor, dentist, accountant, and even video game developer—has a trade or professional group that focuses on its interests. These interest groups take stands on a variety of policy matters, many of which indirectly affect their membership.

Public and Ideological Interest Groups

Public interest groups typically are concerned with a broad range of issues that affect the populace at large. These include social and economic issues such as Social Security reform and revision of the federal tax structure, as well as environmental causes such as clean air

TABLE 7.1

Top 10 Crops Receiving Federal Subsidies as Direct Payments to Farmers (1995–2009)

Rank	Program	Subsidy Total 1995–2009
1	Corn	$12,927,171,703
2	Wheat	$6,969,982,923
3	Soybeans	$4,133,353,401
4	Upland cotton	$3,820,779,718
5	Rice	$2,637,683,165
6	Sorghum	$1,207,917,786
7	Barley	$497,873,693
8	Peanuts	$481,060,291
9	Sunflower	$ 91,536,061
10	Canola	$34,389,538

SOURCE: The Environmental Working Group, http://farm.ewg.org/farm/region.php?fips=00000.

> The Sierra Club and other public interest groups that lobby Congress about environmental issues work to protect public lands such as the Denali National Wildlife Refuge, home to herds of caribou and other species.

and clean water. Examples of public interest groups include the National Taxpayers Union, Common Cause, and the Sierra Club. Usually, the results of the efforts of a particular public interest group's advocacy cannot be limited to the group's members; rather, these results are **collective goods** (sometimes called *public goods*)—outcomes that are shared by the general public. Collective goods are "collective" and "public" because they cannot be denied to people who are not group members. For example, if the Sierra Club succeeds in winning passage of an environmental bill that improves water and air quality, *everyone* shares in the benefits. Specifically, it is impossible to make pure drinking water and clean air a privilege restricted to Sierra Club members.

The nature of collective goods—the fact that they cannot be limited to those who worked to achieve them—creates a **free rider problem,** the situation whereby someone derives a benefit from the actions of others. You are probably familiar with the free rider problem. Suppose, for example, that you form a study group to prepare for an exam, and four of the five members of the group come to a study session having prepared responses to essay questions. The fifth member shows up but is unprepared. The unprepared group member then copies the others' responses, memorizes them, and does just as well on the exam. The same thing happens to interest groups that advocate for a collective good. The group may work hard to improve the quality of life, but the benefits of its work are enjoyed by many who do not contribute to the effort.

Economist Mancur Olson asserted in his **rational choice theory** that from an economic perspective it is not rational for people to participate in a collective action designed to achieve a collective good when they can secure that good without participating. So, in the study group example, from Olson's perspective, it is not economically rational to spend your time preparing for an exam when you can get the benefits of preparation without the work. Of course, taking this idea to the extreme, one might conclude that if no one advocated for collective goods, they would not exist, and thus free riders could not derive their benefit.

Current scholarship on civic engagement has focused on the free rider problem. Researchers have investigated the increased benefits of widespread citizen participation in interest groups, citing evidence that groups with higher levels of public participation may be more effective, and may provide greater collective benefits, than groups with lower rates of participation. Studies also indicate that through the act of participating in civic life, individuals derive some benefit themselves in addition to the benefits created by their work. So, if the fifth person in the study group prepares for the exam, too, *all* members of the group may perform better on the exam. And if more people are civically involved in groups, then their potential to have an impact on their government increases. In addition, civic engagement scholars cite the psychic benefit to an individual of knowing that a collective good was achieved in part because of *her* participation, and these researchers also mention the other benefits derived from collective action, including solidary and purposive benefits.

CONSUMER INTERESTS   Well before attorney and activist Ralph Nader gained nationwide attention as a Green Party candidate for the presidency in 2000, he founded numerous organizations to promote the rights of consumers. In the 1970s and 1980s, these organizations lobbied primarily—and successfully—for changes in automotive design that would make cars safer. One result was the mandatory installation of harness safety belts in rear seats, which then typically had only lap belts. In 1971 Nader founded the interest group Public Citizen, which lobbies Congress, the executive branch, and the courts for openness in government and consumer issues, including auto safety, the safety of prescription drugs, and energy policy. Each year in December, the group issues a list of unsafe toys to guide gift-buyers' holiday purchases.

ENVIRONMENTAL INTERESTS   Many groups that advocate for the protection of the environment and wildlife and for the conservation of natural resources came about as a result of a broader environmental movement in the 1970s, although the Sierra Club was founded more than a century ago, in 1892. Some environmental groups, particularly Greenpeace, have been criticized in the media and by their opponents for their use of confrontational tactics. But many environmental activists say that the power of corporate in-

collective goods
outcomes shared by the general public; also called *public goods*

free rider problem
the phenomenon of someone deriving benefit from others' actions

rational choice theory
the idea that from an economic perspective it is not rational for people to participate in collective action when they can secure the collective good without participating

terests (with which they are frequently at odds) is so pervasive that they can succeed only by taking strong, direct action to protect the natural environment, thus rationalizing their sometimes extreme tactics. And so while some environmentalists follow the conventional route of lobbying legislators or advertising to raise public awareness of their causes, others camp out in trees to attempt to prevent their removal or sit on oil-drilling platforms to halt drilling into a coral reef. In addition to stalling the undesired action, the confrontational protest tactic also has the advantage of attracting media attention, which serves to increase public awareness.[27] Such environmental groups hope that they can prevent environmental destruction by embarrassing the corporation or government involved.

RELIGIOUS INTERESTS   For a long time, organized religions in the United States were essentially uninvolved in politics, partly because they were afraid of losing their tax-exempt status by becoming political entities. But formal religions increasingly have sought to make their voices heard, usually by forming political organizations separate from the actual religious organizations. Today, religious interests are among the most influential interest groups in U.S. politics.

In the early stages of their activism, Christian organizations typically were most politically effective in the Republican presidential nomination process, when the mobilization of their members could alter the outcome in low-turnout primaries. During the 1970s, several conservative Christian organizations, most notably the Moral Majority, founded by the late Reverend Jerry Falwell, were a force in national politics. The Moral Majority helped to elect Ronald Reagan, a Republican, to the presidency in 1980 and was instrumental in shaping the national agenda of the Reagan years, particularly regarding domestic policy. In 1989, another conservative Christian organization, the Christian Coalition, took shape, marking a new era in the politicization of religious groups. The Christian Coalition advocates that "people of faith have a right and a responsibility to be involved in the world around them" and emphasizes "pro-family" values.[28] During its first decade, the Christian Coalition's influence grew gradually. During the 2000 election, the organization was an important supporter of George W. Bush's candidacy for the presidency, and with his election, the group's influence has grown considerably. In the 2004 presidential election, conservative Christian organizations proved enormously important in activities such as voter registration and get-out-the-vote campaigns, thus aiding President Bush's reelection efforts.

The Christian Coalition and other religious groups—including Pax Christi USA (the national Catholic peace movement), B'nai Brith (an interest group dedicated to Jewish interests), and the Council on American-Islamic Relations (CAIR, a Muslim interest group)—also advocate for the faith-based priorities of their members. Many of these organizations have become increasingly active in state and local politics in recent years. For example, in 2010, members of CAIR vocally advocated for the construction of an Islamic center at the site of the World Trade Center, which had been destroyed in the September 11, 2001 terrorist attacks.

Foreign Interest Groups

In the United States, advocacy by interest groups is not limited to U.S.-based groups. Foreign governments, as well as international corporations based abroad, vigorously press for U.S. policies beneficial to them. Foreign governments might lobby for U.S. aid packages; corporations might work for beneficial changes to tax regulations. Often a foreign government will rely on an interest group made up of U.S. citizens of the foreign nation's heritage to promote its advocacy efforts. Indeed, one of the more influential interest groups lobbying for foreign concerns is the U.S.-based American Israel Public Affairs Committee (AIPAC), which has 65,000 members. AIPAC lobbies the U.S. government for pro-Israel foreign policies such as the grant of nearly $2.5 billion in economic and military aid for Israel in 2007. Despite its relatively small membership, AIPAC is considered highly influential because of its financial resources and well-connected membership base, which enjoys access to many policy makers.

Sometimes it is readily apparent when foreign interests are lobbying for their own causes—as, for example, when a trading partner wants better terms. But in other cases, particularly when international corporations are lobbying, it is difficult to discern where their "American" interest ends and their "foreign" interest begins. So although only U.S. citizens and legal immigrants can contribute to federal PACs, American employees of foreign companies do form and contribute to PACs. Many people would be surprised at the large amounts of money that international corporations' PACs contribute to both of the major U.S. political parties. But because many subsidiaries of these corporations are important American businesses, their lobbying activities are not necessarily a foreign encroachment on U.S. politics.

Interest Group Strategies

Interest groups use two kinds of strategies to advance their causes. *Direct strategies* involve actual contact between representatives of the interest group and policy makers. *Indirect strategies* use intermediaries to advocate for a cause or generally to attempt to persuade the public, including policy makers, to embrace the group's position.

Direct Strategies to Advance Interests

Groups often opt for direct strategies when they seek to secure passage or defeat of a specific piece of legislation. These strategies include lobbying, entering into litigation to change a law, and providing information or expert testimony to decision makers.

LOBBYING, ISSUE NETWORKS, AND IRON TRIANGLES   Interest groups hire professionals to **lobby,** or communicate directly with, policy makers on the interest groups' behalf. President Ulysses S. Grant coined the term *lobbyist* when he walked through the lobby of the Willard Hotel in Washington, D.C., and commented on the presence of "lobbyists" waiting to speak to members of Congress.

Today, lobbying is among the most common strategies that interest groups use, and the practice may include scheduled face-to-face meetings, "buttonholing" members of Congress as they walk through the Capitol, telephone calls, and receptions and special events hosted by the interest groups. The professional lobbyists whom interest groups hire are almost always lawyers, and their job is to cultivate ongoing relationships with members of Congress

lobby
to communicate directly with policy makers on an interest group's behalf

(and their staff) who have influence in a specific policy area. In many situations, lobbyists help navigate access to these policy makers for industry and interest group members.

Interest groups have learned that one of the most effective ways of influencing government is to hire former government officials, including cabinet officials, members of Congress, and congressional staffers, as lobbyists. Because these ex-officials often enjoy good relationships with their former colleagues and have an intimate knowledge of the policy-making process, they are particularly effective in influencing government. Frequently, this practice creates an **issue network,** the fluid web of connections among those concerned about a policy and those who create and administer the policy.

Similarly, an interest group's efficacy often depends on its having close relationships with the policy makers involved in decisions related to the group's causes. During the rough-and-tumble policy-making process, the interaction of mutual interests among a "trio" comprising (1) members of Congress, (2) executive departments and agencies (such as the Department of Agriculture or the Federal Emergency Management Agency), and (3) organized interest groups is sometimes referred to as an **iron triangle,** with each of the three players being one side of the triangle (see Figure 7.2). Although each side in an iron triangle is expected to fight on behalf of its own interests, constituents, or governmental department, the triangle often seeks a policy outcome that benefits all parts of the triangle. Often this outcome

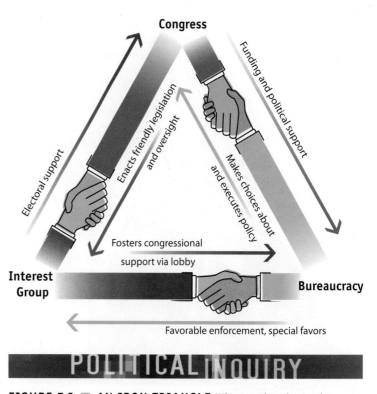

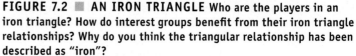

FIGURE 7.2 ■ AN IRON TRIANGLE Who are the players in an iron triangle? How do interest groups benefit from their iron triangle relationships? Why do you think the triangular relationship has been described as "iron"?

occurs because of close personal and professional relationships that develop as a result of the interactions among the sides in an issue-based triangle. And sometimes the individual players in a triangle that is focused on a particular issue—say, military policy or subsidies for tobacco growers—share a personal history, have attended the same schools, come from the same region of the country, and have even worked together at one time. Such long-term relationships can make it difficult for opposing interests to penetrate the triangle. (See Chapter 13 for further discussion of the role of iron triangles in policy making.)

LITIGATION BY INTEREST GROUPS Sometimes, interest groups challenge a policy in the courts. For example, the 2010 U.S. Supreme Court case that resulted in a drastically altered political landscape for campaign funding came as the result of a lawsuit filed by an interest group. In *Citizens United v. Federal Election Commission,* the interest group Citizens United argued that federal bans on corporate and union expenditures to promote or target candidates for federal office violated the organization's right to free speech. A 5–4 majority of Supreme Court justices agreed with the interest group, and lifted the ban.[29]

In other instances, interest groups sue to prevent a particular public policy from being enacted or to prompt a court ruling on the constitutionality of an issue. The latter was the case in 1992, when Planned Parenthood of Pennsylvania, an abortion-rights advocacy group, sued the state's governor, claiming that the state's Abortion Control Act violated the constitutional protections on abortion outlined in the Supreme Court's decision in *Roe v. Wade* (1973). In particular, Planned Parenthood argued that the clauses in the state legislation that required a pregnant woman to notify her husband, a pregnant teen to get parental consent, and any abortion seeker to satisfy a twenty-four-hour waiting period after receiving counseling presented an undue burden and violated the spirit of *Roe v. Wade.* In *Roe,* the Supreme Court had ruled that a woman's right to abortion was essentially guaranteed in the first trimester, could be regulated by the states in the second, and could be banned by the states in the third. The Supreme Court agreed to hear the Planned Parenthood case and struck down some components of the Pennsylvania legislation, including the requirement

issue network
the fluid web of connections among those concerned about a policy and those who create and administer the policy

iron triangle
the interaction of mutual interests among members of Congress, executive agencies, and organized interests during policy making

for spousal notification, while allowing other components not specified in *Roe*, including the parental consent requirement and the twenty-four-hour waiting period, to stand.

By litigating, interest groups can ensure that laws passed by legislatures and signed by executives are in keeping with current constitutional interpretation. By bringing their causes before the courts, they also can shape policy and encourage enforcement by executive agencies.

PROVIDING INFORMATION AND EXPERT TESTIMONY

Interest groups are one of the chief sources of information for policy makers. Interest groups have the resources to investigate the impact of policies. They have access to data, technological know-how, and a bevy of experts with extensive knowledge of the issues. Most interest groups provide information to policy makers, and policy makers understand that the information received is slanted toward the group's interest. But if competing interest groups supply information to policy makers, then policy makers can weigh the merits of the various sets of information.

Sometimes interest groups use celebrities as "experts" to testify, knowing that they will attract greater attention than most policy experts. Elmo, the furry red *Sesame Street* Muppet, testified in 2002 on behalf of a bill that would provide $2 million in federal funding to public schools for music education. The House Appropriations Subcommittee on Labor, Health and Human Services, and Education heard testimony from Elmo, who apparently is an authority on music education. Elmo told the subcommittee: "Elmo loves to sing and to dance and to make music with all his friends on *Sesame Street*. It helps Elmo learn ABCs and makes it easier for Elmo to remember things. Sometimes it makes Elmo excited, and sometimes it calms Elmo down. Elmo's teacher really likes that! My friend [American Music Conference Executive Director] Joe Lamond says some kids don't have music in school. That makes Elmo sad."[30] Other celebrities who have testified on behalf of causes important to them include Bono, the lead singer of the group U2, who testified concerning debt relief for African nations; actor Michael J. Fox, who testified about Parkinson's disease, from which he suffers; actor Goldie Hawn, who testified against granting permanent, normal trade status to China; and actor Julia Roberts, who spoke on behalf of those who suffer from Rett Syndrome, a nervous system disorder disproportionately suffered by women.

> Celebrity "experts" frequently offer testimony before Congress on many issues. School music education was the subject of Elmo's appearance before a hearing of the House Labor, Health and Human Services, and Education Appropriations Committee in 2002.

Indirect Strategies to Advance Interests

Reaching out to persuade the public that the interest group's position is right, deploying citizens as grassroots lobbyists, and electioneering are some of the indirect strategies interest groups use to pursue their public policy agendas. Indirect tactics are likely to be ongoing rather than targeted at a specific piece of legislation, although that is not always the case.

PUBLIC OUTREACH Interest groups work hard—and use a variety of strategies—to make the public, government officials, their own members, and potential members aware of issues of concern and to educate people about their positions on the issues. Some interest groups focus solely on educating the public and hope that through their efforts people will be concerned enough to take steps to have a particular policy established or changed. In doing so, the groups promote civic engagement by informing individuals about important policy concerns, even if the information they provide is skewed toward the group's views. The groups also encourage civic discourse by bringing issues into the public arena. Often they do so by mounting advertising campaigns to alert the public about an issue. NARAL

Pro-Choice America used such a strategy during the 2008 elections when the league took out ads in many traditionally Democratic states urging the election of pro-choice senators and alerting the public to the important role the U.S. Senate plays in confirming U.S. Supreme Court nominees. The ads stressed that the balance of the Court could shift in favor of an overruling of abortion protections if a sitting justice were to retire and be replaced by a pro-life justice.

Sometimes interest groups and corporations engage in **climate control,** the practice of using public outreach to build favorable public opinion of the organization or company. The logic behind climate control is simple: if a corporation or an organization has the goodwill of the public on its side, enacting its legislative agenda or getting its policy priorities passed will be easier because government will know of, and may even share, the public's positive opinion of the organization. For example, when Wal-Mart started to see opposition to the construction of its superstores in communities across the country, it relied on public relations techniques, particularly advertising, to convince people that Wal-Mart is a good corporate citizen. As critics complained about Wal-Mart's harmful effects on smaller, local merchants, the firm's ads touted Wal-Mart's positive contributions to its host communities. When opponents publicized the company's low-wage jobs, Wal-Mart countered with ads featuring employees who had started in entry-level positions and risen through the ranks to managerial posts. These ads would be viewed both by policy makers (municipal planning board members, for example) and by citizens, whose opinions matter to those policy makers. This type of climate control is designed to soften opposition and increase community goodwill.

Other groups, especially those without a great deal of access to policy makers, may engage in protests and civil disobedience to be heard. Sometimes leaders calculate that media attention to their actions will increase public awareness and spark widespread support for their cause.

ELECTIONEERING Interest groups often engage in the indirect strategy of **electioneering**—working to influence the election of candidates who support their issues. All the tactics of electioneering are active methods of civic participation. These techniques include endorsing particular candidates or positions and conducting voter-registration and get-out-the-vote drives. Grassroots campaign efforts often put interest groups with large memberships, including labor unions, at an advantage.

Campaign contributions are considered a key element of electioneering. The importance of contributions puts wealthier interest groups, including corporate and business groups, at an advantage. Figure 7.3 shows the breakdown of contributions by incumbency status. From Figure 7.3, we can see that incumbent candidates have a significant edge in raising money from political action committees. These data indicate that most PACs recognize that incumbents—who are most likely to win reelection—are best situated to look after their interests after the election.

The issue of party affiliation also matters to political action committees. Business PACs and individuals with business interests make up the largest sources of revenue for political candidates and tend to favor Republicans over Democrats. Labor groups and individuals associated with them give overwhelmingly to Democratic candidates, but they contribute a great deal less money than do business PACs. Ideologically driven PACs and individuals are nearly evenly divided between Democrats and Republicans. (See "Analyzing the Sources" on page 234.)

Interest groups also commonly use the tactics of endorsements and ratings to attract support for the candidates whom they favor and to reduce the electoral chances of those whom they do not. Through endorsements, an interest group formally supports specific candidates and typically notifies its members and the media of that support. An endorsement may also involve financial support from the interest group's PAC. And by the technique of rating candidates,

climate control
the practice of using public outreach to build favorable public opinion of an organization

electioneering
working to influence the elections of candidates who support the organization's issues

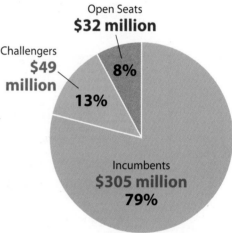

Contributions to 2008 Congressional Candidates by Political Action Committees

POLITICAL INQUIRY

FIGURE 7.3 ▪ Roughly half of the congressional candidates running for office in 2008 were challengers, who netted only 13 percent of the PAC contributions donated to candidates. What are some of the reasons PACs are more likely to contribute to incumbents? What might be the effect of contributing to challengers?

SOURCE: Federal Election Commission, www.fec.gov/press/press2009/20090415PAC/20090424PAC.shtml.

ANALYZING THE SOURCES

TO WHICH CANDIDATES DO POLITICAL ACTION COMMITTEES CONTRIBUTE?

The following chart shows PAC contributions and percentages by candidates' political party over several election cycles.

PAC Contributions by Political Party
(in Millions of Dollars)

Year	Democrat			Republican
2008	$46	46%	54%	$54
	$186	60%	40%	$123
2006	$35	42%	58%	$48
	$126	44%	56%	$160
2004	$33	44%	56%	$42
	$101	43%	57%	$131
2002	$32	46%	54%	$38
	$105	49%	51%	$107
2000	$24	39%	61%	$37
	$99	51%	49%	$96
1998	$21	43%	57%	$27
	$78	49%	51%	$81

Senate
House

SOURCE: Federal Election Commission, www.fec.gov/press/press2009/20090415PAC/20090424PAC.shtml.

Evaluating the Evidence

① In general, what is the trend with regard to the amount of money PACs are contributing to congressional candidates? Are they contributing more than they used to?

② What is the trend with regard to the partisan breakdown of contributions? Do Republicans or Democrats usually receive more contributions, does it vary, or are contributions nearly evenly divided?

③ Are there differences between the level of financial support given to Democrats and that given to Republicans in the House and the Senate?

the interest group examines candidates' responses to a questionnaire issued by the group. Sometimes a group rates members of Congress on the basis of how they voted on measures important to the group. The ratings of a liberal interest group such as the Americans for Democratic Action (ADA) or a conservative interest group such as the American Conservative Union (ACU) can serve as an ideological benchmark. So, for example, as senators in 2007, both Hillary Clinton and Barack Obama had ADA ratings of 75, while Republican John McCain had an ADA rating of 10. McCain had an ACU rating of 82, and Clinton and Obama each had about an 8. Interest group ratings are used by voters and the media to evaluate candidates and also by candidates themselves, who may advertise their rating to targeted constituencies.

Interest Groups, Politics, and Money: The Influence of Political Action Committees

The influence of money on politics is not a recent phenomenon. Louise Overacker, one of the first political scientists to do research on campaign finance, wrote in 1932, "Any effective program of control must make it possible to bring into the light the sources and amounts of all funds used in political campaigns, and the way in which those funds are expended.... Negatively, it must not attempt to place legal limitations upon the size of contributions or expenditures."[31] Years later, Congress saw the wisdom of Overacker's analysis and enacted regulations stipulating that a group that contributes to any candidate's campaign must register as a political action committee (PAC). For that reason, most interest groups form PACs as one arm of their organization, though federal law now permits corporations and labor unions to use their financial resources to purchase advertisements for federal campaigns directly.

Whereas an interest group pursues a group's broad goals by engaging in a variety of activities, its PAC raises and spends money to influence the outcome of an election. Typically it will do so by contributing to candidates' campaigns. Funding campaigns helps an interest group in various ways. For one thing, it establishes the interest group as a formal supporter of one or more candidates. And importantly, campaign contributions are a door opener for an interest group's lobbyists. For a lobbyist, access to policy makers is crucial, and campaign contributions provide a means of contact and help ensure that a phone call will be returned or an invitation responded to, even if the policy maker does not support the group's position on every issue.

Table 7.2 on page 236 lists the PACs that contribute the most money to U.S. campaigns and highlights the party their contributions favor. As the table illustrates, many business

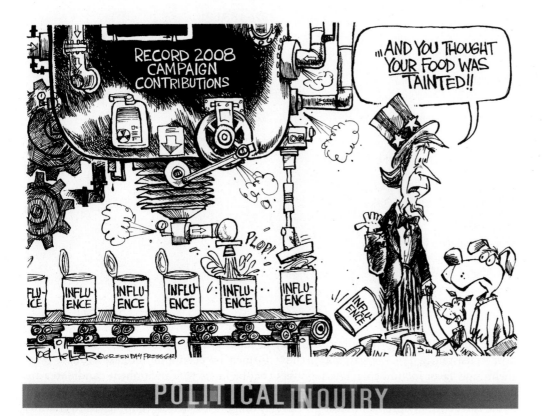

POLITICAL INQUIRY

What point does this cartoon make about the nature of 2008 political campaign contributions? Exactly what are these contributions buying, according to the cartoonist?

© Joe Heller, 2008. www.cagle.com

TABLE 7.2

Top All-Time Donors, 1989–2010

Rank	Organization	Total '89–'09	Tilt
1	AT&T Inc.	$44,214,960	On the fence
2	American Federation of State, County & Municipal Employees	$41,941,811	Strongly Democrat
3	National Association of Realtors	$35,595,518	On the fence
4	Goldman Sachs	$31,437,825	Leans Democrat
5	American Association for Justice	$31,424,029	Solidly Democrat
6	International Brotherhood of Electrical Workers	$31,407,507	Solidly Democrat
7	National Education Association	$30,097,067	Strongly Democrat
8	Laborers Union	$28,978,400	Strongly Democrat
9	Service Employees International Union	$27,933,232	Strongly Democrat
10	Carpenters & Joiners Union	$27,767,683	Strongly Democrat
11	Teamsters Union	$27,728,124	Strongly Democrat
12	Citigroup Inc.	$27,101,058	On the fence
13	Communications Workers of America	$27,025,396	Solidly Democrat
14	American Federation of Teachers	$26,282,491	Strongly Democrat
15	American Medical Association	$26,282,446	Leans Republican
16	United Auto Workers	$25,774,502	Strongly Democrat
17	Machinists & Aerospace Workers Union	$25,105,777	Strongly Democrat
18	National Auto Dealers Association	$24,344,808	Leans Republican
19	United Parcel Service	$24,183,691	Leans Republican
20	United Food & Commercial Workers Union	$24,123,333	Strongly Democrat
21	American Bankers Association	$22,414,966	On the fence
22	National Association of Home Builders	$21,864,655	Leans Republican
23	EMILY's List	$21,239,168	Strongly Democrat
24	National Beer Wholesalers Association	$21,038,345	Leans Republican
25	Time Warner	$20,041,510	Strongly Democrat

LEGEND: Republican   Democrat   On the fence

= Between 40% and 59% to both parties

= Leans Democrat/Republican (60%–69%)

= Strongly Democrat/Republican (70%–89%)

= Solidly Democrat/Republican (over 90%)

and corporate PACs favor Republicans, whereas labor groups tend to support Democrats. More consistently, PACs, particularly those formed by economic interest groups, overwhelmingly favor incumbents. PACs' powers-that-be know that incumbent candidates are most likely to be reelected, and thus the PACs support their reelection bids. As we will examine further in Chapter 9, interest groups rely on political action committees to channel their support to candidates that espouse their views.

Interest groups are a powerful vehicle by which individuals can join forces and collectively persuade policy makers to take legislative action on their goals. As such, interest groups play a strong role in the policy-making process. Throughout U.S. history and continuing today, the prevalence of interest groups is testimony to people's desire to influence the pathways of their society and government.

Interest groups are one of the great leveling devices in U.S. politics. They are organizations that enable "regular Jills and Joes" to influence policy through collective action and organization. And although not all Americans are equally likely to join and form interest groups, interest groups represent an avenue of participation open to all, and with enough variety in tactics and strategies to offer appealing means of civic participation to a broad spectrum of the population. Particularly today, with the Internet providing a highly accessible medium for participation, interest groups give individuals the opportunity to increase their own social capital—to improve their own lives and the life of their community by making government more responsive to their needs and concerns and by increasing the effectiveness of the public policy-making process.

Although there are competing opinions about the role and value of interest groups in U.S. politics, their influence in policy making is unquestioned. Thus interest groups offer enormous potential for people who wish to become civically engaged. The abundance of groups for virtually every cause (and the ability of anyone to form his or her own group) means that like-minded individuals can work together to ensure that government policy represents their views. How does the number of groups available today differ from decades past? What is the result of that difference in terms of potential members?

Today, through the Internet and other digital technology, interest groups can provide individuals with instantly accessed information and organizational tools. Advances in computing, telephone communications, and television have opened the doors to participation in politics and government in ways that were undreamed of a few decades ago. Thanks to technology, the potential exists for interest groups to reach new and ever-widening audiences. As we have seen, however, the potential audience, at least in the present day, excludes many members of the working class, who may not have been socialized to take part in groups and who may lack the time and means to access computer technology. This lack of access poses a challenge to interest groups as they rely ever more heavily on digital recruiting, communicating, organizing, and fund-raising. How will new technologies continue to alter the landscape for interest groups?

In becoming increasingly dependent on relatively low-cost technological tools, interest groups also have to deal with the challenges of paying for the expertise needed to design, build, and maintain their Web sites and Weblogs. Once such issues are resolved, and once access is opened to those not currently wired, digital strategies will further strengthen the clout and efficacy of interest groups and these groups will speak for a broader swath of Americans.

Summary

STUDY NOW

1. The Value of Interest Groups

Interest groups offer individuals a vehicle for engaging in civic actions and improving their communities and the nation as a whole. The positive impacts of improved social capital are reciprocal: as participation benefits individuals, it also benefits communities and larger governments, which in turn provide benefits to individuals, and so on. Interest groups also have some downsides: they can allow well-organized minority views to dominate over less well-organized majority viewpoints; they emphasize the role of money in politics; they strengthen the incumbency advantage of elected officeholders; and they tend to draw participants disproportionately from among society's elites.

2. Who Joins Interest Groups, and Why?

Although interest groups serve as an accessible channel for citizen participation, not everyone is equally likely to join or form an interest group. In general, people with high incomes, individuals who are upper-middle and middle class, and those with high levels of education are more likely to join interest groups than are people with low incomes, those who are lower-middle and working class, and those who have less education. In addition, some people join interest groups related to their occupation. People typically join interest groups for a variety of reasons that can be categorized as solidary incentives, purposive incentives, and economic incentives.

3. How Interest Groups Succeed

Interest groups succeed by using their organizational resources and maximizing the effectiveness of their organizational environment. Organizational resources consist of groups' membership and financial resources. The organizational environment comprises the group's leadership and the presence of opposing or competitive interest groups in the policy-making environment.

4. Types of Interest Groups

Interest groups typically fall into one of three categories. Economic interest groups, such as business, agricultural, or labor union groups, advocate for financial benefits for their members in the form of subsidies or wage policies, for example. Public and ideological interest groups lobby for policies that affect public, or collective, goods and include abortion-rights groups and environmental groups. Foreign governments and corporations also use interest groups to influence a wide variety of policies, especially trade and military policy.

5. Interest Group Strategies

Interest groups usually combine direct and indirect strategies in their attempts to influence the policy process. Direct strategies typically involve lobbying a policy maker, and indirect strategies may include using public outreach to build favorable public opinion of the organization (climate control), using campaign contributions and electioneering to influence who will be making policy, and educating the public so that they share a group's position and can convey that view to policy makers.

6. Interest Groups, Politics, and Money: The Influence of Political Action Committees

PACs are the tool by which interest groups contribute to electoral campaigns. Some PACs are partisan, but in general PACs tend to support incumbent candidates, making it difficult for nonincumbents effectively to challenge those already in office.

Key Terms

climate control 233
collective goods 228
economic incentives 222
electioneering 233
elite theory 216
free rider problem 228
interest groups 214

iron triangle 231
issue network 231
lobby 230
pluralist theory 216
political action committee (PAC) 224
purposive incentives 220

rational choice theory 228
social capital 214
solidary incentives 220
umbrella organizations 226

For Review

1. Explain in detail how the pluralist and elite theories differ in their views of interest groups in U.S. democracy.
2. Why do people join interest groups? Who is most likely to join an interest group? Why?
3. What kinds of interest groups exist in the United States? Which types are the most influential? Why are they most influential?
4. What resources help determine how powerful an interest group is?
5. How do political action committees attempt to influence government action?

For Critical Thinking and Discussion

1. Were you brought up in a family in which joining groups was important? Do your parents belong to any interest groups? Do you? If not, why do you think that is the case?
2. What kinds of interest groups are you and your friends most likely to be involved in (even if you are not)? Why are the issues these groups advocate important to you?
3. How has the Internet changed how interest groups operate? What kinds of groups has it made more effective? Has it made any groups less effective?
4. Select a controversial issue such as abortion or gun control, and use the Internet to search for and learn about the interest groups that represent opposing views. What tactics does each group use? Is one strategy more effective than the other?
5. The Supreme Court has ruled that political expenditures constitute a form of free speech. Do you agree? Can you think of any other ways in which "money talks"?

MULTIPLE CHOICE: Choose the lettered item that answers the question correctly.

1. The idea that a group of wealthy, educated individuals wields most political power is called
   a. pluralist theory.
   b. elite theory.
   c. rational choice theory.
   d. democratic theory.

2. The motivation to join an interest group based on a belief in the group's cause from an ideological standpoint is called a(n)
   a. solidary incentive.
   b. purposive incentive.
   c. economic incentive.
   d. organizational incentive.

3. A restaurant owner who joins a trade association interest group because it advocates for wage policies that would benefit the business is an example of someone motivated by
   a. solidary incentives.
   b. purposive incentives.
   c. economic incentives.
   d. organizational incentives.

4. A group that raises and spends money to influence the outcome of an election is called
   a. an interest group.
   b. a bundling organization.
   c. a political action committee.
   d. a social compact.

5. The phenomenon of someone deriving benefit from others' actions is called
   a. the problem of collective action.
   b. the bundling problem.
   c. the free rider problem.
   d. the slacker problem.

6. A direct strategy to advance the interest of an interest group is
   a. lobbying.
   b. public outreach.
   c. electioneering.
   d. contributing to political parties.

7. The fluid web of connections among those concerned about a policy and those who create and administer the policy is called
   a. political action committee.
   b. a congressional quorum.
   c. an issue network.
   d. a social network.

8. The interaction of mutual interests among members of Congress, executive agencies, and organized interests during policy making is called
   a. a social network.   c. a square cube.
   b. an iron triangle.   d. an issue network.

9. The practice of using public outreach to build a favorable public opinion of the organization is called
   a. climate control.   c. agenda setting.
   b. interest outreach.   d. maximizing spin.

10. Working to influence the election of candidates who support the organization's issues is called
    a. interest group bias.
    b. incumbency advantage.
    c. agenda setting.
    d. electioneering.

FILL IN THE BLANKS.

11. To social scientists, the ways in which our lives are improved by social connections is called _____ .

12. The motivation to join an interest group based on the companionship and the satisfaction derived from socializing with others is called _____ .

13. A group that represents collective groups of industries or corporations is called a(n) _____ .

14. Outcomes shared by the general public are called _____ .

15. The idea that it is not economically rational for people to participate in collective action when the resultant collective good could be realized without participating is the essence of _____ .

Internet Resources

Center for Responsive Politics
www.opensecrets.org This nonpartisan Web site provides information on the campaign financing of candidates for federal office.

Common Cause
www.commoncause.org This Web site features a special section on money and politics and provides links to sites related to its endorsed reform measures.

Federal Election Commission
www.fec.org You'll find a plethora of information about campaign financing, including regulations, contributions and expenditures, specific candidates, individual donors, political action committees, and political parties.

Internet Activism

Join an online interest group that supports a cause you believe in. Google any of your interests with the term "interest group" to find groups that identify with causes you believe in. Examples might include conservative or liberal organizations, environmental groups, groups centered on demographic characteristics, and groups concerned with specific policies. After finding an organization, determine what membership requirements are, and how the group facilitates online participation.

Facebook and Twitter
You can follow or become a fan of hundreds of interest groups on Twitter and Facebook. On Twitter, search the group name. On Facebook, search the group name and click "groups."

Recommended Readings

Alexander, Robert M. *Rolling the Dice with State Initiatives: Interest Group Involvement in Ballot Campaigns.* Westport, CT: Praeger, 2001. A probing analysis of the impact of interest groups on gambling initiatives in California and Missouri that, unlike most treatments of interest group activity, focuses on interest group initiatives within states and on lobbying in a nonlegislative arena.

Berry, Jeffrey M., and Clyde Wilcox. *The Interest Group Society,* 5th ed. New York: Longman, 2008. Analyzes the proliferation of various types of interest groups in the United States, as well as the strategies interest groups use to sway policy makers.

Cigler, Alan J., and Burnett A. Loomis. *Interest Group Politics,* 7th ed. Washington, DC: CQ Press, 2007. A classic analysis, first published in 1983, detailing the impact of interest groups in modern American politics.

Franz, Michael M. *Choices and Changes: Interest Groups in the Electoral Process.* Philadelphia: Temple University Press, 2008. A comprehensive examination of interest groups' use of electioneering tactics, especially campaign contributions, and how electioneering strategies are shaped by the campaign regulatory environment.

Hays, Richard A. *Who Speaks for the Poor: National Interest Groups and Social Policy.* New York: Routledge, 2001. An examination of how the poor gain political representation in the policy process through the efforts of interest groups.

Herrnson, Paul S., Ronald G. Shaiko, and Clyde J. Wilcox. *The Interest Group Connection: Electioneering, Lobbying, and Policymaking in Washington,* 2nd ed. Washington, DC: CQ Press, 2004. A collection of essays describing the role of interest groups on the federal level. The essays focus on elections, Congress, the president, and the judiciary.

Wright, John. *Interest Groups and Congress (Longman Classics Edition).* New York: Longman, 2002. A study of the influence of both historical and modern interest groups, asserting that interest groups' practice of providing specialized information to members of Congress increases their influence there, has an impact on the resultant policy, and shapes opinion.

Movies of Interest

Thank You for Smoking (2005)
Aaron Eckhart stars as a lobbyist in this satirical comedy about the big tobacco lobby.

Erin Brockovich (2000)
Starring Julia Roberts, this film is based on the true story of Erin Brockovich, an activist fighting for the rights of a community whose water supply has been contaminated.

The Pelican Brief (1993)
Based on the John Grisham novel of the same name, this film, starring Julia Roberts and Denzel Washington, spotlights competition between big business and the environmental movement and illuminates how interested parties can use the courts to make policy.

Paths of Glory (1957)
This Stanley Kubrick film delves into the realities of trench warfare during World War I, but through it we see how organizations may succeed or fail at motivating individuals.

Political Parties

THEN

Political parties relied on patronage and voter loyalty to become powerful entities in American politics.

NOW

Voter loyalty has declined, but parties remain an important force for mobilizing citizens.

NEXT

Will the dominance of the Democratic and Republican parties continue?

Will political parties decline in their ability to perform key functions?

How will digital technologies further shape parties' strategies and expand their reach—and change the membership of parties?

Political parties are essential

channels for the realization of American democracy. Political parties serve the American system in many crucial capacities, from recruiting candidates, to conducting elections, to distributing information to voters, to participating in governance. One of their essential functions is to provide an open arena for participation by civic-minded individuals, while reaching out to involve those who do not participate.

Because Americans place high value on independent thought and action, some citizens view political parties with suspicion. For such observers, the collective activity of parties brings worries about corruption and control by elite decision makers. But even though party insiders sometimes do exert considerable power, parties remain one of the most accessible forums for citizens' participation in democracy. Indeed, political scientist E. E. Schattschneider, who believed that parties represented the foremost means for citizens to communicate with political decision makers—and in this way to retain control over their government—wrote that "modern democracy is unthinkable save in terms of political parties."[1]

Parties Today and Their Functions

In the United States today, two major political parties—the Democratic and the Republican parties—dominate the political landscape. Generally speaking, a **political party** is an organization of ideologically similar people that nominates and elects its members to office in order to run the government and shape public policy. Parties identify potential candidates, nominate them to run for office, campaign for them, organize elections, and govern. But given some overlapping roles, political scientists agree that parties can be distinguished from other political organizations, such as interest groups and political action committees, through four defining characteristics.

Defining a Political Party

First, political parties run candidates under their own label, or affiliation. Most candidates who run for office are identified by their party affiliation. Running a candidate under the party label requires party functions such as recruiting candidates, organizing elections, and campaigning.[2] And political parties typically are the only organizations that regularly run candidates for political office under the party label on a ballot.

Second, unlike interest groups, which hope to have individuals sympathetic to their cause elected but which typically do not want to govern, *political parties seek to govern.* Political parties run candidates hoping that they will win a majority of the seats in a legislature or control the executive branch. Such victories enable the party to enact a broad partisan agenda. For example, the Democratic victories in the 2008 presidential and congressional elections paved the way for President Obama and the Democratic leadership in the U.S. House of Representatives and the U.S. Senate to act on the party's stated agenda, particularly in reforming the nation's health care system.

A third defining characteristic is that *political parties have broad concerns, focused on many issues.* The major parties in the United States are made up of coalitions of different groups and constituencies who rely on political parties to enact their agendas. That is to say, if we were to look at a party's **platform**—the formal statement of its principles and policy objectives—we would find its stance on all sorts of issues: war, abortion rights, environmental protection, the minimum wage. These positions are one articulation of the interests

---

political party
an organization that recruits, nominates, and elects party members to office in order to control the government

platform
the formal statement of a party's principles and policy objectives

of that party's coalition constituencies. Typically, interest groups have narrower issue concerns than parties do, and some focus on only a single issue. For example, we know that the National Rifle Association opposes governmental controls on gun ownership, but what is this interest group's position on the minimum wage? On the environment? Chances are high that the NRA does not have positions on those matters because its concern is with the single issue of gun ownership.

Finally, *political parties are quasi-public organizations that have a special relationship with the government.* Some functions of political parties overlap with governmental functions, and some party functions facilitate the creation and perpetuation of government (running elections, for example). The resulting special status subjects political parties to greater scrutiny than private clubs and organizations.

How Parties Engage Individuals

Political scientists who study the nature of Americans' civic engagement recognize that political parties represent one of the main channels through which citizens can make their voices heard. A fixture in the politics of American communities large and small, parties today are accessible to virtually everyone.

Historically, political parties excluded various groups from participating. For example, in many states, women were shut out of party meetings until the mid-twentieth century.[3] African Americans were formally excluded from voting in Democratic primaries in the South until the U.S. Supreme Court banned the practice in 1944, though it took decades before the party complied with that decision.[4] But in recent times, political parties have increasingly embraced and championed diversity. They have encouraged various groups beyond the traditional white European American male party establishment to get involved formally in the party organization, to participate in campaign activities, and to vote. As a result, parties today are much more inclusive of women, ethnic and racial minorities, and students, providing an important avenue for those traditionally excluded from political life to gain valuable experience as party activists, campaign volunteers, and informed voters. This increasingly diverse participation has also contributed to the parties' health, because it has caused them to recognize that to be successful, candidates must reflect the diverse identities and interests of voters.

What Political Parties Do

As we have seen, by promoting political activity, political parties encourage civic engagement and citizen participation and in that way foster democracy. Parties provide a structure for people at the **grassroots** level to volunteer on party-run campaigns, make campaign contributions, work in the day-to-day operations of the party, and run for office. During the 2010 congressional elections, Democratic and Republican activists registered, canvassed, and mobilized voters. Both parties focused their efforts on competitive districts where Democratic incumbents were at risk of being unseated. In some cases, those Democrats were vulnerable because their districts had large numbers of conservative voters; in other cases, they were vulnerable because of their comparatively short tenure in the House. In general, representatives who have served only a term or two are more likely to be defeated than their more senior counterparts.

On the local level, a political party's ability to promote citizen participation varies with its relative influence within the community. Viable political parties—those that effectively contest and win some elections—are more effective at promoting citizen participation than weak political parties. A party that typically is in the minority in a local government—on the town council, in the county legislature—will find it more difficult to attract volunteers, to bring people out to fund-raisers, and to recruit candidates. And it naturally follows that parties that are better at attracting public participation are more likely to win elections.

Political parties also foster cooperation between divided interests and factions, building coalitions even in the most divisive of times. For example, in 2010 when Democratic and Republican wrangling over health care reform reached a crescendo, a bipartisan group of

grassroots organizing
tasks that involve direct contact with voters or potential voters.

> Political parties provide an easy avenue for citizens to participate in the civic life of their communities and nation. One way to participate is to volunteer at a national political party convention, or to try to become a convention delegate.

responsible party model
political scientists' view that a function of a party is to offer a clear choice to voters by establishing priorities or policy stances different from those of rival parties

senators joined forces to support a Clean Air bill, which would reduce the emissions of sulfur dioxide, nitrogen oxides, and mercury. The bill had the support of Senators Tom Carper (D-Delaware), Lamar Alexander (R-Tennessee), Amy Klobuchar (D-Minnesota), Jeanne Shaheen (D-New Hampshire), Judd Gregg (R-New Hampshire), Charles Schumer (D-New York), and Joseph Lieberman (I-Connecticut). The Clean Air bill was able to attract bipartisan support partially because it was considered a less controversial alternative to sweeping climate-change reform legislation. Civic engagement researchers point out that political parties' work in building coalitions and promoting cooperation among diverse groups often occurs away from the bright lights of the media-saturated public arena, where the parties' differences, rather than their common causes, often are in the spotlight.

Political parties also grease the wheels of government and ensure its smooth running. Nearly all legislatures, from town councils to Congress, consist of a *majority party,* the party to which more than 50 percent of the elected legislators belong, and the *minority party,* to which less than 50 percent of the elected legislators belong. Thus, if five of the nine members of your town council are Republicans and four are Democrats, the Republicans are the majority party and the Democrats are the minority party. The majority party elects the legislature's leaders, makes committee assignments, and holds a majority on those committees.

By serving as a training ground for members, political parties also foster effective government. This role of parties is particularly important for groups that traditionally have not been among the power brokers in the government. Historically, African Americans, Latinos, and women have gained valuable knowledge and leadership experience in party organizations—by volunteering on party-run campaigns, assisting with candidate recruitment, or helping with fund-raising endeavors—before running for office.[5] Party credentials established by serving the party in these ways can act as a leveling device that can help make a newcomer's candidacy more viable.

Perhaps most important, political parties promote civic responsibility among elected officials and give voters an important "check" on those elected officials. There is no doubt that the 2010 congressional elections were a mandate on the Obama presidency, even though the president's name was not on the ballot. When an elected leader, particularly a chief executive, is the crucial player in enacting an important policy, the existence of political parties enables voters to hold party members responsible *even if that particular elected official is not running for reelection.* The system thus provides a check on the power of elected officials, because it makes them aware that the policy or position they are taking may be unpopular.

Historically, according to one theory, political parties have also made government more effective and have provided important cues for voters. The **responsible party model,** developed by E. E. Schattschneider, posits that a party tries to give voters a clear choice by establishing priorities or policy stances different from those of the rival party or parties. Because a party's elected officials tend to be loyal to their party's stances, voters can readily anticipate how a candidate will vote on a given set of issues if elected, and can thus cast their vote according to their preferences on those issues.

The Three Faces of Parties

American political parties perform their various functions through three "faces," or spheres of operation.[6] The three components of the party include the party in the electorate, the party organization, and the party in government (see Figure 8.1).

Voter Registration Application
Before completing this form, review the General, Application, and State specific instructions.

> Most states offer voters the opportunity to declare their party affiliation when registering to vote. Affiliated voters are the party in the electorate.

The Party in the Electorate

All the individuals who identify with or tend to support a particular party make up the **party in the electorate.** Several factors influence which party an individual will identify with, including personal circumstances, race, and religion, as well as the party's history, ideology, position on issues of importance to the voter, and candidates.[7]

MEASURING THE PARTY IN THE ELECTORATE The term **party identifier** refers to an individual who identifies himself or herself as a member of one party or the other; party identifiers typically are measured by party registration. In most states, party registration is a legal process in which a voter formally selects affiliation with one political party. This declaration of affiliation often occurs when a person registers to vote; the prospective voter selects his or her party identification by filling out a voter registration form or party declaration form. Depending on the state, a voter may select the Democratic or the Republican Party, a variety of third parties, or no party. When a voter does not select a party, he or she is technically an unaffiliated voter, but often analysts refer to such a voter as an **independent.**

People's party identification sometimes does not match their actual voting preferences. When we refer to the party in the electorate, we also consider those individuals who express a tendency to vote for one party or a preference for that party.

DETERMINING WHO BELONGS TO EACH POLITICAL PARTY Although we commonly speak in terms of which groups affiliate with and "belong to" each of the political parties, those are just generalizations, with many exceptions. In general, each political party counts specific demographic groups as part of its base of support. A party will often draw party activists and leaders from the ranks of this bloc of individuals whose support can be counted on.

Although whites, men, and people with some college education are naturally found in both parties, they are more likely to be Republicans. For the Democrats, key voting blocs include African Americans, ethnic minorities, women, and people with no college education. Individuals with a college degree or more are evenly divided between the two parties. Social class also plays a role in party preference. The working class is largely Democratic; the upper-middle class is largely Republican; and the middle class, by far the largest class in the United States, is divided between the two parties. But the best predictor of a person's party identification is his or her ideology. People who identify themselves as conservative are much more likely to be Republicans; people who identify themselves as liberal are much more likely to be Democrats. (See the discussion of ideology in Chapter 1.)

DIFFERENCES BETWEEN DEMOCRATS AND REPUBLICANS We can trace some of the differences—in both ideologies and core constituencies—between today's Democrats and Republicans to the 1930s. That was the era of the Great Depression, a time of devastating economic collapse and personal misery for people around the world. President Franklin D. Roosevelt's drive to expand the role of government by providing a safety net for the most vulnerable in society has remained part of the Democratic agenda to this day. In the past several decades, this agenda has centered on pressing for civil rights for African Americans and for the expansion of social welfare programs. Today, key components of the Democratic agenda include gay rights, environmental protection, and freedom of choice with respect to abortion.

Traditionally, Republicans have countered that position by advocating a smaller government that performs fewer social welfare functions. Many members of the Tea Party movement argue that smaller government should be the focus of the modern Republican party. But a major priority for the Republican Party today is advocacy of a stronger governmental role in regulating traditional moral values. Because of this stance, a solid voting bloc within the Republican Party comprises conservative Christians, sometimes called the Christian Right or the Religious Right, who agree with the Republicans' pro-life position on abortion (which includes support for an increased regulation of abortion) and appeals for a constitutional amendment banning gay marriage. Republicans also emphasize protection of business and business owners and generally support a decreased role for the federal government,

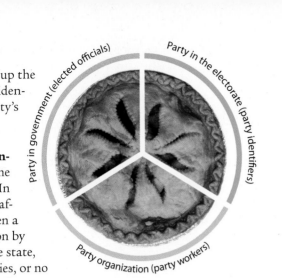

FIGURE 8.1

The Three Faces of Parties

party in the electorate
individuals who identify with or tend to support a party

party identifiers
individuals who identify themselves as a member of one party or the other

independent
a voter who does not belong to any organized political party; often used as a synonym for an unaffiliated voter

particularly with respect to the economy and social welfare issues, and a corresponding larger role for state governments.

More recent analysis of the differences between Democrats and Republicans reveals how much the world has changed in the past several years. Research on party identifiers between 2005 and 2010 shows how the perception of a party's level of assertiveness in foreign affairs is a defining characteristic of Democrats and Republicans.[8] Previous analyses, conducted before the wars in Afghanistan and Iraq, showed that this factor had very little bearing on party identity. The more recent research also indicates that positions on social issues, once a defining feature of the parties, have declined tremendously as a key determinant of partisanship.

In concrete terms, these differences mean that Republicans are more likely to believe that a foreign policy emphasizing military action is the right course, and that Democrats are more likely to oppose war (such as the war in Iraq) and to believe that foreign policy should stress diplomacy over military action. In general, Democrats remain committed to a larger government role in providing an economic safety net.

It is not surprising that the base constituencies of the parties are drawn from the groups that each party's platform emphasizes. The base of the Democratic Party prominently includes women, the majority of whom, since 1980, have voted for the Democratic presidential nominee. Since Franklin Roosevelt's New Deal social welfare policy during the 1930s, African Americans have been an important voting bloc within the Democratic Party, although they have faced struggles and strife in asserting and securing their rights, particularly during the civil rights movement of the 1960s. Other ethnic minorities, including Latinos and Asian Americans, also tend to support the Democratic Party (as described in Chapter 6), as do many working-class voters. The base of the Republican Party prominently includes many small-business owners, citizens who identify themselves as being very religious, and upper-middle-class voters.[9]

party organization
the formal party apparatus, including committees, party leaders, conventions, and workers

The Party Organization

Thomas P. "Tip" O'Neill (D-Massachusetts), Speaker of the House of Representatives from 1977 until 1987, is often quoted as saying, "All politics is local." In no case is that statement truer than it is for American political parties.

Party organization refers to the formal party apparatus, including committees, headquarters, conventions, party leaders, staff, and volunteer workers. In the United States, the party organization is most visible at the local level. Yet county and local parties tend to be *loosely* organized—centered predominantly on elections—and may be dormant when election season passes.[10] Except during presidential elections, state and local political parties typically function quite separately from the national party. Although the number of individuals who actually participate in the party organization is quite small when compared with the party in the electorate, on the local level, political parties offer one of the most accessible means for individuals to participate in politics.

But with respect to political *power,* county and local parties are the most important components of a party organization. Theoretically, political parties' organization resembles a pyramid (see Figure 8.2), with a broad base of support at the bottom and power flowing up to a smaller group at the state level and then to an even smaller, more exclusive group at the national level.[11] In reality, the national committees of both major U.S. political parties exist separately from the committees of the state and local parties (see Figure 8.3), and real political power can usually be found at the local or county party level, as we will see in the following discussion.

National committee

State committees

County committees

Municipal committees

Precinct or ward organizations

FIGURE 8.2

Theoretical Structure of Political Parties: A Hierarchical Model of Party Organizations

THE NATIONAL PARTIES Every four years, political party activists meet at a national convention to determine their party's nominee for the presidency. Here the delegates also adopt rules and develop a party platform that describes the party's policy priorities and positions on issues.

The national party committees (the Democratic National Committee, or DNC, and the Republican National Committee, or RNC) are the national party organizations charged with conducting the conventions and overseeing the operation of the national party during the interim between conventions. The national committee elects a national chair, who is often informally selected by the party's presidential nominee. The national chair, along with the paid staff of the national committee, oversees the day-to-day operations of the political party.

But the role of the national chair depends to a large extent on whether the party's nominee wins the presidency. If the party's nominee is victorious, the national chair has a less prominent role because the president serves as the most public representative of the party. If the party's nominee loses, however, the national chair may take on a more public persona, serving as the spokesperson for the **loyal opposition**—the out-of-power party's objections to the policies and priorities of the government in power. In recent years, regardless of whether the party's nominee has won or lost, one of the most important roles of the national chair has been to raise funds. Money donated to the national parties is often redirected to the state and local parties, which use it to help contest elections and mobilize voters.

FIGURE 8.3

Modern Structure of Political Parties: Power Diffused Through Many Party Organizations

STATE PARTIES Both national parties have committees in each state (the Illinois State Democratic Committee, for example) that effectively *are* the party in that state. State committees act as intermediaries between the national committees and county committees. Typically, state committees are made up of a few members from each county or other geographical subdivision of a given state.

Historically, state parties were important because of their role in the election of U.S. senators, who until 1913 were elected by their states' legislatures. Since the ratification of the Seventeenth Amendment in that year, the voters of each state have directly elected their senators by popular election.

Later in the twentieth century, state political parties began a rebound of power, partly because of the U.S. Supreme Court's decision in *Buckley v. Valeo* (1976). In this case, the Court ruled that political parties are entities with special status because their functions of educating and mobilizing voters and contesting elections help to ensure democracy.[12] This ruling created the so-called **soft money loophole,** through which the political parties could raise unlimited funds for party-building activities such as voter registration drives and get-out-the-vote (GOTV) efforts, although contributions to specific candidates were limited. The Court's decision strengthened the influence of the state parties, which the national parties often relied upon to coordinate these efforts. The Bipartisan Campaign Reform Act of 2002 eliminated the soft money loophole, but until that time state parties were strengthened by their ability to channel those contributions to political parties. (See Chapter 9 for further discussion of soft money.)

COUNTY AND LOCAL PARTIES County committees consist of members of municipal, ward, and precinct party committees. The foot soldiers of the political parties, county committees help recruit candidates for office, raise campaign funds, and mobilize voters. The importance of a given county committee's role largely depends on whether its candidates are elected and whether its party controls the government. Party success tends to promote competition for candidates' slots and for seats on the county committee.

In most major cities, ward committees and precinct committees dominate party politics. Because city council members are often elected to represent a ward, ward committees are a powerful force in city politics, providing the grassroots organization that turns voters out in city elections. Precinct committees (a precinct is usually a subdivision of a ward) also help elect city council members.

Besides fund-raising, county and local political parties still play key roles in shaping both community engagement and individual participation in the political process, as they have done historically. During election season (in most places, from the end of August through the first week in November), county and local parties recruit and rely on volunteers to perform a host of functions, including answering phones in party headquarters, registering voters, coordinating mailings, doing advance work for candidates, compiling

loyal opposition
a role that the party out of power plays, highlighting its objections to policies and priorities of the government in power

soft money loophole
Supreme Court interpretation of campaign finance law that enabled political parties to raise unlimited funds for party-building activities such as voter registration drives and get-out-the-vote (GOTV) efforts

ANALYZING THE SOURCES

THE PEOPLE'S OPINION OF THE PARTIES

The figure below shows the percentage of survey respondents who have a favorable view of the Republican and Democratic parties at selected dates between September 2001 and May 2010.

Evaluating the Evidence

① What is the general trend with regard to party favorability ratings? Is one political party consistently viewed more favorably than the other? What is the trend over time regarding the favorability of Democrats versus Republicans?

② Look at particular high and low points for each political party. What events may have caused people's opinions of the parties to increase or decline?

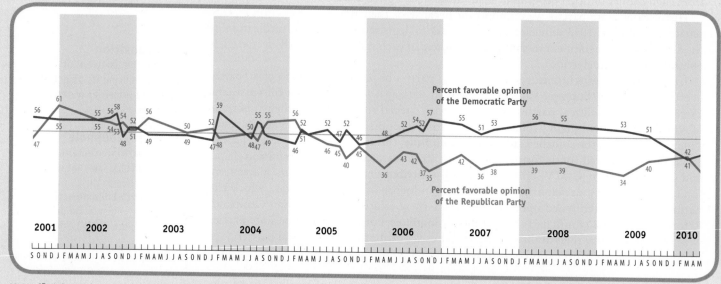

SOURCE: "Party Images," www.gallup.com/poll/24655/Party-Images.aspx.

lists for get-out-the-vote efforts, supervising door-knocking campaigns, and staffing phone banks to remind voters to vote on election day.

The Party in Government

party in government
the partisan identifications of elected leaders in local, county, state, and federal government

When candidates run for local, state, or national office, their party affiliation usually appears next to their name on the ballot. After an elected official takes the oath of office, many people do not think about the official's party affiliation. But in fact, the **party in government**—the partisan identification of elected leaders in local, county, state, and national government—significantly influences the organization and running of the government at these various levels.

In most towns, the party identification of the majority of the members of the legislative branch (often called *city council* or *town council*) determines who will serve as the head of the